T5-BBX-691

The Asia & Japan Business Information Sourcebook

The Asia & Japan Business Information Sourcebook

Christopher Engholm

John Wiley & Sons, Inc.
New York • Chichester • Brisbane • Toronto • Singapore

This text is printed on acid-free paper.

Published by John Wiley & Sons, Inc.

This publication is designed to provide accurate and authoritative information in regard to the subject matter covered. It is sold with the understanding that the publisher is not engaged in rendering legal, accounting, or other professional services. If legal advice or other expert assistance is required, the services of a competent professional person should be sought. *From a Declaration of Principles jointly adopted by a Committee of the American Bar Association and a Committee of Publishers.*

Library of Congress Cataloging-in-Publication Data:
Engholm, Christopher.
The Asia & Japan business information sourcebook / by Christopher Engholm.
p. cm.
ISBN 0-471-30466-2 (alk. paper)
1. East Asia—Commerce—Bibliography. 2. Asia, Southeastern—Commerce—Bibliography. 3. Business information services—East Asia—Bibliography. 4. Business information services—Asia, Southeastern—Bibliography. I. Title. II. Title: Asia and Japan business information sourcebook.
Z7164.C8E54 1994
[HF3820.5]
016.33095—dc20 93-47219

Printed in the United States of America

10 9 8 7 6 5 4 3 2 1

This volume is dedicated to Diana Rowland, with appreciation and thanks for a memorable apprenticeship

PREFACE

The purpose of this book is to assist readers in finding usable business information about the fastest growing economic region of the world: the Asia-Pacific. It was written to help researchers, consultants, and entrepreneurs perform the modern alchemy of turning raw data into usable commercial intelligence. It does this by providing a comprehensive yet rigorously edited listing of more than 1,000 sources of business information about the Asia-Pacific and Japan, including a description of each source and comments about its practical value to the Western businessperson.

The task of obtaining timely and accurate business information is the first, and I would argue the most critical, endeavor of Western firms that hope to prosper in Asia. Unhappily, researchers face a number of frustrations when looking for information, whether they are analyzing a country's economy, investment climate, social conditions, or consumer market for a new product.

Challenge 1: Data collecting is now a multimedia affair. The days of browsing the stacks at the library are gone for the serious researcher. Information is now available in many different media, ranging from familiar forms, such as books, magazines, and newsletters, to more contemporary formats, such as computer floppy disks, on-line electronic bulletins, CD-ROM laser discs, facsimile bulletins, and telephone information hot lines. The researcher faces the annoying task of finding out on what format the needed information exists.

Challenge 2: The information business has gone international. Some of the best information and research resources are now being compiled outside of the United States. Thus, Western researchers must confront the dual problem of searching overseas databases from the United States and finding out whether a source is available in their native language.

Challenge 3: Sources of quality information have multiplied. A growing mountain of Asia business literature now exists, but this hasn't made gathering information easier. Data sources have become highly specialized and thus are not readily available at local libraries or universities. Half of the researcher's battle is now the hunt for exactly the right information to fulfill specific needs.

Challenge 4: Information has become very expensive. With business newsletters costing up to $450 for a year's subscription, journals running $250 on average per year, and specialized directories and databases priced for corporate buyers rather than personal consumers, a core challenge for the modern researcher is to buy only essential information in the most cost-effective media format. For example, it might be better to use a printed database at a cost of $200 per year than an on-line database that costs $5,000 per year and provides the same information!

Challenge 5: "Garbage information" has multiplied, too. The other side of the information age coin is the terrible proliferation of outdated, irrelevant, and poorly presented information that frustrates far more than it informs. Because of this, time-saving "information guides" must now be added to the business researcher's arsenal. These guides must become more tightly focused to be of use to professionals. The many directories of business information sources currently bending the reference shelves at public libraries lack usefulness because they try to cover the globe under one cover. They're unwieldy and too general. In addition, they do not categorize sources based on the businessperson's needs.

This guide to business information addresses all five of these research challenges. It provides sources of business information that are relevant to Asia and Japan as well as essential data regarding the content, usefulness, accuracy, price, and availability of those sources.

I have divided the sources first by region—East Asia and Southeast Asia—and then by country. Each section is introduced with an overview that describes the region or country, including current economic conditions and trends in trade and investment. The sources in each section are divided by subject category (such as Economy or Industry), based on the practical needs of working scholars and businesspeople. The sources are listed in alphabetical order by title. The guide also contains two indexes: an author index (the publisher's name is used when no author is provided) and a title index.

CHRISTOPHER ENGHOLM

La Costa, California
July 1994

ACKNOWLEDGMENTS

A number of people were instrumental in helping me collect and appraise business information sources related to Asia. Foremost, I am indebted to Scott Grimes, who is earning a master's degree at the Graduate School of International Relations and Pacific Studies (IRPS) at the University of California at San Diego. His skilled and tireless research assistance on this project was indispensable.

I would also like to thank the people at the IRPS Library for their patience and assistance and Russell Cole, Robert Hecht-Nielson, Jack Lewis, and Chalmers Johnson for reviewing the manuscript, noting omissions, and politely protesting some of my commentaries.

Thank you also to Julie Castiglia, my agent; John Mahaney, my editor at John Wiley & Sons; Dave Fletcher, who checked and corrected facts in the manuscript; typists Helen Bloomfield and Linda Luke; and my partner in work and play, Jeanie Engholm.

C.E.

How to Use This Book

Let's suppose you need to find information about tax policy in Japan. Turn to the table of contents. Under the heading for Japan, there is a list of subject categories, like the ones that follow. One of these is Taxation. Turn to the page indicated to find a number of information sources on taxation in Japan, listed in alphabetical order by title.

The following subject categories have been included in this book, where applicable. Note that for many countries, sources simply do not exist for every subject. For example, the category for Advertising does not appear in the section on Vietnam because nothing has been published on that subject.

- **Accounting, Banking, and Finance**
- **Advertising**
- **Business Leaders**
- **Company Directories** (includes company financial profiles)
- **Country Profiles** (includes general descriptions of the political, economic, trade, and investment climates)
- **Dictionaries and Language Studies**
- **Distribution** (includes only sources that focus on distribution systems)
- **Economy**
- **Etiquette and Protocol**
- **General Business** (includes all how-to-do-business sources of a nonlegal nature, e.g., how to set up a business, how to negotiate)
- **History and Society** (includes sources on culture and sociology)
- **Industry** (includes sources specific to industrial organization as well as selected industrial sectors)
- **Information Sources** (includes bibliographies and reference sources)
- **Intellectual Property**
- **Laws and Regulations** (includes copyright, patent, and trademark law)
- **Management** (includes sources on domestic as well as international management issues)

- **Market Data and Analysis** (includes sources of data on the domestic market)
- **Politics and Government** (includes who's who directories of officials)
- **Research and Development** (includes technology transfer and directories of research organizations)
- **Taxation**
- **Travel Advice**
- **U.S.-Japan Relations** (includes sources on U.S.-Japan industrial and security relations)

When possible, I have provided the following information about each source listed in this book:

- **Title.** The complete title is listed as it appears on the copyright page of the publication. For bilingual publications, only the English title is given.
- **Date.** For books, the date of publication is normally given as a certain year. For periodicals and on-line databases, the frequency of publication is given instead, such as annual or updated daily.
- **Format.** Here I've noted the types of media in which the information can be obtained, such as hardcover, CD-ROM, or bound newsletter.
- **Author.** The authors are listed first name first and last name last.
- **Editor.** In the case of periodicals, anthologies, or directories, the editor's name is provided.
- **Publisher.** The full name of the publisher is translated into English when it appears in another language. The mailing address of the publisher is provided, as well as telephone and facsimile numbers, when possible, to help the reader purchase a source if it cannot be found in a local library.
- **Pages.** For periodicals, the number of pages is listed as "varies." For books, the number of pages given includes the book's index and endnotes.
- **Exhibits.** Under this heading, I've listed the type of illustrations that appear in the source, such as cartoons, photographs, or tables. This usually "varies" in the case of periodicals.
- **Price.** The price of the source is given only when it is listed on the publication.
- **Commentary.** I have reviewed each source for content, timeliness, style of presentation, and publication value, roughly in that order. Using the commentaries, you should be able to make an informed choice about which source you want to seek first, second, third, and so forth, in your research. You will also be able to avoid pursuing sources that don't readily meet your specific needs. Every source listed is worthwhile and has been selected from a large body of sources reviewed. Given the voluminousness of the literature,

there was no room to include seriously flawed or hard-to-find sources in a single volume like this.

One last tip about using this book: Don't take my commentaries on sources as gospel. They reflect my personal opinions, based on seven years of research on Asian business topics, but you might not agree with what is said about certain sources. I urge you to evaluate as many sources as you can and to formulate your own opinions.

Contents

Part Two: Southeast Asia

The Asia & Japan Business Information Sourcebook

INTRODUCTION

THE NEW TAO OF BUSINESS INFORMATION

Imagine that you wake up one morning and find that your computer monitor has this message: Welcome to Infotopia—The data seeker's paradise. Sitting down at your keyboard, you find that you've stepped into a futuristic virtual environment for the business professional. Moving with ease through multicolored menus, you sample Infotopia's business information features, such as free access to television broadcasts from other countries, translated simultaneously by an on-line service. You click through a selection of international television shows that range from a Chinese stock market report to a live news conference with Indonesia's General Suharto.

Another few clicks and you find a real-time translation service providing a selection of Asian radio broadcasts. Next, you scan through a list of 500 on-line business data services, all instantly available. While on line, you skim through completely indexed electronic books, journals, and newspapers as well as statistical databanks produced in foreign languages but translated into English. All of this costs nothing; you don't even have to pay long-distance telephone charges.

And Now the Real World of Business Information

Unfortunately, Infotopia has yet to be realized in the here and now. The business information industry has only reached adolescence in terms of both information content and the hardware needed to obtain access to it. Finding current business information suited to your specific needs still requires a lot of hard work. Although heaps of information is now available, there is surprisingly little "commercial intelligence" generated from it and made available to the public.

Worst of all, business information is expensive. If you wanted to subscribe to, say, three on-line data services, five management journals, two trade magazines, and five corporate newsletters, you would pay in the neighborhood of $20,000 per year, depending on the quality of the on-line services. That amount doesn't include the on-line telephone charges, which tend to accrue faster than you'd think possible.

Today, You Must Have an Information Strategy

The hoopla surrounding new information technologies like multimedia, hypertext, and CD-ROM promises instant information access at the push of a button. However, although there now exists an abundance of raw data, obtaining the exact commercial information you need remains a frustrating and expensive task. Nowadays, business information users must be smarter about locating and selecting information sources *before* they dive into the data morass. In short, you've got to have an information strategy. If you don't, you'll be smothered by data—most of it useless data—and you'll never solve the problems that you set out to solve by using information.

INFORMATION IS CRITICAL TO SUCCESS IN THE ASIA-PACIFIC

For Western companies doing business in Asia, effective information gathering and intelligence making (which are two distinct tasks) can mean the difference between success and failure, just as in other regions. They are uniquely critical for success in Asia, however, for a number of reasons.

First, there is a general lack of transparency in business bureaucracies in Asian countries. Government decision making is customarily accomplished through consensus building, referred to as the *ringi* system in Japan, the *pummi* system in Korea, and the *Mufakat* in Indonesia. Every Asian country values collective decision-making systems that operate behind closed doors. Decision making is hardly the public process that it is in the West, done by the book and under the scrutiny of the press. In Asia, official decisions are the product of endless personal meetings to build agreement among a wide spectrum of officials. Foreigners are neither invited to participate in nor apprised of these processes. For this reason, sophisticated information gathering and intelligence making take on a heightened importance.

Second, Asians place a high value on information. Most tend to covet it, in fact, because traditionally the possession of information was synonymous with power. Today, especially in East Asia, those who have access to sensitive information wield power over those who do not. Thus, as a rule, inside information is never given freely. The best business information in Asia is still passed personally between cohorts rather than published in the morning edition of the paper. Recent corporate surveys in Japan show that Japanese executives obtain one-third of their business information through networks of personal relationships—people provide valuable information in exchange for something else of value, often other information. Again, foreigners are excluded from this rich source of data. There is an ethnic element at play, too, that works against Anglo-Americans. John So, one of the first joint-venture American managers working in China for Hewlett-Packard, told me recently, "The Chinese tell me more just because I am Chinese." As an "outsider," you must ultimately gather your own commercial intelligence by evaluating published data, researching who's who in Asia, and getting to know the people who have access to the information that you need. You must know who can provide the necessary clout to give you access to emerging opportunities. Many of the sources included in this book will get you started on finding out who these people are.

Third, East Asian businesspeople, with the exception of the Taiwanese and Hong Kong Chinese, tend to conduct business within the framework of large groupings of corporations, called *keiretsu* in Japan, *chaebols* in Korea, and *jituan* in China. (In China, these industrial groupings are a recent phenomenon.) Foreigners who wish to engage with these conglomerates in an appropriate manner must undertake serious research. Most large companies in East Asia are members of larger conglomerates, and it behooves foreign businesspeople to avoid dealing with members of competing conglomerates at the same time. One American executive I know made this mistake. He sat down to negotiate with a Korean supplier to provide production inputs for his joint venture, a venture co-owned by a Korean firm that was a member of the supplier's competing conglomerate. The meeting was abruptly terminated when the Korean negotiator realized the American's mistake. How could the American have prevented this blunder? He could have gathered information from sources such as those listed in this book.

Fourth, we have all heard about the role that the Japanese government plays in providing for the welfare of its people by "guiding" industry in developing new technology and value-added manufacturing. The government harnesses domestic competitors together during the earliest phases of applied R&D and product prototyping, supplying the seed money to conduct studies and lining up the financial backing to bring products to the marketplace. Foreign competitors are typically excluded from this process and deprived of the information gathered. This is yet another reason to gather critical information effectively from outside Japan.

Japan has become the second largest source of international grants and loans. Information gathering about Japanese-financed aid projects in developing countries is an essential first step in participating in these lucrative projects. The alternative to setting up a liaison office inside Japan is diligent and strategic information gathering from home. For a growing number of Western firms, entering the Japanese marketplace is no longer merely an option; it is essential for survival. Yet Japan is the most expensive place in the world to do business. One of the keys to success in Japan is to monitor carefully the business activities of Japanese competitors. This task requires you to become a true insider by positioning your firm inside the flow of timely, relevant, and applied information. There is simply no way to compete in Japan without high-quality information, much of which, fortunately, can be gathered outside Japan. Moreover, to enter the Japanese market, you need personal connections. Obtaining appropriate high-level introductions through solid trust-based relationships requires an emphasis on "people research." You need to know who people are and what influence they wield inside public and private organizations. Ground-level information gathering about key individuals and organizational relationships can and should be conducted before blindly stumbling into Japan.

There is one last critical reason for Westerners to acquire and use information about Asia before doing business there. As anyone who has dealt with Japanese, Chinese, Korean, Thai, or Malaysian businesspeople will tell you, the hidden influence of culture continues to affect the manner in which business is conducted within the region and with Western businesses. Westerners who have learned the cultural ropes, which differ markedly from one country of the Asia-Pacific to another, gain a competitive edge. To understand how Asian businesspeople behave, negotiate, communicate, and perceive their relationship to you and how they will honor a signed contract, you must be culturally informed. This means learning something about a country's history, society, business culture, and protocol.

I have included many sources on these topics in this book because American businesspeople are often ignorant or ill-informed in these areas. Here's just one example of how our collective ignorance of Asian cultures gets us into trouble: A group of egalitarian-minded Westerners forgot that East Asian societies tend to place a high priority on recognizing a person's social standing and behaving accordingly. The Taiwanese, for example, often use both a limousine and a van for transporting delegations of business visitors from the West; the CEO rides in the limo, and the rest of the delegation ride in the van. This selective treatment backfired when an American delegation, calling on a company in Taipei, balked at the unequal treatment. Its members rotated leaders so that each of them could have a ride in the limo. The Taiwanese CEO was greatly offended and considered such frivolity in poor taste. The blunder was an affront to the hierarchical system on which Chinese culture and business are founded. The American delegation projected an image of itself as immature, insensitive, and unaccountable—in short, a risk to do business with.

ASIAN INFORMATION SOURCES

Not long ago, a Western business could find out about Asia's commercial environment in one of two ways: by hiring a consultant or by setting up an office in Asia close to the flow of current information. Both methods were expensive, and thus, relatively few American companies set out to conquer Asia-Pacific markets. In China by the time of the Tiananmen Square uprising, only 300 American companies had set up offices or made investments in the market of 1 billion customers. In Indonesia, with its population of 170 million, the number was far fewer. Without information conduits in place, firms tend to avoid making commitments to new markets; the front-end costs to a company of collecting data about an emerging marketplace can be prohibitive.

Thankfully, all this has changed in regard to most of the Asia-Pacific. You can now collect business information about Asia in a variety of ways, even about the once-insular People's Republic of China. Today, you can

- Subscribe to any number of English-language magazines and journals, many produced in Asian countries, that cover trade and investment.
- Read books written by international experts on specific Asian business topics.
- Consult specialized business reports issued by public and private organizations around the world.
- Use on-line data services (there are now roughly 50 that are directly relevant to Asian business).
- Attend conferences held by trade associations, chambers of commerce, and government entities, both here and in Asia.
- Subscribe to daily "fax bulletin" news-update services.
- Share and obtain information by subscribing to an on-line computer bulletin board.
- Acquire customized information from an Asian or a Western think tank (most serve private customers as well as governments).
- Watch business television programs that cover Asia.

Perhaps most important, today it's possible to engage in electronic conversations with businesspeople in Asia via e-mail, fax, telephone, or video conferencing. All of these conversation methods can now be simultaneously translated by specialized communications services, though many are still in their infancy.

This book is designed to assist you in undertaking all of these cutting-edge methods of information gathering, which seemed all too futuristic only a few years ago.

What *Isn't* Included in This Book

Two caveats must be mentioned about what has been included in this single volume. First of all, the total number of sources had to be limited to roughly 1,000. These include books, on-line services, journals, recurring government and nongovernment reports, data sources on CD-ROM, company directories, fax bulletins, tapes, and videos. Note that this sourcebook does not list specialized articles concerning Asian business; thousands of these are published every year. It does, however, list bibliographies to assist readers in pursuing short articles.

Second, the Japanese propensity for producing top-quality literature about technical topics has produced a seemingly limitless technical literature, including articles in trade journals, reports on high-tech production machinery and processes, and on-line patent information. With literally thousands of technical and scientific sources to choose from, I could not list all of them in this volume. However, for technical people seeking specialized Japanese technical literature, I have provided bibliographies of technical sources to make the search easier. The technical literature that is produced in other Asian countries and is available in English is not plentiful, and the majority of these sources have been included.

Tips for Business Information Users

I have spoken already about the importance of pursuing an information strategy when collecting and synthesizing Asian business data. Here are some tips for using the Asian business information sources reviewed in this book. It is hoped they will make your plunge into this ballooning mecca of data more of a pleasure than a torture.

Know exactly what you want to accomplish before searching for information. This will save you time and money and will reduce frustration. That said, remember that merely looking for general ideas about what you want to accomplish is a perfectly acceptable reason to seek information.

Achieve one objective at a time; again this will save you time in the long run and will reduce the anxiety associated with getting lost in the huge amount of data that is now accessible.

Don't expect to find all of the information you seek in a single source. Be prepared to scan for usable information in many sources and in different styles and formats. For example, you must be willing to look for data in an on-line format, skim a newsletter, and read through an academic monograph to find what you need.

Pay special attention to appraising the features of a source before digging it up. You can learn much about a source's usefulness by checking the date of release; the number of pages; whether the publication contains tables, graphs, and illustrations; and where it was published. By making keen assessments in this way, you can steer yourself to the best sources for your needs.

If you want to purchase information sources, it is crucial to find out what the publication costs and what it contains relative to other formats and publications. For example, the same data may exist in both journal and on-line formats. The total cost of subscribing to an on-line database for 10 employees might be $10,000 per year. A subscription to a journal that has the same data might run $250 per year. The 10 employees might be able to use the data in journal form more cost effectively. Ten subscriptions of the journal would still cost only one-fourth of what the on-line service costs.

This book tries to help information users in all of these tasks. It offers a comprehensive selection of business information sources from which to choose. It tells you what each source contains and who might benefit most from the information, for example, marketers, political risk analysts, investors, and so on. This book also provides price and ordering addresses in case you want to obtain the source straightaway, and it recommends certain texts over others to guide you toward a first-choice source when more than one source exists.

SUCCESSFUL INTELLIGENCE GATHERING

"Comparisons give rise to victories."—Sun Tze

"By the comparisons of measurements you know where victory and defeat lie," Cao Cao advises in *The Art of War*, the classic Chinese book of tactical war strategies that many modern Asian executives apply in their business dealings. Westerners who have negotiated in Asia know how much Asian executives value detail in formulating their business decisions; they consider information gathering to be at the heart of a negotiation. Westerners, on the other hand, are more likely to want to move beyond information gathering to the process of persuasion and give-and-take that precede signing a deal. In fact, how large or small your company is, what sort of technological know-how it possesses, its financial strength—all of this will likely be the focus of intense information gathering long before the negotiation opens. A concerted effort may also be underway to transfer to the Asian side as much as possible of your company's technical knowledge free of charge through strategic and seemingly unending questioning. To the consternation of many Western companies, an alliance entered for the purpose of know-how exchange becomes a case of "information draw." Sometimes, the Asian side plans from the outset to reverse-engineer the Westerner's product through the collaboration. Because the effort is usually a concerted, team objective for the Asian side, I call this negotiating strategy team-driven intelligence gathering. If your company's negotiators are not able to thwart it, your firm is likely to find itself the victim of an imbalanced exchange of information that can translate into huge financial losses.

Pursuing a Team-Driven Information Strategy

Once you have engaged with Asian businesspeople, the task of sharing and providing information becomes critically important to your company's competitiveness. Savvy Westerners doing business in Asia know the value of information, and they know how vital it is to exchange it skillfully with their Asian counterparts. The corporate literature is rife with anecdotes about Westerners' inability to acquire Asian know-how while the Asians acquire huge caches of technical information from us. Japan expert Diana Rowland uses a tongue-in-cheek way to describe an American-Japanese joint venture: It's when a Japanese firm sends 24 people to a U.S. company to find out everything the Americans know, and the Americans then reciprocate by sending *one* person to Japan to *tell* them everything he knows. This jest highlights a serious need for more savvy and more intelligent information-gathering skills on our part. One of the Big Three auto companies entered into a strategic alliance with a Japanese auto company to share manufacturing technology and techniques. More than 1,000 Japanese technicians were to work shoulder-to-shoulder with their American counterparts. The American side provided only three Japanese speakers to facilitate the exchange, whereas most of the Japanese had English language skills. Naturally, the technology flowed primarily toward the Japanese.

We need to be better at learning from others and concealing precious know-how in our international dealings. American engineers tend to be verbose when discussing their individual research accomplishments during negotiations. Taken together with the comments made by American co-workers, a skilled Japanese team can solicit a complete proprietary picture at no charge, while the American team learns nothing substantial from the Japanese. As Rowland says, "Many American companies have been slow in realizing how much they have to gain by effectively gathering information and how much they have to lose by not monitoring what they give away." One reason Asian companies are so competitive in Western markets is that they have learned to generate commercial intelligence from business information collected and gathered in the West.

The Asian ideal of sharing in your company's know-how without paying for it may be partially cultural in origin: the remnants of an ancient agrarian method of technological innovation. When members of early agrarian societies in Asia innovated, they did so in broad daylight, out in the communally farmed rice fields. A breakthrough in irrigation or planting technology directly benefited everyone in the village. No notion of propriety information took root because new technologies were instantly shared by all. Knowledge was immediately made public, and to imitate someone else's methodology or adopt it on one's own farm was considered resourceful as well as a great compliment to the originator. Borrowing know-how was not considered to be thievery or unethical. Feeling little or no reservation about imitating the techniques of others, the Japanese conducted a policy of "selective borrowing" from foreigners. This policy started when they sent an envoy to China who reproduced the imperial palace architecture in Japan. Over the past two centuries, industrial Japan has borrowed extensively from the West and has adapted to its production and quality control techniques. In fact, until the United States brought marketing to Japan in the 1950s, no such word even existed in Japanese.

This is not to suggest that Asia hasn't developed technologies on its own. The Koreans perfected the first movable metal type printing technology in 1234, two hundred years before Gutenberg. The Chinese invented gunpowder in the tenth century, the printing press in the eleventh century, and the magnetic compass in the twelfth century. Although these inventions had a revolutionary impact on the European continent, their origins went largely unrecognized and unappreciated by Westerners.

Much the same myopia persists today. Most Western firms have not taken the necessary initiative to gather and translate good information about Asian markets and business conditions in order to generate the commercial intelligence needed to make informed business decisions. Asian managers can often read English and sometimes German as well as their own language, which puts them in touch with a diversity of management theories. The typical American manager reads only English. There are currently 15,000 Japanese earning MBAs in the United States, not for the purpose of finding jobs in the West, but to gain knowledge of our business systems to help Japanese companies compete with the West.

Intelligence-Gathering Techniques

Increasingly, North American corporations have found it necessary to forge so-called strategic alliances with Asian companies (mostly Japanese) to acquire know-how from Asia, rather than vice versa. Facilitating the flow of technical information and human know-how has proved easier said than done. Here are some hints to help you counter the team-driven information-gathering strategy and better elicit technical information from your Asian counterparts.

Prepare your technical team before conducting a technical exchange. Debrief your negotiators as to what information is shareable and what is not before the exchange opens. Differences in personality between American and Asian "techies" can cause information to flow in one direction only. North Americans have a natural tendency to expound on their scientific achievements and proprietary work when asked. Asian scientists do not as readily reveal their achievements, however, considering such behavior in violation of Confucian precepts about humility. Getting Asian technicians to reveal the information you need can be a struggle for this reason. In addition, they might be under strict limitations on what they can say.

Gather as much technical information about the products produced by your Asian partner company before the meeting by researching their patents, attending trade fairs, and participating in technical seminars. Decide exactly what technological know-how you are after. Determine how much of the "technological puzzle" you have already obtained from other sources before writing the questions that you plan to ask during meetings.

Assign a leader who will be responsible for the exchange to ensure that your team doesn't accidentally deliver know-how to the other side. Before answering a question, an engineer on your team should confer with the negotiation leader. Reconvene your team after formal meetings to discuss the technology puzzle you are attempting to assemble and to discern the technical objectives of the Asian side from their line of questioning. Fill in newly acquired pieces of information, and select those to be sought at the next meeting. You may have to be adamant with your hosts to gain the necessary time for your team to do this in private.

The entire technical exchange will be a waste of resources if no one records it by taking copious notes at every meeting. To ensure continuity of an exchange over time (and through changes in your technical personnel), submit technology exchange "minutes" to be filed at the home office. Circulate the information gleaned in Asia, and capitalize on it to the fullest extent possible.

When attempting to extract technical information from Asian negotiators, remember that certain information might be proprietary to their firm or sensitive to their country's national security. You must remain patient during a technical exchange as the Asian negotiators consider any number of issues before answering your questions: Can they answer without violating government-imposed technology restrictions? Can they answer without violating proprietary know-how guidelines issued by their superiors? How should they formulate the answer so it will be clear to the Westerners after being translated? Unfortunately, North Americans often interrupt their Asian counterparts while they consider these issues, curtailing the flow of information to their side. Don't hound your Asian partners to answer questions they seem reticent to respond to.

Sometimes, questions that are impossible to get answered on Monday are forthrightly answered on Tuesday after approval has been granted behind the scenes. Continue to ask the same questions in new ways on different occasions. A statement of misinformation sometimes elicits the information that you are seeking. For example, you might note, "With all these shipping crates piled on the dock ready to go overseas, your factory must be exporting at least 50 percent of its production," eliciting the response, "Actually, the figure is much lower."

Formalize a "turn-taking" procedure. Asians may not feel comfortable exchanging information by taking turns. They may not feel at ease "bouncing ideas around," as is the habit of informal North American engineers at meetings. "In my own experience," says Hiroshi Ishi of Nippon Telephone & Telegraph, "I found that turn-taking is most difficult for me to learn to adapt to in discussions with Americans. Situation-oriented non-verbal cues for turn-taking in Japanese meetings are much more clear to me. In Japan it is very rude to interrupt other people while they are speaking. We have been taught to be patient, to listen until others are finished talking." In the West, as we all know, sometimes you *have* to interrupt if you are to be heard at all. There are two rules to follow. First, after speaking, ask your partners to please add their comments or response to the discussion. (Do not motion with your hands or signal with your eyes.) Then, wait for them to formulate their ideas and speak. Do not break the silence while they are gathering their ideas.

Sidestep questions skillfully. If you cannot answer a technology-related question, say, "This subject area is proprietary" or "This is outside the agreement we have made about this exchange" or "Our company has not released that information as of yet." Be gentle but firm, and make sure that every member of your team uses the same basic reply.

Finally, never expect your Asian partners to protect your proprietary information from being counterfeited in their country. Actively protect it yourself by registering the proper patents in Asia and policing the market on your own. Should your product or technology get knocked off or stolen, you might be able to extract royalties, but it will take a lengthy, expensive, and unpleasant lawsuit to do so.

Part One

East Asia

EAST ASIA

OVERVIEW

Since 1983, the United States has conducted more trade across the Pacific than across the Atlantic. Exports to the Far East have grown 1,200 percent since 1960, constituting a larger increase in U.S. exports in a shorter period of time than in any other region of the world. Of America's 20 largest trading partners, eight are now in the Pacific region. Our yearly trade with Asia was just $77 billion in 1978; now it's well over $200 billion annually and growing rapidly.

The Asia-Pacific region is twice the geographic size of Europe and the United States combined. One-half of the world's population lives in Asia, and more important, by the year 2000 two-thirds of the world's inhabitants will live there. By that time, the Europeans will actually shrink as a percentage of the world's population, down to about 6 percent. At its current rate, U.S.-Asian trade will be double that of U.S.-European trade. In their book *Megatrends 2000* (William Morrow and Co., 1990), John Naisbitt and Patricia Aburdene write, "Asia will have 80 million new consumers by the year 2000." On the other hand, they predict only 11 million new consumers in Europe. Moreover, what country in Europe, besides Germany, could compare to the cash reserves now held by Japanese and Taiwanese banks, which combined amount to more than $150 billion? Residents of Hong Kong, Korea, Singapore, and Taiwan save as much as 35 percent of their earnings; figures like these promise that Asia will remain the world's main source of business capital into the next millennium.

With their relentless work ethic, rapid technological progress, and export zeal, the South Koreans have the Japanese seriously asking themselves whether they can continue to dominate in East Asia beyond the year 2000. In fact, a recent study conducted by Nihon Keizai, an industrial association in Japan, found that more than three-fourths of Japanese executives fear that South Korea will be the greatest competitive threat of the four East Asian newly industrialized economies (Taiwan, Hong Kong, China, and South Korea).

Greater China Unites

The Chinese-speaking countries of East Asia are combining to forge the most dynamic economic region on earth. Former Communist Party Secretary Zhao Ziyang coined the term *Greater China* to refer to a reunified China of the future: Hong Kong, Taiwan, and the People's Republic merged into one interdependent mega-China. In 1997, Hong Kong and the Mainland will indeed unite, but Taiwan will remain politically independent into the foreseeable future. The three Chinas are uniting commercially, however, and the entrepreneurial synergy generated by that unity fuels an economic growth that is now unsurpassed in the world. Guangdong Province in South China, for instance, has sustained an astounding 12.5 percent annual economic growth rate since 1985.

Political and commercial divisions between China's Three Dragons are rapidly disappearing, and the three Chinas now exist in a state of permanent symbiosis. The Chinese town of Shenzhen, which was a coastal fishing village 10 years ago, now features a skyline crammed with office towers, financed by Hong Kong banks, with flashing neon corporate logos written in classic Chinese characters, the written language of Nationalist Taiwan, rather than the simplified characters of Communist China. Guangdong's surging real estate and stock markets, stoked by overseas Chinese investment from around the globe, have turned many Southern Chinese teenagers into tycoons and many school teachers into land developers. Mainland Chinese labor sustains Hong Kong's continued expansion as a locus of entrepôt trade—a "classroom for laissez-faire capitalism" based on its British legal tradition. Hong Kong firms now employ an estimated 3 million workers in South China and supply 70 percent of the foreign investment flowing into Guangdong Province. Taiwanese companies now dot Southern China, too, after a decade of conducting "invisible" trade across the Taiwan Strait and trading indirectly in China through trading companies in Hong Kong. The island's (now politically correct) exports to China ballooned from $3 to $6 billion annually in 1991 alone. The China Triangle now dwarfs other high-growth regions of the world as a market for Western goods and services.

The commercial needs of the Three Dragons differ markedly. Hong Kong strives to upgrade its financial, transportation, and telecommunications infrastructure so it can compete with Taiwan and Singapore and remain Asia's financial and trade hub. The "Pearl of the Orient" seeks Western technical services in civil engineering, high-tech computing, and communications. Taiwan, on the other hand, strives to move up the world's production technology ladder, seeking from Western suppliers state-of-the-art manufacturing know-how and patent licenses for sophisticated products and processes. The Taiwanese have been increasingly willing to part with their $80 billion in cash reserves to carry forward this effort; annual imports to Taiwan have tripled in the past seven years, growing to $63 billion. Finally, the vast People's Republic of China continues to expand its share of world export markets, from which it has amassed $40 billion in cash reserves. The People's Republic seeks help to privatize its massive socialist enterprises, upgrade its technology, and satisfy its legions of product-starved consumers. As part of the bargain, China offers offshore export manufacturers its limitless supply of inexpensive, yet increasingly skilled, laborers.

Polyglot Peoples and Cultures

The Asia-Pacific is normally divided into East Asia—including Japan, Korea, China, Taiwan, and Hong Kong—and Southeast Asia—including the countries of the Association of Southeast Asian Nations (ASEAN). The countries of ASEAN include Singapore, Indonesia, Thailand, Malaysia, Brunei, and the Philippines. Ethnically, East Asia is comprised of Chinese and the ethnic groups that have evolved racially and culturally from the Chinese as well as cultures that were influenced by China when they became independent states, often tribute states of China. In short, a tie to China is the commonly recognized feature of East Asian ethnic identity, a commonality that unites peoples as diverse as the Islamic Hui-hui who live in China's northwest, the Japanese, and the Tadzhiks of Central Asia. Groups do exist in East Asia that have been influenced by China yet have remained independent, but for the vast majority of East Asians, China is their cradle of civilization.

Due to the heavy cultural and political influence of Confucian China throughout the region, East Asia is often labeled Confucian Asia. Japan, Korea, and Taiwan not only adopted China's lineage state form of government and its methods of rice cultivation, but these peoples also stand under a common umbrella of customary law and ritual. Although Japan's state religion was traditionally Shintoism, most Japanese are a Buddhist-Shintoist-Confucian blend in their religious outlook. This code of law and ritual was spelled out in China's ancient philosophical literature, which originated with the works of Confucius (551–479 B.C.).

Racial intermixing in East Asia over millennia prohibits us from talking about distinct races of people inhabiting the region today. The Japanese "race" is, for example, the result of the mixing of northern and southern Mongoloids with the Ainu, an even earlier occupant of the Japanese islands. We can, however, talk about ethnic groups in East Asia that are differentiated by language, culture, religion, beliefs, and so on. We can speak of a Hakka Chinese from Taiwan as we might talk about a Slovak from Central Europe.

The divisions of groups in East Asia can be said to be more linguistic than they are racial. More than 1,000 languages are spoken throughout East and Southeast Asia. The Sinitic, or Sino-Tibetan, category is the largest language group in Asia, and Chinese languages are the largest subdivision. More people speak Mandarin than any other language on earth. Mao Tse-tung declared Mandarin (*Putunghua*, "the common language") the national language of China, but dialects other than Mandarin—Fukienese, Amoy, Hakka, and Cantonese, for example—are spoken by 20 percent of the population. The Cantonese dialect is spoken in Hong Kong and by most overseas Chinese, since most come from the southern region of mainland China where Cantonese is spoken.

Taiwan's 19 million inhabitants speak dialects of Fukienese and Hakka, but the ruling elite, which arrived after the Communist victory on the Mainland, speaks Mandarin. The Japanese language is a composite of Austronesian, Altaic, and Chinese. Koreans speak and write Korean, which is similar to Japanese but emphasizes the Altaic. During the Japanese occupation of Korea (1910–1945), however, all schooling was in Japanese, and thus most Koreans over 45 can read both Japanese and Korean.

Ethnically, East Asia is not just Chinese. The Koreans originated from Mongol populations that migrated south out of Northern Manchuria. The Japanese evolved from an aboriginal people called the Ainu, who still exist as a minority centered on Hokkaido. Hong Kong Chinese migrated from South China originally, and Taiwan's population, with the exception of the island's "mountain minorities," is largely Fukinese, a people originating on the southern coast of China.

The East Asian Diaspora

Recent Chinese immigrants to the United States, called *San Yi Man*, are the third largest immigrant group after Mexicans and Filipinos. More than 400,000 Chinese entered the United States between 1965 and 1984, about the same number that entered between 1849 and 1930. Sixty percent of new Chinese immigrants settle in California or New York; Manhattan's Chinatown boasts a population of more than 100,000.

Only 10,000 Koreans entered the United States during 1960, but more than 500,000 came in 1985, and 100,000 of those settled in New York. More than 150,000 Koreans now live in Los Angeles's Koreatown; signs written in Han'gul lining Olympic Boulevard mark Korean-owned grocery stores, barbershops, gas stations, and restaurants. Seventy percent of the Koreans who come to America possess a college degree. They come not as migratory workers, but as *yumin*, people who remain as settlers. Many get their start with the help of the *Kae* credit-rotating system brought from Korea, which allows them to capitalize new businesses. Population pressure in urban Korea encourages people to emigrate; South Korea is second only to Bangladesh in population density.

Between 1965 and 1985, more than 90,000 Japanese entered the United States. This is just 3 percent of the total number of Asians that came to live here during those years.

ACCOUNTING, BANKING, AND FINANCE

Title: *Asia Money and Finance*
Date: Monthly
Format: Periodical
Editor: Graham Field
Publisher: Euromoney Publications, Ltd.
Quadrant Subscription Services
Oakfield House
Perrymount Rd.
Haywards Heath
Sussex RH16 3DH, United Kingdom
Pages: Varies
Exhibits: Graphs, photographs, and tables
Price: $265/year

A finely published 55- to 60-page color magazine, this publication offers general information about Asian economic development, key entrepreneurs, and development policy in Asia. It also has a "database" section that provides financial forecasts for the region, including a list of new loans and equity listings. It is a recommended update for the active or armchair investor in the region, though its value might not warrant its high price.

Title: *The Asia-Pacific Region: Its Emerging Economies and Stock Markets*
Date: 1989
Format: Paperback
Author: Nomura Research Institute and Nomura Computer Systems
Publisher: Nomura Securities Co., Ltd.
No 2 Edobashi Bldg. 10-1 Nihonbashi
1-chome, Chuo-ku
Tokyo 103, Japan
Pages: 149
Exhibits: Maps, graphs, and tables

This book is an attractive fact-packed overview of Asian economies and their stock markets. Japan, Indonesia, and China are not included. It covers finances, foreign investment, politics, real estate, and more—an amazing amount of information stuffed into a compact handbook. It is recommended to investors as a desktop reference.

Title: *Asian Development Review*
Date: Semiannual
Format: Periodical
Editor: Hakchung Chao
Publisher: Asian Development Bank
P.O. Box 789
Manila 1099, Philippines
Tel: (63)(2)711-3851
Fax: (63)(2)741-7961
Pages: Varies
Exhibits: Graphs and tables
Price: $8/year

This journal is perhaps the best source of analysis on Asia's financial sector, including articles on capital markets, fiscal policy, economic development, current account balances, exchange rate policy, and other issues of special interest to bankers, accountants, and investment planners. You might also find well researched and well-presented articles about trade and investment flows.

Title: *Asian Finance*
Date: Monthly
Format: Periodical
Editor: Amitabha Chowdhury
Publisher: Asian Finance Publications, Ltd.
3rd Floor, Hollywood Centre
233 Hollywood Rd.
Hong Kong
Tel: (852)815-5221
Fax: (852)854-2794
Pages: Varies
Exhibits: Tables
Price: $35/year

Meant for bankers and financiers, this attractive 75-page magazine offers features and news updates related to Asia's banking scene. It offers perspectives on top banking CEOs, Asian borrowing patterns, debt, currencies, equities, and export markets. It includes coverage of India and Bangladesh and is recommended as a rich source of financial information at a low price.

Title: *The Asian Venture Capital Journal*
Date: Monthly
Format: Periodical
Editor: Robert Lewis
Publisher: Asian Venture Capital Journal, Ltd.
18th Floor, Sincere Insurance Building
4 Hennessy Rd.
Hong Kong
Pages: Varies
Exhibits: Tables
Price: $590/year

For investors and financiers, this 20- to 25-page magazine provides information on investment funds, stock markets, securities, and important venture capital deals in Asia. It is recommended for participating venture capitalists.

Title: *Bankers Handbook for Asia*
Date: 1990
Format: Hardcover
Editor: Amitabha Chowdhury
Publisher: Asian Finance Publications, Ltd.
3rd Floor, Hollywood Centre
233 Hollywood Rd.
Hong Kong
Tel: (852)815-5221
Fax: (852)854-2794
Pages: 469
Exhibits: None

This useful volume begins with a series of overview articles on the banking conditions in each country of Asia. These are followed by a directory of banks and financial companies. Country coverage includes Fiji, Macau, and Papua New Guinea. This book provides asset and account information for each bank and gives the names of major shareholders and bank officers.

Title: Datastream Company Accounts Services
Date: Updated as company results are published
Format: On-line database
Publisher: Datastream International, Ltd.

Monmouth House
58-64 City Rd.
London EC1Y 2AL, United Kingdom
Tel: (44)(71)250-3000
Fax: (44)(71)253-0171

Exhibits: None
Price: £750/year

This on-line database displays five years of financial figures on more than 100,000 international companies, including Japanese and Hong Kong firms. Users may access the company's profit-and-loss accounts, balance sheet, accounting ratios, company profile, and general financial news.

Title: *International Accounting and Auditing Trends*
Date: 1991
Format: Paperback
Editor: Vinod B. Bavishi
Publisher: Center for International Financial Analysis and Research, Inc.
211 College Rd. East
Princeton, NJ 08540
Tel: (609)520-9333
Fax: (609)520-0905
Pages: 231
Exhibits: Tables

Strictly for professional accountants, this enormous study of accounting and auditing practices around the world was first undertaken in 1989 to "facilitate the better understanding of international financial statements and to study global trends in international accounting and auditing." The hundreds of survey tables that are the result will answer specific questions about accounting practices and policies in a number of Asian countries, including Japan, Hong Kong, and Korea. It also contains a multilanguage lexicon of accounting terms.

Title: *International Accounting Summaries: A Guide for Interpretation and Comparison*
Date: 1991
Format: Hardcover
Author: Coopers & Lybrand
Publisher: John Wiley & Sons
605 Third Ave.
New York, NY 10158-0012
Tel: (212)850-6000
Fax: (212)850-6088
Pages: 857
Exhibits: None

Written in response to the internationalization of economic activity, this survey of accounting standards around the world includes the Asian countries of Hong Kong, Japan, South Korea, and Singapore. Each country section covers general accounting principles and specific accounting practices related to balance sheets and income statements. The organization is uniform for each country, each of which receives 25 to 30 pages in coverage. This resource is recommended to tax lawyers and accountants working in the countries covered.

Title: *Pacific Basin Finance Journal*
Date: Quarterly
Format: Periodical
Editor: S. Ghon Rhee

Publisher: Elsevier Science Publishers
P.O. Box 211
Amsterdam 1000 AE,
The Netherlands
Tel: (31)(20)586-2911
Fax: (31)(20)586-3726

Pages: Varies

Exhibits: Tables

This 100-page academic journal contains articles about the financial markets of the Asia-Pacific. The approach is empirical and theoretical, covering such topics as portfolio management, valuation of assets, prices, financial management theory, capital market development and market mechanisms. The research is rock solid, though this one is for specialists in the field only.

Title: *The Rand McNally Bankers Directory International*

Date: 1989

Format: Hardcover

Publisher: Rand McNally, Financial Publishing Division
P.O. Box 65
Skokie, IL 60076-0916
Tel: (708)673-9100

Pages: 2,051

Exhibits: Maps

This essential directory is designed for bankers and those dealing with banking institutions. It provides individual listings for international banks and their branches, including those in Asia. A glossary and country maps are provided, as are current foreign exchange rates and a directory of banking and trade associations.

Title: *The Spicer and Oppenheim Guide to Financial Statements Around the World*

Date: 1989

Format: Hardcover

Author: Spicer & Oppenheim

Publisher: John Wiley & Sons
605 Third Ave.
New York, NY 10158-0012
Tel: (212)850-6000
Fax: (212)850-6088

Pages: 341

Exhibits: None

This country-by-country overview of accounting and reporting practices around the world includes 4 to 8 pages of coverage each for Hong Kong, Indonesia, Japan, Korea, Malaysia, and Singapore. It briefly describes the financial reporting procedures in each country, though it is not meant to be a comprehensive survey of practices among the countries. Topics for each country include form and content of a company's financial statement, public filing requirements, audit requirements, valuation principles, depreciation, research and development, group financial statements, taxation, unusual and prior period times, price level changes, and retirement benefits.

Title: *Standard & Poor's International Creditweek*

Date: Weekly

Format: Periodical

Editor: Paul Stanwick

Publisher: Standard & Poor's
25 Broadway
New York, NY 10004
Tel: (212)208-1810

Pages: Varies
Exhibits: Tables

This 100-page weekly credit-worthiness watchdog covers industrialized countries around the world. Selected companies, as well as countries, are analyzed. In terms of Asia, the focus is on Japan. It includes special reports on selected industries, many of which concern Asia, and provides timely credit ratings for the serious investor.

ADVERTISING

Title: *Asian Advertising & Marketing*
Date: Monthly
Format: Periodical
Publisher: Travel and Trade Publishing (Asia), Ltd.
16th Floor, Capitol Centre
5-19 Jardine's Bazaar
Causeway Bay, Hong Kong
Tel: (852)890-3067
Fax: (852)895-2378
Pages: Varies
Exhibits: Photographs
Price: $45/year

A magazine of high quality and good value, this 50-page publication is meant for everyone involved in Asia's advertising and media market. Articles focus on consumer attitudes, buyer behavior, consumer research, marketing strategies, and public relations. It is fully illustrated and highly recommended.

Title: *International Media Guide: Asia/Pacific*
Date: Annual
Format: Paperback
Editor: Diane Lieberwitz
Publisher: International Media Enterprises, Inc.
22 Elizabeth St.
South Norwalk, CT 06854
Tel: (203)853-7880
Fax: (203)853-7370
Pages: 281
Exhibits: Maps and tables

This is an indispensable directory of Asian media that carry advertising. Companies are listed alphabetically and are coded by the countries they serve. Media descriptions are listed under industry classification headings, such as Environmental Technology, and include addresses, frequency of publication, advertising rates, size and format specifications, and a description of readership. This book is essential reading for marketers focusing on Asia.

Title: *Media Asia*
Date: Quarterly
Format: Periodical
Editor: Vijay Menon
Publisher: Asian Mass Communication Research and Information Centre
39 Newton Rd.
1130 Singapore
Pages: Varies
Exhibits: Graphs and tables
Price: $24/year

Meant for businesspeople or researchers interested in the technical and sociological aspects of communications in Asia, this is an attractive large-format journal available at a reasonable price. Its fascinating articles focus on, for example, an overview of satellite communications in Asia, television in India, and the social impact of satellite broadcasting in Korea. This publication provides interesting background for businesspeople involved in this growing industry and quality information for those researching the media in Asia.

Title: *Standard Directory of International Advertisers and Agencies*
Date: 1993
Format: Paperback
Editor: Owen O'Donnell
Publisher: Reed Reference Publishing
121 Chanlon Rd.
New Providence, NJ 07974
Tel: (908)464-6800
Fax: (908)464-3553
Pages: 1,430
Exhibits: None

This is an annually updated directory of more than 2,000 overseas companies that actively advertise and more than 2,000 advertising agencies. To be listed in the directory, non-U.S. companies must spend at least $75,000 on advertising per year, and agencies must report annual billings of at least $75,000. The entries for companies contain useful information for those selling advertising services in Asia, including the month in which each company sets its advertising budget, approximate advertising expenditures, the media used, and the agencies employed. Besides general information about each agency, the agency listings include approximate billings per year and a breakdown by media type. The listings are indexed by name of company as well as by geographic region. This is the best sourcebook of its type.

BUSINESS LEADERS

Title: *Barons Who's Who of the Asian Pacific Rim*
Date: 1992
Format: Hardcover
Editor: John L. Pellam
Publisher: Barons Who's Who
412 N. Coast Hgwy., B-110
Laguna Beach, CA 92651
Tel: (714)497-8615
Fax: (714)786-9818
Pages: 705
Exhibits: Portraits

Who's who directories are usually frustrating for users because the people they look up never seem to be listed. This one is surprisingly complete, containing biographies of 6,145 prominent Asian individuals, listing their profession, education, and major accomplishments. It also lists 4,262 of the largest Asian companies as well as governmental agencies and religious organizations in the region.

COMPANY DIRECTORIES

Title: *Asian Company Handbook*
Date: 1990
Format: Hardcover
Publisher: Toyo Keizai, Inc.
1-2-1, Nihonbashi
Hongokucho
Chuo-ku
Tokyo 103, Japan
Tel: (81)(3)246-5470
Fax: (81)(3)270-4127

Pages: 811
Exhibits: Tables
Price: $52 (airmail)

An indispensable handbook and companion to *Japan Company Handbook*, this book, updated quarterly, provides one detailed table-format page on each of 763 selected companies in Asia, excluding Japanese corporations. The information about each firm includes name, activities, outlook, number of employees, branches, bankers, financial data, stock information, sales performance, and results of sales efforts. Listings are grouped by country and cross-indexed alphabetically by company name.

Title: *Asia-Pacific/Africa-Middle East Petroleum Directory*
Date: Annual
Format: Paperback
Editor: Jonelle Moore
Publisher: Penwell Directories
Box 21278
Tulsa, OK 74121
Tel: (918)835-3161
Fax: (918)932-9319
Pages: Varies
Exhibits: None

This volume contains a comprehensive listing of companies in Asia and the Middle East that are involved in petroleum, including drilling, exploration, production, marketing, and refining. The directory is broken down by country and includes text overviews of the Asian oil industry. Company profiles are followed by a list of current executives. Company and geographical indexes are included.

Title: *Asia-Pacific Business & Trade Directory*
Date: Annual
Format: Hardcover
Publisher: Universal Business Directories, Ltd.
360 Dominion Rd.
Mt. Eden
Auckland 3, New Zealand
Tel: (64)(9)689-959
Fax: (64)(9)607-505
Pages: 846
Exhibits: Maps and tables
Price: Contact for subscription prices

This directory is meant for salespeople trying to locate buyers in every country of Asia, including the South Pacific countries of the Cook Islands, Guam, and tiny Nauru. The listings are divided by country, and each section is introduced with handy country maps. Addresses of key government departments and country overviews are included. The many paid advertisements may also assist the buyer or seller.

Title: *Asia Pacific Handbook*
Date: Semiannual
Format: Paperback
Publisher: Extel Financial, Ltd.
Fitzroy House
13-17 Epworth St.
London EC2A 4DL, United Kingdom
Pages: Varies
Exhibits: Tables
Price: £180 for annual subscription (2 vols.)

This listing of top companies in each Asian country is designed for those who want to invest in them via local stock markets. Company activities, dividend dates, shareholdings, major shareholders, and key financials are given. It also includes brief profiles of the corporate structure in each country, that is, taxation, stock markets, accounting practices, and so on.

Title: *Directory of Corporate Affiliations International*
Date: Annual
Format: Paperback; also available on database
Editor: Thomas Bachmann
Publisher: National Register Publishing/Reed Reference Publishing
121 Chanlon Rd.
New Providence, NJ 07974
Tel: (908)464-6800
Fax: (908)464-3553
Pages: 1,784
Exhibits: None

This is a four-volume directory of public and private businesses throughout the world. Volume IV lists all non-U.S. companies, public and private, including their subsidiaries, whether located in the United States or overseas. Companies are listed alphabetically but a master index cross-references them by both location and standard industrial code, that is, area of activity. Asia coverage is adequate.

Title: *Directory of the World's Largest Service Companies*
Date: 1990
Format: Paperback
Publisher: United Nations Centre on Transnational Corporations and Moody's Investors Service
Dun & Bradstreet Corp.
99 Church St.
New York, NY 10007
Tel: (212)593-4163
Fax: (201)605-6930
Pages: 834
Exhibits: Tables

This volume provides 2- to 4-page summaries of the financial standing of the world's largest service corporations, a growing number of which are Asian. Listings are categorized by industry, such as advertising, legal services, and wholesale trade. Each entry includes a description of the company, its structure and products, a table of sales, and addresses of subsidiaries.

Title: *Dun's Asia/Pacific Key Business Enterprises*
Date: Annual
Format: Hardcover
Publisher: Dun & Bradstreet Information Services
15th Floor, 100 William St.
Sydney NSW 2011, Australia
Tel: (61)(2)368-2100
Fax: (61)(2)368-2150
Pages: 1,189
Exhibits: None
Price: Contact for subscription prices

This monumental directory lists prominent companies and firms throughout Asia, by country in Volume I and by industrial category in Volume II. It includes a listing of the 2,000 best-performing Asian companies, with addresses and contact names for each company. The best directory of its kind, it includes the People's Republic of China.

Title: *Global Company Handbook: An Analysis of the Financial Performance of the World's 7,500 Leading Companies*
Date: Annual
Format: Paperback
Editor: Vinod B. Bavishi
Publisher: Center for International Financial Analysis and Research, Inc.
211 College Rd. East
Princeton, NJ 08540
Tel: (609)520-9333
Fax: (609)520-0905
Pages: 231
Exhibits: Tables

This is a two-volume directory of the 7,500 largest global corporations, hundreds of which are Asian. Volume I ranks the companies in terms of sales, assets, net income, market value, and number of employees. Comparisons between countries might be useful to the researcher of global competitiveness. Volume II offers detailed profiles of the companies by country; Asian countries are represented. Information provided on each firm includes industrial activity, stock name, stockholders, stock market listing name, and number of employees as well as basic financial data and stock value data. Recommended for the Asia investor.

Title: *The International Directory of Company Histories*
Date: 1988
Format: Hardcover
Editor: Thomas Derdak
Publisher: St. James Press
233 E. Ontario St.
Chicago, IL 60611
Tel: (800)345-0392, ext. 1422
Fax: (313)961-6083
Pages: 3,750 (5 vols.)
Exhibits: None

This five-volume compendium of "company biographies" offers well-written 3,000- to 5,000-word entries on thousands of international companies, listed by industry rather than country. Asian companies receive good coverage. This is a splendid source of company history and business activities, as opposed to financial data. It might be especially useful as part of qualifying a potential partner firm in Asia.

Title: *The International Directory of Importers*
Date: Annual
Format: Hardcover
Author: Interdata
Publisher: The International Directory of Importers
1480 Grove St.
Healdsburg, CA 95448
Tel: (707)433-3900
Fax: (707)433-8920
Pages: 365
Exhibits: None
Price: Contact for subscription prices

This directory is specifically designed to assist exporters in locating customers in Asian countries. It provides current information about firms that import products and services. The publisher gathers this information through the use of a corporate questionnaire. The book is indexed by commodity and country for easy use. In each country section, importers are listed by commodity, and each entry includes a list of key imports and contact information. This book is suggested for marketers who are trying to expand their customer base in Asia.

Title: *Macmillan Directory of Multinationals*
Date: 1989
Format: Hardcover
Author: D.C. Stafford and R.H.A. Purkis
Publisher: Stockton Press
15 E. 26th St.
New York, NY 10010
Tel: (212)673-4300
Fax: (212)673-9842
Pages: 1,441 (2 vols.)
Exhibits: Tables

This five-volume listing of multinational companies includes those based in Asia, primarily Japan. Entries include company activities, members of management and supervisory boards, company structure, product lines, and company evolution. Company data are rendered in table form. Addresses of subsidiaries are provided.

Title: *Major Companies of the Far East and Australasia*
Date: Annual
Format: Hardcover
Editor: Jennifer L. Carr
Publisher: Graham and Trotman
Sterling House
66 Wilton Rd.
London SW1V 1DE, United Kingdom
Tel: (44)(71)821-1123
Fax: (44)(71)630-5229
Pages: 362
Exhibits: None

This volume includes a company directory for Brunei, Indonesia, Malaysia, Philippines, Singapore, and Thailand. Each entry includes the address, senior executives, principal activities, parent company, shareholders, and number of employees. This source is recommended for anyone who is researching companies in these countries. An index provides a list of companies categorized by business activity.

Title: *Moody's International Manual*
Date: 1992
Format: Hardcover
Editor: Robert P. Hanson
Publisher: Moody's Investors Services, Inc.
99 Church St.
New York, NY 07054-3890
Tel: (212)553-0300
Fax: (201)605-6930
Pages: 2,347
Exhibits: Tables

The 4,700 international companies included in this magnum opus, many of which are based in Asia, are listed by country and indexed alphabetically. The reader learns not only about a company's history, business activities, and assets, but also about how the company rates on the Moody's Corporate Board Ratings, from Aaa to C. This is an essential sourcebook for investors.

Title: *Principal International Businesses*
Date: 1991
Format: Hardcover
Publisher: Dun's Marketing Services
Dun & Bradstreet Corp.
99 Church St.
New York, NY 10007
Tel: (212)593-4163
Fax: (212)605-6930
Pages: 4,367
Exhibits: None

This volume, which is as thick as a brick, provides the most comprehensive listing of international companies by geographic area, product classification, and company name. Companies are also listed by "D-U-N-S Number" and characterized as an importer, exporter, or both. This resource is indispensable to the international marketer.

Title: *Transnational Corporations: A Selective Bibliography*
Date: 1988
Format: Hardcover
Author: United Nations Centre on Transnational Corporations
Publisher: United Nations Publications
2 United Nations Plaza
New York, NY 10017
Tel: (212)593-4163
Fax: (212)605-6930
Pages: 442
Exhibits: None

This now slightly dated bibliography is unique in that it collates, by author and title, the literature relevant to transnational corporations, including those headquartered in Asia. It is recommended for the serious researcher of transnational organizations and of activity in specific industries in Asia, for example, semiconductor manufacturing in Southeast Asia.

Title: *Who Owns Whom*
Date: 1993
Format: Hardcover
Editor: Kim Fountain
Publisher: Dun & Bradstreet, Ltd.
Holmers Farm Way
High Wycombe
Bucks HP12 4UL, United Kingdom
Tel: (44)(494)422-000
Fax: (44)(494)422-260
Pages: 1,426 (1 vol.)
Exhibits: None

This is an essential guide to parent and subsidiary relationships worldwide; one volume in the series focuses on Australasia and the Far East. Entries provide an address for the parent company, a list of its subsidiaries and associates, and explanatory notes on each. Companies are listed by country. This is a very useful resource for anyone who is researching a potential partner or customer.

Title: *World Business Directory*
Date: 1992
Format: Hardcover

Editor: Meghan A. O'Meara and Kimberley A. Peterson

Publisher: Gale Research, Inc.
835 Penobscot Building
Detroit, MI 48226-4904
Tel: (313)961-2242
Fax: (313)961-6083

Pages: 3,814 (3 vols.)

Exhibits: None

This three-volume directory of 100,000 companies involved in international trade worldwide lists companies in 190 countries, including the People's Republic of China. Listings are categorized by geographic area, product line, principal business, and name. Company profiles include the number of employees, financial data, and products traded. This directory is useful to marketers who are developing customer lists for Asia.

Title: *Worldscope Industrial Company Profiles*

Date: Monthly

Format: Bound newsletters or CD-ROM

Publisher: Wright Investors' Service
Wright International
Financial Center
1000 Lafayette Blvd.
Bridgeport, CT 06604
Tel: (203)333-6666
Fax: (203)579-0424

Pages: Varies

Exhibits: Tables

For the stock investor, this financial newsletter provides detailed information on the status of stock markets throughout Asia and the world. It lists numerous Asian companies and provides information about their five-year annual growth rates and accounting practices. In addition, it includes tables summarizing the company's fiscal status, income, debt, equity, foreign sales, and so on. Even more interesting are the country profiles. A group of companies in each country, including Asian countries, are analyzed for six years of performance; a clear financial and economic picture of the country is offered. For the serious Asia investor, this newsletter is recommended.

Title: *Worldscope Profiles*

Date: Updated quarterly

Format: CD-ROM

Publisher: Wright Investors' Service
Wright International
Financial Center
1000 Lafayette Blvd.
Bridgeport, CT 06604
Tel: (203)333-6666
Fax: (203)579-0424

Exhibits: None

Price: $2,000

This CD-ROM resource contains financial descriptions, analysis, and stock performance records for companies listed on stock exchanges across the globe. The data cover 1980 to the present, and information on more than 4,900 companies is provided.

Title: *World Trade Database*

Date: Updated quarterly

Format: CD-ROM

Publisher: American Directory Corp.
9200 Lower Azusa Rd.
Rosmead, CA 91770
Tel: (818)287-0417
Fax: (818)287-2440

Exhibits: None
Price: $495

This database profiles more than 120,000 companies worldwide, and it is updated quarterly. Entries include the name of the company, contact information, basic financial data, business scope, and products imported and exported.

Title: *Worldwide Franchise Directory*
Date: 1991
Format: Hardcover
Editor: Susan Boyles Martin
Publisher: Gale Research, Inc.
835 Penobscot Bldg.
Detroit, MI 48226-4094
Tel: (313)961-2242
Fax: (313)961-6083
Pages: 619
Exhibits: Tables

This is a unique directory of franchises worldwide, but Japan is the only Asian country represented. Each franchise listing includes a description of the business and its parent, a list of locations, start-up costs, and a profile of prospective franchisees. Because franchising continues to grow as a mode of entry into Asian markets, it is hoped that future editions of this volume will include additional Asian countries.

Title: *Yearbook of International Organizations*
Date: Annual
Format: Hardcover
Editor: Union of International Associations
Publisher: K.G. Saur Verlag KG
Heilmannstrasse 17
D-8000 Munich 71, Germany
Tel: (49)(89)791-040 (Munich)
Tel: (908)665-3576 (U.S.)
Fax: (908)771-7792 (U.S.)
Pages: 1,200 (2 vols.)
Exhibits: None

Extremely useful to the businessperson, this enormous directory lists international organizations of all types by geographic area and by name of organization. All Asian countries are represented. This resource provides contact name, address, and phone numbers.

COUNTRY PROFILES

Title: *The Asia and Pacific Review*
Date: Annual
Format: Paperback
Author: World of Information
Publisher: Hunter Publishing
300 Raritan Center Pkwy.
Edison, NJ 08818
Tel: (908)225-1900
Fax: (908)417-0482
Pages: Varies
Exhibits: Maps and tables

A handy introduction to Asia, this annual publication provides overviews of every Asian country written by expert contributors. The information provided includes recent events, economic indicators, detailed maps, key facts, country profiles, and a business guide that lists useful addresses and travel information. This well-written, fact-packed, and attractively published book is suggested for business travelers in need of a quick summary before arriving in Asia.

Title: *The Asian Century*
Date: 1989
Format: Hardcover
Author: Julian Weiss
Publisher: Facts on File
460 Park Ave. South
New York, NY 10016
Tel: (212)683-2244
Fax: (212)213-4578
Pages: 231
Exhibits: None

Starting with the premise that the British Century and the American Century are past, this book is a general reader about the coming century of Asian dominance. Each chapter offers a readable narrative about a single country's economic emergence. The book covers major trends in economic development and technological advancement as well as the cultural impact of modernization in each country. It provides a good thumbnail sketch in a nonacademic style for the businessperson who is seeking an introduction to the region. However, it is now dated in many respects, particularly in regard to Japan and China.

Title: *Asia Yearbook*
Date: Annual
Format: Hardcover
Editor: Michael Malik
Publisher: Far Eastern Economic Review
G.P.O. Box 160
Hong Kong
Tel: (852)508-4300
Fax: (852)503-1549
Pages: Varies
Exhibits: Maps, graphs, and tables

Now in its 35th edition, this 250-page yearbook covers every country in Asia as well as selected other subjects, such as population, refugees, trade, military balance, and various key industries. For businesspeople who haven't had time to keep up with Asian news, politics, economy, and society, this well-written and illustrated yearbook is a good way to play catch-up at year's end.

Title: *Bulletin of Labour Statistics*
Date: Quarterly
Format: Periodical
Author: International Labour Office
Editor: Hazel Bennett
Publisher: ILO Publications
CH 1211
Geneva 22, Switzerland
Tel: (41)(22)799-6111
Fax: (41)(22)798-6358
Pages: Varies
Exhibits: Tables
Price: SFr 100/year

In a collection of high-quality tables, this 170-page journal provides data concerning employment, unemployment, wage levels, hours worked, and consumer prices around the world. The coverage of Asian countries varies, depending on the topic, but these figures are hard to find in an updated source elsewhere. The bulletin is trilingual, in English, French, and Spanish.

Title: *Business International Forecasting Services: Asia/Pacific*
Date: Annual
Format: Bound newsletter
Author: Business International Forecasting Services
Publisher: Business International Asia/Pacific, Ltd.
11th Floor, Mount Parker House
Cityplaza, Hong Kong
Tel: (852)567-0491
Fax: (852)566-9150
Pages: Varies
Exhibits: Graphs and tables

This binder newsletter covers all of Asia, offering annual updates on each country's economy, political scene, and financial trends. A summary included in each section provides the busy executive with a quick, useful overview, including a list of "areas of uncertainty." Each country section runs 20 to 40 pages and provides alternative scenarios describing where each country seems to be headed. This newsletter is recommended.

Title: *Chambers World*
Date: 1988
Format: Hardcover
Editor: David Munro
Publisher: W & R Chambers, Ltd./Cambridge University Press
43-45 Annandale St.
Edinburgh EH7 4AZ, United Kingdom
Tel: (44)(31)537-4571
Fax: (44)(31)557-2936
Pages: 733, plus 111-page map atlas
Exhibits: Maps and tables

First published in 1895, this updated gazetteer is a geographical dictionary of places, including those in Asia, listed in alphabetical order. Place names encompass countries, cities, towns, national parks, and economic and cultural regions. Of interest to internationalists of all types, entries provide pronunciation, official name, time zone, population, language, religion, currency, physical description, overview of government and industry, and more. It is an invaluable reference.

Title: *Country Outlooks/Country Data Forecasts/Country Risk Monitor*
Date: Semiannual
Format: Bound newsletters
Author: World Information Services
Publisher: Bank of America/Euromoney Publications
555 California St.
San Francisco, CA 94104
Tel: (415)622-5063
Fax: (415)622-2520
Pages: Varies
Exhibits: Tables

This three-part semiannual series published by the Bank of America is bold and useful, both as a political risk prognosticator and as a predictor of economic trends in each of the countries covered, up to six years beyond publication. That's not to say that it's always correct, but it's nice to have a source like this to buttress one's own business predictions. The country overviews, however, are similar to what can be obtained from the U.S. Department of Commerce at no charge.

Title: *Culturegrams*
Date: Annual
Format: Pamphlets
Editor: V. Lynn Tyler
Publisher: David M. Kennedy School for International Studies
Brigham Young University
Publication Services
280 HRCB
Provo, UT 84602
Tel: (801)378-6197
Fax: (801)378-6347
Pages: Varies
Exhibits: Maps

The product of years of research and input from hundreds of contributors, this series of pamphlets, covering more than 100 countries of the world, is truly one of the best ways to get a cultural overview of any Asian country. These pamphlets distill a tremendous amount of practical advice for the business visitor who wants to play the Asia protocol game like a seasoned pro. They also cover economic and political issues in a nutshell and are highly recommended as a primer.

Title: *The Dawn of the Pacific Century: Implications for Three Worlds of Development*
Date: 1991
Format: Hardcover
Author: William McCord
Publisher: Transaction Publishers
Rutgers–The State University
New Brunswick, NJ 08903
Tel: (908)932-2280
Fax: (908)932-3138
Pages: 222
Exhibits: None

This account of the quick transformation of Asia-Pacific countries into economic powerhouses is based primarily on secondary source research. The author depends heavily on previously published academic works, many of which are noted herein, and does little to make the material entertaining. As a summary, though, it is useful if other similar books are not available.

Title: *DRI International Economic Database*
Date: Updated variously by series
Format: On-line database
Publisher: DRI/McGraw-Hill
Data Products Group
24 Harrtwell Ave.
Lexington, MA 02173
Tel: (617)863-5100
Fax: (708)614-3363
Exhibits: None
Price: Contact for subscription prices

This updated on-line database offers more than 5,000 reports on economic and financial indicators for Japan, China, Southeast Asia, and other major world economies.

Title: *Economic and Social Survey of Asia and the Pacific*
Date: Annual
Format: Paperback
Author: United Nations Economic and Social Commission for Asia and the Pacific Rim (ESCAP)

Publisher: United Nations Publications
2 United Nations Plaza, Room DC2-0853
Sales Section, Publishing Service
New York, NY 10017
Tel: (212)963-8302
Fax: (212)963-3489

Pages: Varies

Exhibits: Graphs and tables

Now in its 45th issue, this annual volume, produced by ESCAP at the United Nations, covers the economic performance and macroeconomic policies of developing countries in Asia. Although the book is a bit dry in style and of rather low quality, the data is useful to the analyst of macro trends in burgeoning markets of the region and of production output in selected industries.

Title: Global Report

Date: Updated continuously

Format: On-line database

Publisher: Citicorp
77 Water St.
New York, NY 10043
Tel: (212)898-7425
(800)842-8405
Fax: (212)742-8769

Exhibits: None

Price: Contact for subscription prices

This updated on-line database provides global business and finance data in six categories: foreign exchange, country reports, money markets, companies, industries, and news. For those following the capital market, this on-line service might mean the difference between success and failure because it is updated continuously. Most of the other information can be found in paper formats for less money than using an on-line database.

Title: *The Henry Holt International Desk Reference*

Date: 1992

Format: Hardcover

Author: Gary McClain

Publisher: Henry Holt and Co.
115 W. 18th St.
New York, NY 10011
Tel: (212)302-6400
Fax: (212)819-9172

Pages: 606

Exhibits: None

This volume bills itself as a desktop source for international business information gatherers. It contains sources of information from around the world pertaining to culture, trade, education, and many other topics. The Asia section includes key countries in alphabetical order, with source categories such as consultants/advisers, chambers of commerce, and economics. The coverage is sparse, but as a first resource, it might be useful to the businessperson who is seeking contact information.

Title: Investext

Date: Updated daily

Format: On-line database (via Dialog)

Publisher: Thomson Financial Networks, Inc.
The Investext Group
11 Farnsworth St.
Boston, MA 02210
Tel: (617)345-2000
Fax: (617)330-1986

Exhibits: None
Price: $96/hour

This on-line database offers more than 320,000 reports on international markets, industries, and companies. It includes in-depth financial analyses of leading companies in each market sector as well as market forecasts for more than 50 industries.

Title: *Investing and Sourcing Sites: Asia/Pacific in the 1990s*
Date: 1991 (Report Q113, vol. 1)
Format: Paperback
Editor: Neal McGrath
Publisher: Business International Asia/Pacific, Ltd.
10th Floor, Luk Kwok Centre
72 Gloucester Rd.
Hong Kong
Pages: 215
Exhibits: Graphs and tables

This well-researched and well-illustrated study covers investment conditions in five Asian countries: China, Hong Kong, South Korea, Singapore, and Taiwan. Each country analysis covers political outlook, economic conditions, investment conditions, investment incentives, and importing and exporting. Each country is appraised as a sourcing site in terms of the government's role in industry, its attitude toward foreign investment, and the past performance of foreign investment.

Title: *Key Indicators of Developing Asian and Pacific Countries*
Date: Annual
Format: Paperback
Author: Economics and Development Resource Center of the Asian Development Bank
Editor: William T.C. Ho
Publisher: Oxford University Press
P.O. Box 789
Manila 1099, Philippines
Pages: Varies
Exhibits: Graphs and tables

A very useful compendium of trade and production data, this annual publication is divided into three parts. The first set of data (much of which is rendered in graphs) compares Asian countries with world development trends; the second offers regional trends; and the third provides data on each country separately. Japan is not included because it is a developed country. This book is a timely, authoritative source of research data for marketers and academics alike.

Title: *Minidragons: Fragile Economic Miracles in the Pacific*
Date: 1991
Format: Hardcover
Editor: Steven M. Goldstein
Publisher: Ambrose Video Publishing, Inc.
Suite 2245
1290 Avenue of the Americas
New York, NY 10104
Tel: (212)265-7772
Fax: (212)265-8088
Pages: 192
Exhibits: Photographs

Conceived as a tabletop companion to the television series "Minidragons," which aired on PBS, this compilation of descriptive country profiles is useful as a brief introduction to Taiwan, Singapore, Hong Kong, and South Korea. The color photography is not spectacular, however, and thus this book cannot be recommended as a gift for business associates.

Title: *Pacific Destiny: Inside Asia Today*
Date: 1990
Format: Hardcover
Author: Robert Elegant
Publisher: Crown Publishers
201 E. 50th St.
New York, NY 10022
Tel: (212)572-6117
Fax: (212)572-6192
Pages: 533
Exhibits: None

Written by a preeminent journalist, this full-length reader provides a colorful tour through modern Asian society. The author keeps the reader's interest with country-specific chapters laced with anecdotes, interview material, and brief but incisive analyses of Asia's economic rise.

Title: *The Pacific Rim Almanac*
Date: 1991
Format: Hardcover
Author: Alexander Besher
Publisher: HarperPerennial
10 E. 53rd St.
New York, NY 10022
Tel: (212)207-7000
Fax: (212)207-7617
Pages: 824
Exhibits: Maps, graphs, and tables

For the cocktail-party Pacific Rimmer, this eclectic compendium of selected articles, survey results, government-issue maps and graphs, and published excerpts provides a fun and useful reader. Most of the material is losing its original timeliness, but for the scope of coverage, this is a recommended desktop resource of general information and interesting facts. The subjects covered range from AIDS in Asia to Zen meditation. It includes a useful list of contacts and business organizations.

Title: *Pacific Rim Intelligence Handbook*
Date: Annual
Format: Bound newsletter
Editor: Karen Kullgren Juh
Publisher: Government Information Services
1611 N. Kent St., Suite 508
Arlington, VA 22209
Tel: (703)528-1082
Pages: Varies
Exhibits: Tables
Price: $187.95

This loose-leaf binder of information includes background notes on all Asian countries, economic overviews, and general marketing information. However, the material appears to be similar to information that is readily obtainable from the U.S. Department of Commerce at no charge.

Title: *Trends in Developing Countries*
Date: Annual
Format: Paperback
Author: The World Bank
Publisher: International Bank for Reconstruction and Development/The World Bank
1818 H St., NW
Washington, DC 20433
Tel: (202)473-1956
Fax: (202)676-0579
Pages: 599
Exhibits: Tables

This large-format paperback compendium is produced by The World Bank each year, and it can't be beat for those who are looking for brief but well-researched overviews of Asian economies. Each 5- to 7-page country entry includes concise updates on economic developments and midterm prospects, all complemented by a complete table of country data, trade trends, and balance-of-payment information.

Title: *The West Pacific Rim: An Introduction*
Date: 1992
Format: Hardcover
Author: Rupert Hodder
Publisher: Belhaven Press
25 Floral St.
Covent Garden
London WC2E 90S, United Kingdom
Pages: 153
Exhibits: Graphs and tables

This slim volume provides an up-to-date overview of the economies of the Asia-Pacific, with an emphasis on Japan and China. It contains two chapters on the region's historical and cultural development and a useful chapter about the Chinese diaspora. Trade, investment, and economic strategies are described, as well. For the businessperson in search of a quick introduction to the economies of the region, this is a good choice.

Title: *Worldcasts—Asia*
Date: Quarterly
Format: Bound newsletter
Editor: George Cratcha
Publisher: Predicasts
11001 Cedar Ave.
Cleveland, OH 44106
Tel: (800)321-6388
Pages: Varies
Exhibits: Tables
Price: $900/year for subscription to all Worldcasts

For the serious marketing manager, these bound newsletters are invaluable once they are understood. All Asian countries are available. Each entry lists products by SIC code. Next, a significant event is noted that affects the market in that country for that product, followed by predictions concerning the product or market (i.e., growth, change, etc.). The publication source from which the information was garnered is also listed. This newsletter is suggested for indefatigable market trackers only.

Title: *The World Factbook*
Date: Annual

Format: Paperback (also available on microfiche, magnetic tape, and computer disks)

Author: Central Intelligence Agency (CIA)

Publisher: U.S. Government Superintendent of Documents
U.S. Government Printing Office
Washington, DC 20402-9325
Tel: (202)783-3238

Pages: 439

Exhibits: Maps, graphs, and tables

Price: Contact for subscription prices

This book provides profiles of 1 to 2 pages each of all of the countries of the world. Color maps and a list of international organizations round out this useful desktop reference.

DISTRIBUTION

Title: *Managing Distribution in Asia/Pacific Markets*

Date: 1992

Format: Paperback

Publisher: Business International Asia/Pacific, Ltd.
10th Floor, Luk Kwok Centre
72 Gloucester Rd.
Hong Kong

Pages: 151

Exhibits: Graphs and tables

This book is of great value to marketers new to the Asian market who seek a general overview of the key problems and solutions in setting up a selling network in the region. This large-format guidebook is informative, clearly written, and convenient to use. Chapters cover the basics of distribution, including a review of market trends in the region, available methods of building a sales network, techniques for supervising the distribution process, typical obstacles, tips for selecting a distributor, suggestions for managing the distributor-principal relationship, and business forecasts for Asian countries. A list of high-profile Asian distributors is included.

ECONOMY

Title: *Asian Development Outlook*

Date: Annual

Format: Paperback

Author: Asian Development Bank

Publisher: Oxford University Press
P.O. Box 789
Manila 1099, Philippines

Pages: Varies

Exhibits: Graphs and tables

Asian countries are treated in country-specific chapters in this 300-page economic outlook reader. The coverage includes gross domestic product (GDP) growth, inflation, trade, debt, and so on, with an emphasis on financial policy issues. Each country outlook runs 3 to 6 pages. This resource includes Laos, Vietnam, Mongolia, Myanmar, and the Pacific Islands (as well as the larger economies of the Asia-Pacific), but it does not cover Japan. Two additional sections examine macroeconomic policy in the region and rural poverty in Asia.

Title: Asian Economic News
Date: Updated weekly
Format: On-line database
Publisher: Kyodo News International, Inc.
50 Rockefeller Plaza, Room 803
New York, NY 10020
Tel: (212)586-4550
Fax: (212)725-3721
Exhibits: None
Price: $120/hour

This on-line database covers business and economics news in the Far East, excluding Japan. It tracks loans by the World Bank and International Monetary Fund (IMF), labor laws, trade regulations, and fiscal and monetary policy, and it provides the full text of articles drawn from regional newspapers and periodicals. It is a rather expensive way to avoid visiting the library to read the same material in paper form.

Title: *Asian-Pacific Economic Literature*
Date: Semiannual
Format: Periodical
Author: National Centre for Development Studies
Editor: H.W. Arndt
Publisher: Beech Tree Publishing
10 Watford Close
Guildford
Surrey GUI 2EP, United Kingdom
Pages: Varies
Exhibits: Graphs and tables
Price: Contact for subscription prices

This useful journal features articles and book reviews. The long articles are presented in academic style and cover topics in trade, investment, and economic development in Asia. The book reviews number almost 100 in each issue and include handy abstracts. Key journal articles are abstracted as well, and an authors' index is provided. This journal is recommended for anyone who is tracking the literature on Asian trade, investment, and economic policy.

Title: *Asia's 'Miracle' Economies*
Date: 1992
Format: Hardcover
Author: Jon Woronoff
Publisher: M.E. Sharpe, Inc.
80 Business Park Dr.
Armonk, NY 10504
Tel: (914)273-1800
Fax: (914)273-2106
Pages: 412
Exhibits: Photographs

If you are going to read one book about the economic rise of the Asian nations, consider reading this one. The author is a talented writer and a solid analyst. In this book he presents a highly readable narrative focusing on the economic ascent of Japan, Korea, Taiwan, Singapore, and Hong Kong. Seven chapters explain Asian economic policies and development models.

Title: *Business Cycles in Asia*
Date: 1991
Format: Hardcover
Editor: Hiroshi Osada and Daisuke Hiratsuka

Publisher: Institute of Developing Economies
42, Ichigaza-Hommura-cho
Shinjuku-ku
Tokyo 162, Japan

Pages: 204

Exhibits: Graphs and tables

With their industrialization since the 1960s, Asian countries have begun to exhibit traceable business cycles. Moreover, because they pursue export-led development strategies while retaining their rural industry alongside manufacturing, the editors believe that these countries have "come to experience the co-existence of manufacturing-based business cycles and agricultural cycles, and also the international diffusion of business cycles." This collection of analytical articles covers these cycles in seven Asian countries. It is suggested for economists and serious-minded corporate strategists.

Title: *The Competitive Advantage of Nations*

Date: 1990

Format: Hardcover

Author: Michael E. Porter

Publisher: The Free Press
866 Third Avenue
New York, NY 10022
Tel: (212)605-9364
Fax: (212)605-9372

Pages: 855

Exhibits: Graphs and tables

In this seminal study, the author of other classics in the field of competitive advantage and global competition asks why particular social groups, economic institutions, and nations advance and prosper. The studies of Japan, Korea, and Singapore provide excellent overviews of industrial policy and corporate competitiveness in these countries. This is a highly recommended and readable volume for American business decision makers.

Title: *Development Challenges in Asia and the Pacific in the 1990s*

Date: 1991

Format: Paperback

Editor: Seiji Naya and Stephen Browne

Publisher: East-West Center
1777 East-West Rd.
Honolulu, HI
Tel: (808)948-5353
Fax: (808)988-6052

Pages: 243

Exhibits: Graphs and tables

This compilation of conference papers by academics examines Asia's challenges in the areas of human development, environmental and natural resource management, and economic reform and management. Articles that might interest businesspeople cover private-sector development in Asia, regional cooperation in Asia, and the political economy of China.

Title: *East Asian Economic Perspectives*

Date: Monthly

Format: Periodical

Publisher: International Center for the Study of East Asian Development

Kaikan Building 13-1, Mainichi-Seibu
Konyamachi, Kokurakita
Kitakyushu City 802, Japan
Tel: (81)(93)511-1311
Fax: (81)(93)511-0404

Pages: Varies

Exhibits: Varies

Price: Contact for subscription prices

This 20-page pamphlet provides monthly updates on Asian economies and long articles on East Asian industrial performance. Selected industries in specific countries are often covered, for example, "Status and Outlook of the Chinese Automobile Industry." Many articles are reprinted research papers from academic organizations throughout the region, and thus there is no lack of content.

Title: *Economic and Social Survey of Asia and the Pacific*

Date: Annual

Format: Paperback

Author: Economic and Social Survey of Asia and the Pacific

Publisher: United Nations Publications
2 United Nations Plaza, Room DC2-0853
Sales Section, Publishing Service
New York, NY 10017
Tel: (212)963-8302
Fax: (212)963-3489

Pages: 237

Exhibits: Graphs and tables

This annual overview of Asian economics is divided into two parts. The first discusses current economic developments in the region and social issues related to poverty and overpopulation; the second examines infrastructural development in the context of sustaining economic growth. The second section also provides detailed information on energy, transportation, education, and health. The text is readable, and the analysis clear and succinct. This is a recommended update for economists and business strategists. When ordering, ask for United Nations Publications Sales no. E.91.II.F.10.

Title: *Economic Cooperation in the Asia-Pacific Region*

Date: 1990

Format: Hardcover

Editor: John P. Hardt and Young C. Kim

Publisher: Westview Press
5500 Central Ave.
Boulder, CO 80301
Tel: (303)444-3541
Fax: (303)449-3356

Pages: 224

Exhibits: Tables

This collection of informative and insightful articles by academic authors is useful to the business reader who seeks background on the growing economic links between Asian nations and on U.S. trade policy in Asia and technology transfer issues. It's tough reading, but the result is an informed big-picture understanding of how Asian countries fit together technologically, economically, and in terms of regional influence and leadership.

Title: *Economic Policy-making in the Asia-Pacific Region*
Date: 1990
Format: Hardcover
Editor: John W. Langford and K. Lorne Brownsey
Publisher: The Institute for Research on Public Policy
P.O. Box 3670 South Halifax
Nova Scotia B3J 3K6, Canada
Tel: (902)609-5315
Fax: (902)700-1057
Pages: 342
Exhibits: Graphs

For those who are tracking political risk factors and shifts in Asian governmental policy, this collection of academic articles explores economic policy making in Asia, devoting one chapter to each country. Not for the casual reader, this book offers much detail on economic decision making in Asian bureaucracies, though it's dated in parts.

Title: Economics and Development Resource Center Report Series
Date: Irregular
Format: Bound monographs
Author: Varies
Publisher: Asian Development Bank
P.O. Box 789
Manila 1099, Philippines
Pages: Varies
Exhibits: Varies

This series appears irregularly on subjects of finance and economic progress in developing Asian economies. Write to the publisher for a current list of published works. The presentation is strictly reportlike in style and theoretical in approach, but these books can be useful to the serious researcher.

Title: *Global Shift: The Internationalization of Economic Activity*
Date: 1992
Format: Paperback
Author: Peter Dicken
Publisher: Paul Chapman Publishing, Ltd.
144 Liverpool Rd.
London N1 1LA, United Kingdom
Tel: (44)(71)609-5315
Fax: (44)(71)700-1057
Pages: 492
Exhibits: Maps, graphs, and tables

This attractive and well-organized textbook will interest businesspeople seeking a comprehensive background in the globalization of trade, investment, and production. It contains in-depth analysis of specific global industries, including textiles, automobiles, electronics, and services. It's loaded with examples, charts, and diagrams and has a complete bibliography. This volume provides good coverage of Japan, Malaysia, Taiwan, Korea, Singapore, Hong Kong, Indonesia, and China.

Title: *Journal of Asian Economics*
Date: Semiannual
Format: Periodical
Author: American Commission on Asian Economic Studies

Editor: M. Jan Dutta
Publisher: JAI Press
55 Old Post Rd., No. 2
P.O. Box 1678
Greenwich, CT 06836-1678
Tel: (908)932-7054
Fax: (908)932-1558
Pages: Varies
Exhibits: Tables
Price: $60 for individuals; $125 for institutions

Recommended for the serious researcher of microeconomic issues in Asian development, this 250-page journal contains 15 to 25 articles of a highly theoretical nature on subjects ranging from income growth to monetary policy. It is pricey, but a good value for those who can use this information.

Title: *The Journal of East Asian Affairs*
Date: Semiannual
Format: Periodical
Editor: Chung No-gwan
Publisher: Research Institute for International Affairs
530-12 Dapsimni 5 Dong
Seoul 150-010, Korea
Pages: Varies
Exhibits: Varies
Price: $14/year

Containing long articles written by academics in the United States, this 300-page journal is published in Korean and thus emphasizes that country in its article roster. The focus is on the macroeconomic aspects of development in East Asian countries. Articles comparing Asian development models are especially useful to business planners tracking these economies. Political topics receive excellent coverage as well and might be useful to anyone who is monitoring political risk in East Asia.

Title: *Looking at the Sun: The Rise of the New East Asian Economic and Political System*
Date: 1994
Format: Hardcover
Author: James Fallows
Publisher: Pantheon Books
Division of Random House, Inc.
201 E. 50th St.
New York, NY 10022
Tel: (212)751-2600
Pages: 517
Exhibits: Map
Price: $25.00

Emphasizing historical and cultural influences on Asian development, this important volume offers a set of working theories about why the economies of the region have boomed, and how they differ markedly from the economic model guiding the U.S. The author provides well-crafted and personal portraits of each country in the region, including those in Southeast Asia. The businessperson will find fresh insights here, an engrossing overview of the entire Asia-Pacific, as well as much grist for constructive debate.

Title: *Pacific Economic Bulletin*
Date: Semiannual
Format: Periodical
Author: National Centre for Development Studies

Editor: Rodney V. Cole and Graeme S. Dorrance

Publisher: Australian National University
G.P.O. Box 4
Canberra ACT 2601, Australia
Tel: (61)(6)249-4705
Fax: (61)(6)257-2886

Pages: Varies

Exhibits: Map and tables

Price: $20

This nicely published 60-page journal is a forum for articles about economic development in Asia, with a welcome focus on the South Pacific islands and Australia. It includes a "statistical annex" of clearly presented data in graphs and tables. It might be of use to business strategists, depending on the focus of the issue.

Title: *Pacific Focus*

Date: Quarterly

Format: Periodical

Author: Center for International Studies

Editor: Kwang Il Baek

Publisher: Inha University
Inchon 402-751, Korea

Pages: Varies

Exhibits: Varies

Price: $40/year

This 175-page journal presents a collection of articles that focus on Asian political trends and economic development. The style of the long articles is theoretical, yet business practitioners might find them helpful in gauging political risk and following macroeconomic developments. Because it is published in Korea, the journal is a good source of information on current political events in Korea.

Title: *Pacific Rim Business Digest*

Date: Bimonthly

Format: Periodical

Editor: John Minthorne

Publisher: Transpacific Communications Co.
1223 Wilshire Blvd., Suite 413
Santa Monica, CA 90403
Tel: (213)394-1467
Fax: (213)395-8058

Pages: Varies

Exhibits: None

Price: $45/year

This general Asia business magazine offers updates on trade, finance, and deal making around the Pacific Rim, with sections dedicated to covering events in every Asian country. This magazine needs a face-lift, and there are similar publications that provide more value for the price.

Title: *Privatisation and Public Enterprise: The Asia-Pacific Experience*

Date: 1991

Format: Hardcover

Editor: Geeta Gouri

Publisher: Oxford & IBH Publishing Co., Pvt. Ltd.
66 Janporn, New Dehli, India 110001
Tel: (011)3324578
Fax: (011)3322639

Pages: 734

Exhibits: Graphs and tables

Published in India, this compilation of research articles covers privatization programs carried out throughout Asia. This detailed examination will be useful to economists, policy makers, and managers who seek to understand the operation and function of state enterprise in the region. Selected articles cover privatization of public enterprises in Thailand, Philippines, Sri Lanka, Malaysia, India, and China. Plentiful case studies of privatized firms make this a one-of-a-kind source.

Title: *Research in Asian Economic Studies*
Date: Semiannual
Format: Hardcover periodical
Editor: M. Dutta
Publisher: JAI Press Inc.
55 Old Post Rd., No. 2
Greenwich, CT 06830
Tel: (908)932-7054
Fax: (908)932-1558
Pages: Varies
Exhibits: Graphs and tables
Price: Contact for subscription prices

The long academic articles in this biannual collection are divided by country and include in-depth analyses of, for example, direct investment in Japan, the earnings of Japanese men, technology assimilation in Bangladesh, and export-led economic development in Korea. Many corporate case studies add value for the serious business reader.

Title: *The Western Pacific: Challenge of Sustainable Growth*
Date: 1992
Format: Hardcover
Author: Alan Burnett
Publisher: Edward Elgar Publishing Co.
Old Post Rd.
Brookfield, VT 05036
Tel: (802)276-3162
Fax: (802)276-3837
Pages: 270
Exhibits: Maps and tables

Written by a professor at the Australian National University, the premise of this volume is "that it is unwise to assume that sustainable growth is a viable concept [in the Western Pacific Rim], given that modern societies need increasing amounts of energy to increase their present rates of economic activity." This book analyzes the potential for long-term growth in the region by looking at demographics, energy consumption, and the environmental impact of development. Businesspeople making long-term projections about the region might find this clearly articulated treatise useful.

Title: Working Paper Series of the Asian Pacific Research and Resource Centre
Date: Irregular
Format: Bound monographs
Author: Varies
Publisher: Asian Pacific Research and Resource Centre, Carleton University
Norman Paterson School of International Affairs
Ottawa
Ontario K1S 5B6, Canada
Pages: Varies

Exhibits: Tables
Price: $5 per report

The topics covered in this series of papers include a comparative study of export processing zones in Asia, a study of the current Indonesian economy, and China's Generalized Agreement on Tariffs and Trade (GATT) membership. Each fully cited academic report runs 30 to 40 pages, single spaced, and provides solidly researched analysis to businesspeople who are exploring specific topics. Write for a current list of reports.

ETIQUETTE AND PROTOCOL

Title: *Asian Customs and Manners*
Date: 1988
Format: Hardcover
Author: Kevin Chambers
Publisher: Meadowbrook, Inc.
18318 Minnetonka Blvd.
Deephaven, MN 55391
Tel: (612)473-5400
Fax: (612)475-0736
Pages: 375
Exhibits: Maps

This easy-to-use reference handbook includes the usual tips on meeting people, general etiquette, body language, and so on, but it also has sections on key phrases in Asian languages and telephone information. For a one-stop source of this important information, this is a good pack-along primer.

Title: *Blunders in International Business*
Date: 1993
Format: Paperback
Author: David A. Ricks
Publisher: Blackwell Publishers
238 Main St.
Cambridge, MA 02142
Tel: (617)225-0401
Fax: (617)225-0412
Pages: 172
Exhibits: None

Like *Do's and Taboos around the World*, this book of entertaining anecdotes delights and informs. The Asia coverage is moderate. Bloopers are divided into those regarding production, foreign names, advertising, translation, management, finance, and law. Reading the book might prevent similar blunders, which is reason enough to recommend it.

Title: *Do's and Taboos Around the World*, 2nd Edition
Date: 1990
Format: Paperback
Editor: Roger E. Axtell
Publisher: John Wiley & Sons
605 Third Ave.
New York, NY 10158-0012
Tel: (212)850-6000
Fax: (212)850-6088
Pages: 183
Exhibits: Cartoons

This is perhaps the largest collection of entertaining business blunders and bloopers, some of which occurred in Asia, for anyone preparing to visit counterparts overseas or who just wants to chuckle at the expense of corporate brethren. The anecdotes, originally collected by the Parker Pen Company, are readable, relevant, and a lot of fun.

Title: *Do's and Taboos of Hosting International Visitors*
Date: 1990
Format: Paperback
Author: Roger E. Axtell
Publisher: John Wiley & Sons
605 Third Ave.
New York, NY 10158-0012
Tel: (212)850-6000
Fax: (212)850-6088
Pages: 236
Exhibits: Cartoons

For those who are preparing to host international guests, including those from Asia, this book is a light and readable source of practical advice. What it lacks in detail, it makes up for in its entertaining presentation. For serious businesspeople who will be hosting Asians, however, additional sources of information should be consulted.

Title: *Protocol: The Complete Handbook of Diplomatic, Official and Social Usage*
Date: 1989
Format: Paperback
Author: Mary Jane McCaffree and Pauline Innis
Publisher: Devon Publishing
2700 Virginia Ave., NW
Washington, DC 20037
Tel: (202)337-5179
Pages: 414
Exhibits: Drawings

The reference book style of this compendium of official government protocol guarantees the book's life as a reference rather than a read, yet for those preparing to host or visit foreign diplomats or royalty, this is your only choice. Chapter topics include titles and forms of address, calling cards, places to entertain, table seating, and flag etiquette. The principal author has served in the office of the Chief of Protocol in the White House. The book is thoroughly illustrated with examples.

Title: *The Traveler's Guide to Asian Customs and Manners*
Date: 1986
Format: Paperback
Author: Elizabeth Devine and Nancy Braganti
Publisher: St. Martins Press
175 Fifth Ave.
New York, NY 10010
Tel: (212)674-5151
Fax: (212)420-9314
Pages: 315
Exhibits: None

This is an easy-to-use country-by-country listing of cultural dos and don'ts, but it offers little for businesspeople other than travel advice and key phrases in Asian languages.

Title: *When Business East Meets Business West: The Guide to Practice and Protocol in the Pacific Rim*
Date: 1991
Format: Hardcover and paperback
Author: Christopher Engholm
Publisher: John Wiley & Sons
605 Third Ave.
New York, NY 10158-0012
Tel: (212)850-6000
Fax: (212)850-6088

Pages: 354
Exhibits: Maps and tables
Price: $24.95, hardcover; $14.95, paperback

This book is a one-stop source of information about business practice and etiquette throughout the diverse countries of the Asia-Pacific. John W. Bruns of McDonnell Douglas Pacific & Asia, Ltd., reviewed the book, saying that it "effectively captures the subtle social aspects of doing business in Asia—exactly where most Westerners are poorly informed." Chapter topics include first impressions, communicating, negotiating, dining, hosting, gift giving, and living in Asia. It includes "culture capsules" that provide historical and political background on each country.

GENERAL BUSINESS

Title: *The Asian Mind Game: Unlocking the Hidden Agenda of the Asian Business Culture: A Westerner's Survival Manual*
Date: 1991
Format: Hardcover
Author: Chin-ning Chu
Publisher: Rawson Associates
Macmillan Publishing Co.
866 Third Ave.
New York, NY 10022
Tel: (212)702-3428
Fax: (212)605-3099
Pages: 271
Exhibits: None

You must form your own opinion about this author's work, which attempts to reveal to Westerners the mysterious and often hidden motivations and agendas of Asian businesspeople. This book is an expanded version of the author's previously published book of the same title. In revealing the hidden secrets of Asian business culture, which is done through a brief analysis of Chinese and Japanese myths and proverbs, it is debatable whether the author is promoting stereotypes or really preparing Westerners to do battle with the economic dragons of Asia. For negotiators, this book will entertain, but it shouldn't be used as a single source of advice.

Title: Asia-Pacific
Date: Updated semimonthly
Format: On-line database
Publisher: Aristarchus Knowledge Industries, Inc.
P.O. Box 45160
Seattle, WA 98108
Exhibits: None
Price: $114/hour; $.65 per full record obtained on-line

This updated on-line database provides business and economic news for Asia and the Pacific. Topics include mergers and acquisitions, political risk, strategic planning, and industry overviews. However, this information is available in any good business library at a fraction of the cost.

Title: *Business Alliances Guide: The Hidden Competitive Weapon*
Date: 1993
Format: Hardcover
Author: Robert Porter Lynch
Publisher: John Wiley & Sons

605 Third Ave.
New York, NY 10158-0012
Tel: (212)850-6000
Fax: (212)850-6088

Pages: 337
Exhibits: Graphs and tables

This compendium of explanation and advice is useful to executives and managers seeking to forge corporate alliances overseas. With the index, businesspeople can find useful references to building alliances in Japan, Korea, and China. Beyond this, however, the material in this how-to guide is general and unfocused.

Title: *Business Networks and Economic Development in East and Southeast Asia*
Date: 1991
Format: Hardcover
Editor: Gary Hamilton
Publisher: Centre of Asian Studies
University of Hong Kong
139 Pokfulam Rd.
Hong Kong
Tel: (852)550-2703
Fax: (852)875-0734
Pages: 333
Exhibits: Tables

Although this compilation of articles is academic in style and theoretical in approach, it is recommended as a one-of-a-kind source of analysis and historical review of corporate networks and commercial relationships among Asian companies. It covers Korean *chaebols*, Japanese *keiretsu* conglomerates, and the family business networks of Taiwan. The insights into the cultural underpinnings of Asian management style and commercial conduct are essential for Western businesspeople who engage with Asian counterparts at any level.

Title: *Corporate Planning and Policy Planning in the Pacific*
Date: 1993
Format: Hardcover
Author: Gavin Boyd
Publisher: St. Martin's Press
175 Fifth Ave.
New York, NY 10010
Tel: (212)674-5151
Fax: (212)420-9314
Pages: 233
Exhibits: None

This volume compares the corporate planning systems at work behind the economic miracles in Asia and compares them with corporate planning in America. The coverage includes Japan, Indonesia, Malaysia, Singapore, Korea, Taiwan, and Thailand. The analysis is useful to serious-minded industrial planners, both corporate and governmental.

Title: *Doing Better Business in Asia: A Handbook of Checklists and Essential Facts for Corporate Managers*
Date: 1988
Format: Hardcover
Publisher: Business International Asia/Pacific, Ltd.
11th Floor, Mount Parker House
Citiplaza
Taikoo Shing, Hong Kong
Tel: (852)567-0491
Fax: (852)588-53279

Pages: 127
Exhibits: Tables

Now rather dated, this guide offers the businessperson well-researched advice on doing business in Asia as an investor. Much of the material is substantiated by useful corporate case studies. Sections cover investing and licensing, managing a venture, marketing, financing, and labor. The section that provides facts and figures suffers the most with the passage of time. This is a good primer for the would-be investor.

Title: *Handbook of International Business*
Date: 1988
Format: Hardcover
Editor: Ingo Walter
Publisher: John Wiley & Sons
605 Third Ave.
New York, NY 10158-0012
Tel: (212)850-6000
Fax: (212)850-6088
Pages: 510
Exhibits: Tables

This is a desktop reference book for students and businesspeople who seek a source of clear explanations and definitions concerning international business. The entries are divided into general topic areas, such as "The System of International Payments" and "Critical Issues in International Business." With the complete index, Asian country information can be easily located in the context of international business topics, for example, "Industrial Policy, Japan."

Title: *International Acronyms, Initialisms & Abbreviations Dictionary*
Date: 1993
Format: Hardcover
Editor: Jennifer Mossman
Publisher: Gale Research, Inc.
835 Penobscot Building
Detroit, MI 48226-4094
Tel: (313)961-2242
Fax: (313)961-6083
Pages: 1,211
Exhibits: None

This volume lists more than 150,000 international acronyms, initialisms, abbreviations, alphabetic symbols, contractions, and other condensed appellations for all countries in all fields. It is helpful to businesspeople who must deal with KOTRA, ASEAN, JETRO . . . you get the idea.

Title: *International Business Communication*
Date: 1992
Format: Paperback
Author: David A. Victor
Publisher: HarperCollins
10 E. 53rd St.
New York, NY 10022
Tel: (212)207-7000
Fax: (212)207-7617
Pages: 280
Exhibits: None

Operating under the perhaps accurate assumption that having excellent international business communication skills is more important to success in dealing with other cultures than possessing excellent technical skills, this book is a comprehensive and heavily cited volume that summarizes key themes in intercultural business communication. It is essential reading for anyone dealing with foreign businesspeople at home or abroad. The author provides practical guidance on critical issues that affect communication patterns across cultures, including language, social organization, the need to save face, high and low contexts for communication, and perceptions of time. Though the business reader must wade through the academic style of presentation, the enormous amount of know-how related warrants the investment.

Title: *International Business Negotiation and Contract Encyclopedia of Terms and Conditions*
Date: 1982
Format: Hardcover
Editor: Michio Morikawa
Publisher: The International Business Practices Education Center
6-5, Toranomon-Tachikawa Building, 1-chome
Nishi-Shimbashi, Minato-ku
Tokyo 105, Japan
Pages: 410
Exhibits: None

This is a finely published encyclopedia of contractual terms and contract forms used in international business, including trade agreements, joint-venture contracts, and technology licensing arrangements. It is suggested for negotiators, mediators, lawyers, and arbitrators.

Title: *International Mergers and Acquisitions*
Date: 1989
Format: Hardcover
Publisher: IFR Publishing, Ltd.
South Quay Plaza II
183 Marsh Wall
London E14 9FU, United Kingdom
Pages: 259
Exhibits: Graphs and tables

This volume contains a chapter about mergers and acquisitions in Japan, including an overview of related laws and regulations as well as a list of deals. It also includes light coverage of China and Indonesia.

Title: *International Negotiation: A Cross-Cultural Perspective*
Date: 1980
Format: Paperback
Author: Glen Fisher
Publisher: Intercultural Press, Inc.
P.O. Box 768
Yarmouth, ME 04096
Tel: (207)846-5168
Fax: (207)846-5181
Pages: 69
Exhibits: None

For international negotiators, this is a useful introduction to the cultural dimension of bargaining overseas. Originally published as a paper prepared for the Foreign Service Institute of the Department of State, the book covers the cultural component of negotiation, styles of decision making, the role of national character in negotiation style, and the dilemma of whether to trust interpreters and translators. The question-and-answer style of presentation and the boldfacing of key concepts make this volume a handy reference guide, though the specific coverage of Asian negotiation behavior is limited to Japan.

Title: *Leasing in Developing Asia*
Date: 1988
Format: Hardcover
Author: Asian Development Bank Workshop
Publisher: Asian Development Bank
P.O. Box 789
Manila 1099, Philippines
Pages: 319
Exhibits: Tables

This is a collection of papers that were presented at a workshop held in 1987 in Manila, sponsored by the Asian Development Bank. For businesspeople involved in leasing, this book will be of interest. The Asian countries covered include Thailand, Taiwan, Sri Lanka, Philippines, Malaysia, Korea, Japan, Indonesia, India, China, and Bangladesh.

Title: *Managing Cultural Differences: High Performance Strategies for Today's Global Manager*
Date: 1987
Format: Hardcover
Author: Philip R. Harris and Robert T. Moran
Publisher: Gulf Publishing
P.O. Bos 2608
Houston, TX 77252-2608
Tel: (713)529-4301
Fax: (713)520-4483
Pages: 608
Exhibits: Tables

First released in 1979 and revised in 1987, this widely used and authoritative textbook is for managers working in cross-cultural situations and for trainers in the intercultural field. The book's four chapters cover the roles of managers as communicators, negotiators, and leaders of cross-cultural teams; how to manage across cultures, deal with differing business protocols, and obtain necessary intercultural training; specific business practices abroad, including 47 pages about Japan, China, and Pacific Basin countries; and a series of appendices including self-tests, a directory of intercultural resources, and organizational cultural assessment testing tools.

Title: *Negotiating Across Cultures: Communication Obstacles in International Diplomacy*
Date: 1990
Format: Paperback
Author: Raymond Cohen
Publisher: U.S. Institute of Peace Press
1550 M. St., NW
Washington, DC 20005
Tel: (202)457-1700
Fax: (202)429-6063
Pages: 193
Exhibits: None

Many of the culture-caused misperceptions and miscommunications that occur during business negotiations have been well-covered in numerous titles. In this book, the author pinpoints similar problems that have occurred in diplomatic negotiations between the United States and other countries—Japan, China, Egypt, India, and Mexico. The case studies are rich in anecdotes, and the tips for cross-cultural statesmanship can be applied to commercial negotiations. This is an interesting and unique study.

Title: *The Pacific Rim Region: A World Marketplace Approach through Trade and Investment*
Date: 1993
Format: Hardcover
Author: Chuck Dangler
Publisher: Madison Books
4720 Boston Way
Lanham, MD 20706
Tel: (301)459-5308
Fax: (301)459-2118
Pages: 161
Exhibits: Maps and tables

Little in this volume redeems it as an introduction to the Pacific Rim. It's incomplete, rather unattractive, and turgidly written. It is included here because it contains sections analyzing the economic development of Japan, Australia, and Chile. For those who are researching trade and investment in these countries, this book might be useful.

Title: *Survival Kit for Overseas Living: For Americans Planning to Live and Work Abroad*
Date: 1984
Format: Paperback
Author: L. Robert Kohls
Publisher: Intercultural Press
P.O. Box 768
Yarmouth, ME 04096
Tel: (207)846-5168
Fax: (207)846-5181
Pages: 98
Exhibits: Tables

The short, step-by-step chapters of this guide make it a great first resource for the person who has accepted a foreign posting. The author, an experienced intercultural trainer, provides a lively introduction to such important cultural concepts as stereotyping, belief systems, and perceptions of Americans overseas. He offers advice about what you should know about your host country, how to be a better communicator there, and how to handle culture shock. The book includes handy checklists to help you prepare to live and work overseas.

Title: *Teaming Up for the 90's: A Guide to International Joint Ventures*
Date: 1991
Format: Hardcover
Author: Timothy M. Collins and Thomas L. Doorley III
Publisher: Business One Irwin
1818 Ridge Rd.
Homewood, IL 60430
Tel: (708)206-2700
Fax: (708)798-6388
Pages: 348
Exhibits: Graphs and tables

This well-researched and well-written textbook/guidebook for corporate strategists occupies the top rung in a growing literature that explains the benefits of entering into strategic corporate alliances across national borders. The interviews conducted for the book include 13 with Japanese firms and three with Korean companies. Based on the first-rate analysis of strategic partnerships in the first part of the book, "golden rules" of setting up alliances are offered in the second half. Filled with examples and attractively designed, this authoritative volume should not be missed.

Title: *The Ultimate Overseas Business Guide for Growing Companies*
Date: 1990
Format: Hardcover
Author: Henry H. Rodkin
Publisher: Dow Jones—Irwin
1818 Ridge Rd.
Homewood, IL 60430
Tel: (708)206-2700
Fax: (708)798-6388
Pages: 201
Exhibits: Tables

"Overseas companies expect certain things from us as Americans." Starting with this premise, this readable how-to book provides advice to businesspeople who are attempting to expand in overseas markets. It covers trademarks, cultural barriers, overseas manners, letters of credit, advertising, and information gathering. It serves as a general primer for the international sales representative.

Title: *World-Class Negotiating: Dealmaking in the Global Marketplace*
Date: 1990
Format: Hardcover
Author: Donald W. Hendon and Rebecca Angeles Hendon
Publisher: John Wiley & Sons
605 Third Ave.
New York, NY 10158-0012
Tel: (212)850-6000
Fax: (212)850-6088
Pages: 270
Exhibits: Tables
Price: $25.95

This book contains useful comparison data about negotiating tactics in different countries, many in Asia. It is of interest to anyone planning strategy for a business negotiation. It includes some coverage of Asian protocol issues, as well.

HISTORY AND SOCIETY

Title: *Beyond Culture*
Date: 1976
Format: Paperback
Author: Edward T. Hall
Publisher: Doubleday
666 Fifth Ave.
New York, NY 10103
Tel: (212)765-6500
Fax: (212)492-9700
Pages: 296
Exhibits: None

Edward T. Hall, called "America's most sensitive ethnologist" by *Sociology* magazine, offers some of his most profound and eclectic essays on humanity and culture in this volume. It contains sections that compare "high-context" cultures like Japan's with "low-context" cultures like America's. The author also explains many communication concepts—both verbal and nonverbal—with which the international businessperson should be acquainted. This is a rich and wise reader for the serious culturalist.

Title: *East Asia: Tradition and Transformation*
Date: 1978
Format: Hardcover
Author: John King Fairbanks
Publisher: Houghton Mifflin
One Beacon St.
Boston, MA 02108
Tel: (617)725-5000
Fax: (617)227-5409
Pages: 969
Exhibits: Photographs and tables

This standard college textbook overview of East Asia, from Peking Man to post–World War II modernity, is a recommended and readable sourcebook. Businesspeople looking to obtain a course in Asian civilization—including ample coverage of philosophic, artistic, and religious traditions—can find it in this well-illustrated volume by one of America's best-known orientalists.

Title: *The Hidden Dimension*
Date: 1982
Format: Paperback
Author: Edward T. Hall
Publisher: Doubleday
666 Fifth Ave.
New York, NY 10103
Tel: (212)765-6500
Fax: (212)492-9700
Pages: 217
Exhibits: Photographs

Have you ever wondered why, when speaking to you, most Asian businesspeople like to stand a little farther away from you than you would like? The difference in comfort zones is what the study of proxemics is all about, and the author of this well-organized and authoritative book is a leading expert in the field. For international businesspeople who want to obtain a deeper understanding of nonverbal communication behavior in general and among the Japanese in particular, this is an extremely insightful and enjoyable read. The topics covered include the language of space, proxemics in a cross-cultural context, and the engineering of space in art and architecture. This is certainly not required reading for the businessperson, but it is enriching nonetheless.

Title: *Pacific Century: The Emergence of Modern Pacific Asia*
Date: 1992
Format: Hardcover
Author: Mark Borthwick (with contributions from others)
Publisher: Westview Press
3500 Central Ave.
Boulder, CO 80301-2847
Tel: (303)444-3541
Fax: (303)449-3356
Pages: 590
Exhibits: Maps, graphs, and photographs

A gigantic undertaking, this is perhaps the first large-scale textbook covering the evolution of the Asia-Pacific into a world economic and political powerhouse. Businesspeople will find it unwieldy and probably too comprehensive, but there isn't a better background on the historic roots of Asian power. This book covers all Asia-Pacific countries, from the Qin Dynasty in China to the rise of Japan and the integration of the Pacific as a unifying trade bloc. It is recommended.

Title: *Strangers from a Different Shore: A History of Asian Americans*
Date: 1989
Format: Paperback
Author: Ronald Takaki
Publisher: Penguin Books
375 Hudson St.
New York, NY 10014
Tel: (212)366-2000
Fax: (212)366-2666
Pages: 569
Exhibits: Photographs

The author of this well-written and heavily researched chronicle of the Asian experience in America is a professor of Ethnic Studies at the University of California at Berkeley. The fast-moving chapters describe the very different experiences of the Chinese, Japanese, Koreans, Indians, Filipinos, and other Asian peoples who have emigrated to the United States throughout history and up to the late 1980s. Rich in detail, quotes, old songs, and Asian terms, this fabulous historical narrative deserves a place next to your favorite armchair.

INDUSTRY

Title: *Asiamac Journal*
Date: Monthly
Format: Periodical
Publisher: Adsale Publishing Co.
14th Floor, Devon House
Taikoo Place
979 King's Rd.
Quarry Bay, Hong Kong
Tel: (852)811-8897
Fax: (852)516-5119
Pages: Varies
Exhibits: Graphs, photographs, and tables
Price: $36/year

This 70-page magazine tracks developments in the machine-building and metalworking industries in Asia. It provides news, conference updates, a list of advertisers, directories of suppliers, and country updates. It is recommended.

Title: *Asian Architect and Contractor*
Date: Monthly
Format: Periodical
Author: International Federation of Asian and Western Pacific Contractor's Associations
Editor: Andrea Forbes
Publisher: Thompson Press, Hong Kong
19th Floor, Tai Sang Commercial Building
24-34 Hennessy Rd.
Hong Kong
Tel: (852)518-3351
Fax: (852)865-0825
Pages: Varies
Exhibits: Photographs
Price: $55/year

This is a glossy industry trade magazine for architects, builders, and contractors. The articles cover new construction projects in Asia, with an emphasis on

East Asia. New technology and building and construction news from around Asia is also included in this 45- to 55-page publication.

Title: *Asian Oil and Gas*
Date: Monthly
Format: Periodical
Editor: Andrew Burns
Publisher: Asian Oil and Gas, Ltd.
14th Floor, Tung Sun Commercial Center
200 Lockhart Rd.
Hong Kong
Tel: (852)511-1301
Fax: (852)507-4620
Pages: Varies
Exhibits: Photographs
Price: $90/year

This full-color, 40- to 50-page glossy industry magazine is published in Hong Kong for companies involved in oil and gas exploration and refining. Monthly sections include Updates, Tech Survey, and Equipment Focus. This resource provides a list of advertisers and conference information and is suggested as an industry updater.

Title: *Asian Shipping*
Date: Monthly
Format: Periodical
Publisher: Asia Trade Journals, Ltd.
P.O. Box 20014
Hennessy Rd.
Hong Kong
Tel: (852)527-8532
Pages: Varies
Exhibits: None
Price: HK$400/year

Covering ports, cargo volumes, and shipping companies in Asia, this rather low-quality magazine reports on rescue and salvage operations as well as shipping news. It takes an unusually keen interest in high-seas shipping disasters.

Title: *Asian Sources Electronics*
Date: Monthly
Format: Periodical
Editor: Mario Percira
Publisher: Trade Media, Ltd.
22nd Floor, Vita Tower
29 Wong Chok Hong Rd.
Hong Kong
Tel: (852)555-4777
Fax: (852)873-0488
Pages: Varies
Exhibits: Photographs
Price: $80/year (surface mail); $225/year (airmail)

This glossy product catalog includes full-color layouts depicting manufactured goods available from Asian suppliers. A product dictionary simplifies use, and an insert card offers three free inquiries to advertisers. This resource is recommended to businesspeople who are looking for new sources of product from Asia. The publication also contains background articles on import barriers, new products, R&D in Asia, and, especially, Asian electronics.

Title: *Asian Textile Association Journal*
Date: Bimonthly
Format: Periodical
Editor: Benjamin Heung
Publisher: Adsale Publishing Co.

14th Floor, Devon House
Taikoo Place
979 King's Rd.
Quarry Bay, Hong Kong
Tel: (852)811-8897
Fax: (852)516-5119

Pages: Varies

Exhibits: Photographs and tables

Price: $54/year (distributed free to qualified individuals)

This magazine-format industry update delivers some strong articles on the textile industry in Asia and provides country-specific coverage. It reports on new technologies, conferences, and trade and tariff laws and is recommended for anyone dealing in this industry inside Asia.

Title: *Asia-Pacific Defense Forum*

Date: Quarterly

Format: Periodical

Author: United States Pacific Command

Editor: P.R. Stankiewicz, Ltd. Col., USAF (Ret.)

Publisher: Commander-in-Chief of the United States, Pacific Command
USINCPAC Staff, Box 13
Camp H.M. Smith
Honolulu, Hawaii 96861
Tel: (808)474-4553
Fax: (808)474-4551

Pages: Varies

Exhibits: Photographs

This magazine reports on U.S. military activities in the Asia-Pacific and elsewhere from a pro-U.S. military point of view. It is useful to businesspeople in the defense industry in tracking U.S. strategy, military activities, and thus customer needs.

Title: *Asia-Pacific Defense Reporter*

Date: Monthly

Format: Periodical; also available on-line

Editor: Denis Warner

Publisher: Peter Issacson Publications, Pty. Ltd.
46-50 Porter St.
Prahran
Victoria 3181, Australia

Pages: Varies

Exhibits: Graphs, photographs, and tables

From the Australian perspective, this trade magazine covers military and defense policy and market opportunities in Asia. Most articles are written by military officials and defense analysts and are divided into regions, such as East Asia, Southeast Asia, and the South Pacific. In-depth country-specific articles cover military purchases, air shows, recent shifts in hardware priorities, and so on. A Newsletter section provides updates on related developments when defense-related news is breaking.

Title: *Asia-Pacific Telecommunications*

Date: Monthly

Format: Periodical

Editor: Eileen Lian

Publisher: Asian Business Press, Pte. Ltd.
100 Beach Rd.
#26-00 Shaw Towers
0768, Singapore
Tel: (65)294-3366
Fax: (65)298-5534

Pages: Varies

Exhibits: Photographs

Price: $70/year (distributed free to qualified individuals)

This large-format glossy newspaper follows the format of *Advertising Age*, presenting hundreds of short pieces on recent deals, new policy decisions, trading regulations, and so on throughout Asia, including India. Interviews with regional decision makers are included. It is a good value for those who need to keep abreast of these developments.

Title: *Cargonews Asia*
Date: Weekly
Format: Periodical
Editor: Martin Savery
Publisher: Far East Trade Press
Block C
10th Floor, Seaview Estate
2-8 Watson Rd.
North Point, Hong Kong
Tel: (852)566-8381
Fax: (852)508-0255
Pages: Varies
Exhibits: Photographs
Price: $59.50/year

This large-format glossy industry newspaper contains all the news fit for the freight forwarder or anyone else following the shipping lanes of Asia. It is the best source of news and updates concerning the cargo and transportation sectors in Asia.

Title: *Information Technology Policy and International Cooperation in Asia*
Date: 1990
Format: Paperback
Publisher: Asian Productivity Organization
4-14, Akasaka 8-chome
Minato-ku
Tokyo 107, Japan
Tel: (81)(3)408-7221
Fax: (81)(3)408-7220
Pages: 185
Exhibits: Graphs and tables

For anyone tracking technology assimilation, technology policy, patent protection, or information technologies in Asia, this study is a one-stop overview. Each country is appraised separately in terms of the status of its information technologies (IT), its IT manufacturing capabilities, computerization, planning, and strategy. Japan is not included.

Title: *Lloyd's ASEAN Shipping Directory*
Date: Annual
Format: Hardcover
Editor: Lee Tong Kuan and S.C. Lim
Publisher: Lloyd's of London Press, Ltd.
1101 Hollywood Centre
233 Hollywood Rd.
Hong Kong
Tel: (852)854-3222
Fax: (852)854-1538
Pages: Varies
Exhibits: Tables

This is an index of shipping companies and vessels. It includes an economic overview of ASEAN, and maritime regulations are noted in country sections. It is an essential directory for freight forwarders.

Title: *Lloyd's List Maritime Shipping*
Date: Monthly
Format: Periodical
Editor: Kevin Chinnery
Publisher: Lloyd's of London Press, Ltd.
1101 Hollywood Centre
233 Hollywood Rd.
Hong Kong
Tel: (852)854-3222
Fax: (852)854-1538
Pages: Varies
Exhibits: Photographs
Price: $160/year

This magazine-format industry updater covers port development and shipping news throughout the Asia-Pacific, including ports of the Russian Far East. The writing is crisp and the coverage wide, making this a good value for the price.

Title: *The Pacific Challenge in International Business*
Date: 1987
Format: Hardcover
Editor: W. Chan Kim and Philip K.Y. Young
Publisher: UMI Research Press
University Microfilms, Inc.
Ann Arbor, MI 48106
Tel: (313)761-4700
Fax: (313)761-1204
Pages: 342
Exhibits: Graphs and tables

In this compilation of academic articles, the reader is introduced to the phenomenal economic development and growth of Asia-Pacific countries. This book is special because it includes a number of in-depth articles about specific industries that will interest businesspeople who are involved with Asian firms in these areas. The industries covered include oil, natural gas, marine minerals, fish products, electronic calculators, apparel, and computer software. As a reader on Asia's assimilation of technology to increase exports, it is also a useful volume.

Title: *Pacific Telecommunications Review*
Date: Quarterly
Format: Periodical
Author: Pacific Telecommunications Council
Editor: James Savage
Publisher: Pacific Telecommunications Council
2454 S. Beretania St., Suite 302
Honolulu, HI 96826-1596
Tel: (808)941-3789
Fax: (808)944-4874
Pages: Varies
Exhibits: Photographs
Price: $25/year

Filled with what its editor calls "polite, friendly, and thoughtful articles" about Asian telecommunications opportunities and policy, this quarterly runs about 30 pages and contains roughly five articles plus a number of book reviews per issue. This publication is new and should prove to be useful to telecommunications companies that want an introduction to broad developments in their industry vis-à-vis Asia. It's a good value.

Title: *Property and Construction in Asia Pacific*
Date: 1991
Format: Paperback
Editor: Anthony Walker and Roger Flanagan
Publisher: Blackwell Scientific
3 Cambridge Center
Cambridge, MA 02142
Tel: (617)225-0401
Fax: (617)225-0412
Pages: 229
Exhibits: Maps, graphs, photographs, and tables

Attractively published, this book is useful to those in the construction industry who seek information about the building industry in Asian countries. Chapters cover Hong Kong, Japan, and Singapore and focus on the business environment, the economy, real estate, and the state of the construction industry. This book gets down to specifics: subcontractors, materials, patterns of investment, and so on.

Title: *Textile Asia*
Date: Monthly
Format: Periodical
Publisher: Kayser Sung Business Press, Ltd.
11th Floor, California Tower
30-32 D'Aguilar St.
Hong Kong
Tel: (852)523-3744
Fax: (852)810-6966
Pages: Varies
Exhibits: Graphs, photographs, and tables
Price: $162/year

With contributing editors throughout Asia, this 170-page magazine provides comprehensive coverage of business news related to the textile industry in all Asian countries. It is highly recommended as a source of timely information on tariffs, quotas, new projects, conferences, trade shows, new products, and textile technology. Articles are divided into country sections for easy reference. It is a good value for the price.

INFORMATION SOURCES

Title: *Access Asia: A Guide to Specialists and Current Research*
Date: Annual
Format: Paperback
Editor: Kimberly A. Wilhelm
Publisher: National Bureau of Asian Research
715 Safeco Plaza
Seattle, WA 98185
Tel: (206)632-7370
Fax: (206)632-7487
Pages: 418
Exhibits: None

The first clearinghouse of Asian specialists, this who's who directory lists each expert's address, expertise, publications, and current research. This is a first stop for companies that are looking for consultants and advisers with specific areas of experience. Individuals are listed alphabetically, and a location index is included.

Title: *Asian Bibliography*
Date: Semiannual
Format: Hardcover

Author: Economic and Social Commission for Asia and the Pacific

Publisher: United Nations Publications
2 United Nations Plaza, Room DC-0853
Sales Section, Publishing Service
New York, NY 10017
Tel: (212)963-8302
Fax: (212)963-3489

Pages: 125

Exhibits: None

This bibliography of articles and books is cross-indexed by author, area, and subject. Subject headings include commodities, environment, law, and science and technology. Most of the articles are research papers of particular value to anyone conducting an in-depth literature search.

Title: *Asian Markets: A Guide to Company and Industry Information Sources*

Date: 1988

Format: Hardcover

Publisher: Washington Researchers Publishing
2612 P. St., NW
Washington, DC 20007
Tel: (202)333-3533
Fax: (202)625-0656

Pages: 371

Exhibits: None

This directory of business information sources is meant for marketers who are trying to sell to Asian countries. The organizations listed include U.S. government departments, international organizations, and private-sector companies. On-line databases are included. In the country sections, Asian government and business organizations are listed, and the book includes country-specific publications. Although it is becoming dated, it is highly recommended as a sourcebook for the Asia marketer. The information provided by each organization is not listed, however, nor are publications in the country sections critiqued.

Title: *Bibliography of Asian Studies*

Date: Annual

Format: Paperback

Editor: Wayne Surdan

Publisher: Association for Asian Studies
108 Lane Hall
University of Michigan
Ann Arbor, MI 48109-1290
Tel: (313)988-7265
Fax: (313)936-2948

Pages: 425

Exhibits: None

The articles and monographs listed in this bibliography are divided by geographic region and by subject. An author index is provided, as well. Most of the material comes from research journals and newsletters printed in the United States and abroad. In addition to articles, slightly more than 300 books are included in each edition. Entries provide reference information only. The section on economics is quite complete, but the subject categories do not include business or industry.

Title: *A Bibliography of Asia-Pacific Studies*
Date: 1992
Format: Paperback
Author: Diana Chan and Painan Wu
Publisher: Chinese University of Hong Kong
Shatin, New Territories
Hong Kong
Tel: (852)695-2508
Fax: (852)604-6692
Pages: 560 (3 vols.)
Exhibits: None

The authors of this handy bibliography of publications on the political, social, and economic scene in Asia are working librarians associated with the Chinese University of Hong Kong and its libraries (one author is now deceased). They have produced an easy-to-use listing of core sources in the university's libraries, divided first by country and then into sections: reference sources, political scene, social scene, economic scene, and business scene. Each entry contains reference information only, with the library location (all in Hong Kong) and call numbers. All of the countries of Asia and Southeast Asia are represented.

Title: *Biblio List Updates in Print*
Date: Monthly
Format: Periodical
Publisher: Joint Bank–Fund Library
Reference Desk, IS6-1000
The World Bank
Office of the Publisher
1818 H St., NW
Washington, DC 20433
Tel: (202)473-1956
Fax: (202)676-0579
Pages: Varies
Exhibits: None

This 50-page stapled folder provides a monthly update of periodical articles and working papers recently collected by the Joint Library of The World Bank and the International Monetary Fund. The articles are divided by country; reference information only is provided. This source is for serious researchers of specific topics in international policy, development issues, and economics.

Title: *Business Periodicals Index*
Date: Monthly
Format: Periodical
Publisher: H.W. Wilson Co.
950 University Ave.
Bronx, NY 10452
Pages: Varies
Exhibits: None
Price: $190/year

This 300-page monthly publication lists business periodicals published in English and is divided into subject categories, including accounting, economics, electronics, and trade. Articles from several hundred publications are listed, and addresses are provided for each periodical. Each entry includes the title and subtitle, author's name, list of illustrations, and reference information. This handy source is available in most business libraries.

Title: *The Directory of International Sources of Business Information*
Date: 1991
Format: Hardcover
Author: Sarah Ball

Publisher: Pitman Publishing
128 Long Acre
London WC2E 9AN,
United Kingdom
Tel: (44)(71)379-7383
Fax: (44)(71)240-5771

Pages: 859

Exhibits: None

This directory of organizations that provide international business information focuses on companies, markets, finance, securities, and economics. Asia receives moderate coverage. The sources are divided into country data sources, industry data sources, and on-line databases, the latter being the most useful to the Asia business researcher. Addresses and phone numbers are provided, but the information offered by each organization is not critiqued. This is a comprehensive and up-to-date resource.

Title: *Federal Staff Register*

Date: Annual

Format: Hardcover

Editor: Ann L. Brownson

Publisher: Staff Directories, Ltd.
P.O. Box 62
Mount Vernon, VA 22121-0062
Tel: (703)739-0900
Fax: (703)739-0234

Pages: 1,588

Exhibits: None

This annual directory lists contact information for 32,000 key executives and staff members of the executive branch of the U.S. government and includes 2,600 biographies. It will help researchers locate people, agencies, committees, and departments involved in Asia-Pacific trade, politics, technology, agriculture, and so on. A subject index makes this well-known directory easy to use.

Title: *Gale Directory of Databases*

Date: Annual

Format: Paperback

Editor: Kathleen Young Moraccio

Publisher: Gale Research, Inc.
835 Penobscot Building
Detroit, MI 48226-4094
Tel: (313)961-2242
Fax: (313)961-6083

Pages: Varies

Exhibits: None

This massive sourcebook provides exhaustive coverage of on-line sources of information for business researchers. It is perhaps the best guide to accessing the international business data available on the global information highway.

Title: *Global Guide to International Business*

Date: 1983

Format: Hardcover

Editor: David S. Hoopes

Publisher: Facts on File Publications
460 Park Ave. South
New York, NY 10016
Tel: (212)683-2244
Fax: (212)213-4578

Pages: 847

Exhibits: None

This now slightly dated directory of business information sources contains sections on each Asian country, with short descriptions of each source. Information sources under each country heading are further broken down by subjects, such as business and economic publications, directories, background, and travel.

Title: *How to Find Information about Foreign Firms*

Date: 1990

Format: Hardcover

Publisher: Washington Researchers Publishing
2612 P. St., NW
Washington, DC 20007
Tel: (202)333-3533
Fax: (202)625-0656

Pages: 104

Exhibits: None

This is a step-by-step handbook for finding information about international companies, including those in Asia. It shows business researchers how to use directories, periodicals, and databases and how to access federal regulatory agencies. It is a good starting point for those who want to analyze an Asian company completely and efficiently.

Title: *Index to International Statistics: Abstracts*

Date: Annual

Format: Hardcover

Editor: Susan I. Jover

Publisher: Congressional Information Services, Inc.
4520 East-West Hgwy.
Bethesda, MD 20814
Tel: (301)654-1550
Fax: (301)654-4033

Pages: 360

Exhibits: None

For those seeking statistical information about population, business and financial activities, foreign trade, education, health, and political characteristics of a country, this is the source. The publications indexed are published by intergovernmental organizations (IGOs) and contain authoritative data collected throughout the world. Each entry lists the issuing organization, title, language, address of publisher, and price and includes a descriptive abstract of the material. This comprehensive monthly index can be found in most local libraries in the government documents section.

Title: *Index to the Foreign Broadcast Information Service—Daily Reports East Asia*

Date: Monthly

Format: Periodical

Editor: Greg Dean

Publisher: Newsbank, Inc.
58 Pine St.
New Canaan, CT 06840
Tel: (802)875-2910

Pages: 99

Exhibits: None

The Foreign Broadcast Information Service (FBIS) is a U.S. government agency that monitors overseas broadcasts, news agency transmissions, periodicals and newspapers, and statements made by government officials. The reports cover East Asia, China, the Near East, and South Asia, among other regions, and are conveniently indexed by country and subject. The index is best used in a library that also subscribes to the Daily Reports produced by FBIS.

Title: *International Business Bibliography*
Date: 1989
Format: Hardcover
Author: William R. Slomanson
Publisher: William S. Hein and Co, Inc.
1285 Main St.
Buffalo, NY 14209
Tel: (716)882-2600
Fax: (716)883-8100
Pages: 407
Exhibits: None

This bibliography provides sources of information about international business topics in key countries and regions of the world. Topic areas are listed alphabetically from accounting to transnational legal practice, and country divisions are provided under each topic heading. Asia and Japan coverage is sufficient, but prices and publisher addresses are not provided. Also, the volume is becoming dated.

Title: *The International Directory of Business Information: Sources and Services*
Date: 1986
Format: Hardcover
Editor: Alan Oliver
Publisher: Europa Publications, Ltd.
18 Bedford Square
London WC1B 3JN, United Kingdom
Tel: (44)(71)580-8236
Fax: (44)(71)636-1664
Pages: 378
Exhibits: None

This directory of organizations that provide business information includes Japan and Australia but no other Asian countries. The organizations listed include chambers of commerce, business libraries, and trade-promoting organizations. Addresses and phone numbers are provided, but no description or critique of the information is given.

Title: *International Directory of Centers for Asian Studies*
Date: 1989
Format: Hardcover
Publisher: Asian Research Service
G.P.O. Box 2232
Hong Kong
Tel: (852)(5)733-641
Fax: (852)(5)838-4849
Pages: 60
Exhibits: None

Ever wonder what's going on at the Institut fuer Orientalistik in Austria or the Bhandarkar Oriental Research Institute in India? This list of Asian studies organizations provides a comprehensive list of places where the businessperson can seek specialized information and research and academic contacts. Each entry includes the organization's address, research interest, person in charge, number of staff, and recent publications. This bibliography is also handy as a mailing list of organizations and experts that are interested in Asia.

Title: *The International Directory of Marketing Information Sources*
Date: 1988
Format: Hardcover
Editor: Marina Norman
Publisher: Euromonitor Publications, Ltd.

87-88 Turnmill St.
London EC1M 5QU,
United Kingdom
Tel: (44)(71)251-8024
Fax: (44)(71)608-3149

Pages: 362

Exhibits: None

Yet another directory of marketing information, this one provides addresses for official organizations and publications by country (including Asian countries), major libraries, research companies, databases, and business journals. It contains information about each organization (operating hours, information provided, etc.) that is not found in similar sourcebooks.

Title: *International Research Centers Directory*

Date: Annual

Format: Hardcover

Editor: Darren L. Smith

Publisher: Gale Research, Inc.
835 Penobscot Building
Detroit, MI 48226-4094
Tel: (313)961-2242
Fax: (313)961-6083

Pages: 1,327

Exhibits: None

Listing more than 6,600 scientific research organizations around the world, including the countries of Asia, this volume is useful to those involved in technology-related businesses of any kind. The research centers are indexed alphabetically and by country. Addresses and phone numbers are accompanied by a description of research activities, publications and services, and affiliates and subsidiaries.

Title: *Marketing Information: A Professional Reference Guide*

Date: 1987

Format: Hardcover

Editor: Jac L. Goldstucker

Publisher: Business Publishing Division
College of Business Administration
Georgia State University
University Plaza
Atlanta, Georgia 30303-4253
Tel: (706)542-2830
Fax: (706)542-0601

Pages: 436

Exhibits: None

Although this volume is not specifically targeted at Asia, it does provide a worldwide listing of marketing firms, advertising agencies, special libraries, and consulting companies, many of which provide Asia-related information and services. The section on international marketing is subcategorized by country and lists sources pertaining to marketing in Asia. It is suggested as an auxiliary source of marketing information concerning Asia.

Title: *NIRA's World Directory of Think Tanks*

Date: 1993

Format: Hardcover

Editor: Hajime Ishida

Publisher: National Institute for Research Advancement
37th Floor, Shinjuku Mitsui Building
2-1-1, Nishi-Shinjuku
Shinjuku-ku
Tokyo 163-04, Japan

Pages: 536
Exhibits: None

This handsomely published directory, compiled in Japan, includes descriptions of more than 350 of the world's most active public policy research institutes, otherwise known as think tanks. The entries are divided by country, including China, Indonesia, Japan (only three institutes listed), South Korea, Malaysia, Singapore, Thailand, and Vietnam. Each entry provides the name of the executive officer, areas of research, geographic focus, availability of research findings, funding sources, chief researchers, and a publication list. This resource is very useful for information hounds or professional researchers who seek to cooperate with Asian think tanks.

Title: *Predicasts F & S Index: International*
Date: Annual
Format: Hardcover
Editor: Concetta M. Caporuscio
Publisher: Predicasts
11001 Cedar Ave.
Cleveland, OH 44106
Tel: (800)321-6388
Pages: 391
Exhibits: None

If you are looking for specific published business information of a timely nature, this updated index is perhaps your best bet. It lists articles published in business newspapers and magazines from around the world. All of the Asian countries receive coverage. Each entry provides the publication name, date, page, and a one-line abstract of the article's content. In the three separate sections of the index you can look up materials by subject (e.g., cargo aircraft), country, or company. Most large libraries subscribe to the index, which is of particular use to commodities traders, market researchers, and anyone tracking the activities of an Asian company.

Title: *World Sources of Market Information*
Date: 1982
Format: Hardcover
Editor: Euan Blauvelt and Jennifer Durlacher
Publisher: Gower Publishing Co., Ltd.
Croft Rd.
Aldershot
Hants Gull 3HR, United Kingdom
Tel: (44)(252)331-551
Fax: (44)(252)344-405
Pages: 287
Exhibits: Tables

This book provides overviews of key world markets, including most Asian countries, as well as a listing of more than 1,100 reports available for purchase, most providing market research. A product and topic index is provided for each country, and a list of market research companies and organizations is given. This resource is becoming dated.

LAWS AND REGULATIONS

Title: *East Asian Executive Reports*
Date: Monthly
Format: Periodical
Editor: Stephen M. Soble

Publisher: International Executive Reports
717 D St., NW, Suite 300
Washington, DC 20004
Tel: (202)628-6900
Fax: (202)628-6618

Pages: Varies

Exhibits: Varies

Price: $455/year

This 25- to 40-page collection of articles written by practitioners in the field covers Asian business policy and law and typically includes one or more corporate case studies of Western firms doing business in Asia. This periodical covers all of Asia, with an emphasis on burgeoning economies. It is recommended especially to lawyers and contract negotiators.

Title: *The Foreign Corrupt Practices Act*

Date: 1982

Format: Hardcover

Author: George C. Greanias

Publisher: D.C. Heath and Co.
125 Spring St.
Lexington, MA 02173
Tel: (617)862-6650
Fax: (617)860-1202

Pages: 187

Exhibits: None

This book provides a comprehensive overview of the evolution and content of U.S. laws pertaining to bribes and gift giving by U.S. companies doing business abroad.

Title: *Pacific Basin Legal Developments Bulletin*

Date: Monthly

Format: Periodical

Editor: Peter T. Dwight and Nadaisan Logaraj

Publisher: Baker & McKenzie
One Prudential Plaza Suite 2800
130 Randolph Dr.
Chicago, IL 60601
Tel: (312)861-2915
Fax: (312)861-2899

Pages: Varies

Exhibits: None

Issued by the law firm of Baker & McKenzie, this 25- to 35-page monthly booklet contains clearly articulated and very useful legal updates for countries of the Asia-Pacific. The coverage includes taxation, copyright law, insider trading, and immigration, focusing on significant legal changes.

Title: *Trade Control Measures*

Date: Updated regularly

Format: CD-ROM

Publisher: United Nations Conference on Trade and Development
Division for Data Management
Palais des Nations
Geneva CH-1211, Switzerland
Tel: (41)(22)734-6011
Fax: (41)(22)733-9879

Exhibits: None

Price: Contact for subscription prices

This updated database reviews current trade barriers of major global economies, including those in Asia.

Title: *UCLA Pacific Basin Law Journal*
Date: Semiannual
Format: Periodical
Author: UCLA School of Law
Editor: Julie Yeh and M. Elizabeth Deen
Publisher: Regents of the University of California
UCLA Pacific Basin Law Journal
School of Law
405 Hilgard Ave.
Los Angeles, CA 90024
Tel: (310)825-7411
Fax: (310)206-4723
Pages: Varies
Exhibits: None
Price: $25/year

This is a journal-style collection of articles dealing with trade, tax, and intellectual property issues in the Asia-Pacific. This 180- to 200-page publication also includes book reviews. It would certainly be of interest to lawyers working in the region.

Title: *World Trade Resources Guide*
Date: 1992
Format: Hardcover
Editor: Kenneth Estell
Publisher: Gale Research, Inc.
835 Penobscot Building
Detroit, MI 48226-4094
Tel: (313)961-2242
Fax: (313)961-6083
Pages: 891
Exhibits: Maps

This list of import and export resources is divided by country, includes most Asian countries, and provides the names and addresses of organizations and agencies, publications and information sources, and transportation and shipping contacts. Each country receives 3 to 15 pages of coverage. Country facts and descriptions of the activities of selected organizations are provided. Also included are computerized databases and business libraries in each country.

MANAGEMENT

Title: *The Asian Manager: Recruiting, Training, and Retaining Executives*
Date: 1982
Format: Paperback
Author: Richard G. Payne
Publisher: Business International Asia/Pacific, Ltd.
1111/1119 Mount Parker House
City Plaza, Taikoo Shing, Quarry Bay, Hong Kong
Pages: 144
Exhibits: Tables

Rather dated now, this large-format booklet helps companies plan for human resources management in Asia by pinpointing potential problems and offering solutions. The chapters deal with one country at a time, including Hong Kong, Indonesia, Korea, Malaysia, Philippines, Singapore, Taiwan, and Thailand. Recruiting, training, and retaining of managers is the focus. This is a recommended guide on a subject that receives too little attention.

Title: *Asia Pacific International Journal of Business Logistics*
Date: Monthly
Format: Periodical
Editor: Dr. John Gattorna
Publisher: MCB University Press, Ltd.
60-62 Toller Lane
Bradford
West Yorkshire BD8 9BY, United Kingdom
Tel: (44)(274)499-821
Fax: (44)(274)547-143
Pages: Varies
Exhibits: Varies
Price: Contact for subscription prices

This is a unique publication. It tracks more than 100 trade journals and synopsizes key articles in the form of easy-to-read abstracts. The abstracts are divided by topics, such as logistics and distribution strategy, just-in-time management, and supply-chain management. It is recommended for managers who want to remain on the edge of new production theories and techniques, many of which emanate from Asia. Note, however, that the abstracts are not made from the Asian managerial literature; in fact, relatively few titles concern Asian firms.

Title: *Asia Pacific Journal of Management*
Date: Annual
Format: Periodical
Editor: Wang Kie Ann
Publisher: National University of Singapore
School of Management
10 Kent Ridge Crescent
0511, Singapore
Tel: (65)7765641
Fax: (65)7771296
Pages: Varies
Exhibits: Varies
Price: $32/year

One of the few journals dedicated to informing English readers about how Asians manage their firms, this 100-page publication of 6 to 8 articles will interest managers who intend to work in Asia or want to try new techniques at home. From budgetary control systems to tactics in managerial networks, the approach is theoretical yet compares Asian and Western managerial styles. This journal is suggested for the serious surveyor of management theory.

Title: *California Management Review*
Date: Quarterly
Format: Periodical
Editor: David Vogel
Publisher: University of California
350 Barrows
Haas Graduate School of Business Administration
Berkeley, CA 94720
Tel: (510)642-4247
Fax: (510)643-7127
Pages: Varies
Exhibits: Graphs and tables
Price: $45/year for individuals; $58/year for institutions

This is a first-rate 130- to 150-page journal covering current management practice worldwide. Numerous articles deal with Asian companies, especially Japanese firms. Case studies and surveys provide an in-depth view of Asian managerial technique. Browsing through old issues may turn up information that is valuable to the manager or executive working in Asia.

Title: *Developing Effective Global Managers for the 1990s*
Date: 1991
Format: Hardcover
Publisher: Business International Corp.
215 Park Ave. South
New York, NY 10003
Tel: (212)460-0600
Fax: (212)995-8837
Pages: 117
Exhibits: Graphs and tables

Offering a body of advice for corporations facing the task of training globally competent managers, this large-format volume is useful as an organizational template. Most useful to the executive or human resource director, 19 corporate case studies (AT&T, NEC, etc.) are included as examples of firms that are training managers to meet the global challenge of the nineties. This publication is recommended.

Title: *Global Human Resource Development*
Date: 1993
Format: Hardcover
Author: Michael J. Marquardt and Dean W. Engel
Publisher: Prentice-Hall
13 Sylvan Ave.
Englewood Cliffs, NJ 07632
Tel: (212)373-8000
Fax: (212)698-7007
Pages: 320
Exhibits: Graphs

This book opens with the premise that culture-sensitive human resource development programs are essential to a firm's successful globalization. Of use to managers of offices and factories in Asia, the authors present chapters on South Central Asia, East Asia, Japan, and the South Pacific region. In each of these chapters, local human resource development activities and priorities are discussed in relation to the local economy, and case stories of prominent companies in the country are presented to illustrate how local policies are being enacted in the workplace.

Title: *Managing in Developing Countries*
Date: 1990
Format: Hardcover
Author: James E. Austin
Publisher: The Free Press
866 Third Ave.
New York, NY 10022
Tel: (201)592-2000
Fax: (201)592-2824
Pages: 465
Exhibits: Graphs and tables

This specialized book by a Harvard management professor is invaluable to the overseas manager. It's well organized and clearly written and covers every conceivable management challenge in developing countries. It has ample coverage of

Japan, Malaysia, Korea, Indonesia, Philippines, Taiwan, and Thailand. The book instructs on how to handle problems in financing, production, technology management, marketing, and ownership strategies. Cultural issues are also covered. This is a first-class textbook for the serious practitioner.

Title: *Managing the Multinational Subsidiary*
Date: 1986
Format: Hardcover
Editor:s: Hamid Etemad and Louise Segun Dulude
Publisher: Croom Helm, Ltd.
6th Floor, Suite 4
64-76 Kippax St.
Surry Hills NSW 2010, Australia
Pages: 225
Exhibits: Tables

One of only a few books on the subject of managing an overseas subsidiary, this compilation of articles by academics contains some coverage of Asian countries. Topics include the strategic management of subsidiaries, world product mandating, specialization, and choice of technology. This book is useful to managers of operations in Asia.

Title: *Transnational Management: Text, Cases, and Readings in Cross-Border Management*
Date: 1992
Format: Hardcover
Author: Christopher A. Bartlett and Sumantra Ghoshal
Publisher: Richard D. Irwin, Inc.
20 Park Plaza, Suite 320
Boston, MA 02116
Tel: (708)798-6000
Fax: (708)798-6296
Pages: 914
Exhibits: Maps, graphs, and tables

Meant for managers of overseas operations, this college textbook is a reader about global strategy, marketing, and managing. With numerous reprinted articles, case studies, and well-researched chapter introductions, the book provides the background and real-incident material to guide executives through strategy formulation, overseas marketing tactics, and dealing with specific cross-border management challenges. Case studies include many Asian companies and market environments. It is highly recommended.

MARKET DATA AND ANALYSIS

Title: *ADB Business Opportunities*
Date: Monthly
Format: Periodical
Publisher: Asian Development Bank
P.O. Box 789
Manila 1099, Philippines
Pages: Varies
Exhibits: None
Price: $30/year

For companies that seek to bid on projects funded by the Asian Development Bank, this is an essential publication. It lists proposed projects, procurement notices, and contract awards, each entry noting the executing agency, loan amount, objective of project, and needed goods and services.

Title: Asia Forecast
Date: Updated quarterly
Format: On-line database
Publisher: The WEFA Group
401 City Line Ave., Suite 300
Bala Cynwyd, PA 19004-1780
Tel: (215)660-6300
Fax: (215)660-6477
Pages: Varies
Exhibits: None
Price: Contact for subscription prices

This quarterly on-line database provides macroeconomic forecasts for the countries of East and Southeast Asia. It covers national accounts, imports, exports, prices, debt, balance of payment, labor, and population statistics.

Title: Asia-Pacific Dun's Market Identifiers
Date: Updated monthly
Format: On-line database
Publisher: Dun & Bradstreet Information Services
One Diamond Hill Rd.
Murray Hill, NJ 07974-0027
Tel: (201)665-5000
Fax: (201)665-5418
Exhibits: None
Price: Contact for subscription prices

This on-line database covers more than 250,000 corporations in 40 countries. It provides mailing information, company descriptions, names of key personnel, sales figures, and volume of imports and exports.

Title: *Asia-Pacific International Journal of Marketing*
Date: Monthly
Format: Periodical
Author: Graduate School of Management, University of Queensland
Editor: Oliver H.M. Yau
Publisher: MCB University Press, Ltd.
60/62 Toller Lane
Bradford
West Yorkshire BD8 8BY, United Kingdom
Tel: (44)(274)499821
Fax: (44)(274)547143
Pages: Varies
Exhibits: Graphs and tables
Price: Contact for subscription prices

With 3 to 5 articles presented in each issue, this journal published by the University of Queensland offers some eclectic yet well-researched articles. Each issue focuses on marketing in the broadest sense, with topics including rural outshopping in Australia, price accuracy in the New Zealand supermarket, and so on. With a little browsing, market analysts might find just what they are looking for in this attractive journal.

Title: *Cracking the Pacific Rim: Everything Marketers Must Know to Sell into the World's Newest Emerging Markets*
Date: 1992
Format: Hardcover
Author: Oliver C. Dziggel and Allyn Enderlyn
Publisher: Probus Publishing Co.

118 N. Clinton St.
Chicago, IL 60614
Tel: (312)868-1100
Fax: (312)868-6250

Pages: 252

Exhibits: Maps and tables

Most of the information in this volume can be obtained free of charge from the U.S. Department of Commerce, though as a one-stop source, this book offers convenience for the price. Each chapter covers a single country of Asia and provides information on basic data, approaching the market, the investment climate, financial aspects, licensing and patents, and advice for travelers. The style is clear and factual but hardly entertaining; the material is entirely instructive and not anecdotal. The book contains a list of information sources.

Title: *Global Purchasing: How to Buy Goods and Services in Foreign Markets*

Date: 1992

Format: Hardcover

Author: Thomas K. Hickman and William M. Hickman, Jr.

Publisher: Business One Irwin
1818 Ridge Rd.
Homewood, IL 60430
Tel: (708)206-2700
Fax: (708)798-6388

Pages: 237

Exhibits: Tables

A primer for buyers of goods and services from abroad, this volume offers advice on how to qualify suppliers, deal with diverse business cultures, negotiate in foreign areas, control the costs of importing and payment transactions, and manage a good business relationship to achieve performance and quality control. The authors offer would-be importers some useful business advice when they discuss the brass tacks of the buying transaction, but they miss the mark when covering the cultural aspects of doing business abroad. This book is a good source of definitions of trading terms and contains an explanation of the documentation steps necessary to import.

Title: *The National Trade Data Bank* (NTDB)

Date: Updated monthly

Format: CD-ROM

Author: Office of Business Analysis, Economics and Statistics Administration, U.S. Department of Commerce

Publisher: U.S. Department of Commerce
Main Commerce Building
14th and Constitution Ave., NW
Washington, DC 20230
Tel: (202)482-1405
Fax: (202)482-2164

Exhibits: None

Price: $300/year

This subscription CD-ROM database provides a vast array of statistical and text data regarding international business climates, market analysis, economic indicators, and political developments. It lists publications from more than two dozen U.S. government agencies, including the International Trade Administration, the Department of Labor, the Department of State, and the Central Intelligence

Agency. The dollar values and amounts of U.S. imports and exports by product line are provided, as well as a list of importing companies around the world that are interested in doing business with U.S. suppliers. This is an absolutely indispensable source of global marketing information at a very reasonable price.

Title: *Predicasts F&S Index Plus Text*
Date: Monthly
Format: CD-ROM
Publisher: Predicasts, Inc.
11001 Cedar Ave
Cleveland, OH 44106-3088
Tel: (216)795-3000
Fax: (216)229-9944
Exhibits: None
Price: $2,500/year

This monthly CD-ROM database describes global business activities from more than 1,000 trade, industry, and government publications. It covers manufacturing and service industries, focusing on markets, products, and companies. Most business libraries carry the printed version of this publication.

Title: *Statistical Yearbook for Asia and the Pacific*
Date: 1990
Format: Paperback
Author: Economic and Social Commission for Asia and the Pacific
Publisher: United Nations Statistical Office
United Nations Publications
2 United Nations Plaza, Room DC2-0853
Sales Section, Publishing Service
New York, NY 10017
Tel: (212)963-8302
Fax: (212)963-3489
Pages: 465
Exhibits: Tables

The data collected for this volume concern population, labor, national accounts, agriculture, forestry and fishing, industry, energy, transport and communications, trade, wages, prices, and finance. The data are divided into country sections, with each country receiving 15 to 20 pages of tables in coverage. When ordering, ask for UN publication sales no. E/F.91.II.F.1.

Title: *Trade Opportunities: International and Domestic Trade Information*
Date: Updated regularly
Format: CD-ROM
Publisher: U.S. Department of Commerce/Update Publications
1736 Westwood Blvd.
Los Angeles, CA 90024
Tel: (310)474-5900
Exhibits: None
Price: $299/year

This CD-ROM database provides access to a variety of Department of Commerce publications, including the Trade Opportunities program, *Commerce Business Daily*, and *Selling to International Markets*.

POLITICS AND GOVERNMENT

Title: *Asian Bulletin*
Date: Monthly
Format: Periodical
Editor: Anna Y. Yang
Publisher: Asian Peoples' Anti-Communist League Publications
8th Floor, 102 Kuangfu Rd.
Taipei, Taiwan 110
Tel: (886)(2)752-3366
Fax: (886)(2)777-4656
Pages: Varies
Exhibits: Graphs, photographs, and tables
Price: Contact for subscription prices

This erudite monthly is published in Taipei, and thus all articles pertaining to the People's Republic fall under the heading of "Communist China." With its 100 pages packed to the margins with text and black-and-white photos, this journal presents itself correctly as a monthly news digest of political and international affairs. The coverage is Asia-wide, including perspective reports on international developments. Articles are roughly 2 to 5 pages in length and are divided by region. This is a recommended source of Asia-wide news analysis presented in a *New York Times* writing style.

Title: *Asian Business*
Date: Monthly
Format: Periodical
Editor: Brian Caplen
Publisher: Far East Trade Business
Block C, 10th Floor, Seaview Estate
2-8 Watson Rd.
North Point, Hong Kong
Tel: (852)566-8381
Fax: (852)508-0197
Pages: Varies
Exhibits: Photographs and tables
Price: Free to qualified individuals;
$45/year (surface mail);
$95/year (airmail)

This general Asian business magazine has staff stationed throughout Asia. Its focus is on financial news in each Asian country, how-to advice for investors, new marketing opportunities, and company profiles. With more than 70 pages of news, features, and photographs, this periodical packs a lot of value for the money.

Title: *Asian Business Information*
Date: Monthly
Format: Periodical
Publisher: Asian Business Information, Ltd.
Chinese Periodical Distribution
716 N. Figueroa St.
Los Angeles, CA 90012
Tel: (213)626-0389
Pages: Varies
Exhibits: Photographs
Price: Contact for subscription prices

This full-color monthly features articles concerning industrial development in East Asia, with a clear emphasis on the People's Republic of China. Most of the advertisements are from China, as well. This is a strange publication in need of focus, but it will interest those who want to learn about selected industrial projects in Asia.

Title: *The Asian Political Dictionary*
Date: 1985
Format: Hardcover
Author: Lawrence Ziring and C.I. Eugene Kim
Editor: Jack C. Plano
Publisher: ABC-Clio, Inc.
Riviera Campus
Box 4397
2040 Alameda Padre Serra
Santa Barbara, CA 93140-4397
Tel: (805)963-4221
Fax: (805)966-4861
Pages: 438
Exhibits: Maps and tables

This exhaustive and fact-packed "dictionary" is more like an encyclopedia containing historical descriptions of political terms, figures, and events. From the Asian Highway to the Hukbalahop Uprising, the political researcher is sure to find helpful, complete, and insightful information. The definitions are divided by topic, such as diplomacy and political geography.

Title: Asian Political News
Date: Updated weekly
Format: On-line database
Publisher: Kyodo News International, Inc.
50 Rockefeller Plaza, Room 803
New York, NY 10020
Tel: (212)586-4550
Fax: (212)725-3721
Exhibits: None
Price: $156/hour

This on-line database contains the full text of articles drawn from regional Asian newspapers and periodicals. It covers only current events and political developments in East and Southeast Asia. It is of interest to political risk analysts and journalists.

Title: *Asian Power and Politics: The Cultural Dimensions of Authority*
Date: 1985
Format: Paperback
Author: Lucian W. Pye
Publisher: Belknap Press/Harvard University Press
29 Garden St.
Cambridge, MA 02138-1499
Tel: (617)495-2600
Fax: (617)495-8924
Pages: 414
Exhibits: None

Authored by a foremost orientalist, this pithy volume explores the nature of social and political power in Asia and sheds light on bureaucratic decision making there. This is a great source for business-people who want to acquire background knowledge of Asian society and business culture.

Title: *Asian Security 1992–93*
Date: 1992
Format: Hardcover
Author: Research Institute for Peace and Security
Publisher: Brassey's, London
Macmillan Publishing Co.
1st Floor, 8000 Westpark Dr.
McLean, VA 22102
Tel: (703)442-4535
Fax: (703)790-9063
Pages: 249
Exhibits: Tables

Beginning with the premise that international politics in Asia "was never as straightforward as the confrontation of two camps with a single overriding East-West orientation," this volume surveys the security issues prevalent in each country of Asia in the post–cold war world order. Engaging in style, this book provides a good introduction for political risk analysts as well as businesspeople in the defense industries.

Title: *Asian Studies Center Backgrounder*
Date: Irregular
Format: Periodical
Author: Asian Studies Center
Publisher: The Heritage Foundation
214 Massachusetts Ave., NE
Washington, DC 20002-4999
Tel: (202)546-4400
Pages: Varies
Exhibits: Varies
Price: Contact for subscription prices

This 10-page newsletter, published by a well-known American think tank, stresses the need for America to maintain a leadership role in Asia and offers strategic plans for American officials to achieve this goal. It is useful to businesspeople who track U.S. relations to Asian countries and must weigh domestic sources of political risk to Asian ventures.

Title: *Asian Survey*
Date: Monthly
Format: Periodical
Author: Institute of International Studies, University of California, Berkeley
Editor: Robert A. Scalapino, Leo E. Rose, and Joyce K. Kellgren
Publisher: University of California Press
2120 Berkeley Ave.
Berkeley, CA 94720
Tel: (510)642-4247
Fax: (510)643-7127
Pages: Varies
Exhibits: Varies
Price: $44/year for individuals; $92/year for institutions

This journal, edited by the illustrious Asia commentator Robert Scalapino, is a good value for its low subscription price, especially for businesspeople following political and policy trends in selected countries of Asia, particularly Japan and China. The 10- to 25-page articles are academic in style and approach, but for those who need in-depth analysis of issues in Asian politics, economy, energy policy, technology, trade negotiations, and so on, this is a recommended journal.

Title: *Asian Wall Street Journal*
Date: Daily
Format: Newspaper
Editor: Urban C. Lehner
Publisher: Dow Jones Publishing Co. (Asia), Inc.
2nd Floor, AIA Building
G.P.O. Box 9825
Hong Kong
Pages: Varies
Exhibits: Diagrams, graphs, and tables
Price: $650/year

High-priced but highly recommended for the businessperson, this 20- to 25-page newspaper appears three times a week and provides Asia-related business news in the *Wall Street Journal* format. It also includes European news, commentary, and arts and leisure reports, as well as stock listings for Asia markets, currency rates, interest rates, and so on.

Title: *Asia-Pacific Outlook*
Date: Quarterly
Format: Periodical; also available on-line
Author: Economist Intelligence Unit
Publisher: Business International Corp.
40 Duke St.
London EC14 8PD, United Kingdom
Tel: (44)(71)493-6711
Fax: (44)(71)499-9767
For on-line version, contact:
Maid Systems, Ltd.
Maid House, 18 Dufferin St.
London EC1Y 8PD, United Kingdom
Tel: (44)(71)253-6900
Pages: Varies
Exhibits: Graphs and tables
Price: Contact for subscription prices

Each issue of this 20-page pamphlet provides an analysis of a regional trend underway in the Asia-Pacific (e.g., "The Emergence of Greater China"), which is followed by short pieces that amount to an economic overview of the region. It is recommended to businesspeople who do not want to miss out on the next economic wave in Asia. The publication is concise and of high quality.

Title: *Asia Today*
Date: Monthly
Format: Periodical
Editor: Florence Chong
Publisher: East Asia News and Features, Ltd.
Box N7
Grosvenor Place Post Office
Sydney 2000 NSW, Australia
Tel: (61)(2)256 2110
Fax: (61)(2)241 4126
Pages: Varies
Exhibits: Varies
Price: $105/year

A rather dull-looking magazine published in Australia, this 30-page monthly focuses on new markets opening in Asia, business deals struck between Asian and Western companies, and trade policy in Asian countries. For those who follow the activities of Australian firms in the region, this magazine may be worth looking at, though the price is high relative to that of similar magazines. If you're looking for the Australian perspective, this one is your choice.

Title: *Asiaweek*
Date: Weekly
Format: Periodical
Editor: Michael O'Neill
Publisher: Asiaweek, Ltd.
34th Floor, Citicorp Centre
18 Whitfield Rd.
Causeway Bay, Hong Kong
Pages: Varies
Exhibits: Varies
Price: $153/year

With staff correspondents stationed throughout Asia, this glossy color weekly covers Asian society, politics, and business developments in the style of *Time Magazine* and *Newsweek*. It provides book reviews, travel advice, macroeconomic data, well-researched and entertaining features, great photography, human interest tidbits, and surveys of Asian attitudes and perceptions. A recommended general magazine to keep the Asia businessperson up to speed conversationally. It also includes an overview of regional stock markets.

Title: *Comparative Business-Government Relations*
Date: 1990
Format: Hardcover
Author: George Cabot Lodge
Publisher: Prentice-Hall
113 Sylvan Ave.
Englewood Cliffs, NJ, 07632
Tel: (201)592-2000
Fax: (201)592-2824
Pages: 447
Exhibits: Graphs and tables

This compilation of articles and case studies for the Harvard Business School course of the same title examines "the different roles and relationships of business and government in key countries of Asia" and elsewhere and offers advice to managers who will have to contend with these changes. Asia-related topics include the Japanese government's targeting of the computer industry, cooperation between Japan and the United States, Japanese-American competition in microelectronics, and Japan's high-technology policy.

Title: *Current World Affairs*
Date: Quarterly
Format: Periodical
Editor: George A. Daoust
Publisher: Current World Affairs
Hero Books
1336 Kingston Ave.
Alexandria, VA 22302
Tel: (703)356-1151
Fax: (703)827-2683
Pages: Varies
Exhibits: None
Price: $170/year

This index is a quarterly compilation of periodical articles, government documents, research reports, books, and monographs. Materials are listed by subject, and entries provide short abstracts. This is a recommended first source for researchers of political topics and news events.

Title: *Daily Report—East Asia*
Date: Daily
Format: Periodical, hardcover, or microfiche
Author: Foreign Broadcast Information Service
Publisher: Newsbank, Inc.
P.O. Box 2604
Washington, DC 20013
Tel: (202)338-6735
Pages: Varies
Exhibits: None
Price: Contact for subscription prices

This daily 75-page pamphlet is a little-read but absolutely essential publication for anyone tracking current political and economic developments in Asia. This collection of key articles is translated from Asian publications and delivered to subscribers two days after their original appearance in print. The report tracks hundreds of publications and divides articles by country.

Title: *East Asian Dynamism: Growth, Order, and Security in the Pacific Region*
Date: 1990
Format: Paperback
Author: Steve Chan
Publisher: Westview Press
5500 Central Ave.
Boulder, CO 80301
Tel: (303)444-3541
Fax: (303)449-3356
Pages: 134
Exhibits: Maps and tables

Part of the Dilemmas in World Politics series, this monograph draws on the history of Asian-international relations to predict future geopolitical scenarios, all of which might interest political risk analysts and those seeking a brief overview of Asian political economy and security issues.

Title: *Far Eastern Affairs*
Date: Bimonthly
Format: Periodical
Author: The Institute of the Far East
Editor: V.B. Vorontsov
Publisher: U.S.S.R. Academy of Sciences
27 Krasikov St.
Moscow, Russia
Tel: (7)(095)124 09 04
Pages: Varies
Exhibits: Varies
Price: Contact for subscription prices

A 200-page, rather low-budget journal published by the Academy of Sciences in Russia, this collection of articles is insightful and entertaining. It includes interviews with experts, science news, political forecasts, business news, and historical articles, all focusing on the Russian Far East but including articles on Japan, Korea, and Russian-Asian relations. For businesspeople heading for the Russian Pacific Rim, this journal might provide background.

Title: *Far Eastern Economic Review*
Date: Weekly
Format: Periodical
Editor: L. Gordon Crovitz

Publisher: Dow Jones and Co.
25th Floor, Citicorp Centre
18 Whitfield Rd.
Causeway Bay, Hong Kong

Pages: Varies

Exhibits: Graphs, photographs, and tables

Price: $159/year

This renowned publication is a bargain for its price. It is highly recommended for a weekly update on Asian politics, economy, business, and society. The full-color glossy magazine consists of regular features, regional news, arts and society reports, and a strong business section. The writing is first-rate, as is the analysis. For those who must subscribe to a single publication about Asia, this should be it.

Title: *Global Outlook*

Date: Quarterly

Format: Periodical; also available on-line

Author: Economist Intelligence Unit

Publisher: Economist Intelligence Unit, Ltd.
40 Duke St.
London EC14 8PD, United Kingdom
Tel: (44)(71)493-6711
Fax: (44)(71)499-9767
For on-line version, contact:
Maid Systems, Ltd.
Maid House
18 Dufferin St.
London EC14 8PD, United Kingdom
Tel: (44)(71)253-6900

Pages: Varies

Exhibits: Graphs and tables

Price: Contact for subscription prices

With roughly 15 pages of facts and current analysis of global economic trends (much of which is rendered in tables and graphs), this full-format pamphlet is of use to businesspeople who want to view Asian development, trade, and investment opportunities from a global perspective. It is also a recommended resource for finding out how world events are affecting business activities in Asia.

Title: *International Political Science Abstracts*

Date: Monthly

Format: Periodical

Publisher: International Political Science Association
27, rue Saint-Guillaume
75337 Paris Cedex 07, France

Pages: Varies

Exhibits: None

Price: Fr 1,180/year

This compendium of abstracts covers the topics of political science theory and method, political thinkers and ideas, government institutions, the political process, national area studies, and international relations. With the index, researchers can locate specialized articles on Asia-related political topics, including trade policy. The abstracts are complete and clearly written.

Title: *Northeast Asia Program Newsletter*

Date: Monthly

Format: Periodical
Author: Research School of Pacific Studies
Publisher: Australian National University
G.P.O. Box 4
Canberra ACT 2601, Australia
Tel: (61)(62)316-9444
Fax: (61)(62)316-9484
Pages: Varies
Exhibits: Varies
Price: $A 40/year for individuals; $A 100/year for institutions

This rather pricey unbound newsletter features 2 to 5 articles written by faculty members at the Research School of Pacific Studies at the Australian National University. Most articles focus on political change and make prognostications. This resource is of use to those who make political risk assessments.

Title: *Pacific Affairs*
Date: Quarterly
Format: Periodical
Author: Institute of Pacific Relations
Editor: Ian D. Slater
Publisher: University of British Columbia
6344 Memorial Rd.
Vancouver, B.C. VGT 1Z2, Canada
Tel: (604)822-3259
Fax: (604)822-6083
Pages: Varies
Exhibits: Varies
Price: $35/year for individuals; $50/year for institutions

This 100-page quarterly collection of academic research articles covers macro trends in Asian development and politics. For analysts tracking political risk and economic policy, this is a useful source, at least on occasion, as the coverage is Pan-Asian and the number of articles is limited to 4 to 6. The book reviews are useful to those trying to select reading material for a specific research task. Asian writers are well represented.

Title: *Pacific-Asia and the Future of the World-System*
Date: 1993
Format: Hardcover
Editor: Ravi Arvind Palat
Publisher: Greenwood Press
88 Post Rd. West
Westport, CT 06881
Tel: (203)226-3571
Fax: (203)222-1502
Pages: 207
Exhibits: Graphs and tables

A collection of papers presented at the Conference on the Political Economy of the World-System in 1991, this volume is useful to the Asia-Pacific economist or anyone interested in the evolution of the "Pacific Rim Century." The topics covered include the political economy of the Pacific Rim, the rise of East Asia, China's economic reform, and others. The writing is in the style of spoken lectures.

Title: *The Pacific in the 1990s: Economic and Strategic Change*
Date: 1990
Format: Hardcover

Author: Janos Radvanyi
Publisher: University Press of America, Inc.
4720 Boston Way
Lanham, MD 20706
Tel: (301)459-3366
Fax: (301)459-2118
Pages: 158
Exhibits: None

This anthology covers geopolitical issues and security issues in the Pacific region while concentrating on the "complex interactions between social, political, and economic forces and changing security postures" in the Asia-Pacific. It contains articles on Japan's self-defense forces, the modernization of China's defense apparatus, and regional security issues. It is now dated but still useful to political risk analysts and those in the defense industry.

Title: *Pacific Review*
Date: Quarterly
Format: Periodical
Author: International Institute for Strategic Studies
Editor: Gerald Segal
Publisher: Oxford University Press
23 Tavistock St.
London WC2E 7NQ, United Kingdom
Tel: (44)(71)379-7676
Fax: (44)(71)836-3108
Pages: Varies
Exhibits: Varies
Price: $70/year for individuals; $142/year for institutions

This rather pricey, full-format journal of 200 pages includes a collection of articles, written mainly by academics, on subjects such as economic cooperation between Asian countries, developments in key Asian industries, country relations, and technology. It includes book reviews of popular titles. This is a good source of analysis for anyone tracking macro development and political issues in Asia, as well as U.S.-Asian relations.

Title: *Political and Economic Encyclopedia of the Pacific*
Date: 1985
Format: Hardcover
Editor: Gerald Segal
Publisher: Longman Group U.K., Ltd.
Westgate House
The High
Harlow
Essex CM20 1YR, United Kingdom
Tel: (914)993-5000 (U.S.)
Fax: (914)997-8115 (U.S.)
Pages: 293
Exhibits: Maps

With entries from Emperor Akihito to zinc, this handy desktop encyclopedia covers key political and economic events, personalities, terms, and concepts in an easy-to-use two-column format. It includes a general index. The only drawback is that this book is quickly becoming dated.

Title: *Political Handbook of the World*
Date: Annual
Format: Hardcover
Editor: Arthur S. Banks
Publisher: CSA Publications

State University of New York
Box 6000
Binghamton, NY 13902-6000
Tel: (607)777-2168
Fax: (607)777-2408

Pages: 956

Exhibits: None

Containing political overviews of all countries of the world, this hefty handbook is a useful reference for business researchers and political risk analysts. Each country section covers government, the current political scene, political parties, and an overview of government structure.

Title: Reuter TEXTLINE

Date: Updated daily

Format: On-line database (via Dialog)

Publisher: Reuters, Ltd.
85 Fleet St.
London EC4P 4AJ, United Kingdom

Exhibits: None

Price: $96/hour

This on-line database indexes and provides either abstracts or complete text for more than 2,000 financial and business newspapers, newsletters, and journals. Stored publications include the *Asian Wall Street Journal*, the *Japan Times*, and *Jiji Press*.

Title: *RIM: Pacific Business and Industries*

Date: Quarterly

Format: Periodical

Author: Center for Pacific Business Studies

Publisher: Sakura Institute of Research
2-16-6, Shinjuku
Shinjuku-ku
Tokyo 160, Japan

Pages: Varies

Exhibits: Graphs and tables

Price: Contact for subscription prices

This publication was started in 1991 and contains the results of research undertaken by the Sakura Institute of Research in Japan. *RIM* stands for both the Pacific Rim and Research for International Management. The 3 to 5 articles in this 40-page journal cover global and regional developments in trade, investment, technology, environment, and diplomatic relations. Typical of research of this sort conducted in Japan, the articles are concise yet comprehensive, providing detail in extremely well-rendered graphs and tables. This resource is suggested for businesspeople who want to stay abreast of global commercial trends and who want to understand the Japanese perspective of these trends.

Title: *South China Morning Post*

Date: Daily

Format: Newspaper

Publisher: South China Morning Post
Tong Chong St.
Quarry Bay, Hong Kong
Tel: (852)565-2222

Pages: Varies

Exhibits: Graphs, photographs, and tables

One of the world's great newspapers, this Hong Kong–based daily is a highly recommended source for Chinese news analysis, Hong Kong business updates, and Asian news in general. It includes sections on real estate, business, and stocks. It's also a great place to research job opportunities throughout Asia.

Title: *Trade Warriors: The Guide to the Politics of Trade and Investment*
Date: 1990
Format: Hardcover
Editor: Richard J. Whalen and R. Christopher Whalen
Publisher: The Whalen Co., Inc.
1717 K St. NW, Suite 706
Washington, DC 20006
Tel: (202)293-5540
Fax: (202)293-1627
Pages: 467
Exhibits: Photographs

For businesspeople seeking to lobby the U.S. government, this very handy set of government biographies (including photo portraits) will excite and inform. For example, the section on Lloyd Bentsen notes, "Bentsen dismisses fears of [Japanese trade] retaliation against the U.S., saying, 'I spent 16 years building a business. I look at the Japanese with a $60 billion trade surplus with this country. Retaliate? In business I learned never to run off my No. 1 customer, and neither will the Japanese.'" Each biography lists major campaign contributors, committee membership, and political tendencies on economic and trade issues. This is a useful insider's guide to the folks who, for better or for worse, directly affect corporate America's business relationships in Asia.

RESEARCH AND DEVELOPMENT

Title: *Pacific Research Centres: A Directory of Organizations in Science, Technology, Agriculture, and Medicine*
Date: 1988
Editor: Lindsay Karpera
Format: Hardcover
Publisher: Longman House
Burnt Mill, Harlow
Essex CM20 2JE, United Kingdom
Pages: 517
Exhibits: None

For technical directors of companies that want to link up with research centers in any of the East Asian and Southeast Asian countries, this directory provides details of about 3,500 industrial, government, and academic laboratories and research centers, listed by country and then alphabetically by name. Each entry includes the organization name, contact information (including telephone numbers but no fax numbers), the name of director, section names, the number of graduate research staff, annual expenditures, publications, and research activities. This resource includes an index of organization names and an index of research subjects.

Title: *Science and Technology in Australasia, Antarctica and the Pacific Islands*
Date: 1989
Format: Hardcover
Author: Jarlath Ronayne and Campbell Boag

Publisher: Longman House
Burnt Mill, Harlow
Essex CM20 2JE, United Kingdom
Tel: (914)993-5000 (U.S.)
Fax: (914)997-8115 (U.S.)

Pages: 335

Exhibits: Graphs and tables

This volume of Longman's series of related titles contains a section on science and technology in the islands of the South Pacific, including Cook Islands, Fiji, and Papua New Guinea. The section includes a readable overview of the region's geography, science and technology organizations, and key research activities. It includes a description of prominent research organizations and their activities, including contact information.

TAXATION

Title: *The CCH Journal of Asian Pacific Taxation*

Date: Bimonthly

Format: Periodical

Editor: Felicity Paton

Publisher: CCH Australia, Ltd.
CCH International
Talavera and Khartoum Rds.
P.O. Box 230
North Ryde NSW 2113, Australia

Pages: Varies

Exhibits: Graphs and tables

Price: $215/year

For accountants and tax lawyers, this 60- to 70-page magazine provides updates and overviews of taxation issues throughout Asia. Conference information and a professional directory are included. Expert contributors add regional perspectives.

Title: *Corporate Taxes—A Worldwide Summary*

Date: 1991

Format: Hardcover

Publisher: Price Waterhouse
1251 Avenue of the Americas
New York, NY 10020
Tel: (212)489-8900
Fax: (212)790-6620

Pages: 585

Exhibits: Tables

For the tax lawyer or accountant, this is a nicely published guide to tax regimes in all countries. Each country receives 3 to 5 pages of coverage, including basic rates for major types of taxes, notes on income determination, deductions, and tax incentives. It is recommended as a desktop reference.

Title: *Taxation in Asia and the Southwest Pacific: International Business Guide*

Date: 1990

Format: Paperback

Publisher: DRT International
1633 Broadway
New York, NY 10019-6754
Tel: (212)489-1600
Fax: (212)492-2005

Pages: 201

Exhibits: Tables

This guide to taxation in Asia covers Australia, China, Hong Kong, India, Indonesia, Japan, Korea, Macao, Malaysia, New Zealand, Pakistan, Philippines,

Singapore, Sri Lanka, Taiwan, and Thailand. For each country, the reader will find concise coverage of the main types of business activities, tax rates, and investment incentives as well as appendixes of tables. This is certainly a useful overview for expatriates and accountants.

TRAVEL ADVICE

Title: *All-Asia Guide*
Date: 1991
Format: Hardcover
Editor: Michael Malik
Publisher: Far Eastern Economic Review
Review Publishing Co., Ltd.
G.P.O. Box 160
Hong Kong
Pages: 764
Exhibits: Diagrams, maps, photographs, and tables

This comprehensive traveler's guide covers all of Asia under one cover, with different authors tackling each country. Vietnam, Cambodia, Brunei, and North Korea receive coverage along with the more common destinations. Each country section includes a historical overview, maps, hotel information, health advice, and a list of interesting sites. The coverage on a particular country may be incomplete, but as a single source of essential travel information that includes every Asian country, this book will suffice.

Title: *Asia: Guide to Business Travel*
Date: 1987
Format: Hardcover
Author: Robert K. McCabe
Publisher: International Herald Tribune
A&C Black (Publishers), Ltd.
35 Bedford Row
London WC1R 4JH, United Kingdom
Tel: (44)(71)240-946
Fax: (44)(71)831-8478
Pages: 186
Exhibits: Maps

This travel guide is especially designed for businesspeople. It is divided into the capital cities of Asia and covers little outside these cities. The author rates the cities as to overall quality (Shanghai ranks lowest and Hong Kong highest) and focuses on providing basic but essential traveler's information: arriving, tipping, money, communications, what to wear, languages, doing business (very brief coverage), and useful phone numbers. Restaurant, hotel, and sightseeing information is very useful to businesspeople who are not traveling on a shoestring.

Title: *Guide to the Orient*
Date: 1987
Format: Hardcover
Editor: Geoffrey Eu
Publisher: APA Productions (HK) LD
302-308 Hennessy Rd.
Wanchi, Hong Kong
Tel: (852)838-7873
Fax: (852)834-6175
Pages: 417
Exhibits: Photographs

This well-researched and well-photographed book is a good armchair travel guide to all of Asia. Different authors cover each East and Southeast Asian country, providing background history and descriptions of key sites. Guide sections at the book's end give information about travel arrangements, accommodations, and local languages. This book is more of a visual introduction than a take-along guide.

Title: *A Traveler's Guide to Asian Culture*
Date: 1989
Format: Hardcover
Author: Kevin Chambers
Publisher: John Muir Publications
P.O. Box 613
Santa Fe, NM 87504
Tel: (509)982-4079
Fax: (509)988-1680
Pages: 214
Exhibits: Maps

This is a handy primer that can enhance the business traveler's appreciation of Asian cultural sights, though the author is not a historian or an orientalist. This is a light read.

Title: *The Wall Street Journal Guide to Business Travel: Pacific Rim*
Date: 1991
Format: Paperback
Editor: Edie Jarolim
Publisher: Fodor's Travel Publications
201 E. 50th St.
New York, NY 10022
Tel: (212)872-8254
Fax: (212)572-2248
Pages: 537
Exhibits: Maps and tables

A compact companion to take along while traveling in Asia, this Fodor's guide, marketed under the *Wall Street Journal* moniker, covers the key business cities of Asia. All of the Asian capitals are included, as are other major cities, including Shanghai, Osaka, and Canton. Each city section provides essential information (such as government trade office addresses), notes on local business practice, a list of hotels, a city map, restaurant information, and tips on what to do with your free time.

JAPAN

OVERVIEW

Despite the economic downturn of the early 1990s, Japan remains one of the world's strongest economies, with massive purchasing power and an unparalleled commitment to manufacturing excellence. Although still considered by many to be a closed market, Japan has proved profitable for many companies that have maximized the hard-won gains of U.S. trade negotiators and have committed to a long-term presence in the country.

Japan at a Glance

Population:	124,040,000
Religion:	Buddhist, Shinto, Christian
Government:	Constitutional monarchy/parliamentary democracy
Language:	Japanese, English
Currency Name:	Yen (¥)
Total Trade (1993):	$330.9 billion total exports; $198 billion total imports

Japan is the world's second-largest economy, with an annual gross national product of nearly $3 trillion. Despite its current recession, Japan has sustained its traditional pattern of investing huge amounts of capital in its manufacturing base. The Japanese economy has also been buoyed by the government's fiscal policy, which has included a record $85.6 billion economic stimulus package. On average, Japan outinvested the United States in the upgrading of plants and equipment in the early nineties by more than $400 billion per year, investing more than $3 trillion annually. Moreover, the country maintains an annual trade surplus with the world of more than $130 billion, $45 billion of which is with the United States.

Economic Conditions

Japan's Nikkei stock market lost one-half of its value between 1989 and 1992, and land values have dropped by 20 percent since their peak in 1990. A new frugality has set in among consumers, and speculative commercial activities have virtually disappeared. However, publicly funded projects in infrastructural development have begun, including airports, roads, bridges, and housing. This is a massive program of investment throughout the country. Budgeted in the trillions of dollars, this program encompasses bridges, airports, telecommunications systems, medical centers, and the construction of technologically sophisticated "smart buildings." The result is a wide range of potential markets for U.S. products.

Japan is the second largest importer of U.S. products in the world, after Canada. Through 1994 and beyond, the country will remain an important focus of U.S. sales and marketing efforts. Japan's continuing global search for the very best in technology offers important opportunities to U.S. business. This nation's investment in Japan is being encouraged by a more relaxed attitude on the part of the Japanese government as well as the declining value of land in Japan. At the same time, most barriers to the import of U.S. products have been eliminated, and imports from the United States are actively encouraged by the Japanese government in order to redress Japan's chronic trade imbalance with the United States. Most trade barriers are now concentrated in a few segments of the Japanese economy, such as agriculture and food products.

Three strong trends in the Japanese population offer the greatest promise for U.S. exports: (1) the aging of the population, (2) the need to "deminiaturize" and expand living space, and (3) the maturing of a new consumer class of young professionals. Most Americans would be surprised that, as of 1984, the Japanese have spent an average of $583 each—or 6 percent of their total income—to buy American-made products, whereas Americans spent only $289 each on Japanese products—or just 2 percent of their income. To begin an effort to crack the Japan market, U.S. firms should set up direct lines of communication with one or more of the 61 personnel who operate the United States and Foreign Commercial Service of the Department of Commerce in Japan.

Historical Background

Although Japan's state religion was traditionally Shintoism, early rulers did not suppress Buddhism or Confucianism, and most Japanese are a Buddhist-Shintoist-Confucian blend in their religious beliefs. Shintoism contributes the ideals of loyalty to one's clan, group, or company. Like the Shintoist samurai warrior, the Japanese value sacrifice to their leaders, whether statesmen or managers, and apologies and atonement for their mistakes or breeches of responsibility. Buddhism contributes the ideal of mentorship in the master/disciple relationship of Zen Buddhism as well as the ethic of frugality, silent meditation, and formality. Confucianism contributes values of duty and family piety.

Japan is an island culture of almost total ethnic homogeneity, where collective unity is easily enforced. Just as some Westerners harbor a cultural superiority complex, some Japanese harbor a uniqueness complex. If we were to take Japanese explanations for the trade imbalance as truth, we'd have to accept that Japanese brains are different, Japanese snow is different, and even their rice is unique. Articles appear in the Japanese press explaining that the inherent qualities of the "traditional Japanese mind" make the Japanese uniquely suited to perform production tasks that other people can't. One article explained that a tradition of cleanliness (inspired by Buddhism) and of discipline (inspired by Shintoism) is behind Japan's prowess at maintaining the cleanest "clean rooms" for producing the most defect-free computer microchips. The tradition starts, one article contends, with the habit of leaving one's shoes at the door of one's home and ends with the worker's nightly bath in the deep tub called an *ofuro*.

Many experts have observed that the Japanese company is really a secondary village in its organization and system of values. As in the rice farming village of ancient Japan, tasks are separated among divisions in which people are bonded socially in such things as drinking together after hours, recalling the festival-like atmosphere of togetherness of Shinto rituals of long ago. Seniority in the Japanese company is based on length of service just as leadership in the early village was based on age and amount of experience. The large family feudal system has no doubt declined, but it has been replaced by universities and large companies in which individual worth is tied to the importance of company and school in the economic life of the country. There is another similarity between the rice farm and the Japanese corporation: On the farm, everyone had to be a generalist and learn every aspect of the operation, from planting to harvesting. The same system exists today in Japanese companies.

Most Japanese workers and managers are hired for entry-level positions directly out of college. They typically receive automatic pay raises and promotions. Status and seniority are tied to length of service. Workers participate in after-hours gatherings of their co-workers to foster harmony and cooperation in their division. They're loyal to their company, more so sometimes than to their family. Japanese managers tend to originate from the rank and file, working their way up the company ladder from lower levels. They make an active commitment to preserve harmony through intricate social rituals, such as gift giving, bowing to superiors, and honorific language to show deference.

ACCOUNTING, BANKING, AND FINANCE

Title: Atlas
Date: Updated throughout the day
Format: On-line database
Publisher: Technical Data
11 Farnsworth St.
Boston, MA 02210
Tel: (617)345-2526
Exhibits: None
Price: Contact for subscription prices

This continuously updated on-line database offers financial data and analysis of the Japanese bond markets as well as those of other major economies. It provides bond histories and short-term predictions and includes buying and selling recommendations.

Title: *Daiwa Bank Monthly Research Report*
Date: Monthly
Format: Periodical
Editor: Daiwa Research Institute, Inc.
Publisher: The Daiwa Bank Ltd., Research Division
2-1, Bingomachi 2-chome
Chuo-ku
Osaka 541, Japan
Tel: (81)(6)271-1221
Fax: (81)(6)268-1723
Pages: Varies
Exhibits: Graphs and tables
Price: Contact for subscription prices

Meant for bankers, economists, and financiers, this 6-page newsletter, published by Daiwa Bank in Japan, provides a monthly financial update on Japan's economic condition. The report also includes industry outlooks on an irregular basis. It carries a table of interest rates and economic indexes, as well as a list of Daiwa overseas branches.

Title: Dataline
Date: Updated weekly
Format: On-line database
Publisher: Textline/Reuters, Ltd.
85 Fleet St.
London EC4P 4AJ, United Kingdom
Tel: (44)(71)250-1122
Exhibits: None
Price: £75/hour

This database provides company financial data and forecasting for 16 industrialized countries, including Japan. It covers more than 3,000 traded companies, offering multiple financial forecasts based on user-provided assumptions.

Title: *DKB Economic Report*
Date: Semimonthly
Format: Periodical
Author: Dai-Ichi Kangyo Bank Research Institute Corp.
Publisher: Dai-Ichi Kangyo Bank, Ltd.
1-5, Uchisaiwaicho 1-chome
Chiyoda-ku
Tokyo 100, Japan
Tel: (81)(3)596-1111
Pages: Varies
Exhibits: Graphs and tables

Price: Contact for subscription prices

Published by the Dai-Ichi Kangyo Bank, this 12-page newsletter provides recent economic indicators for Japan as well as text analysis of the country's economic and financial outlook. It also includes industry outlooks on an irregular basis, a table of major economic indicators, and a list of Dai-Ichi Kangyo branches overseas.

Title: *Financial Reporting in Japan*

Date: 1992

Format: Hardcover

Author: T.E. Cooke and M. Kikuya

Publisher: Blackwell Publishers
108 Cowley St.
Oxford OX4 1JF, United Kingdom
Tel: (44)(1)404-4101

Pages: 356

Exhibits: Graphs and tables

For accountants and tax lawyers, this volume provides an in-depth explanation of accounting principles and practices in Japan. The first part of the book reviews the evolution of these practices within the framework of Japan's commercial environment; the second part contains an analysis of accounting practices based in part on the authors' survey of Japanese accounts. The book covers such topics as the history of Japanese enterprise, the accounting regulatory framework, international influences on practices, disclosure principles, asset valuation, and a survey of accounts. This is a clearly articulated body of useful research.

Title: Information Service International—Dentsu, Ltd.

Date: Updated daily

Format: On-line database

Publisher: Information Service International—Dentsu, Ltd.
11-10, Tsukiji 1-chome
Chuo-ku
Tokyo 104, Japan
Tel: (81)(3)3214-1111

Exhibits: None

Price: Contact for subscription prices

This database provides information on stocks and bonds listed on the Tokyo and Osaka stock exchanges. It gives all prices in the first section of the Tokyo Stock Exchange, the first and second sections of the Osaka Stock Exchange, and other daily listings.

Title: *Inside Japanese Financial Markets*

Date: 1988

Format: Hardcover

Author: Aron Viner

Publisher: Dow Jones-Irwin
1818 Ridge Rd.
Homewood, IL 60430
Tel: (708)206-2700
Fax: (708)798-6388

Pages: 364

Exhibits: Tables

For would-be investors in Japan, this book provides a readable overview of all Japanese financial markets as well as a review of the "social and political imperatives" that make these markets the most regulated in the free world.

Title: *Invest Japan*
Date: 1992
Format: Hardcover
Author: William T. Ziemba and Sandra L. Schwartz
Publisher: Probus Publishing Co.
1925 N. Clynbourn Ave.
Chicago, IL 60614
Tel: (312)868-1100
Fax: (313)368-6250
Pages: 589
Exhibits: Graphs and tables

For the serious-minded investor, this hefty volume offers an in-depth review of Japan's financial markets: how they function and how they have performed up to 1992. It includes solid coverage of valuation techniques, hedging strategies, and stock market risks and offers suggestions for potential prospective investors.

Title: *Japanese Finance and Industry*
Date: Quarterly
Format: Periodical
Publisher: Industrial Bank of Japan, Ltd.
Nihonbashi Annex
2-16, Yaesu 1-chome
Chuo-ku
Tokyo 100, Japan
Tel: (81)(3)5252-6046
Fax: (81)(3)3273-6260
Pages: Varies
Exhibits: Graphs and tables
Price: Contact for subscription prices

This 25- to 40-page booklet carries one long article per issue on a topic relevant to Japan's industrial economy. It also has an overview section that provides recent trends and future outlooks for Japan's major industries. Of particular value to businesspeople is the long (15- to 20-page) article, which delivers much in content, insight, and topic relevancy. Previous articles have focused on Japan-U.S. relations from an industrial viewpoint, Japan's middle class, and Japanese women as a consumer market. It is recommended as an enlightening read as well as an industry updater for Japan.

Title: *The Japanese Financial System*
Date: 1987
Format: Hardcover
Editor: Yoshio Suzuki
Publisher: Clarendon Press/Oxford University Press
Walton St.
Oxford OX2 6DP, United Kingdom
Pages: 358
Exhibits: Tables

This volume provides both an overview of the structure of Japan's financial system and an in-depth examination of the various parts of the system, including financial assets, markets, institutions, and banks. It is clearly written and rich in detail.

Title: *Japanese Management Accounting: A World Class Approach to Profit Management*
Date: 1989
Format: Hardcover
Editor: Yasuhiro Monden and Michiharu Sakurai

Publisher: Productivity Press
P.O. Box 3007
Cambridge, MA 02140
Tel: (617)497-5146
Fax: (617)868-3524

Pages: 546

Exhibits: Graphs and tables

For corporate accountants, this well-illustrated and clearly written textbook provides a complete explanation of accounting practices in Japanese corporations. The five sections of the volume cover cost management systems for manufacturing, profit planning and control systems, cost accounting practices and standards, organizational aspects of managerial accounting, and other specialized accounting practices. It is highly recommended.

Title: *Japan's Securities Markets: A Practitioner's Guide*

Date: 1989

Format: Hardcover

Author: Takeji Yamashita

Publisher: Butterworths and Co. (Asia), Pte. Ltd.
30 Robinson Rd., #12-01
Tuan Sing Towers
0104, Singapore
Tel: (65)220-3684
Fax: (65)225-2939

Pages: 310

Exhibits: Graphs and tables

For the sophisticated investor, this volume explains the structure and performance of Japan's securities market, including the markets for stocks, equity, and futures and the short-term money market. It is detailed and clearly written.

Title: *Monthly Finance Review*

Date: Monthly

Format: Periodical

Publisher: Information Systems Department
Institute of Fiscal and Monetary Policy
Ministry of Finance, Japan
3-1-1, Kasumigaseki
Chiyoda-ku
Tokyo 100, Japan
Tel: (81)(3)581-4111

Pages: Varies

Exhibits: Tables

Price: Contact for subscription prices

Issued by the Ministry of Finance in Japan, this 20- to 25-page booklet provides short articles summarizing trends in current business conditions in Japan (e.g., domestic demand, production, employment, balance of payments, prices, etc.). These are followed by a set of tables accompanied by short text descriptions tracking "economic events" in Japan (e.g., the release of an economic report by the government, recent trade figures, or a new policy measure ratified by the government). This is a useful updater that includes a poster-size table of key economic indicators for the current month.

COMPANY DIRECTORIES

Title: *Access Nippon*

Date: 1993

Format: Paperback

Publisher: Access Japan, Inc.

Yamaguchi Building
2-8-5, Uchikanda
Chiyoda-ku
Tokyo 101, Japan
Tel: (81)(3)5256-1541
Fax: (81)(3)3258-1487

Pages: 423

Exhibits: None

The first five chapters of this handbook provide a readable, fact-packed primer for foreigners who wish to initiate business dealings with Japan. Selected topics include the Japanese economy, market research, distribution, office space, taxes, getting information, travel advice, and a useful overview of all sectors of Japanese industry. The next 250 pages make up a directory of Japanese companies, listed by industry. Entries include a company overview, characteristics of overseas business, overseas partners, annual sales, and more. This is a useful and rich compendium of practical information.

Title: *The Complete Directory of Japan*

Date: Annual

Format: Hardcover

Publisher: Asia Press
Dowa Building
2-22, Ginza 7-chome
Chuo-ko
Tokyo 104, Japan

Pages: 1,350

Exhibits: None

This convenient one-volume directory contains short listings of national and local government entities, domestic commercial and industry contacts, foreign diplomats and organizations, institutions of higher learning, and Japanese businesses abroad. As a general directory, this volume does the job, but the company listings provide names and addresses only; marketers will need to consult one or more of the other company directories listed herein.

Title: COSMOS

Date: Updated monthly

Format: On-line database

Publisher: Teikoku Databank, Ltd.
5-20, Minami Aoyama
2-chome
Minato-ku
Tokyo 107, Japan
Tel: (81)(3)3404-4311

Exhibits: None

Price: Contact for subscription prices

This on-line database contains descriptive data on more than 950,000 Japanese companies. It also provides contact information, financial data for the last two years, and company characteristics.

Title: *Diamond's Japan Business Directory*

Date: Annual

Format: Hardcover

Editor: Tetsuji Yamada

Publisher: Diamond Lead Co.
4-2, Kasumigaseki 1-chome
Chiyoda-ku
Tokyo 100, Japan
Tel: (81)(3)3504-6791
Fax: (81)(3)3504-6798

Pages: 1,500

Exhibits: Tables

Meant for stock investors, this hefty directory lists Japanese companies by name and industrial category. A second section lists brand and trade names used by these companies. The company profiles are each two pages long and provide a text commentary on company performance and future prospects; the statistical information given includes stock share ratios, profit-and-loss statements, assets, liabilities, and general company descriptions.

Title: *Directory of Affiliates and Offices in Japanese Firms in the ASEAN Countries*
Date: 1982
Format: Paperback
Publisher: Japan External Trade Organization (JETRO)
2-5, Toranomon 2-chome
Minato-ku
Tokyo 105, Japan
Tel: (81)(3)582-5511
Fax: (81)(3)582-7508
Pages: 254
Exhibits: None
Price: ¥ 5,000

Written by the staff of the *Nikkei Weekly*, this fact-packed and well-illustrated almanac of articles covers key trends, economy, finance, and industry in Japan, with a chronology of the year's events in review. A section of statistics lists government agencies, political parties, key economic indicators, and market shares. Separate articles cover every industrial sector and all aspects of the economy, including international trade and foreign investment. Each article is two pages in length. This is a highly recommended yearly review of the Japanese business scene for those who don't have the time to read the *Nikkei Weekly*.

Title: *Directory of Japanese-Affiliated Companies in the USA and Canada*
Date: Annual
Format: Paperback
Publisher: Japan External Trade Organization (JETRO)
2-5, Toranomon 2-chome
Minato-ku
Tokyo 105, Japan
Tel: (81)(3)3582-3518
Pages: 800
Exhibits: None

Published by JETRO, this directory lists Japanese affiliates in the United States and Canada by state or province. The list includes 9,168 affiliates in the United States and 702 in Canada. An affiliate is defined as any business in which a Japanese company owns a share of 10 percent or more. Each entry includes company name, address, phone number, and names of key executives. A supplemental index lists the companies by industry or service.

Title: *Japan Business Directory*
Date: Annual
Format: Hardcover
Publisher: The Japan Press, Ltd.
12-8, Kita Aoyama 2-chome
Minato-ku
Tokyo 107, Japan
Tel: (81)(3)3404-5161
Fax: (81)(3)3423-2358
Pages: 2,000 (2 vols.)
Exhibits: None
Price: ¥ 72,100

More like a phonebook of Japanese companies and business organizations than a directory, this resource lists companies alphabetically and provides minimal information on each: name, address, president, and products imported and exported. No cross-listing by product or service is provided. The book is tabbed for easy use.

Title: *Japan Company Datafile*
Date: 1991
Format: Hardcover
Publisher: Toyo Keizai, Inc.
1-2-1, Nihonbashi
Hongokucho
Chuo-ku
Tokyo 103, Japan
Tel: (81)(3)3246-5621
Fax: (81)(3)3241-5543
Pages: 1,199
Exhibits: None

Meant particularly for stock investors, this directory includes 1,178 Japanese companies listed on the first sections of Japan's three main stock exchanges in Tokyo Osaka, and Nagaya. Companies are categorized by industry and are indexed by name as well. Each company is described in one page, including corporate history, sales breakdown, shareholders, capital changes, subsidiaries, branch offices, number of employees, average monthly pay, and more.

Title: *Japan Company Handbook*
Date: Quarterly
Format: Paperback
Publisher: Toyo Keizai, Inc.
1-2-1, Nihonbashi
Hongoku-cho
Chuo-ku
Tokyo 103, Japan
Tel: (81)(3)3246-5655
Fax: (81)(3)3241-5543
Pages: 1,200
Exhibits: Graphs

This directory lists 2,326 Japanese-affiliated companies located in the member countries of the Association of Southeast Asian Nations (ASEAN): Singapore, Philippines, Malaysia, Thailand, Brunei, and Indonesia. The companies are grouped by industry within each county section. They are also cross-indexed in a master list by name. Company profiles provide the name of the local firm, address, phone, type of business, and the names (and equity share) of shareholders.

Title: *Japan Directory of Professional Associations*
Date: 1988
Format: Hardcover
Publisher: Intercontinental Marketing Corp.
Wako 5 Building
1-19-8, Kakigaracho
Tokyo 100-31, Japan
Pages: 390
Exhibits: None

This is an alphabetical listing of 5,800 Japanese professional organizations, "including nearly all academic, business, commercial, industrial, professional, technical, and trade groups" that international businesspeople might need to contact for information, specialized publications, or membership. Cultural associations and government and corporate research institutes are also listed. The directory is cross-indexed by subject category. The list of publication sources published by the associations is not available elsewhere.

Title: *Japan Economic Almanac*
Date: Quarterly
Format: Paperback
Author: The *Nikkei Weekly*
Publisher: Nihon Keizai Shimbun, Inc.
1-9-5, Otemachi
Chiyoda-ku
Tokyo 100-66, Japan
Tel: (81)(3)3270-0251
Pages: 2,500 (2 vols.)
Exhibits: Graphs
Price: $59.50/year

The best all-around, convenient directory of Japanese firms, this quarterly handbook provides recent financial information on Japanese corporations listed on the first and second sections of the Tokyo, Osaka, and Nagoya stock exchanges. Published in two volumes, one for the first section and one for the second, each volume profiles more than 1,000 firms, one firm per page. The profiles include company description, business outlook (the most valued part of these handbooks), financial data, sales breakdown, stock prices, investments, and more. It is highly recommended to investors.

Title: Japanese Company Factfinder
Date: Updated quarterly
Format: CD-ROM
Publisher: Dialog Information Services
3460 Hillview Ave.
P.O. Box 10010
Palo Alto, CA 94304-1396
Tel: (800)334-2564
Price: $3,200/year

Since 1900, Teikoku Databank in Japan has been tracking the credit worthiness of more than 2 million Japanese companies. Information about 186,000 of those companies is now available on CD-ROM—by far the most comprehensive database of Japanese firms in any format. Each entry includes the company name, contact information, annual sales, profits, taxable income, net-worth and dividend ratios, sales ranking, credit rating, number of shareholders, and banks with which the company conducts business. You can search for companies by name, geographic location, or industrial classification.

Title: *Japanese Investment in U.S. and Canadian Real Estate Directory*
Date: 1990
Format: Hardcover
Publisher: Mead Ventures, Inc.
P.O. Box 44952
Phoenix, AZ 85064
Tel: (800)669-6323
Fax: (602)234-0076
Pages: 619
Exhibits: None

This directory lists Japanese-owned real estate companies doing business in the United States and Canada and is of special interest to marketers targeting this customer base. The company profiles list addresses, key contacts, business activities, and general information about the real estate activities of the companies. The companies are cross-indexed by state. An appendix includes important addresses, and a glossary of Japanese real estate terms and a list of Japanese media are given.

Title: *Japanese Overseas Investment: A Complete Listing by Firms and Countries*
Date: Annual
Format: Hardcover
Publisher: Toyo Keizai
1-2-1, Nihonbashi Hongoku-cho
Chuo-ku
Tokyo 103, Japan
Tel: (81)(3)3246-5621
Fax: (81)(3)3241-5543
Pages: 800
Exhibits: None

Divided by geographic region and country, this directory lists 13,000 Japanese firms around the world that are either partially or wholly capitalized by Japanese firms. Each entry provides the name of the Japanese investing entity, the percentage of shareholding, other investors' addresses and telephone numbers, the number of employees, gross assets, and business profit-making results. This is the best worldwide directory of its type.

Title: *Japan Trade Directory*
Date: Annual
Format: Hardcover
Publisher: Japan External Trade Organization (JETRO)
2-5, Toranomon 2-chome
Minato-ku
Tokyo 105, Japan
Tel: (81)(3)3582-3518
Fax: (81)(3)3582-7508
Pages: 1,300
Exhibits: Maps and tables
Price: ¥ 30,900

Published by JETRO, this directory lists, both alphabetically and by commodity, 3,000 Japanese companies involved in international trade. The directory also lists trade associations, banks, law and patent offices, and other entities involved in trade. The product listing is divided into exports and imports, making this an ideal directory for marketers. The company profiles include type of business, number of employees, overseas offices, annual sales, languages spoken by contact personnel, and specific products and services for export and/or import. It is recommended as a first-choice directory.

Title: *Membership Directory*
Date: Annual
Format: Paperback
Publisher: The American Chamber of Commerce in Japan
7th Floor, Fukide Building No. 2
4-1-21, Toranomon
Minato-ku
Tokyo 105, Japan
Tel: (81)(3)3433-5381
Fax: (81)(3)3463-1446
Pages: 150
Exhibits: Photographs

Like the other membership directories of the American Chamber of Commerce in Asian countries, this one lists members alphabetically by company name and, in an index, alphabetically by member's last name. The directory provides job titles and portraits but no other professional information about members. It's a good source of contacts and services for firms setting up in Japan.

Title: *Standard Trade Index of Japan*
Date: Annual
Format: Hardcover
Publisher: The Japan Chamber of Commerce and Industry
2-2, Marunouchi 3-chome
Chiyoda-ku
Tokyo 100, Japan
Pages: 1,200
Exhibits: None
Price: ¥ 23,690

This directory lists 7,000 manufacturers, exporters, importers, trade service organizations, and foreign firms located in Japan. Firms are listed alphabetically and by commodity or service, and those that are interested in trade with foreign companies are marked with an asterisk. The profiles include only contact information and line of business.

COUNTRY PROFILES

Title: *CITEC Review*
Date: Monthly
Format: Periodical
Publisher: Japan External Trade Organization (JETRO)
1221 Avenue of the Americas
New York, NY 10020
Tel: (212)997-0400
Pages: Varies
Exhibits: Maps, graphs, and tables
Price: Contact for subscription prices

Providing news updates on Japan-foreign technological and investment cooperation, this four-page newsletter published by JETRO often includes useful corporate surveys and information about Japanese investment environments. For those investing in Japan, this is a useful supplemental resource.

Title: *Country Forecast—Japan*
Date: Quarterly
Format: Periodical
Publisher: The Economist Intelligence Unit
P.O. Box 154
Dartford
Kent DA1 1QB, United Kingdom
Tel: (44)(322)289-194
Fax: (44)(322)223-803
Pages: Varies
Exhibits: Graphs and tables
Price: Contact for subscription prices

Like others in its series, this 35- to 40-page booklet provides a five-year macroeconomic forecast for Japan on a quarterly basis. Sections cover politics, economy, demographic and social trends, and the business environment. A concluding set of tables provides economic statistics for the previous five-year period and projections for the coming five-year period. The writing is clear, and the publication is well-illustrated. The one-page executive summary is a handy updater. This resource is recommended.

Title: *Inside the Japanese System*
Date: 1988
Format: Paperback
Editor: Daniel I. Okimoto and Thomas P. Rohlen

Publisher: Stanford University Press
Ventura Hall
Stanford, CA 94305-4115
Tel: (415)723-1712
Fax: (415)723-0758

Pages: 286

Exhibits: Graphs and tables

This compilation of erudite articles by some of the foremost academics in the field of Japan studies asks whether Japan should make structural changes in its industrial-economic system to accommodate U.S. demands (first made in 1989) that it do so to level the trade imbalance between the countries. Selected article topics include U.S.-Japan trade, trade problems, and relations; Japanese business groups and the U.S. demand for structural change; and built-in impediments in the Japanese system. For trade negotiators and researchers these expert articles grapple with issues that remain relevant today.

Title: *Japan Almanac*

Date: Annual

Format: Paperback

Publisher: Asahi Shimbun
5-3-2, Tsukiji
Chuo-ku
Tokyo 104-11, Japan
Tel: (81)(3)3545-0131

Pages: 320

Exhibits: Maps, graphs, and tables

This handy, palm-size almanac, covers a galaxy of topics, from population and politics to communications and crime, each topic receiving one page of text and graphic coverage. An amazing volume of information is rendered in easy-to-read tables and diagrams, divided under the main headings of national land/politics, economy/industry, society/life, and culture/leisure. This is a recommended desktop reference for anyone who uses country data.

Title: Japan Economic Newswire (JEN)

Date: Updated daily

Format: On-line database (via Dialog)

Publisher: Kyodo News International, Inc.
50 Rockefeller Plaza, Room 803
New York, NY 10020
Tel: (212)586-4550
Fax: (212)725-3721

Exhibits: None

Price: $96/hour

This on-line database covers Japanese domestic affairs and international news as it relates to Japan. It provides the complete text of hundreds of thousands of English-language articles. News about business and industry receives ample coverage, making this a valuable, though expensive, source for investors, strategists, and journalists.

Title: *Japan 1994: An International Comparison*

Date: Annual

Format: Paperback

Editor: Kokichi Morimoto

Publisher: Keizai Koho Center
6-1, Otemachi 1-chome
Chiyoda-ku
Tokyo 100, Japan

Pages: 102
Exhibits: Maps, graphs, and tables

Published by the nonprofit organization Keizai Koho Center, this annual pocket booklet of comparison tables and charts will come in handy for anyone researching Japan. The data compare Japan to 10 to 20 other countries in nearly 100 categories, such as population, trade, food supply, industry, overseas aid, taxes, wages, and so on. This is a highly recommended desktop reference.

Title: *JEI Report*
Date: Weekly
Format: Periodical
Publisher: Japan Economic Institute
1000 Connecticut Ave., NW
Washington, DC 20036
Tel: (202)296-5633
Pages: Varies
Exhibits: Tables
Price: Contact for subscription prices

Published by the Japan Economic Institute, this 10-page newsletter carries articles that briefly examine Japan's political and economic climate. The articles offer insightful analysis and predictions for future trends. News briefs provide economic updates.

Title: Nikkei Economic Electronic Databank System (NEEDS)
Date: Varies by file
Format: On-line database service
Publisher: Nihon Keizai Shimbun (NIKKEI)
Databank Bureau
1-9-5, Otemachi
Chiyoda-ku
Tokyo 100, Japan
Tel: (81)(3)5294-2407
Fax: (81)(3)5294-2411
Exhibits: None
Price: ¥ 1,500/month;
¥ 1,000/connection

This on-line service offers access to seven on-line databases that provide information on current events, business, economics, and finance. NEEDS provides the full text of articles in English and Japanese from Japan's leading newspapers as well as company profiles, stock information, and historical financial data.

Title: NIFTY
Date: Updated regularly
Format: On-line database service
Publisher: NIFTY Corp.
8th Floor, Omori Bell Port A
26-1 Minami
Ohi 6 chome,
Shinagawa 140, Japan
Tel: (03)5471-5241
Fax: (03)5471-5890
Exhibits: None
Price: Contact for subscription prices

This on-line service provides information in English and Japanese through a number of databases. The topics covered include the Japanese economy, current events, biotechnology, industrial technology, and telecommunications.

Title: *Quality of the Environment in Japan*
Date: Annual

Format: Paperback

Publisher: Environment Agency
Government of Japan
1-2-2, Kasumigaseki
Chiyoda-ku
Tokyo 100, Japan

Pages: 540

Exhibits: Graphs and tables

Issued by the Japanese Environment Agency, this annual report delivers a detailed and well-illustrated accounting of the state of Japan's environment, with a section covering trends in the world environment as well. It covers global environmental issues, local initiatives to improve the environment, current conditions of the environment, government policy, air pollution, water pollution, pollution disputes, surveys on environmental protection, and the promotion of international environmental protection.

Title: *White Papers of Japan*

Date: Annual

Format: Hardcover

Editor: Itaru Umeza and Haruhisa Takeuchi

Publisher: The Japan Institute of International Affairs
19th Floor, Mori Building
2-20, Toranomon 1-chome
Minato-ku
Tokyo 105, Japan

Pages: 228

Exhibits: Graphs and tables

For researchers, marketers, and political analysts, this book contains annual abstracts of official reports and statistics gathered by the Japanese government, including text summaries of trends in Japanese politics and economy. It also includes key policy speeches by Japanese leaders and tables of basic statistical data. The topics include foreign policy, defense, economy, trade, and life of the nation. The abstracts are well organized and are well illustrated with graphs and tables.

DICTIONARIES AND LANGUAGE STUDIES

Title: *Essential Kanji*

Date: 1987

Format: Hardcover

Author: P.G. O'Neill

Publisher: John Weatherhill, Inc.
7-6-13, Roppongi
Minato-ku
Tokyo 106, Japan
Tel: (212)223-3008 (U.S.)
Fax: (212)223-2584 (U.S.)

Pages: 325

Exhibits: Japanese characters

The Japanese written language comprises a combination of phonetic signs and ideographic characters, based on the Chinese characters, that the Japanese call Kanji. The phonetic systems present no real barrier for foreigners learning Japanese, but the 2,500 necessary Kanji require years of memorization. This dictionary provides explanations and stroke orders for 2,000 of the most common characters, with samples of how they are used in Japanese. The characters are also indexed alphabetically by their romanized "reading"—a convenient feature.

Title: *Japanese Business Glossary*

Date: 1983

Format: Hardcover

Publisher: Mitsubishi Corp.

2-6-3, Manrunouchi
Chiyoda-ku
Tokyo 100-66, Japan
Tel: (81)(3)3210-2121
Fax: (81)(3)3210-8051

Pages: 220

Exhibits: Japanese characters

This is a bilingual version of a dictionary of terms produced by Mitsubishi and called *Tatemae and Honne*. This version provides a complete translation of business terms and definitions into Japanese script.

Title: *Japanese Business Language: An Essential Dictionary*

Date: 1987

Format: Hardcover

Author: Mitsubishi Corp.

Publisher: KPI, Ltd.
11 New Fetter Lane
London EC4P 4EE, United Kingdom

Pages: 221

Exhibits: Japanese characters

Meant for expatriates or anyone who seeks a deeper understanding of Japanese business culture, this one-of-a-kind directory of Japanese terms is invaluable. Terms like bucho, nemawashi, and sensei are fully defined, with Japanese language translations of each term provided as well. (In case you were wondering, a bucho is the chief of a division, nemawashi refers to Japan's consensus decision making, and sensei is a title used to address a teacher.)

Title: *Japanese-English Learner's Dictionary*

Date: 1992

Format: Paperback

Editor: Shigeru Takebayashi

Publisher: Kenkyusha, Ltd.
11-3, Fujimi 2-chome
Chiyoda-ku
Tokyo 102, Japan
Tel: (81)(3)3291-2301
Fax: (81)(3)3293-1194

Pages: 1,121

Exhibits: Drawings, maps, and Japanese characters

This is an attractive and portable compilation of definitions of Japanese words, without English-to-Japanese definitions. Each entry includes pronunciation, characters, definition in English, and examples of the phrase in Japanese, with English translations.

Title: *Japanese: The Spoken Language in Japanese Life*

Date: 1981

Format: Paperback

Author: Osamu Mizutani

Publisher: The Japan Times, Ltd.
5-4, Shibaura 4-chome
Minato-ku
Tokyo 108, Japan
Tel: (81)(3)3453-5311
Fax: (81)(3)3453-8023

Pages: 180

Exhibits: None

For serious students of the Japanese language or culturalists who want to understand Japanese values and psychology as expressed in spoken language, this book is required reading. The author grapples with such topics as the situational nature of Japanese, the language behavior of the average Japanese, how the Japanese speak to avoid openly disagreeing with one another, and how speech is adjusted between people of differing levels of status. Although chock-full of profound sociological insights, this book has been included here as a dictionary because it explains cultural traits as expressed in speech term by term; thus, the book is a valuable reference.

Title: *Kodansha's Compact Kanji Guide: A New Character Dictionary for Students and Professionals*
Date: 1991
Format: Paperback
Publisher: Kodansha International
17-14, Otowa 1-chome
Bunkyo-ku
Tokyo 112, Japan
Tel: (81)(3)3944-6491
Fax: (81)(3)3944-5560
Pages: 894
Exhibits: Japanese characters

For those learning to use Jōyō Kanji, the nearly 2,000 commonly used characters in modern Japanese writing, this is a handy comprehensive dictionary. It's user-friendly and has easy-to-understand advice on how to look up Kanji characters, a task far more difficult than looking up alphabetized English words. Ample coverage is given to words from the business world, including business jargon and financial terms, which are highlighted for immediate use by the businessperson.

Title: *Martin's Pocket Dictionary: English-Japanese; Japanese-English*
Date: 1990
Format: Hardcover
Author: Samuel E. Martin
Publisher: Charles E. Tuttle Co.
2-6, Suido 1-chome
Bunkyo-ku
Tokyo 112, Japan
Tel: (81)(3)3811-7741
Fax: (81)(3)5689-4926
Pages: 724
Exhibits: None

For the traveler, here is a pocket-size two-way dictionary that includes romanized pronunciation and no Japanese characters. For the serious student of Japanese, both spoken and written, this dictionary of Japanese grammatical terms and characteristics is a potential lifelong companion. Each entry explains a term or phrase and gives its part of speech, meaning, function, English counterpart, and related expressions. Examples follow. The authors include a complete descriptive overview of Japanese grammar and an English and Japanese index.

Title: *The Oxford-Duden Pictorial Japanese and English Dictionary*
Date: 1989
Format: Paperback
Publisher: Oxford University Press
800 Madison Ave.
New York, NY 10016
Tel: (212)679-7300
Fax: (212)725-2972
Pages: 864

Exhibits: Drawings and Japanese characters

Each page of this extraordinary dictionary provides English and Japanese names for items depicted in an adjacent drawing. The reader looks up, say, photography, and finds a page of drawings of a camera, its parts, and related equipment and accessories, each numbered and translated. This book represents a fantastic achievement, except for the omission of romanized pronunciations of each Japanese word, which would have made this the perfect business traveler's dictionary.

Title: *Tatemae and Honne*
Date: 1988
Format: Hardcover
Author: Mitsubishi Corp.
Publisher: The Free Press
Macmillan, Inc.
866 Third Ave.
New York, NY 10022
Tel: (212)605-9364
Fax: (212)605-9372
Pages: 182
Exhibits: None

Extremely useful to anyone working with the Japanese, this is a well-organized dictionary of Japanese terms relating to the practice of business. Definitions are clear and complete, but the Japanese script of each term is not supplied.

ECONOMY

Title: *Balance of Payments Monthly*
Date: Monthly
Format: Periodical
Editor: Akira Nagashima
Publisher: Bank of Japan
1-1, 2-chome, Hongoku-cho
Nihonbashi, Chuo-ku
Tokyo 103, Japan
Tel: (81)(3)3279-1111
Pages: Varies
Exhibits: Tables
Price: ¥ 770/issue

Issued monthly by the Bank of Japan, this 80- to 90-page booklet provides raw statistical data on Japan's balance of payments, that is, exports and imports (by country and commodity), services and transfers, long-term capital assets and liabilities, gold and foreign exchange reserves, and balance of monetary movements. The figures are given in U.S. dollars.

Title: COMLINE
Date: Updated daily
Format: On-line database service
Publisher: Comline International Corp.
1st Floor, Meiji Building
1-5-15, Jinnan
Shibuya-ku
Tokyo 150, Japan
Tel: (81)(3)3770-5501
Exhibits: None
Price: $180/hour

This on-line service provides multiple databases that cover aspects of the Japanese economy and offer daily updates on Japanese commercial sectors, including electronics, telecommunications, biotechnology, transportation, and manufacturing. The service also provides a directory of Japanese corporations.

Title: DRI International Cost Forecasting
Date: Updated quarterly
Format: On-line database
Publisher: DRI/McGraw-Hill
Data Products Group
24 Harrtwell Ave.
Lexington, MA 02173
Tel: (617)863-5100
Fax: (708)614-3363
Exhibits: None
Price: Contact for subscription prices

This on-line database provides producer and wholesale price indexes, construction costs and wages, and earnings for Japan as well as other major industrial countries. The coverage includes wholesale price indexes for a variety of commodities, raw materials, and manufactured goods.

Title: DRI Japanese Forecast
Date: Updated 5 times/year
Format: On-line database
Publisher: DRI/McGraw-Hill
Data Products Group
24 Harrtwell Ave.
Lexington, MA 02173
Tel: (617)863-5100
Fax: (708)614-3363
Exhibits: None
Price: Contact for subscription prices

This on-line database offers more than 500 quarterly reports on the Japanese economy on topics including gross national product (GNP), wages, money supply, stock prices, and exchange rates.

Title: *Economic Eye: A Quarterly Digest of Views from Japan*
Date: Quarterly
Format: Periodical
Author: Japan Institute for Social and Economic Affairs
Editor: Katsura Kuno
Publisher: Keizai Koho Center
Otemachi Building
6-1, Otemachi 1-chome
Chiyoda-ku
Tokyo 100, Japan
Tel: (81)(3)3201-1415
Fax: (81)(3)3201-1418
Pages: Varies
Exhibits: Tables
Price: Contact for subscription prices

The publisher of this 30-page newsletter, the nonprofit Keizai Koho Center, works with the *Keidanren* (Japan Federation of Economic Organizations) "to provide domestic and international audiences with an unbiased overview of the Japanese economy." Each issue carries translations of 8 to 10 recent Japanese articles on economic issues. Issues focus on specific topics, such as the educational system, rethinking Japanese management, and so on. This newsletter is recommended as a selective and rich source of insight on focused subjects. It includes a table of key economic indicators.

Title: *Economic Notes*
Date: Monthly
Format: Periodical
Publisher: Japan Development Bank

9-1, Otemachi 1-chome
Chiyoda-ku
Tokyo 100, Japan
Tel: (81)(3)3244-1986
Fax: (81)(3)3270-4099

Pages: Varies
Exhibits: Tables
Price: Contact for subscription prices

Issued by the Japan Development Bank, this 10- to 15-page newsletter is a partial translation of *Keizai Memo* (published by the Economic and Industrial Research Department) and provides a recent economic survey of Japan. The "notes" are categorized by topic—such as industrial activity, capital spending, housing investment, and so on—all accompanied by tables of data. The text summaries of current data offer a time-saving service to executives who track Japan's economy.

Title: *Economic Statistics Monthly*
Date: Monthly
Format: Periodical
Publisher: Bank of Japan
1-1, 2-chome, Hongoku-cho
Nihonbashi, Chuo-ku
Tokyo 103, Japan
Tel: (81)(3)3663-5681
Pages: Varies
Exhibits: Tables
Price: ¥ 1,030/year

Published by the Bank of Japan, this is the best and most comprehensive source of raw statistical data on the Japanese economy. The data cover currency, interest rates, money markets, banking accounts, GNP, and so on, including a business survey section. For the serious analyst, this 250-page compendium includes no text summary or opinion.

Title: *Economic Survey of Japan*
Date: Annual
Format: Hardcover
Publisher: Economic Planning Agency
1-1 Kasumigaseki 3-chome
Chiyoda-ku
Tokyo 10, Japan
Tel: (81)(3)3581-0261, ext. 609
Pages: 289
Exhibits: Graphs and tables

Issued on an annual basis by a Japanese government agency, this volume provides an authoritative and detailed review of economic trends in Japan over the past year. Topics include the overall state of the economy, the agenda for the economy, trends in the business sector, the state of manufacturing, the current account, the labor market, and prices. The book examines the factors behind Japan's business cycles and looks at features of the current cycle.

Title: *Governing the Japanese Economy*
Date: 1993
Format: Hardcover
Author: Kyoko Sheridan
Publisher: Policy Press/Blackwell Publishers
108 Cowley St.
Oxford OX4 1JF, United Kingdom
Tel: (44)(1)404-4101

Pages: 331
Exhibits: Graphs and tables

Providing official foreign aid is one way the Japanese government promotes Japanese exports throughout the developing world. This compilation of clearly written research articles examines Japan's official development assistance (ODA) programs, the participation of the country's private firms in aid-related projects, and the burden sharing of development projects between the United States and Japan.

Title: *Hitotsubashi Journal of Economics*
Date: Monthly
Format: Periodical
Editor: Yukio Noguchi and Kotaro Suzumura
Publisher: Hitotsubashi University and Japan Publications Trading Co., Ltd.
P.O. Box 5030
1, Naka 2-chome
Kunitachi
Tokyo 186, Japan
Pages: Varies
Exhibits: Graphs
Price: Contact for subscription prices

This 50-page journal compiles academic articles on economic subjects. Topics include Japanese investment in Central Europe, taxation in Japan, and other topics relevant to economic trends throughout Asia. Most articles lean toward the theoretical, but there are exceptions that will interest general business researchers.

Title: *Industrial Policy of Japan*
Date: 1988
Format: Hardcover
Editor: Ryutaro Komiya, Masahiro Okuno, and Kotaro Suzumura
Publisher: Academic Press
1250 Sixth Ave.
San Diego, CA 92101
Tel: (619)231-0926
Fax: (619)699-6715
Pages: 590
Exhibits: Graphs and tables

For anyone tracking Japan's official development assistance (ODA) around the world, this is the official annual ODA report. The first chapter discusses the current state of Japanese aid. The second chapter responds to criticism of the aid programs. The final chapter examines future priorities and directions for Japanese aid programs.

Title: *The Internationalization of Japan*
Date: 1992
Format: Hardcover
Editor: Glenn D. Hook and Michael A. Weiner
Publisher: Routledge
11 New Fetter Lane
London EC4P 4EE, United Kingdom
Tel: (44)(71)583-9855
Fax: (44)(71)583-0701
Pages: 325
Exhibits: Graphs and tables

This collection of articles by academics examines the process and implications of Japan's economic internationalization, with selected titles focusing on the automobile industry, Japanese capital, migrant workers, education, and political thought.

Title: *Japan and the Global Economy*
Date: 1991
Format: Hardcover
Editor: Jonathan Morris
Publisher: Routledge
11 New Fetter Lane
London EC4P 4EE, United Kingdom
Tel: (44)(71)583-9855
Fax: (44)(71)583-0701
Pages: 240
Exhibits: Tables

In this compilation, the business researcher will find informative and well-cited academic articles on the subjects of the globalization of Japanese manufacturing and Japanese investment overseas, with an emphasis on the United States, Canada, and the Asia-Pacific.

Title: *Japan and the World Economy*
Date: Quarterly
Format: Periodical
Editor: Ryuzo Sato
Publisher: North-Holland/Elsevier Science Publishers
Journal Department
P.O. Box 211
Amsterdam 1000 AE, The Netherlands
Tel: (31)(20)5803642
Fax: (31)(20)5803598
Pages: Varies
Exhibits: Graphs and tables
Price: Contact for subscription prices

The aim of this small-format academic journal is to address concerns associated with the increasing "economic interdependence between Japan and its trading partners." The topics for original research include economics, finance, managerial sciences, and marketing. This journal is meant for the economist or serious analyst; the articles are highly theoretical.

Title: *Japanese Capitalism Since 1945*
Date: 1989
Format: Hardcover
Editor: T. Morris-Suzuki and T. Seiyama
Publisher: M.E. Sharpe, Inc.
80 Business Park Dr.
Armonk, NY 10504
Tel: (914)273-1800
Fax: (914)273-2106
Pages: 221
Exhibits: Graphs and tables

This hefty textbook provides a broad, fact-based introduction to Japan's economy, and then, state the authors, "subjects those facts to modern economic analysis, both theoretical and empirical." They compare Japanese institutions with similar institutions in America, and compare the economies of each country in terms of overall performance. Although too theoretical for most business readers, this book might interest serious researchers and economists.

Title: *Japanese Economic Indicators Quarterly*
Date: Quarterly

Format: Periodical
Publisher: Economic Planning Agency
Japanese Government
3-1-1, Kasumigaseki
Chiyoda-ku
Tokyo 100, Japan
Tel: (81)(3)3581-0261
Pages: Varies
Exhibits: Graphs and tables
Price: Contact for subscription prices

This 120-page small-format journal carries recent economic statistics in table and graph form. The indicators cover business conditions, production, labor, wages, prices, orders received, public finance, trade, and so on. This journal is intended for the serious analyst; it contains no text overviews.

Title: *Japanese Economic Studies*
Date: Quarterly
Format: Periodical
Editor: Kazuo Sato
Publisher: M.E. Sharpe, Inc.
80 Business Dr.
Armonk, NY 10504
Tel: (914)273-1800
Fax: (914)273-2106
Pages: Varies
Exhibits: Graphs and tables
Price: $423/year

In this 80-page, small-format journal, the business reader will find long articles by Japanese academics on an array of topics broadly related to Japan's industrial economy. Recent articles discussed working hours and the quality of life in Japan, how pay levels are determined in Japan's financial sector, and the formation and development of Japanese medium-size companies. The writing style is clear and not too theoretical. This journal is useful to analysts and executive managers alike.

Title: *The Japanese Economy*
Date: 1992
Format: Hardcover
Author: Takatoshi Ito
Publisher: MIT Press
55 Hayward St.
Cambridge, MA 02142
Tel: (617)253-5646
Fax: (617)258-6779
Pages: 455
Exhibits: Tables

Of interest to historical researchers and, perhaps, managers and executives who seek a deeper understanding of the historical evolution of Japanese management style and industrial organization, this compilation covers such topics as the legacy of Japan's economic growth, monopoly capital, problems of the working class, and foreign trade and industrial imperialism in postwar Japan. This is a readable and well-researched book.

Title: *Japan's Economic Structure: Should It Change?*
Date: 1990
Format: Hardcover
Editor: Kozo Yamamura
Publisher: Society for Japanese Studies
Thomason Hall, DR-05
University of Washington
Seattle, WA 98195
Tel: (206)543-7666
Fax: (206)543-1228

Pages: 377
Exhibits: Tables

Meant as a general reader on topics related to Japanese industrial and social organization, this anthology of engaging background articles covers such topics as the Japanese family, hierarchy in society, the work ethic, the economy, industrial groups, the corporation as a family unit, government institutions, education, innovation, and Japan's vulnerabilities. This is an excellent reader.

Title: *Japan's Foreign Investment and Asian Economic Interdependence*
Date: 1992
Format: Hardcover
Editor: Shojiro Tokunaga
Publisher: University of Tokyo Press
1, Furo-cho, Chikusa-ku
Nagoya 464-01, Japan
Tel: (81)(52)781-5027
Fax: (81)(52)781-0697
Pages: 294
Exhibits: Graphs and tables

In this compilation of erudite articles, the researcher will find solid information on Japan's direct foreign investment and on technology transfer throughout the Asia-Pacific region.

Title: *Japan's Official Development Assistance*
Date: Annual
Format: Hardcover
Publisher: Ministry of Foreign Affairs, Government of Japan, and the Association for Promotion of International Cooperation
23 Mori Building
1-23-7, Toranomon
Minato-ku
Tokyo 105, Japan
Tel: (81)(3)3504-2085
Fax: (81)(3)3504-3889
Pages: 340
Exhibits: Graphs and tables
Price: ¥ 2,060

The result of a two-year joint research project, this textbook on industrial policy in Japan is well written and well organized. It provides a complete and readable analysis from an economic perspective. Sections cover the history of industrial policy, the theory behind it, the promotion of it, industrial adjustment policy, and industrial organization in coordination with industrial policy. This is a recommended source on this much-talked-about topic.

Title: *JCER Report*
Date: Monthly
Format: Periodical
Publisher: Japan Center for Economic Research
Nikkei Kayabacho Building
6-1, Nihombashi Kayabacho 2-chome
Chuo-ku
Tokyo 103, Japan
Tel: (81)(3)3639-2811
Fax: (81)(3)3639-2839

Pages: Varies
Exhibits: Photographs and tables
Price: Contact for subscription prices

Focusing on economic issues as they relate to Japan, this 30-page newsletter carries research articles and papers presented by experts at conferences and symposiums around the world. Both the general business reader and the serious economist will find useful information about Japan's economy in this publication.

Title: *The Journal of Japanese and International Economies*
Date: Quarterly
Format: Periodical
Editor: Masahiko Aoki
Publisher: Academic Press, Inc.
1250 6th Ave.
San Diego, CA 92101
Tel: (619)699-6825
Fax: (619)699-6800
Pages: Varies
Exhibits: Graphs and tables
Price: $146/year

Meant solely for economists, this small-format 100-page academic journal carries highly theoretical research articles on economic issues related to Japan. The book reviews it contains are perhaps as useful as the articles.

Title: *Monetary and Economic Studies*
Date: Semiannual
Format: Periodical
Publisher: Institute of Monetary and Economic Studies
Bank of Japan
Research Division I
CPO Box 203
Tokyo 100-91, Japan
Pages: Varies
Exhibits: Graphs
Price: Contact for subscription prices

Published by an economic research institute in Japan, this 120-page journal of research articles provides information on economic and monetary issues specific to Japan. The articles are highly theoretical and thoroughly cited, covering such topics as optimal currency composition of government debt, monetary stabilization with interest rates instruments, and so on. This journal is best suited for the serious economist.

Title: *Monthly Economic Review*
Date: Monthly
Format: Periodical
Publisher: Bank of Japan
1-1 Nihonbashi Hongo ku-cho 2-chome
Chuo-ku
Tokyo 103, Japan
Pages: Varies
Exhibits: Tables
Price: Contact for subscription prices

Published by the Bank of Japan, this 10-page monthly newsletter provides updates on Japan's monetary and economic conditions. Starting with a three-page text summary of salient trends in personal consumption, housing investment, public works, export volume, the labor market, balance of payments, and so on, the publication then offers several pages of tables of recent statistics, including industrial production, corporate profits, and major economic indicators. This is a useful updater.

ETIQUETTE AND PROTOCOL

Title: *Coping with Japan*
Date: 1985
Format: Hardcover
Author: John Randle with Mariko Watanabe
Publisher: Basil Blackwell, Ltd.
108 Cowley Rd.
Oxford OX4 1JF, United Kingdom
Tel: (44)(1)404-4101
Pages: 175
Exhibits: Maps, pictures, and tables

This readable guidebook covers the essentials of etiquette and customs in Japan for the tourist or businessperson. Short chapters focus on accommodations, advice for emergencies, eating and drinking, holidays and festivals, language, and Japanese script. As a general primer, the book is a readable and useful source and companion, though businesspeople need to consult other sources, as well.

Title: *Culture Shock! Japan*
Date: 1993
Format: Paperback
Author: Rex Shelley
Publisher: Graphic Arts Center Publishing Co.
P.O. Box 10306
Portland, OR 97210
Tel: (503)226-2402
Fax: (503)226-1410
Pages: 280
Exhibits: Maps and tables

Part of a well-known and unique series of books, this one is meant for expatriates and travelers in Japan who want to understand the customs, culture, and etiquette in order to avoid culture shock. Well illustrated and entertaining to read, the book covers communicating, socializing, and doing business with the Japanese, though there are richer sources on business protocol and tactics for businesspeople. This book is recommended as a source of background about daily life and social interaction in Japan.

Title: *How to Be Polite in Japanese*
Date: 1989
Format: Paperback
Author: Osamu Mizutani and Nobuko Mizutani
Publisher: Japan Times, Ltd.
Room 3108, Kasumigaseki Building
2-5 Kasumigaseki 3-chom
Chiyoda-ku
Tokyo 100, Japan
Tel: (81)(3)3453-5311
Fax: (81)(3)3453-8022
Pages: 160
Exhibits: Tables
Price: $18.50

The authors of this guide to being polite while communicating in Japan have provided a great service to business visitors to the country. Visiting executives to Japan have found, often the hard way, that the Japanese put a premium on communication that expresses politeness, respect, and concern for others. The authors of the book instruct the reader how to exhibit—through words, phrases, and gestures—these sentiments and more. Phrases appear in Japanese and English; concepts are in boldface to facilitate use.

Title: *Japanese Business Etiquette, 2nd ed.*
Date: 1993
Format: Paperback
Author: Diana Rowland
Publisher: Warner Books
1271 Avenue of the Americas
New York, NY 10020
Tel: (212)522-7200
Fax: (212)522-7991
Pages: 286
Exhibits: Maps, graphs, and tables
Price: $12.99

This is the best source of clear and readable advice on how to conduct yourself as a businessperson when dealing with the Japanese. It covers dining, gift giving, hosting, communication, negotiation, and much more in a clear and engaging style. This is a very useful and popular book.

Title: *Japanese Etiquette and Ethics in Business*
Date: 1987
Format: Hardcover
Author: Boye De Mente
Publisher: Passport Books
4255 West Touhy Ave.
Lincolnwood, IL 60646-1975
Tel: (708)679-5500
Fax: (708)679-2494
Pages: 182
Exhibits: Diagrams

This is one of many books written by this author on the subject of Japanese culture and business practice. This book offers colorful chapters on Japanese business culture, management style, business entertainment, and the hidden barriers between foreigners and the Japanese. Critics of this author's work claim that critical errors mar this volume, but it is engaging and contains a complete and useful glossary of Japanese terms.

Title: *Japanese Names*
Date: 1989
Format: Paperback
Author: P.G. O'Neill
Publisher: Weatherhill, Inc.
8-3, Nibancho
Chiyoda-ku
Tokyo 102, Japan
Tel: (212)223-3008 (U.S.)
Fax: (212)223-2584 (U.S.)
Pages: 359
Exhibits: Japanese characters

The author claims that this index "covers a wide range of Japanese names, some 36,000 in all, and is in two parts to provide both the readings of names written in characters and the characters of known names." It includes surnames; personal names; place names; literary, historical, and artistic names; and era names. It provides the romanization of names but not the English translation of their meaning.

Title: *With Respect to the Japanese: A Guide for Americans*
Date: 1984
Format: Hardcover
Author: John C. Condon

Publisher: Intercultural Press, Inc.
P.O. Box 700
Yarmouth, ME 04096
Tel: (207)846-5168
Fax: (207)846-5181

Pages: 89

Exhibits: Japanese characters

Most books about Japanese culture focus on the Japanese and offer little in the way of comparison with other cultures. This notable book by a well-known Japan specialist juxtaposes Japanese traits, values, and behaviors with those of Americans. The result is a highly entertaining and instructive guide for businesspeople who want to get to know their Japanese counterparts and build better relationships with them. It also includes a discussion contrasting Japanese and American management styles and contains answers to frequently asked questions about the Japanese.

GENERAL BUSINESS

Title: *American Enterprise in Japan*

Date: 1991

Format: Hardcover

Author: Tomoko Hamada

Publisher: State University of New York Press
State University Plaza
Albany, NY 12246
Tel: (518)472-5000
Fax: (518)472-5038

Pages: 294

Exhibits: Diagrams

Based on actual case studies, this book provides an account of the cultural differences that must be overcome in a company comanaged by Americans and Japanese. The author examines "cross-cultural management from an anthropological perspective," with plenty of historical emphasis on the divergent values adopted in American and Japanese firms. Based on extensive interviews, this is a recommended source for workers and managers in an environment in which Japanese and American cultures are represented. It is also recommended for negotiators involved in U.S.-Japan alliances.

Title: *Doing Business in Japan*

Date: 1991

Format: Hardcover

Publisher: Ernst and Young
787 Seventh Ave.
New York, NY 10019
Tel: (212)830-6000
Fax: (212)489-1745

Pages: 128

Exhibits: Tables

Written "to give the busy executive a quick overview of the investment climate, taxation, forms of business organization, and business and accounting practices in Japan," this guide is a useful handbook for expatriates and accountants. It provides concise explanations of direct taxes, indirect taxes, taxes on domestic and foreign firms, and taxes on individuals, all in numbered sections for easy use.

Title: *Doing Business in Japan*

Date: 1993

Format: Paperback

Publisher: Price Waterhouse

7th Floor, Aoyama Building
2-3, Kita-Aoyama 1-chome
Minato-ku
Tokyo 107, Japan

Pages: 255

Exhibits: None

As an overview of Japan's business environment and taxation regime, this book provides a rich and useful source of current information. Starting with a country profile, it covers the business environment, incentives for investment, the regulatory environment, banking and finance, exporting regulations, and labor relations. Finally, it covers taxation in great depth, including auditing requirements, the tax system and administration, corporate taxes, and individual taxes—all with special emphasis on foreign corporations.

Title: *Doing Business with the Japanese*

Date: 1983

Format: Hardcover

Author: Mitchell F. Deutsch

Publisher: New American Library
1633 Broadway
New York, NY 10019

Pages: 197

Exhibits: None

Price: $14.50

An early "how-to-do-business" guide for Japan, this sensible and easy-to-read book holds up well today. The author worked closely with Sony and speaks from experience, which is not always the case with this sort of general guide. Chapter topics include bargaining, negotiating, and working for the Japanese. There is also a guide to correct behavior. Though probably out of print, this book is worth looking up in a business library.

Title: *Gaijin Kaisha: Running a Foreign Business in Japan*

Date: 1990

Format: Hardcover

Author: Jackson N. Huddleston, Jr.

Publisher: M.E. Sharpe, Inc.
80 Business Park Dr.
Armonk, NY 10504
Tel: (914)273-1800
Fax: (914)273-2106

Pages: 270

Exhibits: None

Written by the man who introduced the American Express Card to Japan, this personal and practical guide to operating a business in Japan is recommended to general managers of Japan-based operations. Based on hands-on experience, selected chapters cover personnel, legal issues, government relations, manufacturing, finance, accounting, marketing, selling, and more. Chapters include subheadings for easy use, and the author provides plenty of corporate anecdotes.

Title: *Gucci on the Ginza: Japan's New Consumer Generation*

Date: 1989

Format: Hardcover

Author: George Fields

Publisher: Kodansha International
114 Fifth Ave.
New York, NY 10011
Tel: (212)727-6460
Fax: (212)727-9177

Pages: 267

Exhibits: None

By the author of *From Bonzai to Levis*, this close to brilliant book provides both insight and philosophic inspiration to marketers targeting Japanese consumers. Though fast becoming dated in its factual content, it remains a delight and is highly recommended. Selected chapters cover style and communication in advertising to Japanese consumers, the professed (and real) uniqueness of the Japanese, and the rise of *shinjinrui* (literally, "the new human species"), referring to a new generation of young Japanese consumers. This book was published in Japan under the title *The Japanese Market Culture*.

Title: *Hidden Differences: Doing Business with the Japanese*
Date: 1987
Format: Paperback
Author: Edward T. Hall
Publisher: Doubleday
666 Fifth Ave.
New York, NY 10103
Tel: (212)765-6500
Fax: (212)492-9700
Pages: 172
Exhibits: None

This volume, written by a preeminent culturalist, is highly recommended as a first book to read about Japanese business culture. Hall begins by defining a few necessary culture concepts concerning space, time, and information flow in communication, then provides an introduction to corporate Japan and its foundation of human relationships. Making allowances for swift cultural change in Japan, this clear and concise analysis of Japanese business values and behavior remains valid today. The final section provides specific cross-cultural advice on marketing in Japan, managing there, and negotiating.

Title: *Honoring the Customer: Marketing and Selling to the Japanese*
Date: 1991
Format: Hardcover
Author: Robert M. March
Publisher: John Wiley & Sons
605 Third Ave.
New York, NY 10158-0012
Tel: (212)850-6000
Fax: (212)850-6088
Pages: 203
Exhibits: None

This is perhaps the only trade book that deals specifically with how to sell and market in Japan. The author, a professor of management in Japan, covers the behavior of Japanese buyers, selling successfully in Japan, understanding customers, and dealing with Japanese buyers outside Japan. The book is too slim to cover its important topics with sufficient depth, but its plentiful case studies of firms that have dealt with the problems of selling in Japan provide important warnings for anyone setting out to peddle products there.

Title: *Japanese Business: Cultural Perspectives*
Date: 1993
Format: Hardcover
Editor: Subhash Durlabhji and Norton E. Marks
Publisher: State University of New York Press

State University Plaza
Albany, NY 12246
Tel: (518)472-5000
Fax: (518)472-5038

Pages: 388

Exhibits: Diagrams

This collection of articles offers culture-based analyses of Japanese business practice. Sections focus on the cultural backdrop of Japanese business, communication and relationships, management and marketing, and manufacturing. This comprehensive and recommended reader was written for practitioners and researchers alike. It includes a glossary.

Title: *The Japanese Economy and the American Businessman*

Date: 1989

Format: Hardcover

Author: Daniel Metraux

Publisher: Edwin Mellen Press
Box 450
Lewiston, NY 14092
Tel: (716)754-2266
Fax: (716)754-4335

Pages: 171

Exhibits: None

This book chronicles the wave of Japanese investment that hit foreign shores throughout the 1980s, only to subside and virtually disappear in the 1990s. There were successes and failures in this surge of direct Japanese investment in Europe and the United States, and this book offers a guided tour of the "economic and social laboratory in which it has been conducted," with an eye for highlighting different strategies pursued by the investors and the varying receptions they received. This is a literate and engaging study in narrative form.

Title: *The Japanese Negotiator: Subtlety and Strategy Beyond Western Logic*

Date: 1988

Format: Hardcover

Author: Robert M. March

Publisher: Kodansha International
17-14, Otowa
Bunkyo-ku
Tokyo 112, Japan
Tel: (81)(3)944-6492
Fax: (81)(3)944-6323

Pages: 197

Exhibits: Charts and tables

An expertly presented analysis of Japanese negotiating behavior and strategy, this recommended volume is of great help to Western negotiators.

Title: *Japan Twenty-First*

Date: Monthly

Format: Periodical

Editor: Shinji Umemura

Publisher: Nihon Kogyo Shimbun
Sankei Building
7-2, Ohtemachi 1-chome
Chiyoda-ku 100
Tokyo Japan
Tel: (81)(3)3231-7111

Pages: Varies

Exhibits: Graphs

Price: $108/year

Formerly titled Business Japan, this 75-page magazine has become a first-class source of information about new technologies and products created in Japan. It also provides an in-depth examination of Japanese industries. Extraordinarily detailed articles on the technological characteristics of new products are followed by corporate surveys, CEO profiles, and economic surveys. For the serious investor, marketer, and analyst, this monthly delivers maximum value for a moderate price.

Title: *The Rising Sun on Main Street: Working with the Japanese*
Date: 1992
Format: Hardcover
Author: Alison R. Lanier
Publisher: International Information Associates, Inc.
P.O. Box 773
Morrisville, PA 19067
Tel: (415)493-9214
Fax: (415)493-9421
Pages: 265
Exhibits: None

Meant for those working or negotiating with the Japanese, this book provides an overview of Japanese attitudes, communication, behavior, business protocol, and negotiation style. The approach is introductory, and most of the material appears in better form elsewhere.

Title: *Setting Up and Operating a Business in Japan: A Handbook for the Foreign Businessman*
Date: 1988
Format: Hardcover
Author: Helene Thian
Publisher: Charles E. Tuttle Co., Inc.
2-6, Suido 1-chome
Bunkyo-ku
Tokyo 112, Japan
Tel: (81)(3)3811-7741
Fax: (81)(3)5689-4926
Pages: 191
Exhibits: Graphs and tables

Practical and easy to use, this guidebook for businesspeople instructs on setting up a company in Japan, financing, taxation, visas, employees, costs, and advertising. It includes a list of helpful business organizations in Japan that can assist foreigners. It is a sensible overview with an emphasis on logistics.

Title: *Setting Up Enterprises in Japan*
Date: 1992
Format: Paperback
Author: TMI Associates, Shimazaki International Law Office, and Chuo Coopers and Lybrand International Tax Office
Publisher: JETRO Publications
2-5, Toranomon 2-chome
Minato-ku
Tokyo 105, Japan
Tel: (81)(3)3582-3518
Fax: (81)(3)3587-2485
Pages: 627
Exhibits: Graphs

For investors, traders, and alliance partners who are ready to take the plunge into Japan, this comprehensive, bilingual, and well-illustrated handbook covers the legal and logistical aspects of setting up business there. It covers all of the steps and documentation necessary to incorporate a company, import technology, export to Japan, transfer capital, and compute taxes. Flowcharts, sample documents, and step-by-step presentation make this indispensable guide the best of its kind. It is highly recommended to corporate planners, negotiators, and contract lawyers working with Japan.

Title: *Smart Bargaining: Doing Business with the Japanese*
Date: 1984
Format: Hardcover
Author: John L. Graham and Yoshihiro Sano
Publisher: Harper & Row, Ballinger Division
10E 53rd St.
New York, NY 10022
Tel: (212)207-7000
Fax: (212)207-7203
Pages: 163
Exhibits: Diagrams and tables
Price: $19.95

Those who plan to negotiate with the Japanese should study this concise and well-organized guide. The advice it contains is based on solid research and a coauthorship that provides authority and credibility rarely seen in the soft science of cross-Pacific negotiating theory. Topics include American versus Japanese negotiation styles, team selection, what happens during a negotiation, and cultural and personality issues. The book features four useful U.S. corporate case studies.

Title: *The Technopolis Strategy*
Date: 1986
Format: Hardcover
Author: Sheridan Tatsuno
Publisher: Prentice-Hall
1230 Avenue of the Americas
New York, NY 10020
Tel: (212)373-8000
Fax: (212)698-7007
Pages: 298
Exhibits: Maps and tables

This compendium of articles comprises a comprehensive study of business-government relations in Japan and the United States, conducted at Harvard Business School. For serious researchers and public policy makers, the book provides in-depth research and case work on topics related to global competition, industrial policy, and U.S.-Japan relations. Important conclusions are offered that help explain Japan's national competitiveness vis-à-vis America.

Title: *283 Useful Ideas from Japan for Entrepreneurs and Everyone Else*
Date: 1988
Format: Hardcover
Author: Leonard Koren
Publisher: Chronicle Books
275 Fifth St.
San Francisco, CA 94103
Tel: (415)777-7240
Fax: (415)777-8887
Pages: 174
Exhibits: Diagrams and pictures

From temporary sidewalks to urine solidifiers, this illustrated book of ideas that the Japanese have brought to the world is entertaining and intriguing. It is recommended to anyone who is stressed out over Japanese "imitation" of others' inventions.

Title: *Venture Japan*
Date: Quarterly
Format: Periodical
Editor: James Borton
Publisher: Investment Dealers' Digest
18th Floor, 2 World Trade Center
New York, NY 10048
Tel: (212)227-1200
Fax: (212)912-9039
Pages: Varies
Exhibits: Graphs and tables
Price: $72/year

This attractive 100- to 120-page compilation of articles examines the practical aspects of entering the Japanese market and identifies fundamental marketing strategies. Informative articles, written in a style that the practitioner will appreciate, cover such subjects as franchising in Japan, the state of Japanese banks, intellectual property protection, U.S.-Japan strategic alliances, selling services in Japan, and so on. Most writers are corporate professionals who offer insight and real-world experience.

HISTORY AND SOCIETY

Title: *Behind the Mask: On Sexual Demons, Sacred Mothers, Transvestites, Gangsters, Drifters and Other Japanese Cultural Heroes*
Date: 1984
Format: Hardcover
Author: Ian Buruma
Publisher: Penguin Books
375 Hudson St.
New York, NY 10014-3658
Tel: (212)366-2000
Fax: (212)366-2666
Pages: 242
Exhibits: Photographs

A penetrating, if not disturbing, exploration of Japanese society, this book obliterates many Western stereotypes and myths about Japan. It is highly recommended as an intellectual guide to Japan's urban underworld. The author provides an incisive social commentary, especially regarding the psychological makeup of Japanese men.

Title: *The Book of Tea*
Date: 1964
Format: Paperback
Author: Kakuzo Okakura
Publisher: Dover
31 E. Second St.
Mineola, NY 11501
Tel: (516)294-7000
Fax: (516)742-6953
Pages: 76
Exhibits: None

A timeless classic, this slim and artfully written volume is a highly acclaimed description of the pseudoreligious tea ceremony in Japan.

Title: *Bushido: Way of the Samurai*
Date: 1975
Format: Paperback
Author: Tanaka Minoru
Editor: Justin F. Stone
Publisher: Sun Publishing
P.O. Box 5588
Santa Fe, NM 87502-5588
Tel: (505)471-5177
Fax: (505)471-6151

Pages: 85
Exhibits: None

A window on the Japanese psyche, this is a readable translation of the classic code of the Samurai.

Title: *The Cambridge Encyclopedia of Japan*
Date: 1993
Format: Hardcover
Editor: Richard Bowring and Peter Kornicki
Publisher: Cambridge University Press
The Pitt Building
Trumpington St.
Cambridge CB2 1RP, United Kingdom
Pages: 400
Exhibits: Maps, photographs, and tables

This beautifully published "encyclopedia" of Japan is set up more in the style of a National Geographic tabletop reader than an alphabetical encyclopedia. The well-written and well-illustrated sections include geography, language and literature, arts and crafts, politics, history, thought and religion, society, and economy. This book is recommended as a reader and as a business gift.

Title: *The Chrysanthemum and the Sword: Patterns of Japanese Culture*
Date: 1946
Format: Hardcover and paperback
Author: Ruth Benedict
Publisher: New American Library
1633 Broadway
New York, NY 10019
Tel: (212)397-8000
Pages: 324
Exhibits: None

Written by one of America's great anthropologists, this classic and readable ethnography of Japanese culture is required reading for businesspeople attempting to understand the roots of Japanese cultural values and social interaction.

Title: *Concise Dictionary of Modern Japanese History*
Date: 1984
Format: Hardcover
Author: Janet E. Hunter
Publisher: University of California Press
2120 Berkeley Way
Berkeley, CA 94720
Tel: (642)642-4247
Fax: (642)643-7127
Pages: 347
Exhibits: None

This handy dictionary provides clear definitions of events, individuals, and organizations that have played a significant role in the modern history of Japan. For the nonspecialist, this is an easy-to-use and compact source of basic information about such things as *Kaizo* (reconstruction), the 1927 financial crisis, Japan's women's movement, and so on.

Title: *Crested Kimono: Power and Love in the Japanese Business Family*
Date: 1990
Format: Hardcover

Author: Matthews Masayuki Hamabata
Publisher: Cornell University Press
P.O. Box 250
124 Roberts Place
Ithaca, NY 14851
Tel: (607)257-7000
Fax: (607)257-3552
Exhibits: None

A revealing inside account of a third-generation Japanese-American's reentry into Japanese business and life-style, this well-written book offers the business-person crucial insights into Japanese character, etiquette, and interaction with foreigners.

Title: *Cultural Atlas of Japan*
Date: 1988
Format: Hardcover
Author: Martin Colcutt, Marius Jansen, and Isao Kumakura
Publisher: Facts on File Publications
460 Park Ave. South
New York, NY 10016
Tel: (212)683-2244
Fax: (212)213-4578
Pages: 240
Exhibits: Maps, photographs, and tables

Here is a beautifully published tabletop atlas rich in illustration and content. It is divided into three parts. The first deals with Japan's ancient beginnings, including maps of its island geography and an overview of what is known about the archaeological origins of Japanese culture and society. The second part covers ancient times to the Edo Period of the 1600s. The third describes the Meiji Restoration, Imperial Japan, and the country's reform and reconstruction after World War II. This book, which includes a bibliography, a chronology of events, a gazetteer, and numerous sidebars on Japan's rich cultural heritage, is both a great reader and a well-chosen business gift.

Title: *The Dance of Life: The Other Dimension of Time*
Date: 1983
Format: Paperback
Author: Edward T. Hall
Publisher: Doubleday
666 Fifth Ave.
New York, NY 10103
Tel: (212)765-6500
Fax: (212)492-9700
Pages: 250
Exhibits: Diagrams

Edward T. Hall, the noted American ethnologist and culture expert, writes in this volume about "time as culture, how time is consciously as well as unconsciously formulated, used, and patterned in different cultures." For anyone who has become frustrated and impatient with the unhurried pace of business practice in Asia, this book is just what the doctor ordered. The coverage is general, though many specific examples refer to the Japanese. (Unfortunately, most busy executives who could benefit from this insightful and enjoyable book won't be able to find the time to read it.)

Title: *The East*
Date: Bimonthly
Format: Periodical
Editor: Morita Tohru
Publisher: The East Publications

19-7-101, Minami-Azabu 3
Minato-ku
Tokyo 106, Japan
Tel: (81)(3)3446-7721

Pages: Varies

Exhibits: Photographs

Price: $35/year

Filled with colorful photographs and excellent writing, this 60-page magazine provides a window on Japanese traditional culture. Selected articles focus on Japanese temple architecture, ancient stories, the symbol of the lotus in Buddhism, art, food, and other things Japanese. This is a recommended read for the cross-culturalist and certainly for the empathetic expatriate. It includes informative advertisements for culture-related books translated from the Japanese.

Title: *The Enigma of Japanese Power: People and Politics in a Stateless Nation*

Date: 1988

Format: Hardcover

Author: Karel Van Wolferen

Publisher: Alfred A. Knopf
201 E. 50th St.
New York, NY 10022
Tel: (212)751-6200
Fax: (212)572-2593

Pages: 496

Exhibits: None

Here is the most current, readable, and illuminating appraisal of modern Japanese politics and society. It is required reading for Japanophiles and anyone contemplating doing business in Japan. The author explores every aspect of Japan's "stateless" political/industrial system, including the bureaucrats, salarymen, managers, and religious leaders. If you were to take one book about Japan to a desert island, this should be the one.

Title: *"Even Monkeys Fall from Trees" and Other Japanese Proverbs*

Date: 1987

Format: Paperback

Author: David Galef

Publisher: Charles E. Tuttle Co.
2-6, Suido 1-chome
Bunkyo-ku
Tokyo 112, Japan
Tel: (81)(3)3811-7746
Fax: (81)(3)5689-4926

Pages: 226

Exhibits: Drawings and Japanese characters

"One cannot always find a fish under a willow." "The protruding nail will be hammered." "Obey the customs of the village you enter." All of these Japanese proverbs are listed in this handy reference, which might be used by businesspeople, writers, or anyone else interested in Japanese values and behavior. It includes a list of English equivalents ("When in Rome, do as the Romans do") but no in-depth cultural analysis.

Title: *The Floating World in Japanese Fiction*

Date: 1959

Format: Hardcover

Author: Howard Hibbett

Publisher: Charles E. Tuttle Co.
2-6, Suido 1-chome
Bunkyo-ku
Tokyo 112, Japan
Tel: (81)(3)3811-7741
Fax: (81)(3)5689-4926

Pages: 232
Exhibits: Drawings

For those interested in the manners, customs, and pastimes of city life in Tokugawa Japan, this collection of "gay stories and novels" from the literary genre called *ukiyo-zoshi*, or "tales of the floating world," will surprise and delight. This was an age that was obsessed with pleasure. To quote from the book, "It was a time of innovations in popular literature, as well as in music, the kabuki theatre, and the graphic arts." The tales in this volume bring to life that earlier time. The author provides an erudite social background of the period, as well.

Title: *A Half Step Behind: Japanese Women Today*
Date: 1991
Format: Paperback
Author: Jane Condon
Publisher: Charles E. Tuttle Co.
2-6, Suido 1-chome
Bunkyo-ku
Tokyo 112, Japan
Tel: (81)(3)3811-7741
Fax: (81)(3)5689-4926
Pages: 351
Exhibits: None

Based on extensive interviews with Japanese housewives, farmers, politicians, teachers, career women, and office workers, the author of this enduring work looks at Japanese women in the family, in the educational system, at work, and in their current role in Japanese society. Chapters cover such topics as marriage, divorce, schools and teachers, and job roles, such as career woman, part-timer, and office worker. Artfully written, insightful, and buttressed by verbatim interviews, this book should not be missed by expatriates, managers, or anyone who deals with Japanese women professionally or socially.

Title: *How to Do Business with the Japanese*
Date: 1986
Format: Hardcover
Author: Herbert F. Jung
Publisher: Japan Times, Inc.
5-4, Shibaura 4-chome
Minato-ku
Tokyo 108, Japan
Tel: (81)(3)3453-5311
Fax: (81)(3)3453-8023
Pages: 143
Exhibits: None

Although somewhat dated now, this slim and readable guide covers many timeless topics of importance to business negotiations in Japan. These include how and why to negotiate indirectly, hearing the unspoken, obligation building, and not taking "yes" for an answer.

Title: *Illustrated Eating in Japan*
Date: 1990
Format: Paperback
Publisher: Japan Travel Bureau, Inc.
Shibuya Nomura Building
1-10-8, Dogenzaka
Shibuya-ku
Tokyo 150, Japan
Tel: (81)(3)257-8311
Fax: (81)(3)257-8325
Pages: 191
Exhibits: Drawings
Price: ¥ 910–1,010

This detailed and useful guide is part of a 13-volume series published in Japan. Plentiful cartoon drawings and concise text make this the best source of information about eating in Japan for Japanese gourmets, expatriates, or visitors. It provides information on types of eating establishments, common dishes, traditional cuisine, drinks, recipes, and table manners. This is a complete, fun-to-use guide.

Title: *Illustrated "Salaryman" in Japan*
Date: 1990
Format: Paperback
Publisher: Japan Travel Bureau, Inc.
Shibuya Nomura Building
1-10-8, Doyenzaka
Shibuya-ku
Tokyo 150, Japan
Tel: (81)(3)257-8311
Fax: (81)(3)257-8325
Pages: 191
Exhibits: Drawings
Price: ¥ 910–1,010

Ever wondered how a Japanese office is laid out or how Japanese employees are encouraged to be so loyal to their companies? Part of a 13-volume set published in Japan, this cartoon-illustrated handbook answers these questions and more. Sections cover the working day; the salaryman's working life, life-style, and manners; and Japanese business terms, gestures, and proverbs. This book includes eye-opening explanations of militarylike morning gatherings, radio calisthenics conducted at work, the wardrobe of the office lady, and "new employee education." Before you run off to work in Japan, read this book.

Title: *Intercultural Encounters with Japan: Communication, Contact, and Conflict*
Date: 1974
Format: Paperback
Editor: John C. Condon and Mitsuko Saito
Publisher: Simul Press
Kowa Building 9
1-8-10, Akasaka Minato-ku
Tokyo 107, Japan
Pages: 259
Exhibits: Graphs and tables

This classic compendium of research on Japanese values and business psychology is essential reading for businesspeople engaging with the Japanese as partners, negotiators, or just as friends. Recent works on this subject typically echo what this pioneering book first made known 20 years ago. A good library might be your best bet in locating a copy.

Title: *Japan and Western Civilization*
Date: 1983
Format: Hardcover
Author: Kuwabara Takeo
Publisher: Columbia University Press
562 W. 113th St.
New York, NY 10025
Tel: (212)316-7100
Fax: (212)316-7169
Pages: 205
Exhibits: Diagrams

For the Japan culture afficionado, this is a fascinating collection of essays exploring the clash of values between Japan and the West. The author is an eminent

Japanese sinologist and the director of the Institute for Humanistic Studies at Kyoto University. He tackles such high-minded issues as the qualities of art, beauty, and classic literature in Japan and compares Japan's cultural heritage with Europe's. This work is eclectic, profound, and a bit avant-garde in presentation.

Title: *Japan: The Hungry Guest*
Date: 1985
Format: Hardcover
Author: Jack Seward and Howard Van Zandt
Publisher: Lotus Press
Chofu P.O. Box 15
Chofu-shi
Tokyo 182-91, Japan
Pages: 294
Exhibits: None

An early important and readable examination of cultural factors that result in ethical differences between Japanese and Americans. Divergent patterns of behavior are discussed in the context of work, trade, politics, negotiations, advertising, contracts, bribery, scandal, and sex-oriented business entertainment. Still topical today, this book is recommended to anyone dealing with the Japanese.

Title: *The Japanese*
Date: 1977
Format: Hardcover
Author: Edwin O. Reischauer
Publisher: Belknap Press/Harvard University Press
79 Garden St.
Cambridge, MA 02138-1499
Tel: (617)495-2600
Fax: (617)495-8924
Pages: 443
Exhibits: Photographs

Now a bit dated but still an entertaining and masterful read, this classic portrait of the Japanese is "must" reading for Japan-bound visitors and businesspeople alike. It is well illustrated and includes chapters on Japanese business organization and international trade as well as long sections on Japan's history and society.

Title: *The Japanese*
Date: 1987
Format: Hardcover
Author: Peter Tasker
Publisher: E.P. Dutton/NAL Penguin, Inc.
2 Park Ave.
New York, NY 10016
Tel: (212)366-2000
Fax: (212)366-2666
Pages: 312
Exhibits: Photographs

For a current portrait of the Japanese, this readable and well-illustrated volume does the trick. It includes chapters on the socialization process in Japan, manufacturing prowess, the media, and politics. The writing is nontheoretical and journalistic, though the author is not afraid of making long-term predictions based on his remarkable body of research.

Title: *Japanese Society*
Date: 1970
Format: Hardcover
Author: Chie Nakane
Publisher: University of California Press

2120 Berkeley Way
Berkeley, CA 94720
Tel: (510)642-4247
Fax: (510)643-7127

Pages: 157

Exhibits: None

This is an excellent academic monograph that explores Japanese character and social mores. The readable style and profound insights in this classic make it a main choice for anyone who wants to understand the Japanese from the inside out. The book's four sections cover the formation of group relations, ranking and status within the group, the structure of Japanese society, and the social values of the Japanese person.

Title: *The Japan Foundation Newsletter*

Date: Monthly

Format: Periodical

Publisher: The Japan Foundation
Park Building
3-6, Kioi-cho
Chiyoda-ku
Tokyo 102, Japan
Tel: (81)(3)2634-4919

Pages: Varies

Exhibits: None

Price: Free

This 25-page newsletter carries articles and news briefs related to Japanese studies and international cultural exchange. For Japanophiles, some of the articles provide enlightening reading. The newsletter includes "cultural highlights" from recent Japanese publications, conference reports, and book reviews.

Title: *Kodansha Encyclopedia of Japan*

Date: 1983

Format: Hardcover

Publisher: Kodansha, Ltd.
12-21, Otawa 2-chome
Bunkyo-ku
Tokyo 112, Japan
Tel: (81)(3)944-6492
Fax: (81)(3)944-6323

Pages: (9 vols.)

Exhibits: Drawings, maps, photographs, and tables

Claiming to be "the first comprehensive encyclopedia seeking to present the totality of a major world culture in a foreign language" (English), this multivolume set represents the contributions of some 680 Japanese and 524 non-Japanese scholars. It includes 9,417 entries in 37 categories of information, ranging from history and economy to folklore and flora and fauna. Each article runs 50 to 2,500 words. For Japanophiles, general researchers on Japan, or corporate gift givers, this is an elegant and authoritative set.

Title: *Meeting with Japan*

Date: 1960

Format: Hardcover

Author: Fosco Maraini

Publisher: Viking Penguin Press
375 Hudson St.
New York, NY 10014
Tel: (212)366-2000
Fax: (212)366-2666

Pages: 467

Exhibits: Photographs, maps, tables

Perhaps the most engrossing book about Japanese history and society from an American publisher, this now somewhat dated work is unmatched in readability, erudition, and illustration. It is out of print but can be found at many used-book stores.

Title: *Nichibunken Newsletter*
Date: Monthly
Format: Periodical
Publisher: The International Research Center for Japanese Studies (Nichibunken)
3-2, Oeyama-cho
Goryo, Nisikyo-ku
Kyoto 610-11, Japan
Tel: (81)(75)335-2222
Fax: (81)(75)335-2091
Pages: Varies
Exhibits: None
Price: Contact for subscription prices

The purpose of this 25- to 30-page newsletter (and the research center that publishes it) is to develop and integrate various areas of Japanese studies. The essays and articles it includes focus on cultural issues, some of which may interest businesspeople—for example, the lifestyle of Japanese working overseas and Japan's internationalization. This newsletter also carries book reviews.

Title: *Pictures from the Water Trade: Adventures of a Westerner in Japan*
Date: 1985
Format: Paperback
Author: John David Morley
Publisher: Harper & Row
Atlantic Monthly Press
351 W. 19th St.
New York, NY 10011
Tel: (212)645-4462
Fax: (212)727-0180
Pages: 259
Exhibits: None
Price: $6.95

Mizu-shobai, or water trade, is the profane term for Japan's illicit nighttime trade, including geisha bars, cabarets, and sex clubs. This is a lively and lyrically written account of a young Western man's plunge into this "underworld of establishments dedicated to the uninhibited pursuit of pleasure." The story is told in the third person as the protagonist confronts the many-layered impediments that divide East and West. This book remains one of the finest, if not most voyeuristic, armchair journeys through a Japan few outsiders ever see.

Title: *The Toyota Foundation Occasional Report*
Date: Irregular
Format: Periodical
Editor: Shukuko Matsumoto
Publisher: The Toyota Foundation
37th Floor, Shinjuku Mitsui Building
2-1-0, Nishi-Shinjuku
Shinjuku-ku
Tokyo 163, Japan
Tel: (81)(3)344-1701
Fax: (81)(3)342-6911
Pages: Varies
Exhibits: Photographs
Price: Contact for subscription prices

Published as a news update about the activities of the nonprofit, grant-making Toyota Foundation, this 12-page newsletter describes the projects that the organization has funded, most of which involve the publishing of Asian research in Japanese. The foundation also conducts seminars and conferences, and this newsletter informs readers about them.

Title: *The Yoke*
Date: Bimonthly
Format: Periodical
Editor: Isao Tanooka
Publisher: Yokohama Association for International Communications and Exchanges
Sangyo Boeki Center Building
2, Yamashita-cho
Naka-ku
Yokohama 231, Japan
Tel: (81)(45)671-7128
Fax: (81)(45)671-7187
Pages: Varies
Exhibits: Graphs and photographs
Price: Free

Published bimonthly by a civic association in Yokohama, this 12-page magazine provides news and opinion from Japan's second-largest city and is useful to anyone doing business there. Selected articles focus on the city's cultural traditions, educational achievements, and the local economy. It is certainly useful reading for expatriates living in Yokohama.

INDUSTRY

Title: *Biotechnology Guide: Japan Company Directory and Comprehensive Analysis*
Date: Annual
Format: Hardcover
Author: Nikkei Biotechnology
Publisher: Stockton Press
15 E. 26th St.
New York, NY 10010
Tel: (212)673-4300
Fax: (212)673-9842
Pages: 591
Exhibits: None

This is a unique directory of Japanese companies involved in the biotechnology industry. It includes company profiles that note the major patents and R&D projects of each firm.

Title: *Built by Japan: Competitive Strategies of the Japanese Construction Industry*
Date: 1988
Format: Hardcover
Author: Fumio Hasegawa and the Shimizu Group FS
Publisher: John Wiley & Sons
605 Third Ave.
New York, NY 10158
Tel: (212)850-6000
Fax: (212)850-6088
Pages: 234
Exhibits: Tables

This book, a compilation of chapters by different authors, offers a one-of-a-kind examination of the Japanese construction industry and describes how it differs from its U.S. counterpart. The book provides in-depth analysis of how Japanese construction firms compete in Japan and abroad. After reading it, the U.S. construction executive might better formulate strategies for competing against Japanese competitors.

Title: *Canon Chronicle*
Date: Bimonthly
Format: Periodical
Editor: Sakio Hirose
Publisher: Corporate Communications Headquarters
Canon Inc.
2-7-1, Nishi-Shinjuku
Shinjuku-ku
Tokyo 163-07, Japan
Tel: (81)(3)3348-2121
Fax: (81)(3)3349-1686
Pages: Varies
Exhibits: Maps, photographs, and tables
Price: Contact for subscription prices

Published by Canon, this 20-page magazine provides updates about corporate activities at Canon and about the company's new products. For those who need to stay abreast of this company, this periodical includes reviews of technological breakthroughs and processes, as well.

Title: *Industrial Groupings in Japan*
Date: Annual
Format: Hardcover
Publisher: Dodwell Marketing Consultants
C.P.O. Box 297
Tokyo 100-91, Japan
Tel: (81)(3)211-4451
Pages: 700
Exhibits: Graphs and tables

This unique directory describes Japan's industrial groupings. It lists the companies that belong to each industrial group, their degree of affiliation, each company's major shareholders, and its annual sales, profits, and other profile information. The volume includes "The Six Major Industrial Groups," "Major Groups and Group Companies," "Leading Multinationals in Japan," and "Group Strength by Industry." This book is highly recommended for investors and alliance builders who need to know how their Japanese partners fit into the larger structure of Japanese industry.

Title: *Information and Communications in Japan*
Date: 1991
Format: Hardcover
Publisher: InfoCom Research
1-1-8, Motoakasaka
Minato-ku
Tokyo 107, Japan
Pages: 243
Exhibits: Tables

This slim but unique directory lists Japanese telecommunications services, including carriers, rates, international communication networks (e.g., INTELSAT), and information services and provides an overview of the new media. For those close to the industry in Japan, this is an essential reference.

Title: *The Invisible Link: Japan's Sogo Sosha and the Organization of the Trade*
Date: 1986

Format: Hardcover
Author: M.Y. Yoshino and Thomas B. Lifson
Publisher: MIT Press
Massachusetts Institute of Technology
55 Hayward St.
Cambridge, MA 02142
Tel: (617)253-5646
Fax: (617)258-6779
Pages: 291
Exhibits: Drawings, graphs, and tables

The large Japanese trading corporation, or sogo sosha, is a primary cog in the international Japanese competitive machine, and it has no counterpart in the United States or Europe. Sogo sosha firms handle roughly one-half of all Japanese imports and exports. This attractive and high-caliber investigation provides detailed coverage of the evolution of these firms, their unique organization, human resource systems, administration, and competitive dynamics. The high level of theoretical analysis in this book should not deter Japan marketers from consulting it in their attempt to understand their large Japanese corporate customers.

Title: *Japan Aviation Directory*
Date: Annual
Format: Hardcover
Publisher: Mitsubishi Heavy Industries, Ltd.
5-1, Marunouchi 2-chome
Chiyoda-ku
Tokyo 100, Japan
Pages: 200
Exhibits: None

This directory is a one-stop reference source for information about Japan's aerospace and aviation markets. The first part provides an overview of the industries, a look at current trends, the defense industry, space activities, air transport, and the activities of selected companies. The second part lists government-related organizations and private firms. Finally, the volume contains a useful who's who for the industry. The listings are categorized by area of activity, including space business, general aviation, and trading houses. Company profiles give contact information, key personnel, and fleet composition.

Title: *Japan Electronics Almanac*
Date: Annual
Format: Paperback
Publisher: Dempa Publications, Inc.
11-15, Higashi Gotanda 1-chome
Shinagawa-ku
Tokyo 141, Japan
Tel: (81)(3)445-6111
Fax: (81)(3)444-7515
Pages: 400
Exhibits: Graphs, photographs, and tables
Price: $55/year

Well worth the price, this information-packed almanac is highly recommended to those who are working in the electronics industry or are tracking the industry in Japan. Overview chapters cover trends in Japan's electronics sector and the outlook for the near term, international activities of the country's electronics firms, and in-depth examination of various subsectors of the electronics industry. A final section provides two-page company profiles of Japan's key electronics firms. This is an extremely well-researched and well-illustrated sourcebook.

Title: *The Japanese Offshore Industry*
Date: 1988
Format: Hardcover
Author: Technical Communications
Publisher: Elsevier Science Publishers, Ltd.
30-32 Eastbury Rd.
London Industrial Park
Beckton
London E6 4LP, United Kingdom
Tel: (44)(81)594-7272
Fax: (44)(81)594-4570
Pages: 146
Exhibits: Graphs, photographs, and tables

For executives and corporate people engaged in offshore oil drilling technology who want to keep abreast of their industry in Japan and for those who wish to export related products and services to Japan, this large-format report will be of interest. The report (current as of 1988) presents, in its words, "an overview of what Japanese industry is doing in offshore technology development, and Japan as a potential market for exporters." It includes a detailed assessment of R&D activities in the offshore oil sector and an appraisal of specific export opportunities.

Title: *Japan's Economic Journal: Diamond Industria*
Date: Monthly
Format: Periodical
Editor: Natsuki Mori
Publisher: Diamond Lead Co., Ltd.
4-2, Kasumigaseki 1-chome
Chiyoda-ku
Tokyo 100, Japan
Pages: Varies
Exhibits: Photographs
Price: $90/year

For executives tracking developments in Japanese industry, this 45- to 50-page magazine offers articles and news briefs about Japan's economy and about selected corporations in key industries. Occasionally, this periodical lists Japan's top firms, and a section for industry news tracks product developments in Japan.

Title: *Japan's Small Businesses Today*
Date: 1988
Format: Hardcover
Publisher: Keiei Joho Shuppan
Tokyo Japan
Tel: (81)(3)291-5791
Fax: (81)(3)291-5793
Pages: 347
Exhibits: Graphs, photographs, and tables

With so much attention given to Japan's corporate conglomerates, it's surprising to learn that Japanese enterprises employing fewer than 300 workers account for 95 percent of the total number of enterprises in Japan and employ 81 percent of its work force. This hefty volume provides brief profiles of Japanese industries in which small and medium-size companies are prevalent, such as construction, light manufacturing, retailing, wholesale, and food service. This is a useful overview of 100 little-discussed segments of the Japanese industrial economy.

Title: *Keidanren Review*
Date: Bimonthly
Format: Periodical
Publisher: Public Affairs Department
Keidanren (Japan Federation of Economic Organizations)
9-4, Otemachi 1-chome
Chiyoda-ku
Tokyo 100, Japan
Tel: (81)(3)3279-1411
Fax: (81)(3)5255-6255
Pages: Varies
Exhibits: None
Price: Contact for subscription prices

Published by Keidanren, a nonprofit organization representing 125 associations and 950 corporations, this four-page newsletter is actually a position paper in which the powerful organization makes policy recommendations to the government. It is of interest to analysts of government-business relations in Japan.

Title: *The Specifications and Applications of Industrial Robots in Japan*
Date: Annual
Format: Hardcover
Publisher: Japan Industrial Robot Association
3-5-8, Shibakoen
Minato-ku
Tokyo 105, Japan
Tel: (81)(3)434-2910
Pages: 850
Exhibits: Diagrams, graphs, photographs, and tables

Meant for production managers and anyone in the robotics industry, this directory provides an illustrated description of the Japanese production robots that are currently available. Each entry supplies robot specifications, control device specifications, and salient characteristics of the robot. The indexes provide a cross-listing by company and task.

Title: *Sumitomo Quarterly*
Date: Quarterly
Format: Periodical
Publisher: Sumitomo Group Public Affairs Committee
C.P.O. Box 229
Tokyo 100-91, Japan
Pages: Varies
Exhibits: Photographs
Price: Contact for subscription prices

Published by the Sumitomo public affairs office, this 25- to 30-page magazine includes articles about Sumitomo Group companies as well as general articles on Japanese society, management, economic trends, and traditional culture. For businesspeople who deal with a Sumitomo-affiliated company, this might be a useful conversation builder.

INFORMATION SOURCES

Title: *Current Japanese Serials in East Asian Libraries of North America*
Date: 1992

Format: Paperback
Author: Yasuko Makino and Mihoko Miki
Publisher: University of Michigan Association for Asian Studies
108 Lane Hall
Ann Arbor, MI 48109-1290
Tel: (313)988-7265
Fax: (313)936-2948
Pages: 485
Exhibits: None

This bibliography lists Japanese-language periodicals held at East Asian university libraries in North America, including journals and newspapers. The list is presented alphabetically by title under the heading of each library. Unfortunately, no subject index is provided, making it difficult for businesspeople to use.

Title: *Database in Japan*
Date: Annual
Format: Paperback
Publisher: Database Promotion Center, Japan
7th Floor, World Trade Center Building
2-4-1, Hammamatsu-cho
Minato-ku
Tokyo 105, Japan
Tel: (81)(3)3459-8581
Fax: (81)(3)3432-7558
Pages: Varies
Exhibits: Graphs and tables

This fascinating examination of the distribution, design, and utilization of information databases in Japan is useful both to those selling and creating databases for the Japanese market and to those interested in using information more efficiently in their companies. The chapters cover such topics as the state of database usage, in-house databases, world development of databases, regional analysis of Japanese databases, and government policy related to Japanese databases. For those connected to the information industry, this is a recommended source; it is both well illustrated and readable.

Title: *Directory of Japanese Databases*
Date: 1989
Format: Hardcover
Publisher: Database Promotion Center
7th Floor, World Trade Center Building
2-4-1, Hammamatsu-cho
Minato-ku
Tokyo 105, Japan
Tel: (81)(3)459-8581
Fax: (81)(3)432-7558
Pages: 233
Exhibits: None

Now slightly dated, this directory lists databases available in Japan, many of which are also available overseas. Keep in mind, however, that this directory lists 1,964 databases that are *available* in Japan, but only 528 of them were created in Japan, and only 100 of these are available to users abroad. This book and other listings of online databases are a prudent first stop for those seeking database information.

Title: *Directory of Japanese Technical Resources in the United States*
Date: 1992
Format: Paperback

Author: Office of International Affairs, National Technical Information Service, U.S. Department of Commerce

Publisher: U.S. Department of Commerce
5285 Port Royal Rd.
Springfield, VA 22161
Tel: (703)487-4636
Fax: (703)487-4009

Pages: 111

Exhibits: None

This directory has three features: (1) a directory of information services with descriptions of commercial services, nonprofit organizations, trade associations, and government organizations that collect, abstract, translate, and distribute Japanese technical information; (2) citations of technical documents translated by the U.S. government and available to the public; and (3) descriptions of university-based technical programs in Japan. Each information-service entry provides contact information, expertise areas, and descriptions of services.

Title: *Directory of Japan Specialists and Japanese Studies Institutions in the United States and Canada*

Date: 1989

Format: Hardcover

Publisher: The Japan Foundation
Park Building
3-6, Kioi-cho
Chiyoda-ku
Tokyo 102, Japan

Pages: 517

Exhibits: None

Meant for anyone seeking advice and consultation from a Japan specialist, this two-volume directory lists experts as well as Japanese studies institutions in the United States and Canada. Personal entries note professional titles, research interests, professional experience, and major publications. The list focuses on academics and does not include most professional consultants working in the private sector.

Title: *How to Find Information about Japanese Companies and Industries*

Date: 1984

Format: Paperback

Publisher: Washington Researchers, Ltd.
2612 P St., NW
Washington, DC 20007
Tel: (202)333-3499
Fax: (202)625-0656

Pages: 331

Exhibits: None

Meant for anyone seeking business information about Japanese companies—especially executive strategists, marketers, and management consultants—this guide to available information sources includes international organizations; Japanese government agencies; U.S. federal, state, and local agencies; and private-sector organizations, such as banks, accounting firms, consultants, and educational organizations. The sources are listed by information needed, including such sections as markets, companies, and statistics. Although it does not include a bibliography of data sources published by the listed organizations, this is a useful directory.

Title: *Japanese Colleges and Universities*
Date: 1991
Format: Paperback
Author: Association of International Education, Japan
Publisher: Maruzen and Co., Ltd.
Export and Import Department
P.O. Box 5050
Tokyo International 100-31, Japan
Pages: 588
Exhibits: None

Meant for students heading to Japan or managers interested in hiring from Japanese educational institutes, this directory lists national and local public and private universities in Japan. It divides schools into nine regions and includes an index of major subject areas, noting the number of foreign students at each.

Title: *Japanese Direct Foreign Investments: An Annotated Bibliography*
Date: 1989
Format: Hardcover
Author: Karl Boger
Publisher: Greenwood Press
88 Post Rd. West
Westport, CT 06881
Tel: (203)226-3571
Fax: (203)222-1502
Pages: 221
Exhibits: None

For anyone researching Japanese investment in the United States, this is a handy, though now somewhat dated, bibliography of books and articles on the subject. Each entry includes an abstract, and a subject index allows easy use.

Title: *Japan's High Technology*
Date: 1991
Format: Hardcover
Author: Dawn E. Talbot
Publisher: Oryx Press
4041 N. Central
Phoenix, AZ 85012-3397
Tel: (602)265-2651
Fax: (602)265-6250
Pages: 171
Exhibits: None

Meant for technology hunters, marketers, and corporate planners, this recent annotated list of business information sources in Japan is a handy resource. The focus is on high technology, but numerous general business sources are included as well. The sources are categorized by media format (e.g., newsletters, directories), and a subject index permits the easy location of information sources on specific technologies. Information for acquiring the sources, including price, is also provided. However, virtually the same information is provided by the National Technical Information Service and updated annually (see pages 164–165).

Title: *Summaries of Selected Japanese Magazines*
Date: Monthly
Format: Periodical
Publisher: Office of Translation Services

Political Section
American Embassy, Tokyo
10-5, Akasaka 1-chome
Minato-ku
Tokyo 107, Japan
Mailing Address:
APO San Francisco, CA 96503
Tel: (81)(3)583-7141

Pages: Varies
Exhibits: None
Price: Contact for subscription prices

Issued monthly by the American Embassy in Tokyo, this 45- to 50-page stapled transcript provides English abstracts of recently published Japanese articles. The focus of the articles is on political issues that directly affect U.S.-Japan relations. This is a useful translation service for political risk analysts and those who track developments inside Japan's government.

Title: *Who's Who in Japan*
Date: Annual
Format: Hardcover
Publisher: Asia Press Co., Ltd.
4th Floor, Dowa Building
2-22, Ginza 7-chome
Chuo-ku
Tokyo 104, Japan
Pages: 700
Exhibits: None

Comprehensive who's who directories frustrate many users because they never seem to list all of the important or topical people, and they usually offer little in-depth information about anyone. This attractive volume might list the person you're looking for, but the information about that person is limited to title, affiliated organization, birthdate, degrees, previous positions, spouse's name, address, and telephone number. People are also indexed by activity, such as bureaucrat/legal, communications, and social science.

INTELLECTUAL PROPERTY

Title: *The Know-How Contract in Germany, Japan and the United States*
Date: 1984
Format: Hardcover
Editor: Herbert Stumpf
Publisher: Kluwer Law and Taxation Publishers
6 Bigelow St.
Cambridge, MA 02139
Tel: (617)354-0140
Fax: (617)354-8595
Pages: 309
Exhibits: None

This volume contains an 80-page section covering the know-how contract in Japan written by a law professor and the director of the Japan Association of Industrial Property. It is meant for lawyers, contract negotiators, and executives involved with the transfer of proprietary information to or from Japan. The authors deliver a very detailed explanation of what know-how is, what know-how contracts are, the regulation of contracts, and the international know-how contract. This is required reading for anyone entering into such a contractual relationship with the Japanese.

LAWS AND REGULATIONS

Title: *Doing Business in Japan*
Date: 1992
Format: Bound newsletter

Publisher: Matthew Bender
11 Penn Plaza
New York, NY 10001-2006
Tel: (212)967-7707

Pages: 300/vol.

Exhibits: None

This binder set is meant to help "those intending to do business in Japan to become aware of some of the pertinent laws and potential legal problems which must be considered in order to engage in intelligent business planning." It is recommended as an English-language legal source for lawyers who represent clients in Japan. It provides comprehensive and civil law in detailed, though not overly legalistic, numbered sections designed for easy updating. It contains informative appendixes and glossaries.

Title: *Environmental Policy and Impact Assessment in Japan*

Date: 1991

Format: Hardcover

Author: Brendan F.D. Barrett and Riki Therivel

Publisher: Routledge
11 New Fetter Lane
London EC4P 4EE, United Kingdom
Tel: (44)(71)583-9855
Fax: (44)(71)583-0701

Pages: 288

Exhibits: Diagrams, graphs, and tables

Part of a series that looks at critical environmental topics, this well-researched monograph "summarizes the current state of environmental policies in Japan and points to possible problems of these policies." The authors begin by emphasizing that Japan produces some of the most sophisticated pollution control technologies and has ratified some of the most stringent environmental laws while remaining one of the world's most destructive polluters. The book provides a clear and succinct explanation of Japan's environmental policy, management, and assessment procedures and includes useful case studies.

Title: *Japanese Labor Law*

Date: 1992

Format: Hardcover

Author: Kazuo Sugeno

Publisher: University of Washington Press
P.O. Box 50096
Seattle, WA 98145-5096
Tel: (206)543-3050
Fax: (206)543-3932

Pages: 714

Exhibits: None

Meant for lawyers and enterprise managers, this comprehensive reference book covers all aspects of labor law in Japan. It was first published in 1985 and is offered here in English translation. This is not a reader but a well-organized compendium of definitions and legal explanations covering the entire gamut of the legal specialty of labor law. Topics include law of the labor market, individual labor relations law, and collective labor relations law.

Title: *The Law of Commerce in Japan*

Date: 1993

Format: Hardcover

Editor: Haig Oghigian

Publisher: Prentice-Hall
Alexandra Distripark
Block 4, #04-31
Pasir Panjang Rd.
0511, Singapore

Pages: 109

Exhibits: None

The concept of this useful volume is simple: have the best-recognized practitioners in the field of Japanese commercial law provide a concise, relevant introduction to their respective areas of practice. The book is especially useful to businesspeople who need an overview of Japanese commercial law before hiring a specialist lawyer. The types of law covered include the sale of goods and commercial law, corporate law, taxation law, intellectual property law, regulations on the issuance of securities, and financing law. The book also covers the rules and protocols for commercial dispute resolution.

Title: *Laws and Regulations Relating to Insider Trading in Japan*

Date: 1989

Format: Hardcover

Author: Kazumi Okamura and Chieko Takeshita

Publisher: Commercial Law Center, Inc.
2-27-10, Hatchobori
Chuo-ku
Tokyo 104, Japan

Pages: 173

Exhibits: None

This book was written for those seeking to understand securities transactions in Japan and the regulations related to insider trading. It offers translations in English of the laws, orders, and ordinances related to the topic. It is useful to lawyers and investors.

MANAGEMENT

Title: *Culture and Management in Japan*

Date: 1988

Format: Hardcover

Author: Shuji Hayashi

Publisher: University of Tokyo Press
1, Furo-cho
Chikusa-ku
Nagoya 464-01, Japan
Tel: (81)(52)781-5027
Fax: (81)(52)781-0647

Pages: 194

Exhibits: Charts and tables

This eclectic but insightful study of Japanese cultural values and their bearing on management practice in Japanese companies will entertain and enlighten expatriates and managers.

Title: *Enterprise Unionism in Japan*

Date: 1992

Format: Hardcover

Author: Hirosuke Kawanishi

Publisher: Kegan Paul International
P.O. Box 256
London WC1B 3SW, United Kingdom
Tel: (44)(71)580-5511
Fax: (44)(71)436-0899

Pages: 467

Exhibits: Graphs and tables

For top management and department heads, this practical and well-illustrated volume provides a complete explanation of what total quality control is and how to promote it as a business operation. Selected topics include process control, attending to the customer, quality control (QC) techniques, problem-solving techniques, standardization, and the QC audit. This volume is highly recommended as a sourcebook and as a step-by-step manual for implementing Japanese-style QC tools and techniques in an enterprise.

Title: *Foreign Competition in Japan*
Date: 1992
Format: Hardcover
Author: Robert J. Ballon
Publisher: Routledge
11 New Fetter Lane
London EC4P 4EE, United Kingdom
Tel: (44)(71)583-9855
Fax: (44)(71)583-0701
Pages: 174
Exhibits: Graphs and tables

For managers and marketers working in Japan, this book provides a comprehensive explanation of Japan's labor environment, including hiring practices, formulas for compensation, and decision-making practices in the enterprise, all with special advice for foreign firms in Japan. The book also includes a detailed section on the Japanese marketplace that focuses on customers and their perceptions of foreign products. A rather eclectic book, it is recommended for its well-supported advice and case examples.

Title: *Gaishi: The Foreign Company in Japan*
Date: 1990
Format: Hardcover
Author: T.W. Kang
Publisher: Basic Books/HarperCollins Publishers
10 E. 53rd St.
New York, NY 10022
Tel: (212)207-7000
Fax: (212)207-7617
Pages: 279
Exhibits: None

For the project manager headed for Japan, this is a personal and practical guidebook that instructs (in a readable and general manner) on how to perform the art of cross-cultural management in a foreign-owned affiliate in Japan. Laced with anecdotes and chock-full of hands-on, practical advice, the book speaks directly to the challenge involved in running an enterprise located in Japan, from hiring workers to implementing quality control techniques. It includes a glossary of Japanese terms and is an excellent overview.

Title: *Honda: An American Success Story*
Date: 1988
Format: Hardcover
Author: Robert L. Shook
Publisher: Prentice-Hall
15 Columbus Circle
New York, NY 10023
Tel: (212)373-8000
Fax: (212)698-7007
Pages: 238
Exhibits: None

Written with the cooperation of the company's management and based on hundreds of interviews with Honda staff members and workers, this readable account tells the story of the Honda Motor

Company and how it became the fourth-largest producer of cars in the United States by integrating Japanese and American management practices. This book is highly praiseworthy for its engaging advice to managers who work with the Japanese here or abroad.

Title: *The Human Side of Japanese Enterprise*
Date: 1988
Format: Hardcover
Author: Hiroshi Tanaka
Publisher: University of Pennsylvania Press
Brockley Hall
418 Service Dr.
Philadelphia, PA 19104-6097
Tel: (215)898-6261
Fax: (215)898-0404
Pages: 269
Exhibits: Photographs

Focusing on the life of a single successful Japanese businessman, this book offers poignant lessons about the cultural value system that underlies and makes possible the successful Japanese management practices that have been written about so often in theoretical terms.

Title: *Implementing Japanese AI Techniques: Turning the Tables for a Winning Strategy*
Date: 1990
Format: Hardcover
Author: Richard Tabor Greene
Publisher: McGraw-Hill
1221 Avenue of the Americas
New York, NY 10020
Tel: (708)615-3360
Fax: (708)614-3363
Pages: 266
Exhibits: Diagrams, graphs, and tables

This book explains how American managers use Japanese methods of introducing and implementing the technology of artificial intelligence (AI) in their enterprises. It is clearly written and well organized.

Title: *Inside Corporate Japan*
Date: 1987
Format: Hardcover
Author: David J. Lu
Publisher: Productivity Press
P.O. Box 814
Cambridge, MA 02238
Tel: (617)497-5146
Fax: (617)868-3524
Pages: 249
Exhibits: None

This is a readable explanation of why Japanese management practices work so well, emphasizing that they are neither mysterious nor inimitable. It describes how Japanese firms become competitive through teamwork, groupism, incremental quality improvements, total quality control, and social responsibility. Plenty of anecdotes and examples make this book readable as well as practical.

Title: *Japanese and European Management*
Date: 1989

Format: Hardcover
Authors: Kazuo Shibagaki, Malcolm Trevor, and Tetsuo Abo
Publisher: University of Tokyo Press
1, Furo-cho
Chikusa-ku
Nagoya 464-01, Japan
Tel: (81)(52)781-5027
Fax: (81)(52)781-0697
Pages: 272
Exhibits: Graphs and tables

Meant for managers in Japan and economists, this book presents a theoretical analysis of Japan's labor markets in terms of, as the authors put it, "how cultural and traditional factors interact with the influence of economic growth." This is an in-depth and thoroughly researched monograph that is useful in comparing European and Japanese management styles.

Title: *The Japanese Business: Success Factors*
Date: 1989
Format: Hardcover
Author: Ryuei Shimizu
Publisher: Chikura Shobo
2-4-12, Kyobashi
Chuo-ku
Tokyo 104, Japan
Pages: 279
Exhibits: Graphs and tables

Well positioned at the Ministry of International Trade and Industry to collect information about Japanese firms, the author of this book comes to useful conclusions about the factors that contribute to the success of a Japanese company. The book makes for rather slow reading, but the data presented are based on a survey of 39,000 Japanese companies—a database that serious researchers of Japan's competitiveness can't ignore.

Title: *The Japanese Firm in Transition*
Date: 1988
Format: Paperback
Author: Iwao Nakatani
Publisher: Asian Productivity Organization
4-14, Akasaka 8-chome
Minato-ku
Tokyo 107, Japan
Tel: (81)(3)408-7221
Fax: (81)(3)408-7220
Pages: 102
Exhibits: Graphs

Concise and readable, this book describes the evolution of Japanese management methods since World War II. The reader completes this book with a solid understanding of how Japanese companies evolved in the postwar period and of interlocking corporate groups, the immobility of the labor market, and Japanese corporate internationalization. The presentation is simple, readable, and straightforward. This is a great first step in learning about management in Japan and the broad challenges it faces.

Title: *The Japanese Labor Market in a Comparative Perspective with the United States*
Date: 1990
Format: Hardcover
Author: Masanori Hashimoto
Publisher: W.E. Upjohn Institute for Employment Research

300 S. Westnedge Ave.
Kalamazoo, MI 49007
Tel: (616)343-5541
Fax: (616)343-3308

Pages: 150
Exhibits: Graphs and tables

This is a compilation of academic articles arising out of the 1987 conference of the Euro-Japanese Management Studies Association. Meant for managers and students of Japanese management practice, the articles examine the unique aspects of Japanese management practice, including lifetime employment, seniority wages, and enterprise unions—to name only a few of the topics explored. Of particular interest are the pieces that focus on the effectiveness of Japanese management techniques in overseas operations.

Title: *Japanese Management: Tradition and Transition*
Date: 1991
Format: Hardcover
Author: Arthur M. Whitehill
Publisher: Routledge, Chapman and Hall, Inc.
29 W. 35th St.
New York, NY 10001
Tel: (212)244-3336
Fax: (212)563-2269
Pages: 299
Exhibits: Tables

This textbook provides a history of Japanese management practice, a review of its cultural underpinnings, and an examination of how Japanese companies manage every aspect of a functioning enterprise. The managerial tasks covered include planning, staffing, leadership, compensation, motivating workers, communication, and improving effectiveness. This book is recommended as a complete description of how Japanese management works.

Title: *Japanese Management in Historical Perspective*
Date: 1988
Format: Hardcover
Editor: Tsunehiko Yui and Keiichiro Nakagawa
Publisher: University of Tokyo Press
1, Furo-cho
Chikusa-ku
Nagoya 464-01, Japan
Tel: (81)(52)781-5077
Fax: (81)(52)781-0697
Pages: 290
Exhibits: None

Based on papers presented at a 1988 conference, this reader provides the serious researcher with a historical overview of key developments in the evolution of Japanese management, management-labor relations, innovation, and business strategy.

Title: *The Japanese Management Mystique*
Date: 1992
Format: Hardcover
Author: Jon Woronoff
Publisher: Probus Publishing Co.
1925 N. Clybourn Ave.
Chicago, IL 60614
Tel: (312)868-1100
Fax: (312)868-6250
Pages: 232
Exhibits: None

Jon Woronoff is perhaps the most prolific author of books that dispel myths about Japanese power and superiority. This volume finds its purpose in examining "the good AND bad points, the strengths AND weaknesses, the achievements AND failures" of Japanese management practice in hopes of encouraging foreign businesspeople to view Japanese managers as something other than invincible. This is an engaging and enlightening book.

Title: *Japanese Management Overseas*
Date: 1989
Format: Hardcover
Author: Hiroshi Komai
Publisher: Asian Productivity Organization
4-14, Akasaka 8-chome
Minato-ku
Tokyo 107, Japan
Tel: (81)(3)408-7221
Fax: (81)(3)408-7220
Pages: 127
Exhibits: Tables

Commissioned by the Asian Productivity Organization, this book sets out to explain how Japanese firms remain productive while Japanese labor endures dehumanizing and, one would think, counterproductive conditions at the hands of management. The book quickly arrives at the positive effects of groupism, the need for harmony, and consensus decision making in the Japanese company. Of particular interest to overseas managers are the chapters on how Japanese management style has been received in Thailand and the United States and on whether it is easily transferable across cultures.

Title: *Japanese Quality Concepts: An Overview*
Date: 1992
Format: Hardcover
Author: Katsuya Hosotani
Publisher: Quality Resources
One Water St.
White Plains, NY 10601
Tel: (914)761-9600
Fax: (914)761-9467
Pages: 270
Exhibits: Graphs and tables

Meant for managers in Japan or researchers of Japanese industrial management, this magnum opus translated from the Japanese provides a detailed examination of the history and function of Japan's enterprise unions. The book is well researched and filled with useful case studies that shed much light on what goes on between Japanese labor and management on the shop floor.

Title: *Japanese Quality Control Circles*
Date: 1988
Format: Hardcover
Author: Maryu Lou Uy Onglatco
Publisher: Asian Productivity Organization
4-14, Akasaka 8-chome
Minato-ku
Tokyo 107, Japan
Tel: (81)(3)408-7221
Fax: (81)(3)408-7220
Pages: 199
Exhibits: Graphs and tables

Based on the author's Ph.D. dissertation and published by the Asian Productivity

Organization, this study includes a number of useful case studies of quality control circles (QCCs) in Japan's banking and electrical industries, shedding light on Japanese attitudes toward the QCC, its evolution, effects, problems, and universality. This book is recommended as a complete introduction for managers and corporate planners.

Title: *Japan's Public Policy Companies*
Date: 1978
Format: Hardcover
Author: Chalmers Johnson
Publisher: American Enterprise Institute for Public Policy Research
1150 Seventeenth St., NW
Washington, D.C. 20036
Tel: (202)862-5831
Fax: (202)862-7178
Pages: 173
Exhibits: Tables

In this early monograph, the well-known Japan specialist contributes to the research on government-business relations in Japan by examining the country's public corporations and mixed public-private enterprises. Not for the novice seeking an introduction, this clearly articulated study is for serious researchers of Japan's political economy.

Title: *Management Japan*
Date: Quarterly
Format: Periodical
Editor: Yoshiaki Nakaune
Publisher: International Management Association of Japan, Inc.
Mori 10th Building
1-18-1, Toranomon
Minato-ku
Tokyo 107, Japan
Pages: Varies
Exhibits: Graphs
Price: $26/year (airmail)

For international managers who need to keep abreast of management technique and theory in Japan, this 35-page magazine-size journal is highly recommended. The well-illustrated articles are written by some of Japan's top industrial managers and academics, covering topics such as management for export promotion, quality control, cultural aspects of managing multinationals, and building alliances as a way to compete in manufacturing.

Title: *Managing Japanese Workers*
Date: 1991
Format: Hardcover
Author: Tadashi Hanami
Publisher: Japan Institute of Labor
7-6, Shibakoen 1-chome
Minato-ku
Tokyo 105, Japan
Pages: 106
Exhibits: None

Published by the Japan Institute of Labor, this slim volume provides the English-reading personnel manager in Japan with a practical book about Japanese labor. It is recommended as a reference on labor law and practice in Japan, including sections on hiring, working conditions, promotion, disputes, unions, firing, and more.

Title: *On Track with the Japanese: A Case-by-Case Approach to Building Successful Relationships*

Date: 1992

Format: Hardcover

Author: Patricia Gercik

Publisher: Kodansha International
Kodansha America, Inc.
114 Fifth Ave.
New York, NY 10011
Tel: (212)727-6460
Fax: (212)727-9177

Pages: 240

Exhibits: None

Price: $19.95

On the widening shelf of books that advise Americans about how to function better in working relationships with the Japanese, this collection of case studies followed by "analysis" sections is the best place to start. The author spent 25 years in Tokyo and is the managing director of the MIT-Japan Program. The four sections of the book, titled "Know Me," "Trust Me," "Believe Me," and "Marry Me," include chapters that describe the experiences of American and Japanese individuals working together. All of the common cultural factors are covered—including "face," after-hours drinking, commitment, and dependency—but here the cool anthropological lessons are well illustrated with very human accounts.

Title: *The Rise of the Japanese Corporate System*

Date: 1991

Format: Hardcover

Author: Koji

Publisher: Kegan Paul International
P.O. Box 256
London WC1B 2SW, United Kingdom
Tel: (44)(71)580-5511
Fax: (44)(71)436-0899

Pages: 276

Exhibits: Tables

The author of this well-written research monograph purports that "a new economic system has developed and been nurtured in Japan inside a shell of capitalism." The new system is described and compared with industrial-economic systems in other developed countries. The analysis of Japanese corporate and management systems will interest the serious researcher.

Title: *The Shift to JIT: How People Make the Difference*

Date: 1992

Format: Hardcover

Author: Ichiro Majima

Publisher: Productivity Press
P.O. Box 3007
Cambridge, MA 02140
Tel: (617)497-5146
Fax: (617)868-3524

Pages: 239

Exhibits: None

This important book by a well-known Japanese management expert presents "a comprehensive and systematic description of Toyota's entire management system," including "not only production management but also research and development (R&D) management, sales management, financial management, cost planning, organizational management, and the planning of international production strategy." There is perhaps no better source of insight and information into the operation of a large Japanese corporation, presented in a more readable manner. Chapters cover financial management, costing, functional management, personnel management, sales management, new product development, production management, and international production strategy.

Title: *Skill Formation in Japan and Southeast Asia*
Date: 1990
Format: Hardcover
Editor: Kazuo Koike and Takenori Inoki
Publisher: University of Tokyo Press
1, Furo-cho
Chikusa-ku
Nagoya 464-01, Japan
Tel: (81)(52)781-5027
Fax: (81)(52)781-0697
Pages: 252
Exhibits: Tables

With the intention of examining how top management's abilities contribute to corporate growth in Japan, the author, a Japanese academic, investigates three performance tasks of top management: providing business vision, making strategic decisions, and providing business management and control. For the study, the author conducted 220 interviews with executives and surveyed 9,000 firms listed on the Tokyo Stock Exchange. For serious researchers, this is a valuable database of empirical research.

Title: *A Study of the Toyota Production System*
Date: 1989
Format: Hardcover
Author: Shigeo Shingo
Publisher: Productivity Press
P.O. Box 3007
Cambridge, MA 02140
Tel: (617)497-5146
Fax: (617)868-3524
Pages: 257
Exhibits: Graphs and tables

The famed author of this manual for setting up quality control in manufacturing invented the just-in-time management system (called the *kanban* system in Japan), which was instrumental in Toyota's production system. This important, highly technical (though readable) book explains Toyota's production system for factory managers who wish to apply it immediately in their plants. The book covers in detail practical aspects of processing, inspection, transportation, and delays.

Title: *Top Management in Japanese Firms*
Date: 1986
Format: Hardcover
Author: Ryuei Shimizu
Publisher: Chikura Shobo
2-4-12, Kyobashi
Chuo-ku
Tokyo 104, Japan
Pages: 212
Exhibits: Graphs and tables

This excellent research monograph asks whether the production skills taught in a Japanese firm are transferable to firms in Southeast Asia. The authors interviewed production workers who work for Japanese firms in Southeast Asia and compared their skills with those in indigenous firms not influenced by the Japanese. The book goes far in explaining "how workers expand and deepen their skills, how workers are motivated by a system of evaluation and renumeration, and how a work force is allocated and mobilized in the workplace." Well illustrated and grounded in hands-on research, this book is suggested reading for overseas production managers or anyone who is seriously intent on understanding Japanese management of worker training.

Title: *Toyota Management System: Linking the Seven Key Functional Areas*
Date: 1993
Format: Hardcover
Author: Yasuhiro Monden
Publisher: Productivity Press
P.O. Box 3007
Cambridge, MA 02140
Tel: (617)497-5146
Fax: (617)868-3524
Pages: 221
Exhibits: Diagrams and tables

Originally published in 1981, this seminal study by a well-known Japanese management expert is a readable and well-researched examination that sets out to accomplish the following: explain the philosophy behind Toyota's production system, highlight the system's most crucial aspects, and provide practical explanations about how to put Toyota's principles into practice. It is highly recommended as a guide to transforming manufacturing operations along the lines originated at Toyota, including techniques for just-in-time production and the *kanban* system.

Title: *Working for the Japanese*
Date: 1990
Format: Hardcover
Author: Joseph J. Fucini and Suzy Fucini
Publisher: The Free Press
866 Third Ave.
New York, NY 10022
Tel: (212)605-9364
Fax: (212)605-9372
Pages: 258
Exhibits: None

The result of research and interviews at Mazda's Flat Rock plant and with local officials and United Automobile Workers (UAW) representatives, this book recounts the often turbulent relationship between Mazda management and American workers and their union. Interestingly, Mazda withdrew their cooperation with the authors midway through the research. This is a recommended and readable source for American managers and workers who are involved with Japanese counterparts.

MARKET DATA AND ANALYSIS

Title: *Consumer Japan*
Date: Annual
Format: Hardcover
Publisher: Euromonitor
87-88 Turnmill St.
London EC1M 5QU, Great Britain
Tel: (44)(71)251-8024
Fax: (44)(71)608-3149
Pages: 350
Exhibits: Tables

Unique and very useful to marketers of consumer product lines, this book provides statistical data on the Japanese market, analysis of trends affecting the market, and profiles of key Japanese manufacturers and retailers. The book's six chapters provide an overview of major aspects of Japan's consumer market, an overview of and statistics about the market, specific details on more than 150 Japanese consumer markets, profiles of key manufacturers and retailers, and sources of consumer market information. This book is commendable, though the definitive how-to book about selling to Japan's consumer market has yet to be written.

Title: *Cracking the Japanese Market*
Date: 1991
Format: Hardcover
Author: James C. Morgan and J. Jeffrey Morgan
Publisher: The Free Press
866 Third Ave.
New York, NY 10022
Tel: (212)605-9364
Fax: (212)605-9372
Pages: 295
Exhibits: Graphs and tables

Written by a father-son team with plenty of experience marketing high-tech production systems to Japan, this is a rich and readable guidebook for marketers. The practical advice includes studying the Japanese market, modes of market entry, and a general set of guidelines for success in Japan. The authors also cover numerous peripheral aspects of the Japanese "challenge" to corporate America and the cultural-philosophical underpinnings of that challenge, and they describe the broad characteristics of Japan's commercial environment.

Title: *Japan Business: Obstacles and Opportunities*
Date: 1983
Format: Hardcover
Author: McKinsey & Company, Inc.
Publisher: John Wiley & Sons
605 Third Ave.
New York, NY 10158-0012
Tel: (212)850-6000
Fax: (212)850-6088
Pages: 208
Exhibits: Graphs and tables

Believing that increased U.S. participation in the Japanese market will reduce trade tensions between the two countries, the United States–Japan Trade Study Group engaged McKinsey & Company to help prepare a study of opportunities in the Japanese market for U.S. firms. Useful to marketers, the book is one of the few that provide an in-depth analysis of selling opportunities in the Japanese market and how U.S. firms can enter it, with special emphasis on the service sector. The book includes plenty of illustrations and examples.

Title: *Japan Business Atlas*
Date: 1987
Format: Hardcover
Publisher: Business International of Delaware, Inc.
4th Floor, Pola Aoyama Building
Minami Aoyama 2-chome
Minato-ku
Tokyo 107, Japan
Tel: (81)(3)404-5672

Pages: 166
Exhibits: Graphs and tables

This business atlas renders much relevant statistical information about Japan's people and economy in visual form. For marketing strategists who need information in the form of charts and graphs, this is a useful source, though the data is years old. The sections of interest to businesspeople include a series of organizational charts of the Japanese bureaucracy and sections on industry, the market, distribution, R&D, Japan's overseas investment, and foreign investment in Japan.

Title: *The Japanese Distribution System*
Date: 1993
Format: Hardcover
Editor: Michael R. Czinkota and Masaaki Kotabe
Publisher: Probus Publishing Co.
1925 N. Clynbourn Ave.
Chicago, IL 60614
Tel: (312)868-1100
Fax: (312)868-6250
Pages: 318
Exhibits: Graphs and tables

Highly recommended to serious-minded Japan marketers, this is perhaps the only in-depth examination of the country's complex distribution system. It's a compilation of articles by experts, but even so, the overall coverage is comprehensive and well organized. Case studies round out this impressive study.

Title: *Japan Exports and Imports*
Date: Monthly
Format: Paperback
Publisher: Japan Tariff Association
4-7-8 Kohji-machi
Chiyoda-ku
Tokyo 102 Japan
Tel: (81)(3)2637-2215
Pages: Varies
Exhibits: Tables
Price: ¥ 228,000/year

Published monthly by the Japan Tariff Association, this 800-page tome is clearly the best source of current statistics about the quantity and composition of Japan's international trade. For marketers making precision analyses of buying and selling patterns, this is an excellent source.

Title: *Japan Marketing Handbook*
Date: 1988
Format: Hardcover
Publisher: Euromonitor Publications, Ltd.
87-88 Turnmill Rd.
London EC1M 5QU, United Kingdom
Tel: (44)(71)251-8024
Fax: (44)(71)608-3149
Pages: 160
Exhibits: Tables

Billed as a practical introduction to the Japanese market, this now rather dated and too-brief book analyzes Japan's changing economic situation, its consumer markets, and its growth industries. It also offers much general advice on how to crack the market. Two chapters—one reviewing the size and nature of the industrial market and the other covering the consumer market—are the most useful, though less dated primers are now available.

Title: *Japan Labor Bulletin*
Date: Monthly
Format: Periodical
Publisher: The Japan Institute of Labor
Chutaikin Building
7-6, Shibakoen 1-chome
Minato-ku
Tokyo 105, Japan
Tel: (81)(3)5470-4064
Pages: Varies
Exhibits: Tables
Price: ¥ 3,600/issue

Meant for anyone working in Japan or managing Japanese workers, this eight-page newsletter carries articles related to labor law, working conditions, the Japanese economy, public policy as it relates to labor, international labor topics, and labor-management relations. Statistics relevant to employment and worker benefits are included. This publication contains useful information that is not readily found elsewhere.

Title: *The JETRO Monitor*
Date: Bimonthly
Format: Periodical
Publisher: Japan External Trade Organization (JETRO)
c/o Dentsu Burson-Marsteller
230 Park Ave. South
New York, NY 10003
Tel: (81)(3)3582-5579 (Japan)
Fax: (81)(3)3582-7508 (Japan)
Pages: Varies
Exhibits: None
Price: Contact for subscription prices

Including two or three short articles and a page of corporate news briefs, this four-page newsletter published by a (sometimes partial) Japanese government agency, is meant for marketers tracking Japanese trade and economic conditions. Of particular use to sellers, the articles typically provide brief analyses of the Japanese market, such as "The Japanese Leisure Market" and "Success in the Japanese Auto Market." The newsletter also includes profiles of American companies in Japan, advice on investing in Japan, and updates on JETRO trade promotion activities.

Title: *Journal of Japanese Trade and Industry*
Date: Bimonthly
Format: Periodical
Editor: Yoshimichi Hori
Publisher: Japan Economic Foundation
11th Floor, Fukoku Seimei Building
2-2-2, Uchisaiwai-cho
Chiyoda-ku
Tokyo 100, Japan
Tel: (81)(3)3580-9291
Fax: (81)(3)3501-6674
Pages: Varies
Exhibits: Graphs, photographs, and tables
Price: $65/year

One of the top sources of general industry news from Japan, this 60-page bimonthly magazine contains articles analyzing Japanese industrial developments, market trends, economic and political developments in Asia, and foreign business in Japan. Articles are clear, opinionated, and well researched—not to mention readable. For marketers and investors, this is an essential updater.

Title: *Marketing Strategies and Distribution Channels for Foreign Companies in Japan*
Date: 1989
Format: Hardcover
Author: Erich Batzer and Helmut Laumer
Publisher: Westview Press
5500 Central Ave.
Boulder, CO 80301
Tel: (303)444-3541
Fax: (303)449-3356
Pages: 302
Exhibits: Tables

Translated from German, this book delivers an admirable explanation of Japanese distribution channels, with an emphasis on the experience of German firms in the market. It includes detailed descriptions of systems of distribution in the following sectors: capital goods and industrial supplies, consumer durables, consumer goods, and food and semi-luxuries.

Title: *MITI and the Japanese Miracle*
Date: 1982
Format: Paperback
Author: Chalmers Johnson
Publisher: Stanford University Press
Ventura Hall
Stanford, CA 94305-4115
Tel: (415)723-1712
Fax: (415)723-0758
Pages: 393
Exhibits: None

An acquaintance with how Japan's Ministry of International Trade and Industry (MITI) operates is crucial for anyone who wants to understand how industrial decision making works in Japan. MITI has played a central role in Japan's economic success and in the formulation of its political policies. This book by one of America's foremost Japan specialists tells the story of MITI from 1925, when Japan's industrial-policy bureaucracy was created, to 1975. The author also reveals "some of the Japanese language of bureaucracy—its concepts, euphemisms, and slogans." Finally, a model of Japan's political economy is offered, one that has remained highly influential among Japan specialists for the past decade.

Title: *Unlocking Japan's Markets*
Date: 1991
Format: Hardcover
Author: Michael R. Czinkota and Jon Woronoff
Publisher: Probus Publishing Co.
1925 N. Clyburn Ave.
Chicago, IL 60614
Tel: (312)868-1100
Fax: (312)368-6250
Pages: 216
Exhibits: None

Recommended to Japan marketers, this volume is one of the few publications that provide a clear explanation of how Japan's distribution system is structured and how it operates. It is not as useful as a guide on entering the market, but it does provide a road map of both wholesale and retail distribution channels.

POLITICS AND GOVERNMENT

Title: Asahi-Shimbun
Date: Updated daily
Format: On-line database
Publisher: Asahi-Shimbun
New Electronic Media Division
5-3-2, Tsujiki
Chuo-ku
Tokyo 104-11, Japan
Exhibits: None
Price: $130/hour

This on-line database provides the complete text of articles and items distributed by the Asahi News Service. It consists primarily of Japanese news items but has some international coverage.

Title: *The Daily Japan Digest*
Date: Daily
Format: Periodical (faxed to subscriber)
Editor: Ayako Doi
Publisher: Japan Digest
205 N. Emerson St.
P.O. Box 3479
Arlington, VA 22203
Tel: (703)528-7570
Fax: (703)528-8123
Pages: Varies
Exhibits: None
Price: Contact for subscription prices

This 5- to 10-page newsletter is published daily and can be received by fax. Most of the short articles focus on political and economic news; other categories include foreign relations, agriculture, education, and society. This is a convenient daily providing timely news from Japan.

Title: *Japan Echo: Japanese Views of Asia*
Date: Quarterly
Format: Periodical
Editor: Ando Yukie
Publisher: Japan Echo, Inc.
Moto-Akasaka Building
1-7-10, Moto Akasaka
Minato-ku
Tokyo 160, Japan
Tel: (81)(3)3470-5031
Fax: (81)(3)3470-5410
Pages: Varies
Exhibits: Photographs and tables
Price: ¥ 1,650/issue

Elegantly published in Japan, this quarterly magazine-format journal is comprised of articles "on a wide range of topics of current interest within Japan." In other words, for marketers and analysts seeking insight into Japanese attitudes, habits, and (indirectly) buying preferences, this is an enlightening and very readable source. The articles combine history, culture, and current affairs and are well illustrated.

Title: *Japan Review of International Affairs*
Date: Quarterly
Format: Periodical
Editor: Nobuo Matsunaga
Publisher: Japan Publications Trading Co., Ltd.
P.O. Box 5030
Tokyo International 102, Japan

Pages: Varies
Exhibits: Tables
Price: $60/year (surface mail)

Published by a nonprofit research institution specializing in international affairs, this 75-page small-format journal focuses on timely topics in international relationships, with an emphasis on Japan. Most issues concentrate on a broad topic, such as Asia-Japan partnerships or Northeast Asia in transition. The journal includes reviews of conferences and lectures. It is recommended as a source for Japan's view of foreign affairs.

Title: *Japan Update*
Date: Monthly
Format: Periodical
Editor: Katsura Kono
Publisher: Japan Business Information Center
Nippon Club Tower
20th Floor,
145 W. 57th St.
New York, NY 10019
Tel: (212)489-6206
Fax: (212)489-6211
Pages: Varies
Exhibits: Photographs
Price: $3.50/issue

This 25-page magazine carries articles written by experts and journalists on topics related to contemporary society and culture in Japan. The articles are readable and informative, covering topics as diverse as Japanese television shows, Japan-Soviet trade, and attitudes toward the Yakuza mafia. For those who are preparing to live in Japan and for Japanophiles, this enlightening reader is recommended.

Title: *Japan's Emerging Global Role*
Date: 1993
Format: Hardcover
Editor: Danny Unger and Paul Blackburn
Publisher: Lynne Rienner Publishers, Inc.
1800 30th St.
Boulder, CO 80301
Tel: (303)444-6684
Fax: (303)444-0824
Pages: 211
Exhibits: Tables

This compilation provides a useful reader on Japan's role in the new world order, with an emphasis on the country's global responsibilities, security priorities, political economy, trade, and technology.

Title: *Japan's Growing Power Over East Asia and the World Economy*
Date: 1990
Format: Hardcover
Author: William R. Nester
Publisher: Macmillan
Houndsmills, Basingstoke
Hampshire RG21 2XS, United Kingdom
Tel: (44)(256)29242
Fax: (44)(256)479-476
Pages: 282
Exhibits: None

In the introduction, the author says that this book "analyzes the reasons behind and implications of the rise of Japan to its present economic superpower status, its hegemony over East Asia, and its growing hegemony over the world economy."

Selected chapters examine Japan's foreign policy since the end of World War II, its power in East Asia, the cultural roots of Japanese neomercantilism, and the future implications for Americans of Japanese dominance in East Asian markets. This book is useful to business historians and geopolitical analysts.

Title: *Liberal Star*
Date: Monthly
Format: Periodical
Author: Liberal Democratic Party of Japan
Publisher: Kazuo Nakano
1-11-23, Nagata-cho
Chiyoda-ku
Tokyo 100, Japan
Tel: (81)(3)3581-6211
Pages: Varies
Exhibits: Graphs and photographs
Price: Contact for subscription prices

With this 12-page newsletter, readers can stay on top of the activities of the Liberal Democratic Party, the ruling party of Japan for 40 years until mid-1993. For government analysts and journalists, this newsletter might strike a nerve, but for most, articles like "Portrait of Former Prime Minister Kaifu Completed" will fall flat.

Title: *MITI Handbook*
Date: Annual
Format: Paperback
Publisher: Ministry of International Trade and Industry/
Japan Trade and Industry Publicity, Inc.
Tornaomon Koohira Kaikan
2-8, Toranomon 1-chome
Minato-ku
Tokyo 105, Japan
Tel: (81)(3)3503-4051
Pages: 50
Exhibits: None
Price: ¥ 4,950

This is an essential handbook for anyone dealing with Japan's Ministry of International Trade and Industry, where a staff of 12,000 manages the Japanese economy and performs a wide range of activities related to international trade and industry. This book provides a detailed road map of the ministry's Byzantine interlocking web of bureaus, agencies, divisions, councils, and external organizations, including task descriptions of each and current telephone numbers. The book, which includes a comprehensive list of trade and industrial organizations, is convenient and highly recommended.

Title: *Organization of the Government of Japan*
Date: 1993
Format: Paperback
Publisher: Institute of Administrative Management
Prime Minister's Office
Government of Japan
P.O. Box 1106
Sun-Shine 60
3-1-1, Higashi-Ikebukuro
Toshimaku
Tokyo 170, Japan
Tel: (81)(3)3981-0441
Pages: 143

Exhibits: None
Price: ¥ 2,000

An essential handbook for lobbyists, journalists, or anyone trying to influence the Japanese government, this book provides brief biographies of members of the lower house, upper house, and committees of the upper house, political party officials, and officials of ministries and agencies. The book includes useful organizational charts, explanations about the structure and composition of Japan's political bureaucracy, and portraits of each person profiled. With the yearly rotations of many Japanese officials, this annually updated volume is especially useful.

Title: *The Weekly Japan Digest*
Date: Weekly
Format: Periodical
Editor: Ayako Doi
Publisher: *Japan Digest*
205 N. Emerson St.
P.O. Box 3479
Arlington, VA 22203
Tel: (703)528-7570
Fax: (703)528-8123
Pages: Varies
Exhibits: None
Price: Contact for subscription prices

This 20- to 30-page compilation of news articles covers Japanese politics, trade, business, and economy and numerous other topics. The articles are indexed by subject and headlined for easy scanning. For those who want a weekly source of Japanese news, this is a recommended publication.

Title: *Who's Who in Japanese Government*
Date: Annual
Format: Hardcover
Editor: Seizaburo Sato
Publisher: International Cultural Association, Japan
30-9, Sakuragaoka-cho
Shibuya-ku
Tokyo 150, Japan
Tel: (81)(3)3463-4633
Fax: (81)(3)3463-4675
Pages: 600
Exhibits: None

Issued under the auspices of the government of Japan, this book is the official explanation of the structure of Japan's government and the functions of its many parts. Starting with 20 pages of handy organizational charts, the book is divided into four sections covering the executive branch, councils, public corporations, and the distribution of personnel working for the national government. The bulk of the book is dedicated to describing the organization and function of the various ministries that exist under the executive branch, such as the Ministry of International Trade and Industry and the Ministry of Labor. This is a useful sourcebook for anyone who works with the Japanese government.

RESEARCH AND DEVELOPMENT

Title: *America vs. Japan*
Date: 1986
Format: Hardcover
Editor: Thomas K. McGraw
Publisher: Harvard Business School Press

535 Albany St.
Boston, MA 02163
Tel: (617)495-6700
Fax: (617)496-8066

Pages: 463

Exhibits: Graphs and tables

Written by a foremost commentator on Japanese technology and innovation, this readable, well-researched, and well-illustrated volume explains Japan's so-called Technopolis Concept (put forward by MITI in 1980), a futuristic plan to build a clonelike network of 19 high-tech cities across Japan. Instead of "Silicon Valley fever," Japan contracted "Technopolis fever," and this fascinating and important book explains the implications for America with a clear-headed journalistic approach underpinned by the author's rich experience and knowledge of the topic.

Title: *Current Science and Technology Research in Japan*

Date: 1990

Format: Hardcover

Publisher: Japan Information Center of Science and Technology
C.P.O. Box 1478
Tokyo 100-91, Japan
Tel: (81)(3)3581-5271
Fax: (81)(3)581-6446

Pages: 1,202

Exhibits: None

For scientists and technology hunters, this directory describes 17,000 research projects currently under way at 615 research institutes. Based on information garnered through questionnaires, the book covers science activities at national laboratories and research organizations, public research organizations, research institutes of special governmental corporations, research institutes of national, public, and private universities, and research institutes of public service corporations. This voluminous work is very useful to the specialist.

Title: *Dialog OnDisc: Japan Technology*

Date: Updated quarterly

Format: CD-ROM

Publisher: Dialog Information Services, Inc.
3460 Hillview Ave.
Palo Alto, CA 94304
Tel: (800)334-2564
Fax: (415)858-7069

Exhibits: None

Price: $4,800/year

The quarterly CD-ROM offers bibliographic information and translated abstracts of scientific, business, and technical articles from Japanese periodicals.

Title: *Directory of Japanese Technical Resources in the United States*

Date: 1992

Format: Paperback

Publisher: Office of International Affairs
National Technical Information Service (NTIS)
U.S. Department of Commerce
5285 Port Royal Rd.
Springfield, VA 22161
Tel: (703)487-4650
Fax: (703)487-4009

Pages: 111
Exhibits: None

This well-indexed directory opens the door to more than 250 commercial, nonprofit organizations, professional and trade associations, and university programs that pertain to technological information services in the U.S. It offers a handy "expertise" index that lists the reporting entities by their particular type of industry expertise. The directory also indexes entities by geographical location. This allows a user friendly approach to sorting out information on the complex Japanese technical market.

Title: *Hitachi Review*
Date: Bimonthly
Format: Periodical
Editor: Toshihiko Ito
Publisher: Hitachi, Ltd.
Ohm-sha Co., Ltd.
1, Kanda Nishiki-cho 3-chome
Chiyoda-ku
Tokyo 101, Japan
Pages: Varies
Exhibits: Graphs, photographs, and tables
Price: ¥ 1,000/issue

Meant for scientists and technology hunters, this 50- to 60-page magazine features 7- to 10-page articles presenting highly technical research findings on subjects ranging from thermal power generation to ultra-high-density recording. Each issue's articles focus on a specific technological area, such as environmentally friendly thermal power plants. This is a highly recommended technical journal, especially for technical people involved with Hitachi-affiliated companies.

Title: *The Japanese Experience in Technology*
Date: 1990
Format: Hardcover
Author: Takeshi Hayashi
Publisher: United Nations University Press
Toho Seimei Building
15-1, Shibuya 2-chome
Shibuya-ku
Tokyo 150, Japan
Tel: (81)(3)499-2811
Fax: (81)(3)3406-7345
Pages: 282
Exhibits: Tables

This excellent compendium of case studies explains the process by which Japan selected and assimilated "appropriate" technologies, which eventually resulted in the country achieving what the author calls technological self-reliance, "the ability to absorb all needed technologies . . . not at a stroke but in stages." Coverage moves from industry to industry, using case studies as data.

Title: *Japan's Growing Technological Capability*
Date: 1992
Format: Paperback
Author: National Research Council
Publisher: National Academy Press
2101 Constitution Ave., NW
Washington, DC 20418
Tel: (202)334-3313
Fax: (202)334-2451
Pages: 235
Exhibits: Graphs and tables

For researchers and corporate strategists following Japan's technological advancement, the articles of this compilation will be of interest. Selected sections compare U.S. and Japanese technological strengths and weaknesses, the economic impact of Japanese technological competitiveness and innovation, the future of competition between the countries, and the implications for U.S. industrial policy. This is a current and very useful book.

Title: *New Technology Japan*
Date: Bimonthly
Format: Periodical
Publisher: Machinery and Technology Department
Japan External Trade Organization (JETRO)
2-5, Toranomon 2-chome
Minato-ku
Tokyo 105, Japan
Tel: (81)(3)3582-5579
Fax: (81)(3)3582-7508
Pages: Varies
Exhibits: Diagrams and photographs
Price: Contact for subscription prices

For businesspeople tracking technological product developments in Japan, this 45-page magazine aims "to promote the international exchange of technology through the introduction of Japanese New Technology." An amazing amount of product information is included, uncluttered by advertising. Typical categories of new technology include advanced materials, electronics and optics, information and communications, and process and production engineering. This publication is of great value to technology hunters and those who are following their Japanese competitors.

Title: *U.S.-Japan Science and Technology Exchange*
Date: 1988
Format: Hardcover
Editor: Cecil H. Uyehara
Publisher: Westview Press
5500 Central Ave.
Boulder, CO 80301
Tel: (303)444-3541
Fax: (303)449-3356
Pages: 279
Exhibits: Graphs and tables

This compilation of highly informative research essays is of interest to technology hunters and alliance seekers heading for Japan or to anyone comparing science and technology activities in Japan and the United States. Selected chapters focus on R&D systems in Japan and the United States, Japanese technical literature, new materials, robotics, computers and communications, biotechnology, and strategic technology alliances. The essays highlight some of the cultural differences between the United States and Japan that affect technology pursuits, exchange, and competitiveness.

TAXATION

Title: *Business Practices and Taxation in Japan*
Date: 1989
Format: Hardcover
Author: Takashi Kuboi
Publisher: Japan Times, Ltd.
5-4, Shibaura 4-chome
Minato-ku
Tokyo 108, Japan
Tel: (81)(3)3453-5311
Fax: (81)(3)3453-8023

Pages: 315
Exhibits: Tables

This is a useful, though rather foreboding, handbook for executives poised to enter the Japanese market and deal with the requisite legal, tax, and regulatory logistics. The presentation is step-by-step, including sections on entering the market, handling the formalities of exporting, setting up an office, and forming a joint venture. The focus is on taxation, including corporate, individual, and foreign corporation tax rates and filing procedures. The book includes translations of Japanese corporate tax return forms and a copy of the U.S.-Japan Tax Treaty. For the accountant or tax lawyer, this is a handy reference.

Title: *Guide to Japanese Taxes*
Date: Annual
Format: Paperback
Author: Yuji Gomi
Publisher: Zaikei Shoho Sha
1-2-14, Higashi Shimbashi
Minato-ku
Tokyo 105, Japan
Tel: (81)(3)3572-0624
Fax: (81)(3)3572-5189
Pages: 440
Exhibits: Tables

Containing the most recent developments in Japan's tax system, this book provides an extensive, up-to-the-minute tax guide for the expatriate, lawyer, and accountant. Starting with an overview of the tax system, the volume covers national income tax, withholding income tax, assessment income tax, corporation tax, inheritance and gift tax, consumption tax, and local tax. It includes sample tax forms.

Title: *Japan: International Tax and Business Guide*
Date: 1991
Format: Paperback
Publisher: DRT International
1633 Broadway
New York, NY 10019-6754
Tel: (212)489-1600
Fax: (212)492-2005
Pages: 131
Exhibits: None

Published by a major accounting firm in Japan, this booklet provides an overview of the country's business environment, investment climate, and taxation. The tax topics covered include corporate taxes, individual taxes, and special taxes. This is an informative primer for expatriates and accountants who are considering taking their firm into Japan.

Title: *An Outline of Japanese Taxes*
Date: 1992
Format: Paperback
Author: Tax Bureau, Ministry of Finance, Government of Japan
Publisher: Printing Bureau, Ministry of Finance
Government of Japan
2-2-4, Toronomon
Minato-ku
Tokyo 105, Japan
Tel: (81)(3)3504-2085
Fax: (81)(3)3504-3889
Pages: 355
Exhibits: Tables
Price: ¥ 3,100

Issued by Japan's Ministry of Finance and authorized by Japan's Tax Bureau, this is the definitive guide to taxation in Japan, written for tax lawyers and accountants. Sections cover individual income tax, corporate tax, surtax, inheritance and gift tax, land value tax, consumption tax. . . . The list is exhaustive, and the coverage is detailed and readable.

TRAVEL ADVICE

Title: *The Economist Business Traveller's Guide: Japan*
Date: 1987
Format: Paperback
Editor: Rick Morris
Publisher: Prentice-Hall
15 Columbus Circle
Western Plaza
New York, NY 10023
Tel: (212)373-8000
Fax: (212)678-7007
Pages: 256
Exhibits: Maps
Price: $17.95

This series of well-organized and attractive business travel guides is perhaps the best ever published. This volume summarizes Japan's complicated industrial scene, political atmosphere, and business landscape in plain English. Other sections acquaint the reader with Japanese business practices, culture, and travel logistics for nine key business cities. Maps are included. It has an amazing amount of information under one cover.

Title: *Illustrated Living Japanese Style*
Date: 1990
Format: Paperback
Publisher: Japan Travel Bureau, Inc.
13-1, Nihonbashi 1-chome
Chuo-ku
Tokyo 103, Japan
Tel: (81)(3)257-8337
(81)(3)257-8391
Pages: 191
Exhibits: Drawings
Price: $10

Part of a 13-volume set published in Japan, this cartoon-illustrated handbook is indispensable reading for anyone moving to Japan to live, though it is recommended for visitors, as well. Helpful diagrams illustrate each page. Twenty-seven chapters cover everything from soaking in the bath (where you should never use soap or shampoo) to what to wear when attending a funeral. This book is infinitely useful and understandable.

Title: *The New Tokyo Bilingual Atlas*
Date: 1993
Format: Paperback
Publisher: Kodansha, Ltd.
12-21, Otowa 2-chome
Bunkyo-ku
Tokyo 112-01, Japan
Tel: (81)(3)3946-6201
Fax: (81)(3)3994-9915
Pages: 152
Exhibits: Maps

An attractive and extremely useful traveler's atlas to Tokyo and the surrounding area, this guide should accompany any English-reading person on a trip to Tokyo. The maps are color-coded, detailed, and labeled in English and Japanese as well as Kanji. The atlas is more than a collection of city maps. It includes the addresses of government offices, schools, and hotels; a subway map; a location map of foreign companies in Tokyo; and other valuable information for the business traveler.

U.S.-JAPAN RELATIONS

Title: *Agents of Influence*
Date: 1990
Format: Hardcover
Author: Pat Choate
Publisher: Alfred A. Knopf
201 E. 50th St.
New York, NY 10022
Tel: (212)571-2600
Fax: (212)572-2593
Pages: 295
Exhibits: Tables

An important book by a well-known political economist, this incendiary volume has lost some of its alarmist spark now that the Japanese economy has slumped and Japanese investment in the United States has declined. However, Japan's ability to lobby the American government, and Americans, is a real phenomenon; the point that the author needs to make clearer is that there is a better response than vilifying foreign lobbying here: The United States must learn to lobby better overseas, especially in Japan where the bureaucracy plays such an active role in the commercial sphere. This book is recommended.

Title: *Common Destiny: Japan and the United States in the Global Age*
Date: 1990
Format: Hardcover
Author: Richard Krooth and Hiroshi Fukurai
Publisher: McFarland and Co., Inc.
Box 611
Jefferson, NC 28640
Tel: (919)246-4460
Fax: (919)246-4460
Pages: 307
Exhibits: None

To get an idea of the premise of this book about U.S.-Japan relations, consider this quote from the introduction: "What happens today between America and Japan has all happened before. Looking back, . . . we find a clear pattern regarding the failings of our nations." The authors provide a well-researched explanation for the strained relationship between the United States and Japan, both as trading partners and as two very different cultures. The book examines our socio-religious differences, our divergent approaches to acquiring national wealth and power, the role of technology in our competitive relationship, and the tendency for both countries to pursue protectionist trade policies. This book is suggested for those seeking a deeper understanding of the long legacy of U.S.-Japan difficulties.

Title: *Cowboys and Samurai*
Date: 1991
Format: Hardcover
Author: Stephen D. Cohen
Publisher: HarperBusiness
10 E. 53rd St.
New York, NY 10022
Tel: (212)207-7000
Fax: (212)207-7617

Pages: 304
Exhibits: Graphs

Admitting that he is no "bona fide expert on Japan," the author of this recounting of U.S.-Japan industrial competition and trade battles presents a well-researched and very readable volume. He begins with the hypothesis "that virtually everyone on both sides has historically underestimated and continues to underestimate the degree and impact of the deeply rooted structural differences between the 'cowboy' and 'samurai' approaches to capitalism."

Title: *Invasion of the Salarymen: The Japanese Business Presence in America*
Date: 1992
Format: Hardcover
Author: Jeremiah J. Sullivan
Publisher: Praeger Publishers
88 Post Rd. West
Westport, CT 06881
Tel: (203)226-3571
Fax: (203)222-1502
Pages: 359
Exhibits: None

The author of this narrative account tells the story of the "invasion" of Japanese investment in the United States up to the early 1990s. The author's ultimate conclusion that the "Japanese 'invasion' of the United States is not a threat to anyone" and that it was "ill-planned and unsuccessful" has gained some credence with the downturn of Japanese investment in the United States in the 1990s. Based on interviews with Japanese managers working in the United States, this is an entertaining read for anyone following Japan's presence in this country.

Title: *Japan Challenges America*
Date: 1992
Format: Hardcover
Author: Harrison M. Holland
Publisher: Westview Press
5500 Central Ave.
Boulder, CO 80301-2847
Tel: (303)444-3541
Fax: (303)449-3356
Pages: 233
Exhibits: None

The purpose of this volume, written by a former U.S. foreign service officer in Japan, "is to alert the public about the growing crisis in U.S.-Japanese relations, the causes and consequences of the crisis, and what can be done to check the drift toward a serious confrontation." It offers a portrait of Japanese society, background on the U.S.-Japan strategic defense relationship, and insight into how the diplomatic relationship between the two economic adversaries has moved from "reason to rhetoric." This is a personal and readable account.

Title: *Japanese Companies in American Communities: Cooperation, Conflict and the Role of Corporate Citizenship*
Date: 1990
Format: Paperback
Author: Daniel E. Bob
Publisher: Japan Society
333 E. 47th St.
New York, NY 10017
Tel: (212)832-1155
Pages: 70
Exhibits: Graphs and tables

Based on surveys of Americans living in areas where Japanese direct investment is heavy, this slim volume examines American attitudes toward that investment, how Japanese firms are behaving as "corporate citizens" on American soil, and the ties that have been built between Japan and America at the community level in the United States. Three detailed case studies, polling of U.S. citizens, and interviews were undertaken by the Japan Society in conjunction with SRI International and the Wirthlin Group. An executive summary provides a convenient overview of the results of this important and interesting study. This book is of particular interest to local government leaders in the United States, Japanese executives, and U.S. community leaders.

Title: *Japan Hands: Who's Who in Japan-U.S. Relations in the U.S. Government*
Date: 1990
Format: Paperback
Author: Saunders & Co.
Publisher: Japan Times, Ltd.
5-4, Shibaura 4-chome
Minato-ku
Tokyo 108, Japan
Tel: (81)(3)3453-5311
Fax: (81)(3)3453-8023
Pages: 457
Exhibits: Photographs

Created to assist foreign observers and lobbyists in locating U.S. officials working in widely dispersed government bureaucracies, this book provides a large set of biographies (photo portraits included) of people who are directly involved in decisions affecting U.S.-Japan relations. Key officials are listed by federal agency and chambers of Congress and appear in alphabetical order in an index. Entries note the person's current responsibilities and interests in U.S.-Japan affairs. This guide is useful to corporate lobbyists in the United States as well as its intended readership.

Title: *Japan Thrice-Opened*
Date: 1992
Format: Hardcover
Author: Hideo Ibe
Publisher: Praeger Publishers
88 Post Rd. West
Westport, CT 06881
Tel: (203)226-3571
Fax: (203)222-1502
Pages: 294
Exhibits: None

This book is a fine translation of *Kaikoku* (Opening of the country), which was published in 1988, and the revised edition titled *Nichi-Bei Kankei* (Japanese-U.S. relations), which was published in 1990. Meant for a general audience, it provides a readable account of U.S.-Japan relations since the first encounter between the countries 140 years ago. It includes chapters on the Japanese social ethos, early historical threats from outside, and Japan's future course in its relationship to America. This is a superb history from the Japanese perspective.

Title: *More Like Us*
Date: 1989
Format: Paperback
Author: James Fallows
Publisher: Houghton Mifflin

One Beacon St.
Boston, MA 02108
Tel: (617)725-5000
Fax: (617)227-5409

Pages: 225
Exhibits: None

By an author who is now associated with the "Japan revisionists," this book is useful to businesspeople for its discussion of Japanese management practice and attitudes toward the West.

Title: *The Reckoning*
Date: 1986
Format: Paperback
Author: David Halberstam
Publisher: Avon Books
1790 Broadway
New York, NY 10019
Tel: (212)399-4500
Fax: (212)261-6895
Pages: 786
Exhibits: None

This readable exposé of the U.S. auto industry battling its competition in Japan is recommended for businesspeople seeking insight into Japanese strategy and government-guided industrial decision making.

Title: *Second to None: American Companies in Japan*
Date: 1986
Format: Hardcover and paperback
Author: Robert C. Christopher
Publisher: Crown
201 E. 50th St.
New York, NY 10022
Tel: (212)572-6117
Fax: (212)572-6192
Pages: 258
Exhibits: None

A literate, journalistic exposé of the American corporate experience in Japan, this book has held up as a readable introduction to most of the problems and pitfalls of doing business in Japan as a foreigner. The author has a brilliant way of weaving practical advice for would-be investors into the story of America's commercial engagement with Japan. Although now dated, this book deserves its popular acclaim.

Title: *The Sun Also Sets: Why Japan Will Not Be Number One*
Date: 1989
Format: Hardcover
Author: Bill Emmott
Publisher: Simon & Schuster
W. Garden Place
Kendal St.
London W2 2AQ, United Kingdom
Tel: (44)288-1900
Fax: (44)221-4467
Pages: 273
Exhibits: None

Japan has become a nation of rampant consumers, pleasure seekers, and speculators—just like America? According to this author, the Japanese "threat" is now just a challenge, and America is still number one. Given the current slump in Japan's economy and the slight upturn in America's, this readable volume of future optimism might prove prophetic.

Title: *Trading Places: How We Allowed Japan to Take the Lead*
Date: 1988
Format: Hardcover
Author: Clyde V. Prestowitz, Jr.
Publisher: Basic Books/HarperCollins
10 E. 53rd St.
New York, NY 10022
Tel: (212)207-7000
Fax: (212)207-7617
Pages: 353
Exhibits: Graphs

This book makes perhaps the best case yet for distrusting Japan as a trading partner. The author thrusts the reader into the ongoing U.S.-Japan trade conflict through the vehicle of the two countries' competing semiconductor industries, with telling insights about how and why the United States continues to fail in trade negotiations with Japan. The author speaks from experience as a trade negotiator for the United States and doesn't pull any punches in his criticism of Japanese intentions. This enduring book is highly recommended.

Title: *Turning the Tables*
Date: 1993
Format: Hardcover
Author: Daniel Burstein
Publisher: Simon & Schuster
Rockefeller Center
1230 Avenue of the Americas
New York, NY 10020
Tel: (212)698-7000
Fax: (212)698-7007
Pages: 272
Exhibits: None

This author, one of America's most readable business journalists, has also written *Yen!*, *Euroquake*, and other titles. Here, he sounds the alarm about Japan's dominance of Asian markets and offers a strategy by which America can turn the tables on Japan. The strategic advice is sound, and the research is based on interviews and periodical sources, though, one should note, few Japanese sources. This is an engaging source of insight and background on the U.S.-Japan economic and strategic relationship.

Title: *Yen!*
Date: 1988
Format: Hardcover
Author: Daniel Burstein
Publisher: Simon & Schuster
Rockefeller Center
1230 Avenue of the Americas
New York, NY 10020
Tel: (212)698-7000
Fax: (212)698-7007
Pages: 335
Exhibits: Tables

Now of somewhat less impact since the recent surcease of Japanese investment in the United States, this controversial and critical view of Japan's economic intentions opened the way for many others. The author presents a readable analysis, based on interviews and primarily non-Japanese sources, of how Japan acquires its wealth, where it invests it, and what the impact is for America. This title is now somewhat dated.

People's Republic of China

OVERVIEW

China's name, *Zhong Guo Ren*, means "the people of the Middle Kingdom." Their collective world view places the Chinese at the center of "all below heaven" (*tian xia*), at the apex of civilization, surrounded by barbarian cultures that occupy the periphery. Western "barbarians" have been trying to get rich in China for 150 years, yet historically few of them have successfully penetrated the "market of one billion." With sweeping economic reform in the People's Republic of China (PRC) and the merging of Hong Kong, Taiwan, and China into a financial and manufacturing powerhouse called Greater China, an increasing number of firms from the West now reap profits there. The People's Republic of China now represents one of the strongest economies in the world. By some estimates, the total size of the Chinese economy may now exceed that of Japan, making it the second largest in the world. China's growth has been driven by a phenomenal increase in foreign trade and investment. With most economists predicting double-digit growth through the 1990s, China offers unparalleled opportunities for U.S. business.

China at a Glance

Population:	1.19 billion
Religion:	Buddhist, Taoist, Muslim, Christian
Government:	Communist Party/Socialist
Language:	Putonghua (Mandarin Chinese), various dialects
Currency:	Renminbi (RMB)
Trade (1993):	$80.5 billion total exports; 72.7 billion total imports

The China market has been booming. Its trade with the United States jumped 26 percent in 1991 and now totals $30 billion a year in two-way trade. American exports to China soared almost 30 percent in 1990, surpassing $6 billion. As China's largest export market, however, the United States suffered a $12.8-billion trade deficit with the PRC in 1991, second only to its deficit with Japan. Export growth and high industrial and agricultural output levels maintained gross national product (GNP) growth of 7 percent annually in the early 1990s.

Economic Conditions

All eyes are on China as it continues to sustain rapid economic growth, increasing two-way trade. There is annual concern that its human rights performance might not improve sufficiently for the United States to renew its "most favored nation" (MFN) status. To these developments can be added the mystery and uncertainty surrounding the health and succession of Deng Xiaoping, China's paramount leader and helmsman since China began its open-door reform program in the late 1970s.

China's GNP growth of 10 percent during Deng Xiaoping's reform program, begun in 1978, outstripped virtually every other country in the world, and the Chinese continue to get richer. In prosperous East China, 5 percent of the people are members of so-called 10,000-yuan households, earning more than $2,700 a year. Retail price inflation, running at 4 percent in 1991, may jump in the mid-1990s, leading to another cycle of economic overheating and recession. Should this occur, austerity measures will throw a wet towel on the economy, as happened in 1986 and 1989.

Through its export drive, China has amassed $44 billion in cash reserves. Combined with renewed lending from The World Bank and the Asian Development Bank since the Tiananmen uprising, this ensures that imports will grow rapidly in the coming years. American companies selling aircraft, cotton, machinery, computers, wood, scientific equipment, iron, and steel cannot ignore this burgeoning market. United States exports to China will increase 10 to 15 percent per year into the foreseeable future, barring major political upheaval in China. At the same time, however, China will concentrate on expanding its export sales to the United States; should the trade imbalance continue to widen, chances improve that the U.S. Congress or President Clinton will either conditionalize or reject China's MFN status.

Another factor that could pull the plug on MFN status is China's continuing use of restrictive measures, such as tariffs, import bans, import licensing requirements, import substitution policies, and unpublished directives (*neibu* laws), to control its foreign trade. Should these practices continue alongside a growing trade imbalance, there will likely be more Section 301 investigations of possible unfair trading by U.S. trade representatives and increasingly tense U.S.-China relations in general.

As China approaches the next millennium, its leaders have clearly set a course toward continued opening and market-oriented reform, though the pace of the implementation of the reform is still a topic of debate. As larger and larger sectors of China's economy become market-oriented and whole regions of the country look increasingly capitalist in organization, the huge state sector continues to burden the economy. Other burdens are the growing budget deficit, the clogged and decaying infrastructure, and the gross inefficiencies in production in all regions outside the Special Economic Zones of the South coast.

One of the unseen dilemmas for China's leaders is to provide a model for a "reformed" style of factory management for its enterprises. With new forms of management style being put into action in economically vibrant areas, the notion of enforcing the implementation of standardized pseudosocialist yet market-responsive management style (market-Leninism) seems more far-fetched with each passing high-growth quarter. Though the short-term outlook for China is very positive (with the caveat that Deng's death may be an interim disruption), the long-term prospects for China depend on how China's leaders deal with the issue of transforming the country's 400,000 state firms into movers for their local economies rather than anchors that, collectively, could be a drag on the country's economy for decades. At present, two-thirds of China's state-owned enterprises face financial difficulties. The U.S. Department of Commerce reports that "perhaps 35 percent or more of state-run enterprises are losing money, while absorbing billions of yuan in subsidies." Much industrial production is of unsalable goods, and almost 63 percent of bank lending to industry is in the form of "working capital loans," which basically cover day-to-day expenses for these firms. Moreover, with the transition to a Western-style tax system to amass government revenue, not enough revenue is available to meet expenditures, in part because new private companies have a propensity to evade paying taxes.

The truly positive factor about China's current situation (and nobody predicted this five years ago) is that the non-state-owned sector is leading the growth in this huge economy. Collective production grew at a rate of 20 percent and the private and foreign-invested industrial sector at 64.4 percent in 1993. The state enterprise growth rate was still admirable at between 8 and 9 percent between 1991 and 1993, but its share of total output fell from 60 percent in 1992 to 52 percent in 1993.

Investing in China is back in vogue after a hiatus following the Tiananmen uprising in June 1989. American companies have established 1,700 joint ventures and wholly owned enterprises in the country, signing contracts worth $548 million in 1991, a 54 percent increase from 1990. As was the case before Tiananmen, the primary strategic reason that U.S. firms have invested in China is to penetrate the huge market for consumer and industrial goods. For a growing number of these firms, investing in the "market of one billion" has proved profitable.

ADVERTISING

Title: *China Media Book*
Date: Annual
Format: Paperback
Editor: Piers R. Tainsh
Publisher: Anglo-Chinese Publications
17 Belmont, Lansdown Rd.
Bath
Avon BA 15 DZ, United Kingdom
Tel: (44)(225)331-118
Fax: (44)(225)330-5441
Pages: Varies
Exhibits: None

This is a one-of-a-kind directory of media that carry advertising in the PRC. This large-format paperback classifies media by province. In each section, media are divided into newspapers, magazines, television, and radio. Each entry notes media coverage, audience, language, rates, frequency, material required (e.g., cassettes), and contact information. This directory is highly recommended to advertisers.

COMPANY DIRECTORIES

Title: *The China Phonebook and Business Directory*
Date: Semiannual
Format: Paperback
Publisher: China Phone Book Company, Ltd.
24th Floor, Citicorp Centre
18 Whitfield Rd.
Hong Kong
Tel: (852)832-8300
Fax: (852)503-1526
Pages: Varies
Exhibits: None
Price: HK$425

This indispensable phonebook is divided into provinces and cities. Under each city heading is a list of categories—such as hotels, light industry, and education—with phone numbers, all of which are essential to the businessperson. This directory includes names of organizations in Chinese and English. It does not list residence or township phone numbers, but it does include company fax numbers.

Title: *Guidebook for Chinese Foreign Economic and Trade Institutions*
Date: 1992
Format: Hardcover
Editor: Department of Policy Research and System Reform
Ministry of Foreign Economic Relations and Trade
Publisher: Ta Kung Pao (HK), Ltd.
342 Hennessy Rd.
Hong Kong
Tel: (5)573-7213
Fax: (5)572-2814
Pages: 458
Exhibits: None

This recently published directory lists key contacts for PRC government organizations, foreign trade representatives, trade promotion bodies, chambers, trade corporations, and manufacturers. The book is divided roughly along these lines with additional sections on the Bank of China, tax bureaus, customs, and so on. Each entry includes telephone and fax numbers, the number of employees, and the amount of capital.

Title: *A Guide to China's Trade and Investment Organizations*
Date: 1989
Format: Hardcover
Author: China Business Forum
Publisher: The U.S.-China Business Council
1818 N St., NW, Suite 500
Washington, DC 20036
Tel: (202)429-0340
Fax: (202)775-2476
Pages: 180
Exhibits: Graphs

Most of this book is devoted to providing a list of general business organizations, key trade organizations, and key investment organizations, all of which are still up-to-date for the most part. An overview of trade decentralization and investment patterns is given, but much of this information is now outdated.

Title: *Register of Chinese Business*
Date: Annual
Format: Hardcover
Publisher: 3W International Digital Publishing Corp.
300 Atrium Way, Suite 252
Mt. Laurel, NJ 08054
Tel: (609)273-9588
Fax: (609)231-0518
Pages: 1,326
Exhibits: None

This monumental directory lists more than 30,000 Chinese companies and 1,500 foreign business agents with offices in China. The information is divided into industry area, such as textiles and garments, engineering and management services, and so on. Each listing includes telephone and cable numbers, name of president, owner (usually listed as "State"), assets in renminbi, number of employees, sales, import/export status, and product lines. This master directory is, as of this writing, one-of-a-kind.

Title: *Trade Contacts in China: A Directory of Import and Export Corporations*
Date: 1987
Format: Hardcover
Publisher: Kogan Page, Ltd.
Gale Research Co.
835 Penobscot Building
Detroit, MI 48226-4094
Tel: (313)961-2242
Fax: (313)961-6083
Pages: 357
Exhibits: None

Though now rather incomplete due to the recent expansion of China's business scene, this directory contains trading corporations throughout China and is perhaps the only list of its type. Of particular use are the text descriptions of the firms, which include an overview of their specific activities.

Title: *U.S.-China Business Services Directory*
Date: Annual
Format: Hardcover
Publisher: U.S.-China Business Council

1818 N St., NW, Suite 500
Washington, DC 20036
Tel: (202)429-0340
Fax: (202)775-2476

Pages: 105

Exhibits: None

This directory is intended for companies seeking China-related business services, including accounting, advertising, consulting, insurance, market research, and shipping services. Each entry provides the company name, address, contact, and services offered.

COUNTRY PROFILES

Title: *China Newsletter*

Date: Bimonthly

Format: Periodical

Editor: Tomozo Morino

Publisher: Japan External Trade Organization (JETRO)
2-5, Toranomon 2-chome
Minato-ku
Tokyo 105, Japan
Tel: (81)(3)3582-5184
Fax: (81)(3)3582-7508

Pages: Varies

Exhibits: Tables

Price: $120/year

A subscription to this 20- to 30-page newsletter, published by a Japanese government agency, is money well spent. Each issue includes 4 to 6 long articles by experts covering China's trade and investment climate, economy, managerial reforms, financial sector, joint ventures, and industry. The writing is well researched without being overly theoretical. Businesspeople involved with China at any level will find this reader crucial to their understanding of China's modernization and commercial imperatives.

Title: *China Report*

Date: Quarterly

Format: Periodical

Author: Centre for the Study of Developing Studies

Editor: Manoranjan Mohanty

Publisher: Sage Publications India
32 M-Block
Greater Kailash 1
New Delhi 110048, India
Tel: (91)(11)641-984
Fax: (91)(11)644-4958

Pages: Varies

Exhibits: None

Price: $32/year for individuals; $62/year for institutions

This small-format journal includes 4 to 6 academic articles, written mainly by Indian authors, on political and economic issues, plus commentary and book reviews. One of many sources on these subjects, this journal contains articles that are useful to businesspeople only intermittently.

Title: *Country Forecast—China*

Date: Quarterly

Format: Periodical; also available on-line

Publisher: Economist Intelligence Unit
40 Duke St.
London W1A 1DW, United Kingdom
Tel: (44)(71)493-6711
Fax: (44)(71)499-9767

For on-line version, contact:
Maid Systems, Ltd.
Maid House
18 Dufferin St.
London ECIY 8PD, United Kingdom
Tel: (44)(71)253-6900

Pages: Varies
Exhibits: None
Price: £160/year

This 10- to 15-page quarterly booklet provides an overview of China's current political scene, an economic forecast, and a snapshot of developments in the country's business environment. It's expensive, but for the executive decision maker with little chance to read widely on China, this is a recommended updater and forecaster. It includes fact sheets and summaries of forecast data for the next five years.

Title: *Information China*
Date: 1989
Format: Hardcover
Author: Chinese Academy of Social Sciences
Editor: C.V. James
Publisher: Pergamon Press
Headington Hill Hall
Oxford OX3 OBW, United Kingdom
Tel: (44)(685)794-141
Fax: (44)(685)60285
Pages: 1,571 (3 vols.)
Exhibits: Photographs and tables

Well-written, well-organized, and well-illustrated, this encyclopedia of China includes selections on land and people, sociopolitical structure, history, economy, armed forces, health, media, technology, and so on. This is a gorgeous tabletop set for the Sinophile and a perfect business gift.

Title: *The Journal of Contemporary China*
Date: Semiannual
Format: Periodical
Editor: Suisheng Zhao
Publisher: Center for Modern China
P.O. Box AK
Princeton, NJ 08540
Tel: (609)497-1294
Pages: Varies
Exhibits: None
Price: $32/year for individuals; $50/year for institutions

A small-format collection of research articles and book reviews, this journal is a source of theoretical analysis of China's economy, political scene, legal atmosphere, international relations, social climate—in short, its focus is wide. An occasional piece on enterprise reform or foreign investment might interest expatriate managers. This journal is for the serious researcher only.

DICTIONARIES AND LANGUAGE STUDIES

Title: *Chinese Calligraphy*
Date: 1986
Format: Hardcover
Author: Edoardo Fazziole
Publisher: Abbeville Press

23rd and 24th Floors
488 Madison Ave.
New York, NY
Tel: (212)888-1969
Fax: (212)644-5085

Pages: 251

Exhibits: Diagrams and Chinese characters

This is a beautifully published book of Chinese characters, with notes on their derivation. It is useful to those learning to read *kanji*.

Title: *Concise English-Chinese/Chinese-English Dictionary*

Date: 1986

Format: Paperback

Author: A.P. Cowie and A. Evison

Publisher: Oxford University Press
18th Floor, Warwick House
Taikoo Trading Estate, 28
Tong Chong St.
Quarry Bay, Hong Kong
Tel: (852)561-0221

Pages: 599

Exhibits: Chinese characters

Here is one of the very few pocket-size two-way English-Chinese dictionaries. It includes pinyin pronunciation and idiomatic bilingual examples and is essential for business travelers to places where Mandarin is spoken.

Title: *A Dictionary of Chinese Idioms*

Date: 1982

Format: Paperback

Publisher: Alharamain Pte., Ltd.
710, Tan Boon Liat
Building
Outram Rd.
Singapore, 0316

Pages: 583

Exhibits: Chinese characters

This one's a keeper. It's a fascinating collection of Chinese idioms used in speech and in writing. Each phrase is provided in Chinese characters along with its pinyin romanization. "To mount the dragon and cleave to the phoenix"—venture to guess what this Chinese idiom means? In this dictionary, which is perhaps more interesting than useful, you will find that it is a description "of a dependent who follows an official in order to get an appointment and to acquire wealth."

Title: *A Dictionary of Chinese Symbols*

Date: 1983

Format: Paperback

Author: Wolfram Eberhard

Publisher: Routledge/Methuer, Inc.
29 W. 35th St.
New York, NY 10001
Tel: (212)244-3336
Fax: (212)563-2269

Pages: 332

Exhibits: Drawings

Here is a compendium of Buddhist and Confucian symbols used in Chinese art, religion, and literature. This is a recommended reference source for the serious cross-cultural researcher, and a source of entertainment for the general reader.

Title: *An Everyday Chinese-English Dictionary*
Date: 1984
Format: Hardcover
Publisher: Joint Publishing Co.
9 Queen Victoria St.
Hong Kong
Tel: (852)523-0105
Fax: (852)5810-4201
Pages: 881
Exhibits: Chinese characters

A hand-sized pocket dictionary, this index of Chinese radicals contains 3,800 single-character entries and 190,000 compound-character entries in common usage. The definitions are clear and brief, and the dictionary is of equal use to Chinese speakers who want to learn English as it is for English speakers who want to learn Chinese. Note, however, that this is not an English-to-Chinese dictionary. It includes a conversion table for complex and simplified forms of Chinese characters, units of weights and measures, and a table of chemical elements. Pinyin pronunciation of each radical is also given.

Title: *Fun with Chinese Characters*
Date: 1983
Format: Paperback
Author: Straits Times Collection
Publisher: Federal Publications Pte., Ltd.
Unit 903-905, Tower B
Hunghom Commercial Centre
37 Ma Tau Wai Rd.
Kowloon, China
Tel: (852)334-2421
Pages: 145
Exhibits: Cartoons

This is an enjoyable primer (part of a series of books) for those who wish to learn to recognize Chinese characters.

ECONOMY

Title: *China Economic News*
Date: Weekly
Format: Periodical
Author: Economic Daily, Beijing
Publisher: EIA Information and Consultancy, Ltd.
12th Floor, 342 Hennessy Rd.
Hong Kong
Tel: (852)573-8217
Fax: (852)833-6889
Pages: Varies
Exhibits: Tables
Price: $390/year

A handsome 20-page bilingual newsletter, this publication runs short articles on economic and industry news from China. Industry specialists and serious China investors will find the detailed and tightly focused articles useful. Recent titles include "Shanghai Company Issues Shares in Hong Kong" and "Hainan Offers Transportation Projects to Investors." This newsletter also includes interviews with Chinese officials, statistics, and news briefs. It is a rich source that warrants its high price.

Title: *China: The Next Economic Superpower*
Date: 1993

Format: Hardcover
Author: William H. Overholt
Publisher: Weidenfield & Nicolson
The Orion Publishing Group
Orion House
5 Upper St. Martins Lane
London WC2H 9EA, United Kingdom
Tel: (71)240-3444
Fax: (71)240-4822
Pages: 293
Exhibits: Charts and maps
Price: $27

Meant for anyone wishing to understand the hows and whys of China's economic takeoff, this upbeat and readable account by an experienced and respected China hand provides perhaps the best introduction to China's economic transition available. Illustrated with numerous charts depicting China's rising socialist market economy, the book includes a chapter on the transition of Hong Kong from British to PRC control, China's emerging financial markets, and much commentary on what the West's political approach to China should be to further both business interests and democracy there.

Title: *Chinese Economic Studies*
Date: Bimonthly
Format: Journal
Publisher: M.E. Sharpe, Inc.
80 Business Dr.
Armonk, NY 10504
Tel: (914)273-1800
Fax: (914)273-2106
Pages: Varies
Exhibits: Graphs and tables
Price: $429/year

This small-format journal carries translations of articles published in Chinese scholarly journals and books. Most articles are taken from Chinese economic and management sources, and thus this is a recommended source for managers working in China who do not read Chinese. It provides selected articles on China's modernization reforms and attempts to transform state enterprises.

Title: *China's Latest Economic Statistics*
Date: Monthly
Format: Periodical
Author: CERD Consultants, Ltd.
Editor: Zhongguo Tongji Xinxibao
Publisher: China's Statistics Information Consultancy Service Center
20th Floor, On Loong Commercial Building
276-278 Lockhart Rd.
Wanchai, Hong Kong
Tel: (852)511-6823
Fax: (852)598-4430
Pages: Varies
Exhibits: Tables
Price: Contact for subscription prices

For analysts, investors, and business strategists, this monthly set of 50 pages of economic statistics will keep you up-to-date on China's quixotic economy. It includes figures on growth, major industrial products, transportation, sales, investment, trade, and major commodities. Clearly presented tables make this data source the best of its kind.

Title: *Economic Reform in China: Problems and Prospects*
Date: 1990
Format: Hardcover
Editor: James A. Dorn and Wang Xi
Publisher: Cato Institute and University of Chicago Press
5801 Ellis Ave.
Chicago, IL 60637
Tel: (312)702-7700
Fax: (312)702-9556
Pages: 383
Exhibits: Tables

With China's economy in rapid transition, the best sources of information are usually compilations of articles presented at conferences by experts, like this volume. Though these pieces were written around the time of the Tiananmen uprising, they are not overly dated. Topics include all aspects of China's reform program: privatization, pricing, science and technology, credit, Hong Kong policy, property rights, and more. This is a recommended reader.

Title: *Economic Theories in China, 1979–1988*
Date: 1988
Format: Hardcover
Author: Robert C. Hsu
Publisher: Cambridge University Press
40 W. 20th St.
New York, NY 10011
Tel: (212)924-3900
Fax: (212)691-3293
Pages: 198
Exhibits: None

This overview of China's enterprise system is recommended to business managers heading for the PRC. In clear scholarly style, the author covers commodities, ownership issues, development of the economy, prices, and wages. Few other books describe in plain language China's economic system and how state enterprises function (or attempt to) within it. The author provides the Chinese names of important concepts and adds his own Chinese perspective.

ETIQUETTE AND PROTOCOL

Title: *Chinese Etiquette and Ethics in Business*
Date: 1989
Format: Paperback
Author: Boye De Mente
Publisher: NTC Business Books
4255 W. Touhy Ave.
Lincolnwood, IL 60646-1975
Tel: (708)679-5500
Fax: (708)679-2494
Pages: 251
Exhibits: Maps

The businessperson might find a few protocol tips in this book, but the material is somewhat dated and poorly organized.

Title: *Coping with China*
Date: 1991
Format: Paperback
Author: Richard King and Sandra Schatzky
Publisher: Basil Blackwell, Ltd.

108 Cowley Rd.
Oxford OX4 1JF, United Kingdom
Tel: (44)(1)404-4101

Pages: 174

Exhibits: None

As an etiquette primer for visitors to China, this slim volume offers the basics in a light and entertaining style (like other books in the series). The topics covered include getting around, money, cuisine, shopping, beliefs, officialdom, language, and holidays. The business section is scant, but the book is a useful companion for travelers.

Title: *Dealing with the Chinese*

Date: 1993

Format: Paperback

Author: Scott D. Seligman

Publisher: Warner Books
1271 Avenue of the Americas
New York, NY 10020
Tel: (212)522-7200
Fax: (212)522-7991

Pages: 350

Exhibits: Tables

This is the most current, accurate, and complete guide available on etiquette and general business protocol in the People's Republic of China. In crisp, briefly drawn chapters, the author provides essential advice about dining, gift giving, hosting, meeting etiquette, and negotiation style. It is a good primer.

GENERAL BUSINESS

Title: *Business P.R.C.*

Date: Bimonthly

Format: Periodical

Publisher: Enterprise International
1604 Eastern Commercial Centre
393-407 Hennessy Rd.
Hong Kong
Tel: (852)573-4161
Fax: (852)838-3469

Pages: Varies

Exhibits: None

Price: $45/year

This colorful, glossy magazine carries short articles covering regional developments in Chinese production, design, and trade, yet its real purpose is to run advertisements of Chinese-made products. Thus, this source is of interest to buyers of light industrial products from China.

Title: *Business Strategies for the People's Republic of China*

Date: 1986

Format: Hardcover

Author: Michael J. Moser

Publisher: Longman Group (Far East), Ltd.
18th Floor, Cornwall House
Tong Chong St.
Quarry Bay, Hong Kong
Tel: (852)811-8168
Fax: (852)565-7440

Pages: 67

Exhibits: None

Rapidly becoming dated, this slim how-to guide provides advice on how to set up a business in China, transfer technology, deal with taxes, set up a joint venture, and more. If nothing similar is available, this book will provide an introduction.

Title: *China Business Guide*
Date: 1986
Format: Paperback
Author: Arthur Andersen and Co.
Publisher: Longman Group (Far East), Ltd.
Address: 18th Floor, Cornwall House
Tong Chong St.
Quarry Bay, Hong Kong
Tel: (852)811-8168
Fax: (852)565-7440
Pages: 233
Exhibits: None

Some of the general information in this book describing the legal climate for business is still up-to-date, including the useful sections on political structure, the economy, business forms allowed, business registration, exchange control, and taxation. If used along with more current sources, this is a useful reference because it contains many laws in complete translation.

Title: *China Business Review*
Date: Bimonthly
Format: Periodical
Editor: Pamela Baldinger
Publisher: China Business Forum
1818 N St. NW, Suite 500
Washington, DC 20036-5559
Tel: (202)775-0340
Fax: (202)775-2476
Pages: Varies
Exhibits: Graphs and tables
Price: $96/year

This bimonthly has downgraded its high-gloss look of the past but still maintains its position as the best all-around source of readable articles on Chinese trade, investment, and economic reform. Each issue normally runs a number of articles focusing on a single business topic, such as telecommunications or energy. With its list of recently signed contracts and book reviews, this periodical is highly recommended as a business source, especially for American marketers and investors.

Title: *China Business Strategies: A Survey of Foreign Business Activity in the P.R.C.*
Date: 1988
Format: Hardcover
Author: Nigel Campbell and Peter Adlington
Publisher: Pergamon Press
660 White Plains Rd.
Tarrytown, NY 10591-5153
Tel: (914)524-9200
Fax: (914)333-2444
Pages: 252
Exhibits: Graphs and tables

Based on extensive surveys of foreign companies in China, this book provides a fascinating glimpse of Japanese, American, and European companies' strategies for profiting in the China market via investment, usually in equity joint ventures. When it first appeared, this book had the added advantage of being current. What it now lacks in relevancy to present-day opportunities in China it makes up for in its unique use of the corporate surveys on which the authors base their advice. It is highly recommended to prospective investors.

Title: *The China Investment Guide*
Date: 1989
Format: Hardcover
Author: China International Economic Consultants
Publisher: Longman Group (Far East), Ltd.
18th Floor, Cornwall House
Tong Chong St.
Quarry Bay, Hong Kong
Tel: (852)811-8168
Fax: (852)565-7440
Pages: 962
Exhibits: Tables

If you're looking for a comprehensive fact book covering foreign capital entering the People's Republic, this is the pick of the litter. It's a massive tome of information, all readable and quite usable for reports, business presentations, business proposals, and market studies. The information is divided into seven sections: political and economic systems, economic survey data, profiles of China's regions, government organizations, foreign investment policies, taxation, and investment laws and regulations. The book's board of advisers reads like a who's who of China, so the book can be said to be authoritative, at least as of 1989. It's not one to curl up with in bed, but as an office reference it packs huge value.

Title: *China's Foreign Trade*
Date: Monthly
Format: Periodcal
Editor: Li Xinyi
Publisher: China's Foreign Trade
1 Fu Ming Xen Wai St.
Beijing, China
Tel: (86)(1)851-3344
Fax: (86)(1)851-1370
Pages: Varies
Exhibits: Tables
Price: $30/year

For the price, this is a good source of trade climate information published in Beijing. It includes 40 to 50 pages of articles on trade promotion, the investment environment, feature development zones of China, selected export commodities, trade law, and statistics. Though the publishing quality is mediocre and the reading is slow going, this source is useful to Western buyers, sellers, and, to a lesser degree, investors.

Title: *China Trade*
Date: Monthly
Format: Periodical
Editor: Bryan Batson
Publisher: Greater China Business Network, Inc.
800 Boylston
Boston, MA 02199
Tel: (617)424-2489
Fax: (617)424-3208
Pages: Varies
Exhibits: Graphs and tables
Price: $225/year

This 7- to 10-page newsletter focuses on business strategies for Hong Kong, Taiwan, and the PRC. Each issue tackles a selected topic, such as risk management strategies for guarding against software piracy in greater China. It includes a summary of commercial news and a market overview. This is a brief but possibly useful newsletter for the marketer who also consults more comprehensive sources on each country of greater China.

Title: *China Trade Handbook*
Date: 1984
Format: Paperback
Editor: Lawrence Fung
Publisher: The Adsale People/Facts on File
460 Park Ave. South
New York, NY 10016
Tel: (212)683-2244
Fax: (212)213-4578
Pages: 329
Exhibits: Tables

Now rather dated, this large-format paperback provides an overview of China's trading environment, trade organizations, buying and selling procedures, and investment climate. It contains a list of ministries and key import/export corporations.

Title: *China Trade Report*
Date: Monthly
Format: Periodical
Editor: L. Gordon Crovitz
Publisher: Far Eastern Economic Review
G.P.O. Box 160
Hong Kong
Tel: (852)508-4300
Fax: (852)503-1549
Pages: Varies
Exhibits: Tables
Price: $375/year

Published by the Far Eastern Economic Review, this attractive 15- to 20-page newsletter is a great one-stop source of news and updates concerning China's trade and investment environment. Articles are brief and informative, the graphics and photographs well rendered, and the writing style crisp and engaging. It lists major contracts signed, economic indicators, and a table of major items traded between China and other countries via Hong Kong. Although overpriced, this periodical is certainly recommended to managers and executives in need of a monthly update.

Title: *Chinese Negotiating Style: Commercial Approaches and Cultural Principles*
Date: 1992
Format: Hardcover
Author: Lucian W. Pye
Publisher: Quorum Books
Box 5007, 88 Post Rd. W.
Westport, CT 06881
Tel: (203)226-3541
Fax: (203)222-1502
Pages: 120
Exhibits: None

Required reading for the Asia negotiator, this is a revised edition of the author's 1982 classic treatise on Chinese negotiating behavior. Chapter topics include sources of negotiation difficultics, the venue of China bargaining, opening moves, an exploration of each step in the bargaining process, negotiating style, and principles to follow when dealing with the Chinese.

Title: *Doing Business in Asia's Booming "China Triangle"*
Date: 1994
Format: Hardcover
Author: Christopher Engholm
Publisher: Prentice Hall
15 Columbus Circle
Western Plaza
New York, NY 10023
Tel: (212)373-8000
Fax: (212)678-7007
Pages: 350
Exhibits: Graphs, tables, and maps

For the trader or investor in "Greater China," including China, Taiwan, and Hong Kong, this practical guide is part of the publisher's Emerging World Market Series. The book's four sections cover country characteristics, selling to the region, investing in mainland China, and etiquette and communication issues in dealing with the Chinese. Written in a handy question-and-answer format, this guidebook offers the interested seller or investor a readable manual for getting started and avoiding pitfalls.

Title: *Doing Business in China*
Date: 1988
Format: Hardcover
Publisher: Ernst & Whinney
1501 Hutchinson House
Hong Kong
Tel: (852)526-5371
Fax: (852)529-7344
Pages: Varies
Exhibits: Graphs and tables

Concentrating on China's tax system, this publication provides coverage of taxation policies as they affect joint ventures, wholly foreign-owned enterprises, and individuals. The coverage is brief, but the book is a useful overview for prospective investors and accountants.

Title: *Doing Business in the People's Republic of China*
Date: 1990
Format: Hardcover
Publisher: Price Waterhouse
China World Tower, Suite 2921
China World Trade Centre
1 Jian Guo Men Wai Ave.
Beijing 100004, People's Republic of China
Tel: (86)(1)505-1524
Pages: 205
Exhibits: None

Like the other guides in this series, this book provides an overview of taxation issues that are relevant to businesspeople working in the PRC. It also includes sections on the business environment, trade opportunities, investment incentives, restrictions on investment, and the regulatory environment. It offers a complete review of the tax system and how it affects businesses and individuals and is useful to prospective investors and accountants.

Title: *The Foreign Experts' Handbook: A Guide to Living and Working in China*
Date: 1988
Editor: Chen Baochen
Format: Hardcover
Author: State Bureau of Foreign Experts, PRC

Publisher: New World Press
Contact: China International Book Trading Corp. (Guoji Shudian)
P.O. Box 399
Beijing 100621, People's Republic of China

Pages: 313

Exhibits: Maps, photographs, and tables

Price: $4.95

Published by the Chinese government, this book contains the laws and regulations applicable to expatriates moving to China. It contains now rather dated information on salaries and living conditions in China for foreign workers, application procedures, living and working tips, and other logistical advice for those who accept a China post.

HISTORY AND SOCIETY

Title: *All the Colours of the Rainbow*

Date: 1983

Format: Paperback

Author: Jiang Zilong

Publisher: Chinese Literature
25 Baiwanzhuang Rd.
Beijing 100037, China
Tel: (86)(1)832-6678
Fax: (86)(1)222-457

Pages: 267

Exhibits: None

This is a wonderful collection of biographical sketches of representative individuals of modern Chinese society. It is useful to anyone working with the Chinese.

Title: *The Art of War*

Date: 1988

Format: Paperback

Author: Sun Tzu (trans. Thomas Cleary)

Publisher: Shambhala Publications, Inc.
Horticultural Hall
300 Massachusetts Ave.
Boston, MA 02115
Tel: (617)424-0030
Fax: (617)236-1563

Pages: 174

Exhibits: None

This is perhaps the most readable translation of the classic book of Asian war strategies. It features an informative introduction to the historical setting in which Sun Tzu wrote his influential manual of war tactics. This book is highly recommended to negotiators in Asia whose counterparts continue to study these subtle but effective ploys for use in the business setting.

Title: *China: An Introduction*

Date: 1978

Format: Hardcover

Author: Lucian Pye

Publisher: Little, Brown and Co.
34 Beacon St.
Boston, MA 02108
Tel: (617)227-0730
Fax: (617)227-4633

Pages: 383

Exhibits: Map and tables

As is the case with all of Lucian Pye's works, this introduction to China is readable and enduring. For businesspeople, it represents a baptism: a thorough enlightenment about things Chinese. Topics include Confucianism, China's reaction to the West, warlordism, the Kuomintang nationalists, the rise of Communism, Mao, the Cultural Revolution, and China's international relations. It is highly recommended as a first book about Chinese history and society.

Title: *The Chinese Heritage*
Date: 1982
Format: Hardcover
Author: K.C. Wu
Publisher: Crown Books
201 E. 50th St.
New York, NY 10022
Tel: (212)572-6117
Fax: (212)572-6192
Pages: 496
Exhibits: Charts, diagrams, and tables
Price: $22.50

This is a not-so-easy-to-read tome that finds the origin of Chinese values in the distant dynasties of the past. Those who seriously wish to deepen their understanding of China's cultural heritage should make the effort to study this impressive book. Study is needed to assimilate its many insights into China's darkest antiquity, but it's worth the effort. The author defines distinctive features of Chinese culture and explores how they took root in the first 1,500 years of Chinese civilization, ending with the close of the Shang Dynasty in 1050 B.C. These cultural distinctions remain largely intact today.

Title: *Chinese Thought and Institutions*
Date: 1957
Format: Hardcover
Editor: John K. Fairbank
Publisher: University of Chicago Press
5801 Ellis Ave.
Chicago, IL 60637
Tel: (312)702-7700
Fax: (312)702-9756
Pages: 438
Exhibits: Diagrams, maps, and tables

This weighty textbook explains Chinese bureaucratic decision making in terms of Chinese philosophy. It is recommended to businesspeople who want to understand the world's oldest bureaucracy by looking at its deepest roots.

Title: *City of Lingering Splendour: A Frank Account of Old Peking's Exotic Pleasures*
Date: 1989
Format: Hardcover
Author: John Blofeld
Publisher: Shambhala Publications, Inc.
Horticultural Hall
300 Massachusetts Ave.
Boston, MA 02115
Tel: (617)424-0030
Fax: (617)236-1563
Pages: 255
Exhibits: None

A lyrically written account of one man's experience in Peking during the early 1940s, that is, before the Communists took control in 1949 and wiped out the "exotic pleasures" this book describes. It is of interest as an engrossing account of being an expatriate in China and of how some aspects of living and working in the Orient haven't changed in half a century.

Title: *The Contemporary Atlas of China*
Date: 1988
Format: Hardcover
Author: Marshall Editions, Ltd.
Publisher: Houghton Mifflin Co.
2 Park St.
Boston, MA 02108
Tel: (617)725-5000
Fax: (617)227-5409
Pages: 199
Exhibits: Drawings, maps, graphs, and photographs

This attractive, medium-size atlas is divided into sections: regions, history, society, culture, and China today. The majority of the maps appear in the first section. Well-illustrated and highly informative text makes up the other sections. This is a sourcebook of information about Chinese culture, land, and society; it is not the best source of detailed maps of the country.

Title: *The Great Chinese Revolution: 1800–1985*
Date: 1986
Format: Hardcover
Author: John K. Fairbank
Publisher: Harper & Row
10 E. 53rd St.
New York, NY 10022
Tel: (212)207-7000
Fax: (212)207-7617
Pages: 396
Exhibits: Maps

In this history of "the Chinese experience in terms that American non-Sinological readers may readily understand," a foremost Sinologist brings to life the span from late Imperial China under Manchu rulers to China under Deng Xiaoping in the mid-1980s. It is recommended with the caveat that the elevated erudition tends to intrude on the readability of the account, especially for the non-Sinophile.

Title: *The Opium War through Chinese Eyes*
Format: Hardcover
Date: 1958
Author: Arthur Waley
Publisher: Stanford University Press
Ventura Hall
Stanford, CA 94305-4115
Tel: (415)723-1712
Fax: (415)723-0758
Pages: 256
Exhibits: None

This is a splendid and engrossing story of events leading to the outbreak of the Opium War between China and Great Britain. It sheds light on both submerged and openly expressed attitudes toward foreigners.

Title: *The Search for Modern China*
Date: 1990
Format: Hardcover
Author: Jonathan D. Spence
Publisher: W.W. Norton & Co.

500 Fifth Ave.
New York, NY 10110
Tel: (212)354-5500
Fax: (212)869-0856

Pages: 876

Exhibits: Maps, photographs, and tables

This monumental achievement in research and erudition should not be missed by those endeavoring to deal with China on a long-term basis. This is historical narrative at its best—informative, fresh, exciting, engaging, dramatic, and wise. Spence has produced many fine histories about China; only this one is included in this bibliography for businesspeople because it covers the period from the Late Ming in the sixteenth century to the Tiananmen uprising. If you were to read only one lengthy history of China, this should be the one. It is well illustrated with maps, color and black-and-white photographs, and tables, and it contains a handy glossary of terms and names.

Title: *Seeds of Fire: Chinese Voices of Conscience*

Date: 1988

Format: Hardcover

Author: Geremie Barme and John Minford

Publisher: Hill & Wang
19 Union Square West
New York, NY 10003
Tel: (212)741-6900
Fax: (212)663-9385

Pages: 491

Exhibits: Drawings

An anthology of dissident writings from China, this attractive volume predated the popular uprising in China in 1989. The book includes many influential articles by well-known Chinese writers and will interest political analysts and anyone interested in understanding the roots of modern political dissidence in the People's Republic.

Title: *Stilwell and the American Experience in China, 1911–1945*

Date: 1970

Format: Hardcover

Author: Barbara W. Tuchman

Publisher: Bantam Books
666 5th Ave.
New York, NY 10103
Tel: (212)765-6500
Fax: (212)765-3869

Pages: 621

Exhibits: Photographs

This highly readable historical narrative of General Stilwell's dealings with Chiang Kai-shek underscores some Chinese negotiating tactics that are still practiced today.

Title: *The Way to Chinese Astrology: The Four Pillars of Destiny*

Date: 1983

Format: Hardcover

Author: Jean-Michel Huon De Kermadec

Publisher: Unwin Paperbacks
11 Newfetter Lane
London EC4 P4EE, United Kingdom
Tel: (44)(71)583-9855
Fax: (44)(71)583-0701

Pages: 143
Exhibits: Diagrams and tables

A rather esoteric introduction to Chinese astrology, this book contains a concise explanation of Taoist concepts and Confucianism. It is perfect for readers who seek a colorful and concise overview of Chinese divinatory practices from ancient times.

INDUSTRY

Title: *China Informatics*
Date: Weekly
Format: Periodical
Editor: Hilary McKown
Publisher: International Data Corporation/China Hong Kong, Ltd.
12th Floor, Seabird House
22-28 Wyndham St.
Hong Kong
Pages: Varies
Exhibits: None
Price: $595/year

This 10-page newsletter covers developments in China's computer industries, focusing on significant Sino-foreign deals and developments at China's leading computer enterprises. It also includes tables of information technology imports to China. It is recommended to the Western marketer of these products.

Title: *Land, Property and Construction in the People's Republic of China*
Date: 1991
Format: Paperback
Author: Anthony Walker
Publisher: Hong Kong University Press
University of Hong Kong
139 Pokfulam Rd.
Hong Kong
Tel: (852)550-2703
Fax: (852)875-0374
Pages: 140
Exhibits: Tables

Part of China's reform has been to adjust the land-tenure system to allow for the modernization of the country's construction industry. By a professor of surveying, this clearly written book covers China's land and propety sector and its construction industry as it has evolved since the open-door policy began. For investors in joint ventures, real estate investors, builders, or land developers in the PRC, this is a one-of-a-kind monograph.

INFORMATION SOURCES

Title: *China Daily Index*
Date: Bimonthly
Format: Periodical
Editors: Chen, Hui and Paul Ivory
Publisher: China Daily/Griffith University Library
China Daily Index Project
University Library
Griffith University
Nathan, Queensland 4111, Australia
Pages: Varies
Exhibits: None

With the exception of stock data, weather, and entertainment information, this index lists all articles published in China Daily and its supplements: Beijing Weekend, Business Weekly, and Shanghai Focus. The articles are listed by subject and/or proper name. Headlines are used in brief descriptions of articles for easy identification of content. Your problem will be finding a library that keeps its *China Daily* newspapers or has the paper on microfiche, which is available from the publisher for $90 per year.

Title: *China Telex & Fax Directory*

Date: Annual

Format: Paperback

Publisher: China Phone Book Co., Ltd.
10th Floor, 1001 Connaught Commercial Building
185 Wandrai Road
Hong Kong
Tel: (852)834-8133
Fax: (852)838-7753

Pages: 313

Exhibits: None

Price: $32

Highly useful to anyone dealing with counterparts in China, this phonebook lists fax and telex numbers for PRC companies and government organizations. Numbers are listed alphabetically, geographically, numerically, and by alphabetically listed telex answer-back code.

Title: *Chinese Studies in English: A Selected Bibliography of Books*

Date: 1991

Format: Paperback

Author: Tsung Shun Na

Publisher: American Institute of Chinese Studies
Charleston, WV

Pages: 215

Exhibits: None

For the business researchers, this is a well-organized selected bibliography, which makes it especially useful. The business how-to books about China are listed in the section on economics. Other sections include history, philosophy and religion, government and politics, law and military, education, foreign relations, and so on. An author index is provided. Unfortunately, the book does not list contact information for the publisher; your best bet for finding it is a university business library.

Title: *Index to the Foreign Broadcast Information Service—Daily Reports China*

Date: Monthly

Format: Periodical

Editor: Greg Dean

Publisher: Newsbank, Inc.
58 Pine St.
New Canaan, CT 06840-5426
Tel: (802)875-2910

Pages: Varies

Exhibits: None

The Foreign Broadcast Information Service (FBIS) is a U.S. government agency that monitors and translates foreign broadcasts, newspapers, periodicals, and government statements. It publishes this material in its FBIS *Daily Reports*. This index lists the information collected by the FBIS in its China edition, which is published monthly. The materials are indexed by subject, and the emphasis is on political and economic affairs. Most large libraries carry this publication as well as the *Daily Reports*.

INTELLECTUAL PROPERTY

Title: *China's Patents and Trademarks*
Date: Irregular
Format: Periodical
Editor: Ding Guoming
Publisher: China Patent and Trademark Publications Office
22nd Floor, Great Eagle Centre
23 Harbour Rd.
Wanchai, Hong Kong
Tel: (852)828-4631
Fax: (852)827-1018
Pages: Varies
Exhibits: Tables
Price: Contact for subscription prices

For companies patenting products and processes in China, this attractively published 110-page magazine covers patents, trademarks, copyright protection, recent cases, statutes and rules, patent statistics, and new technologies. Published in Chinese and English, it contains clearly written analyses and interpretations of China's patent and trademark laws as they relate to specific products, technologies, and processes. It is highly recommended to lawyers and technology vendors.

Title: *Intellectual Property Law in the People's Republic of China*
Date: 1986
Format: Hardcover
Author: Michael D. Pendleton
Publisher: Butterworth and Co. (Asia) Pte., Ltd.
30 Robinson Rd., #12-01
Tuan Sing Towers
Singapore, 0104
Tel: (65)220-3684
Fax: (65)225-2939
Pages: 134
Exhibits: None

For companies transferring technology to China, this is a recommended primer on laws relevant to intellectual property, trademarks, patents, and copyright. The appendix reprints key laws and regulations concerning these areas.

LAWS AND REGULATIONS

Title: *China Trade Agreements*
Date: 1988
Format: Hardcover
Author: Thomas C.W. Chiu
Publisher: Taylor and Francis
242 Cherry St.
Philadelphia, PA 19106-1906
Tel: (215)785-5800
Pages: 315
Exhibits: None

This is an attractive collection of standard contracts used in China, including letter of intent, protocol for cooperation, joint venture, agency service agreement, processing and assembly, and many others, covering the gamut of Sino-foreign business tie-ups. This is a suggested source for negotiators and lawyers.

Title: *Commercial Disputes Settlement in China*
Date: 1985
Format: Hardcover
Author: Eric Lee
Publisher: Lloyd's of London Press,, Ltd.
26-30 Artillery Lane
London E1 7LX, United Kingdom
Tel: (44)(206)772-277
Fax: (44)(206)46273
Pages: 141
Exhibits: None

This is a recommended, all-too-brief explanation of the perception and practice of dispute arbitration (and relevant legislation) in the PRC. The author is an experienced legal expert who thoroughly understands the cultural backdrop of China's judicial priorities. Chapters cover legal development, commercial dispute settlement, arbitration, and rules of arbitration, and the book reprints laws regarding lawyers and civil procedure.

Title: *Foreign Trade, Investment and the Law in the People's Republic of China*
Date: 1987
Format: Hardcover
Editor: Michael J. Moser
Publisher: Oxford University Press
200 Madison Ave.
New York, NY 10016
Tel: (212)679-7300
Fax: (212)725-2972
Pages: 603
Exhibits: None

This compilation of legal essays written by some of the most well-known lawyers and academics involved with China provides, in the words of its editor, "an introduction to the legal framework governing the conduct of business transactions with the People's Republic of China." Each chapter handles a different aspect of law, such as foreign trade, investment, technology transfer, offshore oil, setting up a representative office, contracts, and banking. This is a praiseworthy reader for lawyers as well as corporate planners and executives.

Title: *Journal of Chinese Law*
Date: Semiannual
Format: Periodical
Editor: R. Randle Edwards
Publisher: Center for Chinese Legal Studies
Columbia University School of Law
562 W. 113th St.
New York, NY 10025
Tel: (212)316-7100
Fax: (212)316-7169
Pages: Varies
Exhibits: None
Price: $25/year

Each issue of this attractive journal contains 3 to 5 articles on China's changing legal environment. Book reviews are not included. This is a suggested source of legal background on China's tax, construction, trade, and civil law. Nonlawyers might find it a useful source of insight into Chinese commercial decision making and business climate.

Title: *Law in the People's Republic of China*
Date: 1989
Format: Hardcover
Editor: Ralph H. Folsom and John H. Minan
Publisher: Martinus Nijhoff Publishers
P.O. Box 163
Dordrecht, 3300 AD, The Netherlands
Tel: (31)(7)684-400
Fax: (31)(7)615-698
Pages: 1,076
Exhibits: None

Meant for lawyers and law students, this compendium of essays about aspects of PRC law also includes a collection of laws and regulations relevant to foreign investment and trade. The essays are divided into sections that deal with evolution of law in China, dispute resolution, the legal profession in China, procedural law, substantive law, and laws applying to Hong Kong and Macao. This is certainly the most comprehensive and attractively published reader on the subject. For those seeking background knowledge in this area, this is a good place to start.

MANAGEMENT

Title: *Guide to Labor Management of Enterprises with Foreign Investment in China*
Date: 1989
Format: Hardcover
Publisher: Ministry of Labor
12 Hepingli Zhongjie
Beijing 100621, People's Republic of China
Tel: (86)(1)421-2454
Pages: 1,307
Exhibits: None

For those seeking a source of laws and regulations relevant to investing in and operating an enterprise in China, this compendium is a comprehensive resource, with Chinese translations included. The documents provided include the law on joint ventures and its amendments, laws concerning the encouragement of foreign investment, and laws related to labor management in foreign-invested joint ventures.

MARKET DATA AND ANALYSIS

Title: *China Statistical Abstract*
Date: Annual
Format: Hardcover
Author: State Statistical Bureau of the People's Republic of China
Publisher: Praeger Publishers
88 Post Rd. West
Westport, CT 06881
Tel: (203)226-3571
Fax: (203)222-1502
Pages: 106
Exhibits: Tables

If you cannot locate the *China Statistical Yearbook* (described in the following entry), this condensed version of some of the same data is a second choice. Selected sections include population and labor force, agriculture, industry, investment, science and technology, trade, and finance.

Title: *China Statistical Yearbook*
Date: Annual
Format: Hardcover
Author: State Statistical Bureau of the People's Republic of China
Editor: Fan Ziqing
Publisher: China Statistical Information and Consultancy Service Center
38 Yuetan Nanjie
Sanlihe
Beijing 100826, People's Republic of China
Tel: (86)(1)851-5074
Fax: (86)(1)851-5078
Pages: 777
Exhibits: Tables

For business researchers of China, this is the government-released compendium of annual economic and production data. It is by far the most authoritative source of PRC numerical data. Sections include natural resources, employment, enterprises, population, wages, investment, public finance, prices, people's livelihood, agriculture, industry, energy, trade, patents, and health care. With each passing year, this volume includes more and even better information.

Title: *A Study of China's Population*
Date: 1992
Format: Paperback
Author: Li Chengrui
Publisher: Foreign Languages Press
24 Baiwanzhuang Rd.
Beijing 100037, People's Republic of China
Tel: (86)(1)832-6641
Fax: (86)(1)832-6642
Pages: 275
Exhibits: Graphs and tables

Written by the official in charge of the Census Office of the State Council, this book first reviews China's three census reports up to 1982 and appriases their reliability. In part two, the author analyzes demographic changes between census reports and provides a preliminary analysis of data collected in the census of 1990. The erudition here is not high, but the data presented are credible.

POLITICS AND GOVERNMENT

Title: *China Briefing*
Date: Annual
Format: Hardcover
Publisher: The Asia Society/Westview Press
5500 Central Ave.
Boulder, CO 80301
Tel: (303)444-3541
Fax: (303)449-3356
Pages: Varies
Exhibits: None

This annual compilation is a forum in which the current crop of China experts presents articles on topics ranging from China's educational system to the country's foreign investment policy. A recommended reader that will keep you up-to-date.

Title: *China's Political System: Modernization and Tradition*
Date: 1993
Format: Paperback
Author: June Teufel Dreyer
Publisher: Paragon House
90 Fifth Ave.
New York, NY 10011
Tel: (212)620-2820
Fax: (212)633-0518
Pages: 448
Exhibits: Diagrams and tables

For those seeking background knowledge about China's current political and economic environment, this readable volume, written by a political scientist, fits the bill. The topics covered include the economy, health and family-planning policies, the future of the military, arts and entertainment in relation to politics, environmental issues, and the status of China's ethnic minorities. A number of historical chapters set the stage. This book is a one-stop historical overview from Mao to now.

Title: *Daily Report—China*
Date: Daily
Format: Periodical
Publisher: Foreign Broadcast Information Service (FBIS)
P.O. Box 2604
Washington, DC 20013
Tel: (202)338-6735
Pages: Varies
Exhibits: Tables
Price: Contact for subscription prices

The FBIS *Daily Report* for China is published Monday through Friday and contains translations and transcriptions of current news and information obtained from Chinese radio and television broadcasts, news agency transmissions, newspapers, books, and periodicals. The items are divided into categories: international affairs, national affairs, regional affairs, Taiwan, and Hong Kong and Macao. The subcategory on the economy will interest businesspeople most, but the *Daily* is a highly recommended source of Chinese-related information in general.

Title: *The Directory of Chinese Government Organs*
Date: 1989–1990
Format: Hardcover
Editor: Jim Mingyuan
Publisher: New China News, Ltd.
5 Sharp St. West
Wanchai, Hong Kong
Tel: (852)5-8313510
Pages: 944
Exhibits: Maps

Divided into two parts, this directory lists ministries, commissions, administrative bodies, and bureaus at the state level. Part two lists government organs in China's 30 provinces, municipalities, and autonomous regions. Each entry gives the main functions of the organization (of which there are thousands) and telephone and cable numbers, address, and key personnel.

Title: *Directory of Chinese Officials and Organizations*
Date: 1991
Format: Paperback

Author: Central Intelligence Agency

Publisher: National Technical Information Service
5285 Port Royal Rd.
Springfield, VA 22161
Tel: (703)487-4650
Fax: (703)487-4009

Pages: 156

Exhibits: None

If you are looking for the name of a Chinese official or the name of his or her organization, this book is the place to look. Broken down by government body, sections focus on the Communist Party Central Committee, National People's Congress, judicial system, ministries, commissions, bureaus, and so on, down to the provincial level. The book lists name, title, and department of officials only.

Title: *Mao and China: Inside China's Cultural Revolution*

Date: 1984

Format: Paperback

Author: Stanley Karnow

Publisher: Viking Penguin, Inc.
40 W. 23rd St.
New York, NY 10010
Tel: (212)366-2000
Fax: (212)366-2666

Pages: 592

Exhibits: None

An understanding of Mao Tse-tung and Maoism is essential for businesspeople to gain perspective on where China has been and thus where it is going in the 1990s. This book, by a foremost American journalist, recounts the isolationist chaos of the Cultural Revolution years during the late 1960s, a dark chapter in China's recent national memory but one that Western businesspeople—especially younger ones—should take the time to understand. This is a thoroughly engrossing read.

Title: *Policy-making in China: Leaders, Structures and Processes*

Date: 1988

Format: Hardcover

Author: Kenneth Lieberthal and Michel Oksenberg

Publisher: Princeton University Press
41 William St.
Princeton, NJ 08540
Tel: (609)258-4900
Fax: (609)258-6305

Pages: 445

Exhibits: Diagrams and tables

A classic on the subject of Chinese bureaucratic decision making, this volume is based on a lengthy study of Chinese decision making regarding energy projects, including the exploration of offshore oil, the Three Gorges hydroelectric project, and a large-scale coal project. The study "reveals a fragmented bureaucratic structure of authority, decision making in which consensus building is central, and a policy process that is protracted, disjointed, and incremental." For corporate representatives and anyone working with the Chinese government, this is required, though not necessarily easy, reading. It delivers a detailed explanation of how Chinese government decision making works—or rather, doesn't work.

Title: *Reform and Reaction in Post-Mao China*
Date: 1991
Format: Paperback
Editor: Richard Baum
Publisher: Routledge
29 W. 35th St.
New York, NY 10001
Tel: (212)244-3336
Fax: (212)563-2269
Pages: 209
Exhibits: None

These essays about reform in China first appeared in 1989 in a journal. They have been updated here to include analyses of the forces that led to the Tiananmen massacre in Beijing in mid-1989. The essay authors, well known for their academic work on China, tackle such topics as democratization, urban private business, corruption, technology, and Chinese political change. Although a tad too academic for the business reader, this is a good overview of China's market reforms as of the late 1980s.

Title: *The Spirit of Chinese Politics*
Date: 1992
Format: Paperback
Author: Lucian Pye
Publisher: Harvard University Press
79 Garden St.
Cambridge, MA 02138-1499
Tel: (617)495-2600
Fax: (617)495-5898
Pages: 264
Exhibits: None

In this enduring analysis, a foremost China observer portrays China's political culture as a projection of inherent psychological tendencies in the Chinese personality, such as acceptance of authority, order, hierarchy, and emotional quietism. Originally written in 1968, this new edition contains two post-Tiananmen chapters. Few other sources provide such crystalline insight into Chinese behavior, values, and beliefs, all of which play a role in business relationships in China today. This book is highly recommended.

Title: *Who's Who in the People's Republic of China*
Date: 1991
Format: Hardcover
Author: Wolfgang Bartke
Publisher: K.G. Saur Verlag
Postfach 71 10 09
8000 Munich 71, Germany
Tel: (49)(89)791-040 (Germany)
Tel: (908)665-3576 (U.S.)
Fax: (908)271-7792 (U.S.)
Pages: 899
Exhibits: Photographs

In 1981, the first edition of this large-format who's who contained 2,026 biographies. As its preface states, this new edition of 3,700 biographies contains only 917 of the entries in the first edition "due to deaths, purges, and resignations of the person concerned." About one-half of the biographies are accompanied by portraits, and each entry lists posts held, including dates. This source for political analysts includes noteworthy scientists and dissidents.

RESEARCH AND DEVELOPMENT

Title: *China's Four Modernizations: The New Technological Revolution*
Date: 1980
Format: Hardcover
Editor: Richard Baum
Publisher: Westview Press
5500 Central Ave.
Boulder, CO 80301
Tel: (303)444-3541
Fax: (303)449-3356
Pages: 307
Exhibits: Photographs and tables

Though out-of-date now, this collection of essays provides an overview of China's science and technology policies, science institutions, technological goals, and experience assimilation of foreign technology. The authors are some of the best-known experts in the field. The book includes organizational charts of China's science and technology system.

Title: *Directory of Major Chinese Research Centers*
Date: 1991
Format: Hardcover
Author: The editorial staff of General Guide to Chinese Scientific Research and Technology Development Institutions
Publisher: New World Press
24 Baiwanzhuang Rd.
Beijing 100037, China
Distributed by: China International Book Trading Corp.
35 Chegongzhuan Xilu
P.O. Box 399
Beijing 100044, China
Pages: 925
Exhibits: None

For those interested in research being conducted in the People's Republic, this massive directory provides details about thousands of laboratories and institutes there. The listings are divided into areas of scientific endeaver—such as agricultural sciences, technology, and dynamic engineering—and each entry includes contact information, research tasks, major achievements, and names of directors.

Title: *Technological Change in China*
Date: 1992
Format: Paperback
Author: Richard Conroy
Publisher: Development Centre of the Organization for Economic Co-operation and Development
Head of Publications Service, OECD
2 rue André-Pascal
75775 Paris Cedex 16, France

Distributed by: OECD Publications and Information Centre
2001 L St., NW, Suite 700
Washington, DC 20036-4910
Tel: (202)785-6323
Fax: (202)785-0350

Pages: 276

Exhibits: Charts and tables

For a complete overview of China's science and technology landscape, this is perhaps the most complete source. The clear prose is illustrated with useful tables and is extensively footnoted. The book includes chapters on technology imports to China, the assimilation of foreign technology, and science and technology law in China.

Title: *Technology Transfer to China*

Date: 1987

Format: Hardcover

Author: Office of Technology Assessment, U.S. Congress

Editor: Alan T. Crane

Publisher: U.S. Government Printing Office
Washington, DC 20402-9325
Tel: (202)783-3238

Pages: 245

Exhibits: Graphs, photographs, and tables

Though a bit dated, this is one of the finest (and most readable) U.S. government–sponsored studies of China. The contributors include the core experts in the area of technology transfer to China, and the well-illustrated chapters cover the political, economic, and developmental implications of China's technological modernization. Especially for those who are looking for information concerning U.S. State Department regulations on technological exports to China, this is a great place to start.

TAXATION

Title: *Taxation in the People's Republic of China*

Date: 1991

Format: Hardcover

Author: Jinyan Li

Publisher: Praeger Publishers
88 Post Rd. West
Westport, CT 06881
Tel: (203)226-3571
Fax: (203)222-1502

Pages: 194

Exhibits: None

Meant for international tax lawyers and scholars, this treatise on China's tax system is well organized and clearly written, with chapters covering the evolution of the tax regime, taxation of goods and services, income taxes on individuals, taxes on domestic enterprises, taxes on foreign investment, agricultural tax, local tax, and an evaluation of the current tax system as of 1991. This is a handy overall description.

Korea

OVERVIEW

Korea is a 600-mile-long peninsula the size of Virginia with a restless population of 65 million people. The Korean Peninsula in East Asia is divided at the 38th parallel into the Democratic People's Republic of Korea (DPRK), or North Korea; and the Republic of Korea (ROK), or South Korea. The population is made up almost entirely of ethnic Koreans, 44 million living in the South and 20 million in the North. South Korea's economic "miracle" is the product of hard work, guided industrial policy, and loans from the United States. Education plays a large role in South Korea's development as well; there are more Ph.D.'s in South Korea per capita than anywhere else in the world. As of this writing, dramatic events unfold in North Korea. The death of communist leader Kim Il Sung may result in the country's opening western investment and cultural exchange with South Korea. Sources providing business information about North Korea are virtually nonexistent, though a reflection of policies appear in the pages ahead.

South Korea at a Glance

Population:	43.7 million
Religion:	Buddhist, Protestant, Catholic
Government:	Democratic republic
Language:	Korean
Currency:	Won (W)
Trade (1993):	$71.6 billion total exports; $81.8 billion total imports

The most secure jobs in South Korea are found at companies affiliated with *chaebols* (corporate conglomerates). These firms offer employees lifelong employment and high social standing. However, antipathy toward the *chaebols*, which are family-controlled and highly favored by the government, has fueled labor uprisings in South Korea since the early 1980s. South Korea's manufacturing industry is controlled by as few as 30 *chaebols*.

Economic Conditions

From 1965 to 1990, South Korea was the world's second fastest-growing economy. Korean industry, led by the huge *chaebols*, is perfectly structured to generate rapid growth, which it did up until 1989, when growth dipped from 12 percent to 6.8 percent in real gross national product (GNP) growth. The government reacted in 1989 with a stimulus package that fueled growth rates of 9.3 percent in 1990 and 8.4 percent in 1991, unleashing rampant construction, private consumption, and investment. Inflation increased, and Korea's trade deficit widened to $7 billion in 1991.

Economic austerity measures in 1992 slowed growth to 4 percent in real GNP in 1992. Some applaud the government's success in reducing inflation and the current account deficit, but critics, especially those in private enterprise, claim that stabilization has gone too far and is leading to stagnation. Political pressure on the newly elected government, led by Kim Young-sam, to pursue short-term stimulus of the economy could thwart Korea's long-term effort to develop from an economy dependent on low wages and standardized production to a high-wage, technology-based economy.

With per capita GNP of more than $6,000, the purchasing power of Korea's population of 43 million should not be overlooked by Western marketers. Real wages rose 30 percent between 1988 and 1992. Korea still depends on the United States to purchase 40 percent of its exports, which have soared by 20 to 30 percent each year since 1986. The country has made great strides in liberalizing its market and lowering tariff and nontariff barriers to imports, though protective barriers remain in the financial sector. Observers contend that the country's long-term growth will be threatened if its government cannot push quickly to move financial institutions forward toward market-oriented operation and away from their traditional role as managers of the government's industrial policy. As is the case in Japan, the farming sector in Korea wields immense political power and has successfully lobbied to keep agricultural imports to a minimum.

Korean *chaebols* seem to get bigger, even with the slow proliferation of small and medium-size firms operated by entrepreneurs. This represents a dilemma for Western companies seeking to become involved with Korean industry. Projects or products are either lost in the halls of the mammoth *chaebols* or entrusted to an aggressive (and sometimes not so ethical) Korean agent or partner who lacks the financial power and political clout to make anything happen.

Historical Background

Korea was dubbed *Chosun*, "The Land of Morning Calm," in 2333 B.C. by its first ruler, Tangun. Unfortunately, the history of the Korean people has been anything but calm. A victim of its unfortunate geographic position, Korea is a rabbit-shaped mass of land that dangles into the Yellow Sea on the east and the

Sea of Japan on the west, vulnerable to Japan from the south and to China from the north. The Chinese conquered the northern region of Korea in 108 B.C.; the Koreans retook it in A.D. 313. Mongols invaded Korea in 1259 and remained until the Koreans drove them out in 1368. Japan took its turn in 1592. From the 1600s to the 1880s Korea become the "Hermit Kingdom." In 1876, Japan began to force Korean ports open to initiate trade; in 1910, the Japanese took total control of Korea as an occupying force until the Japanese defeat in 1945. The United States then occupied the South (below the 38th parallel), and the Soviet Union occupied the North. The Korean War (1950–1952) began when troops from the North, backed by China, attacked the South.

Koreans are known euphemistically as a "people of many sorrows." In their folk songs, birds don't sing, they weep. Bells don't ring, they cry. Their collective sorrow takes the form of an ingrained cultural value called *hahn*, the deep-seated feelings of rancor, frustration, shame, and insecurity, bred of centuries of oppression, that have given Koreans a national sense of inferiority. The typical Korean's work ethic is not Christian, Confucian, or Japanese in origin; it is generated by *hahn*, and it is found in both sexes. Korea's postwar leaders have harnessed *hahn* into a tremendous national motivation to achieve, to save face for the republic among the world's community of nations. Up until the late 1980s, most Koreans accepted the country's authoritarian government because they felt it would bring modernization, power, and security—the long-awaited national redemption.

The typical Korean is a complex cultural composite: Confucian, shamanistic, Buddhist, and Christian. Roughly 60 percent of Koreans are Buddhist or Buddhist-Confucian, 25 percent are Christian, and almost all of them remain partly shamanistic. The huge, dark, Christian churches that rise out of the Seoul cityscape are testimony to the large number of Christians in South Korea. (Christians account for only 1 percent of the population in Japan, and the figure is even less in China.) Christianity in Korea quickly associated itself with the independence movement against the Japanese, thereby winning hearts and minds. As a voting bloc, Christian Koreans will enjoy a majority by the year 2000, and their dominance will surely move the country toward democratic reform.

Extremely status-conscious, Koreans divide themselves along class lines; the elite occupy bureaucratic, business, and academic positions. Koreans' social stature is based largely on education and family ties and fits into a hierarchy of dependent relationships based on loyalty and reciprocity. Good-natured, generous, humorous, emotional, sentimental, and short-tempered, the typical Korean views the West with some reservation and ambivalence. Koreans maintain a deep Confucian sense of duty to family, state, and company. Ranking and obedience to authority are ingrained early; military training is required for all Korean men.

A militaristic discipline pervades all levels of South Korean commercial endeavor. The corporate aristocracy is highly competitive and less collectively unified than in Japan. Conflict and competition sometimes supersede harmony. Few Horatio Alger stories come out of Korea. Upward mobility usually depends on nepotism or personal affiliations, yet everyone strives to gain top positions of power and influence. Tenacity, talent, and hard work are needed to get anywhere. Only one out of four Korean students is accepted into the freshman class of Korean universities.

During the Japanese occupation of Korea, roughly 3 million Koreans migrated to Manchuria and parts of China, 700,000 to Siberia, 3 million to Japan, and 7,000 to the United States (mostly Hawaii). At present, 5.5 million Koreans live in the United States, concentrated in Los Angeles and New York City. The Yen-pien Korean Autonomous District in northwest China is home to the majority of ethnic Koreans living in the People's Republic.

The Korean language is a linguistic branch of Ural-Altaic and is related to other agglutinative languages, including Turkish, Mongolian, and Japanese. The written language is *Han'gul*, a phonetic alphabet created in 1443 that is celebrated with an annual holiday on October 9.

ACCOUNTING, BANKING, AND FINANCE

Title: *Foreign Exchange Policy, Monetary Policy, and Capital Market Liberalization in Korea*
Date: 1992
Format: Bound monograph
Author: Jeffrey A. Frankel
Publisher: University of California Press
2120 Berkeley Way
Berkeley, CA 94720
Tel: (510)642-4247
Fax: (510)643-7127
Pages: 24
Exhibits: Graphs

For specialists in the field, this working paper examines recent financial and exchange rate reforms in Korea and looks at the role of U.S. political pressure. The author offers conclusions about whether Korean interest rates have become tied to world interest rates and about whether the Korean won has become more closely tied in value to the U.S. dollar. The author suggests that Korea is becoming more closely tied financially to Japan.

Title: *Korea's Recent Foreign Exchange Rate Systems: MCBP vs. MAR System*
Date: 1992
Format: Paperback
Author: Jin Chun Kim
Publisher: Korea Institute for International Economic Policy
P.O. Box 1906
Yeongdong
Seoul 150-611, South Korea
Tel: (82)(2)528-3333
Fax: (82)(2)528-3311
Pages: 68
Exhibits: Graphs and tables

The multiple currency basket peg (MCBP) system and the market average rate (MAR) system are two exchange rate systems that Korea has adopted to achieve its macroeconomic and liberalization policy goals. Currently, the country plans to adopt a free floating exchange rate system, after evaluating other systems. The objective of this clearly written and well-researched study is to evaluate the MAR system and its predecessor, the MCBP system. For bankers and corporate accountants seeking insight on these topics, this is an authoritative source.

COMPANY DIRECTORIES

Title: *Business Korea Yearbook*
Date: Annual
Format: Hardcover
Publisher: Business Korea Co., Ltd.
Yoido P.O. Box 273
Seoul 150-602, South Korea
Tel: (82)(2)784-4010
Fax: (82)(2)784-1915
Pages: 700
Exhibits: Tables
Price: $270

For those who seek current information about Korea's industry, economy, or large companies, this tabbed volume is the place to look. Sections cover the macroeconomy, finance, *chaebols*, manufacturing, investment, media, tourism, and energy, and there is a manufacturing company index. Company profiles include text briefings on company activities, sales, and prospects as well as tables of financial data. This book is recommended as a benchmark tool and as a resource for prospective investors.

Title: *Directory: The American Chamber of Congress in Korea*
Date: Biannual
Format: Paperback
Publisher: The American Chamber of Congress in Korea
Room 307, Westin Chosun Hotel
87 Sokong-dong, Chung-ku
Seoul 100, South Korea
Tel: (82)(2)752-3061
Fax: (82)(2)755-6577
Pages: Varies
Exhibits: None

For those who are moving to Korea, this directory of members can provide the personal contacts necessary for cultural adjustment. It includes the names, portraits, telephone numbers, titles, and business activities of members.

Title: *Directory of Foreign Companies in Korea*
Date: Annual
Format: Hardcover
Publisher: Korea Economic Report
Yoido P.O. Box 963
Seoul 150-609, South Korea
Tel: (82)(2)783-5283
Fax: (82)(2)780-1717
Pages: 690
Exhibits: None

This country-by-country guide to foreign firms operating in Korea might be of use to marketers. Firms are listed alphabetically in country sections. Each entry includes the names of executives and a paragraph on the company's activities.

Title: *Kompass: Republic of Korea*
Date: 1990
Format: Hardcover
Author: Global Industrial Survey Co., Ltd.
Publisher: Croner Publications Inc.
211-03 Jamaica Ave.
Queens Village, NY 11428
Tel: (718)464-0866
Fax: (718)465-6171
Pages: 1,466 (2 vols.)
Exhibits: Tables

For each of the 15,000 Korean companies listed by name, product line, and industrial group, this two-volume directory provides company address, telephone and fax numbers, names of directors, bankers, share capital, number of employees, and nature of business.

Title: *The Korea Directory*
Date: Annual
Format: Paperback
Publisher: The Korea Directory Co.
C.P.O. Box 3955
Seoul 120-602, South Korea
Pages: Varies
Exhibits: None

This directory of Korean companies categorizes firms by activity, such as manufacturing and importing/exporting. The list includes airlines, trade agents, freight forwarders, foreign firms, schools and colleges, and others. Firms are indexed by name and by product line; entries provide bank reference, capitalization, business territory, name of president, and product line. A who's who section lists foreign residents living in Korea. The volume is tabbed for easy use and includes advertisements.

Title: *Korean Business Directory*
Date: Annual
Format: Paperback
Publisher: The Korea Chamber of Commerce and Industry
C.P.O. Box 25
Seoul 100, South Korea
Tel: (82)(2)316-3114
Fax: (82)(2)757-9475
Pages: 1,200
Exhibits: None

The Korean companies listed in this directory appear in alphabetical order and are indexed by the commodities they handle. They can also be accessed by importing or exporting status. Financial and service industries and economic organizations are also listed. Each company entry notes the name of the president, capital, number of employees, bank, business activities, and items imported and exported.

Title: *Korean Trade Directory*
Date: Annual
Format: Hardcover
Publisher: Korea Foreign Trade Association
Trade Center P.O. Box 100
Seoul 150-602, South Korea
Tel: (82)(2)551-5268 or 5269
Fax: (82)(2)551-5100
Pages: Varies
Exhibits: None

An enormous directory, this volume includes more than 30,000 companies in Korea that are involved in international trade. The four sections provide an alphabetical product index, company information, an alphabetical company index, and a service industries index. Company entries include address, phone number, product line, and list of products imported and exported. This directory is highly recommended.

COUNTRY PROFILES

Title: *The Handbook of Korea*
Date: 1990
Format: Hardcover
Publisher: Korean Overseas Information Service/ Samhwa Printing Co., Ltd.
C.P.O. Box 1307
Seoul 150-100, South Korea
Tel: (82)(2)635-0094
Fax: (82)(2)678-5623
Pages: Varies
Exhibits: Maps, photographs, and tables

This hefty handbook provides "an overview of Korea's long history, a record of accomplishments in modern times and a look at what may be expected in the future." Selected sections, all clearly written and well illustrated, cover geography, history, government, industry, education, sports, and unification policy. Encyclopedic in coverage and very high in publication quality, this is a useful desktop reference for the Koreaphile, and it makes a nice business gift to boot.

Title: *Korea Annual*
Date: Annual
Format: Paperback
Editor: Yim Young Kyu
Publisher: Yonhap News Agency
P.O. Box 1039
Kwanghwamun
Seoul 150-602, South Korea
Tel: (82)(2)390-3114
Fax: (82)(2)738-0820
Pages: Varies
Exhibits: Tables
Price: W 27,000

Really an almanac, this general information storehouse provides current factual data on the Korean government, social affairs, sports, climate, North Korea, and so on. The who's who section lists prominent businesspeople, and the section on government offers a concise overview of its structure and key officials. This is a recommended desktop reference. It includes advertisements.

Title: *Korea Business and Industry Yearbook*
Date: Annual
Format: Hardcover
Editor: Joong-Jin Hahn
Publisher: InfoServ
P.O. Box 923
Yongdungpo-gu
Seoul 150-609, South Korea
Tel: (82)(2)785-0909
Fax: (82)(2)785-5340
Pages: Varies
Exhibits: Tables
Price: $250

This hefty volume provides up-to-date information on Korean industry and business, based on analysis of mountains of government and trade association reports. It offers a warehouse of information on Korean companies, especially the member companies of Korea's *chaebol* conglomerates, as well as a full analysis of the economy and industrial performance for the year. The detailed company profiles include complete financial information. This book includes a transcription of new laws relevant to industry.

Title: *South Korea: Global Forecast*
Date: Quarterly
Format: Periodical
Publisher: The Economist Intelligence Unit
40 Duke St.
London W1A 1DW, United Kingdom
Tel: (44)(71)(322)289-194
Fax: (44)(71)(322)223-803
Pages: Varies
Exhibits: Tables
Price: Contact for subscription prices

This high-quality, large-format, 15-page booklet appears quarterly and includes a fact sheet, an executive summary of its forecast, and an analysis of Korea's political, economic, and business climate outlook for the next five years. For the marketer or investor, this updater is the best of its type: well-organized, succinct, and generally accurate in its predictions.

Title: *South Korea/North Korea: Country Report*
Date: Quarterly
Format: Periodical
Publisher: The Economist Intelligence Unit
40 Duke St.
London, W1A 1DW, United Kingdom
Tel: (44)(71)(322)289-194
Fax: (44)(71)(322)223-803
Pages: Varies
Exhibits: Graphs and tables
Price: Contact for subscription prices

With its analysis of economic and political trends in Korea each quarter, this 40-page publication is suggested for investors and business risk analysts. It provides a concise executive summary and forecasts for growth, wages, taxes, foreign trade, and more. Plenty of easy-to-read tables provide selected data.

DICTIONARIES AND LANGUAGE STUDIES

Title: *Standard English-Korean/Korean-English Dictionary for Foreigners*
Date: 1991
Format: Paperback
Editor: B.J. Jones and Gene S. Rhie
Publisher: Hollym Corp.
18 Donald Place
Elizabeth, NJ 07208
Tel: (908)353-1655
Fax: (908)353-0255

Pages: 394
Exhibits: Korean characters

Beginning with a "Han'gul in a Hurry" chart of pronunciations, this handbook of short definitions of English and romanized Korean words makes a worthy travel companion. It contains an explanation of the Korean alphabet and its sounds and a romanization chart.

Title: *Talking Business in Korean: Dictionary and Reference for International Business*
Date: 1988
Format: Hardcover
Author: Un Bok Cheong
Publisher: Barron's Educational Series
250 Wireless Blvd.
Hauppauge, NY 11788
Tel: (516)434-3311
Fax: (516)434-3723
Pages: 522
Exhibits: None

Containing more than 3,000 terms, this hand-size business dictionary covers accounting, computer terminology, labor relations, and marketing—just about every standard business term you will need to get by in Korea or to help out your interpreter. It contains key phrases and general travel information as well. It is recommended.

ECONOMY

Title: *Asia's Next Giant: South Korea and Late Industrialization*
Date: 1989
Format: Paperback
Author: Alice H. Amsden
Publisher: Oxford University Press
200 Madison Ave.
New York, NY 10016
Tel: (212)679-7300
Fax: (212)725-2972
Pages: 379
Exhibits: Graphs and tables
Price: $12.95

This volume provides a very readable overview and analysis of Korea's industrial development. Written by an economist at the New School for Social Research, it "seeks an answer to the puzzle of why South Korea has grown so much faster than most developing countries, even those that have gone through what is called 'late industrialization'." It includes chapters on Korea's early industrial history, influence from Japan, and development model as well as in-depth analysis of the country's automobile, ship building, and steel industries.

Title: *Korea Economic Report*
Date: Monthly
Format: Periodical
Editor: Kim Chong-tae
Publisher: Korea Economic Report
Yoido P.O. Box 963
Seoul 150-609, South Korea
Tel: (82)(2)783-5283
Fax: (82)(2)780-1717 or 782-7998
Pages: Varies
Exhibits: Graphs and tables
Price: $72/year

This full-length business magazine contains short journalistic articles divided by topic: domestic political news, finance, technology, and business and industry. International relations are covered with respect to their effect on business. This publication is useful as a general fast-paced reader on Korea's economy and business climate.

Title: *Korea Economic Update*
Date: Quarterly
Format: Periodical
Publisher: Korea Economic Institute
1101 Vermont Ave., NW, Suite 401
Washington, DC 20005-3521
Tel: (202)561-1400
Fax: (202)561-1401
Pages: Varies
Exhibits: Graphs
Price: Contact for subscription prices

This four-page newsletter provides a readable economic briefing, including an appraisal of Korea's economic growth, wages, housing, inflation, trade balance, and so on. This resource will interest those in need of a quarterly briefing that is truly brief.

Title: *Korea Leading Developing Nations: Economy, Democracy, and Welfare*
Date: 1992
Format: Hardcover
Author: Sung Moon Pae, Ph.D.
Publisher: University Press of America
4720 Boston Way
Lanham, MD 20706
Tel: (301)459-3366
Fax: (301)459-2118
Pages: 518
Exhibits: Graphs and tables

This magnum opus analyzes Korea's development experience, focusing on trade, investment, the Korean development model, America's role in political development in Korea, and Korea's social welfare services. As a source of background information, this academic volume may be of use to businesspeople studying the living conditions of Korean citizens, for example, housing, pensions, medical care, and insurance.

Title: *Korea's Development Assistance: Performance, Prospects and Policy*
Date: 1992
Format: Paperback
Author: Sooyong Kim and Wan-Soon Kim
Publisher: International Trade and Development Institute
International Center for Economic Growth
243 Kearny St.
San Francisco, CA 94108
Tel: (415)981-5485
Fax: (415)433-6841
Pages: 78
Exhibits: Graphs and tables

This booklet, which describes Korea's past overseas aid performance and examines the country's future foreign aid policy, is the first of its type published in English. The monograph is clear, concise, extensively footnoted, and useful to those researching the evolution and current trends in Korea's shift from being a borrowing nation to a lending one.

Title: *Quarterly Economic Review*
Date: Quarterly
Format: Periodical
Editor: Soo Gil Lee
Publisher: The Bank of Korea
10-2 Kwanchol-dong
Chongno-gu, C.P.O. Box 28
Seoul, South Korea
Tel: (82)(2)759-4114
Fax: (82)(2)759-4890
Pages: Varies
Exhibits: Tables
Price: Contact for subscription prices

This is a handsomely published pamphlet of 35 pages that provides a brief quarterly appraisal of South Korea's economic performance. It is of special interest to bankers and investors because it covers recent developments in capital markets. Each issue focuses on specific aspects of the investment climate and selected industries, all illustrated with a liberal use of tables and graphs.

Title: *Republic of Korea Economic Bulletin*
Date: Monthly
Format: Periodical
Publisher: Economic Planning Board, Republic of Korea/ Center for Economic Education, Korea Development Institute
Tel: (82)561-1400, ext. 264
Fax: (82)561-1410
Pages: Varies
Exhibits: Graphs and tables
Price: Contact for subscription prices

Providing 3 to 5 articles in each 30-page issue, this publication covers Korean trade and economic policy. Of use to business analysts, it contains a handy appendix of statistics, including key indicators, prices, wages, and trade.

ETIQUETTE AND PROTOCOL

Title: *Coping with Korea*
Date: 1987
Format: Paperback
Author: Gary P. Steenson
Publisher: Basil Blackwell
108 Cowley Rd.
Oxford 0X4 1JF, England
Tel: (44)(1)404-4101
Pages: 148
Exhibits: Drawings
Price: $10.00

Written by an American commercial officer, this is a concise guide to essential Korean social etiquette. It includes travel advice and tips on general business protocol.

Title: *Doing Business in Korea*
Date: 1987
Format: Hardcover
Author: Korean American Business Institute
Editor: Arthur M. Whitehall
Publisher: Croom Helm, Ltd.

Provident House
Burrell Row, Beckenham
Kent BR3 1AT, United Kingdom

Pages: 121

Exhibits: Graphs and tables

This not entirely dated though rather eclectic compilation of articles by academics includes a few pieces of interest to businesspeople. One article by Kyong Dong Kim—"Koreans: Who Are They?"—outlines the core characteristics of Korean behavior and personality through an appraisal of cultural values. Other articles focus on trade policy, finance, labor, business law, and entrepreneurship.

Title: *Korean Etiquette and Ethics in Business*

Date: 1988

Format: Paperback

Publisher: NTC Business Books
2466 W. Touhy Rd.
Lincolnwood, IL 60646
Tel: (708)679-5500
Fax: (708)679-2494

Pages: 156

Exhibits: None

This book contains a few useful tidbits on Korean history and business etiquette, but it's poorly organized and incomplete. It does contain a very useful glossary of Korean cultural terms, however.

GENERAL BUSINESS

Title: *Business Korea*

Date: Monthly

Format: Periodical

Editor: Kim Kyong-Hae

Publisher: Business Korea Co., Ltd.
C.P.O. Box 8819
Seoul 100-688, South Korea
Tel: (82)(2)234-4010
Fax: (82)(2)253-4040

Pages: Varies

Exhibits: Graphs, photographs, and tables

Price: $250/year

This publication is pricey but top-notch in terms of content and publishing quality. Articles are divided into categories including corporate strategy, labor, economy, finance, external relations, industries, and investment. This is the most comprehensive and best-written one-stop source available for businesspeople involved with Korea. It includes a table of key economic indicators.

Title: *Doing Business in Korea*

Date: 1991

Format: Hardcover

Publisher: Ernst & Young International
787 Seventh Ave.
New York, NY 10019
Tel: (212)773-6469
Fax: (212)977-9156

Pages: 112

Exhibits: Tables

Concentrating on Korea's tax system, this booklet provides coverage of taxation policies as they affect resident corporations, partnerships, joint ventures, and individuals. Other sections cover auditing practices, the labor force, and investment incentives. It is useful to expatriates, accountants, and prospective investors.

Title: *K.C.C.I. Quarterly Review*
Date: Quarterly
Format: Periodical
Editor: Cha Sang-Pil
Publisher: Korea Chamber of Commerce and Industry
C.P.O. Box 25
Seoul 100-600, South Korea
Tel: (82)(2)316-3114
Fax: (82)(2)757-9475
Pages: Varies
Exhibits: Tables
Price: Contact for subscription prices

This 20-page quarterly contains articles on the Korean economy and business environment—that is, what Korean business interests feel the government should do to bring about improvement in both. Businesspeople will find economic statistics and a list of business opportunities.

Title: *The Key to Successful Business in Korea*
Date: 1988
Format: Hardcover
Author: Song-hyon Jang
Publisher: Yong Ahn Publishing Co.
C.P.O. Box 737
Seoul, South Korea
Tel: (82)(2)753-4531 or 1405
Fax: (82)(2)756-3635
Pages: 227
Exhibits: None

Meant for foreign businesspeople entering Korea to sell and invest, this authoritative book by Korea's leading international business consultant is absolutely essential for anyone doing business with or managing Koreans. It includes much boiled-down knowledge on negotiating, managing, dealing with the Korean bureaucracy, and selling to Korea. This short book is required reading.

Title: *Korea Business World*
Date: Monthly
Format: Periodical
Editor: Lee Kie-Hong
Publisher: Korea Businessworld
Yoido P.O. Box 720
Seoul 150-607, South Korea
Tel: (82)(2)535-5431
Fax: (82)(2)594-7663
Pages: Varies
Exhibits: Graphs, photographs, and tables
Price: $80/yr.

Meant as a general business magazine, this 60- to 80-page publication covers the Korean economy, financial climate, technological developments, and market opportunities. What it lacks in publishing quality it makes up with its comprehensive coverage, written with the serious businessperson in mind.

Title: *Korea Trade and Business*
Date: Monthly
Format: Periodical
Editor: Chulsu Kim
Publisher: Korea Trade Promotion Corp. (KOTRA)

Trade Center P.O. Box 123
Seoul 100-108, South Korea
Tel: (82)(2)551-4181
Fax: (82)(2)551-4477 or 4478

Pages: Varies
Exhibits: Tables
Price: Contact for subscription prices

The news articles in this 60-page business magazine are divided by topic, including government policies, economy, international cooperation, industries, energy, finance, investment, and shipping. Written in clear, well-illustrated prose, this general reader provides the marketer with a useful source of economic analysis and trading information.

Title: *Living in Korea*
Date: 1987
Format: Paperback
Editor: Richard B. Rucci
Publisher: American Chamber of Commerce in Korea
Yongdong P.O. Box 629
Seoul 135-606, South Korea
Tel: (82)(2)469-8326 or 8327
Pages: 300
Exhibits: Maps and photographs
Price: W 12,000

Essential for anyone planning to live in South Korea, this book covers topics such as moving to Korea, health care, things to do, shopping, transportation, and contact information useful to expatriates.

Title: *Trade Korea*
Date: Biweekly
Format: Periodical
Editor: Shin Young Gak
Publisher: Trade Korea, Inc.
42-15 Crescent St., Suite 505
Long Island City, NY 11101
Tel: (718)706-6655
Fax: (718)706-8857
Pages: Varies
Exhibits: Tables
Price: $91/year

This 50- to 60-page magazine provides news and opinion on trade-related topics, including developments in market opening, Korean trade relations, corruption, and trade negotiations. With its detailed focus on Korean markets and the opening of those markets, this is a useful source for marketers and trade analysts, not to mention trade negotiators.

HISTORY AND SOCIETY

Title: *Korean Patterns*
Date: 1978
Format: Paperback
Author: Paul S. Crane
Publisher: The Royal Asiatic Society
Distribution Office
Myung Hwa Co.
C.P.O. Box 7852
Seoul 100, South Korea
Tel: (82)(2)274-5443
Pages: 188
Exhibits: Cartoons

Although a bit dated now, this slim volume, written by a missionary, has withstood the test of time for its concise portrait of Korean cultural values and personality. The author discusses essential etiquette, the nature of Korean personal and public relationships, and Korean versus American personality traits. The descriptions of the Korean family, religious and business practices, and attitudes toward Westerners are as valid today as when the book was written.

Title: *Korean Public Bureaucracy: A Behavioral Perspective*
Date: 1982
Format: Hardcover
Author: Kon Yoon Woo
Publisher: Sung Kyun Kwan University Press
1 Hoeki-dong Dongdaumum-gu
Seoul 130-701, South Korea
Pages: 191
Exhibits: Tables

Based on solid academic research and surveys, this volume provides an early psychological analysis of Korean personality. Chapter topics include the Korean socio-family system, personality characteristics, the political environment, and the behavior of bureaucrats.

Title: *The Koreans*
Date: 1988
Format: Hardcover
Author: Russel Warren Howe
Publisher: Harcourt Brace & Jovanovich
6277 Sea Harbor Dr.
Orlando, FL 32887
Tel: (407)345-2000
Fax: (407)345-9354
Pages: 275
Exhibits: Photographs
Price: $12.95

This is the most complete and literate book covering modern Korean society and culture, though it does not cover Korean business practice. It is recommended as an engrossing reader for those seeking to understand the below-the-surface workings of daily life in modern Korea.

Title: *Korean Ways: Korean Mind*
Date: 1982
Format: Hardcover
Author: Won-dal Yang
Publisher: Tamgu Dang
101-1 Gyeongun-Dong
Jongro-gu
Seoul 110-310, South Korea
Tel: (82)(2)730-8670
Fax: (82)(2)738-4408
Pages: 246
Exhibits: Photographs, maps, and charts

The numerous short chapters of this book explain Korean character by exploring the culture's music, poetry, and history.

INDUSTRY

Title: *Industry in Korea*
Date: 1991
Format: Paperback
Publisher: Korea Development Bank

Chong Nyang
P.O. Box 113
Dongdaemom-gu
Seoul 130-012, South Korea
Tel: (82)(2)967-8811
Fax: (82)(2)961-5092

Pages: 223

Exhibits: Graphs, photographs, and tables

This attractive and well-illustrated book provides a statistical overview of Korean industries, with sections on energy, metal, chemicals, textiles, high technology, and other industries.

LAWS AND REGULATIONS

Title: *Business Laws in Korea*

Date: 1988

Format: Hardcover

Editor: Chan-Jin Kim

Publisher: Panmun Book Co., Ltd.
C.P.O. Box 1016
Seoul, South Korea
Tel: (82)(2)732-5131
Fax: (82)(2)720-5756

Pages: 1,055

Exhibits: None

A hefty volume of essential business regulation in Korea, this book is comprehensive in the body of law it provides in translation and useful in that it offers 150 pages of text articles covering the foundation of Korean law and juridical organization in Korea. The types of law covered include industrial property law, trade law, antitrust law, and tax law. This book is highly recommended to lawyers and business strategists.

Title: *Korea and International Law*

Date: 1993

Author: Choung Il Chee

Format: Hardcover

Publisher: Seoul Press
Institute of International Legal Studies
Korea University
C.P.O. Box 8850
Seoul 100, South Korea
Tel: (82)(2)923-6311

Pages: 390

Exhibits: Maps

This collection of erudite legal articles, written by a Korean-born professor who has been teaching law in the United States, covers critical issues in international law as they relate to South Korea. The issues, discussed in readable 10- to 20-page articles, include the maritime claim of the Republic of Korea, fishery zones, the law of the sea, the United Nations command in Korea, the Soviet attack on a Korean airliner, the diversion of the Han River by North Korea, and other critical and intriguing legal topics. This book is useful to anyone studying Korean international relations and politics.

MARKET DATA AND ANALYSIS

Title: *A Guide to the Korean Import Market*

Date: 1989

Format: Hardcover

Publisher: Korea Trade Promotion Corp. (KOTRA)
Trade Center P.O. Box 123
Seoul, South Korea
Tel: (82)(2)551-4181
Fax: (82)(2)551-4477

Pages: 99
Exhibits: Graphs, photographs, and tables

Opening with the premise that the trade imbalance that the United States suffers with Korea is largely due to lack of information on the part of American executives, this slim volume attempts to answer the key questions about entering the Korean market. Selected chapters cover import policy, import trends, the import environment, import procedures, the distribution system, and advice for sellers in Korea. Although not too detailed and a bit dated, this is an excellent overview of the Korean market and how to crack it.

Title: *Korea and the World: Key Statistics*
Date: Annual
Format: Paperback
Editor: Seh-Hyung Choi
Publisher: Yong-Hak Park
T.C.P.O. Box 100
Seoul, South Korea
Tel: (82)(2)551-5114
Fax: (82)(2)551-5100
Pages: 128
Exhibits: Tables and charts

Compact and convenient, this pocket-size handbook of statistical information includes the latest data on demographics, employment, wages, industry, energy resources, finance, national accounts, trade, and culture. A great one-stop source of key statistics in easy-to-read figures.

Title: *Trade Today of Korea*
Date: Annual
Format: Hardcover
Editor: Gi-Nam Jeong
Publisher: Overseas Media Corp.
C.P.O. Box 6494
Seoul, South Korea
Tel: (82)(2)737-3666
Pages: 1,100
Exhibits: None

Listing the company members of various trade associations in Korea, this volume is useful to businesspeople trying to make contacts in Korea, develop mailing lists, or decide on which trade association to join. It does not classify companies by product line, but it does list companies by business. For marketers, other Korean directories are more useful.

Title: *What to Sell to Korea*
Date: 1990
Format: Paperback
Publisher: Korea Foreign Trade Association
Korea World Trade Center
Trade Center P.O. Box 100
Seoul, South Korea
Tel: (82)(2)551-5273
Fax: (82)(2)551-5100
Pages: 181
Exhibits: None

Meant for small and medium-size exporters who might lack the resources to analyze the Korean market, this book by the Korea Foreign Trade Association serves as a primer in cracking that market. Clearly organized and well illustrated, selected chapters offer information about gaining access to the market, demographics, distribution channels, and the effectiveness of advertising. Very helpful to sellers, this resource includes a directory of key Korean importers.

POLITICS AND GOVERNMENT

Title: *Korea and World Affairs*
Date: Quarterly
Format: Periodical
Editor: Sang-Woo Rhee
Publisher: Research Center for Peace and Unification of Korea
C.P.O. Box 6545
Seoul, South Korea
Tel: (82)(2)777-2628
Fax: (82)(2)755-1853
Pages: Varies
Exhibits: None
Price: $24/year

This collection of academic articles will hold the interest of business investors who must keep tabs on political risk in Korea. Security issues and relations between North and South Korea are the focus. Primary source materials are reprinted for the use of researchers.

Title: *Korea Newsreview*
Date: Weekly
Format: Periodical
Publisher: The Korea Herald
C.P.O. Box 2147
Seoul, South Korea
Tel: (82)(2)752-6170
Fax: (82)(2)757-2049
Pages: Varies
Exhibits: Maps, graphs, photographs, and tables
Price: $108/year

For the Korea watcher, this magazine covers national news, the economy, and Korean culture. The focus is general and the publishing quality wanting. It is a fair value for a weekly update, however.

Title: *Korea Update*
Date: Bimonthly
Format: Periodical
Publisher: Information Office
Embassy of the Republic of Korea
2450 Massachusetts Ave., NW
Washington, DC 20008
Tel: (202)939-5687
Fax: (202)387-4695
Pages: Varies
Exhibits: Photographs
Price: Contact for free subscription

This free six-page newsletter is worth a look to keep track of U.S.-Korean relations and to read over recent speeches by our presidents. It also tracks press coverage of Korea in the U.S. media.

Title: *North Korea Directory*
Date: Annual
Format: Paperback
Publisher: Radiopress, Inc.
R-Building Shinjuku
33-8, Wakamatsu-cho
Shinjuku-ku
Tokyo 162, Japan
Pages: 292
Exhibits: None

This one-of-a-kind directory sets out, in its words, to list "new positions of all important North Korean officials as ascertained from constant and observant checking of official North Korean reports." The text is provided in English and Japanese, and phone numbers and a name index are included. This resource is useful to political analysts and serious businesspeople involved with North Korea.

Title: *North Korea News*
Date: Weekly
Format: Periodical
Editor: Ik-Sang Lee
Publisher: Naewoo Press
42-2 Chuja-dong,
C.P.O. Box 9708
Chung-gu
Seoul 100-240, South Korea
Tel: (82)(2)275-8248
Fax: (82)(2)278-9176
Pages: Varies
Exhibits: None
Price: Contact for subscription prices

For the analyst tracking news from North Korea, this 10-page newsletter, published in the South, summarizes and translates press articles in the North. It provides a useful week-in-review section.

Title: *Vantage Point: Developments in North Korea*
Date: Monthly
Format: Periodical
Editor: Ik-sang Lee
Publisher: Naewoo Press
42-2 Chuja-dong,
C.P.O. Box 9708
Chung-gu
Seoul 100-240, South Korea
Tel: (82)(2)275-8248
Fax: (82)(2)278-9176
Pages: Varies
Exhibits: Tables
Price: Contact for subscription prices

This 30-page publication tracks diplomatic developments in North Korea in medium-length articles. The emphasis is on human rights abuses and diplomatic missions visiting North Korea. It is useful to the business risk analyst.

TAXATION

Title: *Doing Business in Korea*
Date: 1992
Format: Paperback
Publisher: Price Waterhouse
Seihwa Accounting Corp.
C.P.O. Box 4986/5940
Seoul 100-649, South Korea
Tel: (82)(2)745-8500
Fax: (82)(2)738-0447
Pages: 209
Exhibits: Tables

Like the other guides in the series, this book provides an overview of taxation issues relevant to businesspeople working in Korea. It also includes sections on the business environment, trade opportunities, investment incentives, restrictions on investment, and the regulatory environment. It offers a complete review of the tax system and how it affects businesses and individuals. This publication is useful to prospective investors and accountants.

Title: *Guide to Korean Taxes*
Date: Annual
Format: Hardcover

Author: Chong Sang Kim and Yong Kyun Kim

Publisher: CCH International
Talavera and Khartoum Rds.
P.O. Box 230
North Ryde
Sydney NSW 2113, Australia
Tel: (61)(2)888-2555
Fax: (61)(2)888-7324

Pages: 731

Exhibits: Tables

This book contains a comprehensive explanation of Korean tax laws, regulations, and enforcement decrees in English and Korean. Well organized and clearly written, the chapters cover taxation terms and the tax calendar, individual taxes, corporate taxes, value-added taxes, and other taxes. This book is a convenient guide for expatriates, accountants, and tax lawyers.

TRAVEL ADVICE

Title: *South Korea Handbook*

Date: 1988

Format: Hardcover

Author: Robert Nilsen

Publisher: Moon Publications
722 Wall St.
Chico, CA 95928
Tel: (916)345-5473
Fax: (916)345-6751

Pages: 586

Exhibits: Maps and photographs

This guidebook is part of a series of travel guides that began to appear before the ubiquitous Lonely Planet series, and it is perhaps even more informative and more clearly written. The author has plenty of experience in South Korea, having lived there for six years since 1983. Experience matters in a book like this, which takes you well beyond the recommended hotels for a cultural excursion to every region of this country. Korea's history, language (*Han'gul*), and cultural heritage are all covered with plenty of detail and illustrations. The extensive travel advice will keep you poking around the country for years.

Hong Kong

OVERVIEW

Hong Kong, which translates as "fragrant harbor," rose upon a foundation of trade in "foreign mud," that is, opium. In its hundred-year history, it has become the world's greatest entrepôt trading center and the third largest financial center in the world, with more Rolls Royces per hectare than anywhere else. The island possesses the second largest futures market in the world and the second busiest port. About the size of New York City, Hong Kong has 40,000 enterprises, mostly small ones. It is, as the cliché goes, a schoolroom for the study of free-market capitalism. There is duty on only five commodities entering Hong Kong, and no duty on goods leaving it.

Hong Kong was the destination for Cantonese and Fukienese Chinese fleeing war, famine, and political reprisal in Mainland China, especially during the years of civil war in China, which culminated with Communist victory. Historically, these were some of China's hardiest capitalists, and they found fertile ground for cultivating enterprise in British-run, laissez-faire Hong Kong.

The British found Hong Kong, with its deep-water harbor, perfect for mooring their large clipper ships. China gave the island to England as a victory prize after the Opium War in 1842, a gesture that Queen Victoria's Foreign Secretary, Lord Palmerston, accepted with derisive laughter. Of course, it was not with laughter that Margaret Thatcher relinquished Hong Kong to China in a treaty signed in 1984.

Hong Kong at a Glance

Population:	5.8 million
Religion:	Buddhist, Taoist, Christian, with small numbers of Muslims, Hindus, Jews, and Sikhs
Government:	U.K. colonial administration (until 1997)
Language:	English and Cantonese; Mandarin is also spoken
Currency:	Hong Kong dollar (HK$)
Trade (1993):	$119.5 billion total exports; $123.8 billion total imports

Hong Kong has an affluent society and a service-oriented economy in which the per capita gross domestic product exceeds $13,500. With the ongoing economic growth throughout Asia, Hong Kong has benefited as a trade and financial hub. For example, it channels more than $1 billion every year of Taiwanese investment into South China. Its similar role vis-à-vis Vietnam has just begun. Hong Kong is the gateway to the Chinese market; between 2 and 4 million people are now employed by invested enterprises in Guangdong Province, and 30 to 40 percent of China's foreign exchange income comes from or through Hong Kong. However, the "Pearl of the Orient" will soon be a Special Administrative Region of the People's Republic of China. No city or country on earth lives under a heavier onus of uncertainty than Hong Kong. Hong Kong is a city, as Chinese poet Han Su-yin wrote in *Life* magazine in 1959, "on borrowed time in a borrowed place."

Every Hong Kong businessperson has prepared, in his or her own way, for 1997. During the last three years, 150,000 Hong Kong professionals and skilled residents have fled for safe haven abroad. Most are pessimistic about Hong Kong's future. They acknowledge that they're powerless to change China's internal political system, that it is based on a long tradition of political power and authority spanning hundreds of years. Only 25 percent of people in Hong Kong are confident about the "one country, two systems" policy being preserved in the Basic Law. Seventy percent think China will not honor the 1984 agreement after 1997.

Economic Conditions

Hong Kong's economic conditions are closely tied to events unfolding in Mainland China. The treaty signed in 1984 between Great Britain and the PRC, handing over Hong Kong to China in 1997, guarantees the future existence of Hong Kong as a capitalist enclave until 2047. "One country, two systems," as the scenario is termed, has also been envisioned for Macao's relationship to the PRC, as embodied in an agreement with the Portuguese that turns over Macao in 1999. Will Hong Kong and Macao be able to retain their status as laissez-faire "classrooms for capitalism" under China's Communist regime? That's the 64,000-yuan question that Hong Kong residents and potential investors alike have been losing sleep over since the Tiananmen uprising in June 1989. With Hong Kong businesspeople, many of whom now hold two passports just in case, the apprehension about Mainland China's meddling in Hong Kong's economy and civilian life is real; on the other hand, many outside observers feel that the transition will be smooth, predicting that pragmatic China won't kill the goose that lays the golden eggs, that is, foreign exchange earnings.

The U.S. Foreign Commercial Service, for example, "feels that the apprehension about Hong Kong's future has been overstated . . . that the People's Republic of China will abide by the Hong Kong Accords, and will do nothing to impede the economic growth and stability of Hong Kong and Macau" because (1) China is a large investor in Hong Kong, and its investments are profitable; (2) China depends on Hong Kong's port and trading infrastructure to increase exports; (3) China's leaders, including Deng Xiaoping, have used South China and Hong Kong as models for economic progress for China; and (4) Hong Kong's territorial integrity has never before been questioned or threatened militarily by China, even during the cultural revolution.

Even with an unpredictable giant next door, Hong Kong continues to boom. The Hong Sing stock market has soared after its crash during the aftermath of the Tiananmen uprising. Real estate prices increased by 50 percent in 1992! The only blemish is inflation, which is rising at a rate of 10 percent per year. In terms of production, much of Hong Kong's manufacturing activity has been moved into South China. The country's manufacturing sector now generates less than one-third of the GDP; exports from Hong Kong remain roughly stable, whereas re-exports, goods moving through Hong Kong but not produced there, have skyrocketed.

Hong Kong's central Asian location, state-of-the-art communications network, immaculate infrastructure, low taxes (16.5 percent corporate tax), congenial commercial environment, skilled labor force, and proximity to the "market of one billion" all combine to rank Hong Kong as the location of choice for corporate headquarters. The principal investor countries in Hong Kong are Japan ($6.9 billion as of 1991), the United States ($6.4 billion), and China ($2.3 billion). Technology marketers should note that Hong Kong's status for importing sensitive technology is higher than China's; it may lose that status in 1997. Should that status be maintained, higher technology sales to China might become possible through Hong Kong, with the added risk that dual-use technologies purchased in Hong Kong might end up in China.

COMPANY DIRECTORIES

Title: *The American Chamber of Commerce in Hong Kong Members' Directory*

Date: Annual

Format: Hardcover

Publisher: The American Chamber of Commerce in Hong Kong
1030 Swire House
Central, Hong Kong
Tel: (852)(5)260-165
Fax: (852)(5)810-1289

Pages: 500

Exhibits: Photographs and tables

Price: $100

In this directory of members of the American Chamber of Commerce in Hong Kong, the expatriate will find many useful contacts and a source of potential acquaintances in Hong Kong. The directory includes an index of individuals with their office phone numbers.

Title: *Business Directory of Hong Kong, 1992/93*
Date: 1992
Format: Hardcover
Editor: Charles Lau
Publisher: Current Publications Ltd., Hong Kong
G.P.O. Box 9848
1501 Enterprise Building
228 Queen's Rd.
Central, Hong Kong
Tel: (852)543-4702
Fax: (852)815-8396
Pages: 944
Exhibits: Photographs
Price: $120

This comprehensive directory of more than 12,000 Hong Kong firms and organizations is meant as a desktop guide for marketers and buyers. Firms are divided by business activity, such as travel agents or manufacturers—toys. Under each area of activity, companies are listed alphabetically. Only addresses, name of director, and the company's banker are noted. This is a useful phonebook-like directory.

Title: *Directory of Companies with P.R.C. Capital*
Date: 1987
Format: Hardcover
Editor: Thomas M.H. Chan
Publisher: CERD Consultants
Room 1201, Yam Tze Commercial Building
17 Thomson Rd.
Wanchai, Hong Kong
Tel: (852)527-8148
Pages: 331
Exhibits: None

This one-of-a-kind directory, which will presumably become obsolete in 1997, lists companies in Hong Kong that are capitalized, in whole or in part, by Chinese money. The volume lists companies alphabetically and according to the government entities that own them, such as the Guangdong Provincial Government, MOFERT, and central ministries and state departments. Company profiles include contact information, shareholders, directors, scope of business, and relevant comments. The text appears in English and Chinese.

Title: *Directory of Hong Kong Industries*
Date: Annual
Format: Hardcover
Publisher: Hong Kong Productivity Council
Management and Industrial Consultancy Division
HKNC Building
78 Tat Chee Ave.
Kowloon, Hong Kong
Pages: 1,253
Exhibits: Photographs

Containing more than 5,000 Hong Kong companies, this directory lists firms by product offering and provides cross-indexing by name. A list of brand names is also provided in case the reader knows the product but not the maker. Government departments and trade associations in Hong Kong that play a role in facilitating business are listed and described. Each company entry provides address and phone, name of director, number of employees, floor space, products made, turnover, paid-up capital, and brand names. This is a highly recommended and comprehensive directory.

Title: *Federation of Hong Kong Industries: Members' Directory*
Date: Annual
Format: Paperback
Publisher: Membership Relations Division
Federation of Hong Kong Industries
4th Floor, Hankow Centre
5-15 Hankow Rd.
Tsimshatsui
Kowloon, Hong Kong
Tel: (852)723-0818
Fax: (852)721-3494
Pages: 813
Exhibits: None

This directory is aimed at buyers of goods and services offered by the members of the Federation of Hong Kong Industries. Firms can be looked up by product classification or company name. Entries include address, general manager, board of directors, products and services, type of ownership, and annual sales turnover.

Title: *The Hong Kong Exporter's Association Members' Directory*
Date: 1990
Format: Hardcover
Publisher: Hong Kong Exporters' Association
Room 825, Star House
3 Salisbury Rd.
Tsimshatsui
Kowloon, Hong Kong
Tel: (852)730-9851 or 9852
Fax: (852)730-1869
Pages: 176
Price: HK$40

This is a directory of companies in Hong Kong that are members of the Hong Kong Exporters' Association. The book lists them by name and by product line exported. It also contains information on hotels, consulates in Hong Kong, banks, and so on. It is useful to importers of goods from Hong Kong.

Title: *Kompass Hong Kong: Company Information*
Date: 1990
Format: Hardcover
Publisher: SHK International Services, Ltd.
231 F National Mutual Centre
151 Gloucester Rd.
Wanchai, Hong Kong
Tel: (852)832-6100
Fax: (852)838-0639
Pages: 288 (2 vols.)
Exhibits: None

This directory lists 7,000 Hong Kong companies. The first volume lists companies by product line; the second provides company information alphabetically. The directory includes manufacturers, importers/exporters, service companies (including banks), and building contractors. A well-organized and comprehensive directory of Hong Kong firms.

COUNTRY PROFILES

Title: *Country Report—Hong Kong, Macau*
Date: Quarterly
Format: Periodical
Publisher: The Economist Intelligence Unit

P.O. Box 154
Dartford
Kent DA1 1QB, United Kingdom
Tel: (44)(322)289-194
Fax: (44)(322)223-803

Pages: Varies

Exhibits: Graphs and tables

Price: Contact for subscription prices

For anyone tracking political, economic, or business climate changes in Hong Kong and Macao, this is a recommended one-stop source. Following a very handy executive summary of the entire "outlook," the publication includes sections on the political scene, economic policy, trends in demand, employment and wages, industry, finance, and foreign trade. An appendix of current statistics is also provided.

ECONOMY

Title: *The Economic Future of Hong Kong*

Date: 1990

Format: Hardcover

Author: Miron Mushkat

Publisher: Lynne Rienner Publishers
3 Henrietta St.
Covent Garden
London WC2E 8LU, United Kingdom

Pages: 171

Exhibits: None

For economists and risk analysts, this research monograph offers a set of future scenarios for the Hong Kong economy in light of the changeover of sovereignty in 1997. It is readable, though it was drafted before the Tiananmen uprising.

GENERAL BUSINESS

Title: *Agency in Hong Kong*

Date: 1989

Format: Paperback

Author: Gary P. Miller and William G. Magennis

Publisher: Longman Group (Far East), Ltd.
18th Floor, Cornwall St.
Quarry Bay, Hong Kong
Tel: (914)993-5000 (U.S.)
Fax: (914)997-8115 (U.S.)

Pages: 62

Exhibits: None

A great number of companies prefer to do business in Hong Kong through a representative agency rather than an affiliated office, which is expensive. This convenient publication instructs on how to arrange relationships between principals, agents, and third parties in Hong Kong in a legal manner. Written by two solicitors experienced in Hong Kong, selected chapters cover setting up an agency to represent your firm in Hong Kong, writing an appropriate contract with an agency, and dealing with disputes. The book includes sample agreements.

Title: *Doing Business in Hong Kong*

Date: 1992

Format: Paperback

Publisher: Price Waterhouse, Hong Kong
22nd Floor, Prince's Building
Hong Kong

Pages: 224

Exhibits: Tables

This handy book offers an overview of Hong Kong's investment climate, with an emphasis on taxation and accounting. The topics covered include banking and finance, exporting, labor relations, tax administration, corporate taxation, and personal taxation. This resource is useful for expatriates and accountants as well as businesspeople thinking about entering the Hong Kong market.

Title: *Doing Business in Hong Kong*
Date: 1990
Format: Hardcover
Publisher: Ernst & Young
15th Floor, Hutchinson House
10 Harcourt Rd.
Central, Hong Kong
Tel: (852)846-9888 or 526-5371
Fax: (852)868-4432 or 845-9208
Pages: 90
Exhibits: Tables

Compiled by a well-known accounting and consulting firm, this slim volume provides a clear overview of Hong Kong's investment climate, taxation, forms of business organization, and business and accounting practices. Starting with an executive summary, the nine chapters present regulatory information in an easy-to-use format. An appendix of tables provides statistics up to 1989.

Title: *Doing Business in Today's Hong Kong*
Date: 1991
Format: Paperback
Publisher: American Chamber of Commerce, Hong Kong
1030 Swire House
G.P.O. Box 355
Central, Hong Kong
Tel: (852)526-0165
Fax: (852)810-1289
Pages: 390
Exhibits: Graphs and tables
Price: HK$245

Published by the American Chamber of Commerce in Hong Kong, this handy guidebook covers the island's business environment, business services, and major industries in clear and practical prose. For the expatriates or the executive heading to Hong Kong, this guide instructs on taxation, finance, insurance, standards and testing, and other areas of business logistics. The approach is step-by-step, resulting in an easy-to-read and practical book. Industry overviews provide updates on key developments for those who are just getting their feet wet.

Title: *Establishing a Business in Hong Kong*
Date: 1989
Format: Paperback
Author: Stephen Terry and Scott Brodsky
Publisher: Longman Group (Far East), Ltd.
18th Floor, Cornwall St.
Quarry Bay, Hong Kong
Tel: (914)993-5000 (U.S.)
Fax: (914)997-8115 (U.S.)
Pages: 108
Exhibits: Tables

The purpose of this book is to provide a "practical guide to the establishment of a business in Hong Kong through the use of a private limited liability company." Written by two lawyers experienced in Hong Kong's commercial environment, the book describes the requirements for setting up and running such a firm and delivers a complete and succinct outline of the local tax system. Selected chapters instruct on how to incorporate a company, define the role of directors and managers, and deal with shareholders. For those seeking advice about the specific legal and documentary logistics of operating a corporation in Hong Kong, this is a useful companion.

Title: *Hong Kong Digest*
Date: Semimonthly
Format: Periodical
Publisher: Hong Kong Economic and Trade Office
222 Kearny St., Suite 402
San Francisco, CA 94108
Tel: (415)397-2215
Fax: (415)421-0646
Pages: Varies
Exhibits: None
Price: Contact for subscription prices

This 10-page loose-leaf news brief runs news abstracts dealing with Hong Kong business, investment, consumer behavior, finance, large projects, and so on, on a semimonthly basis. It is useful to the Hong Kong business news hound.

Title: *Hong Kong Industrialist*
Date: Monthly
Format: Periodical
Publisher: Federation of Hong Kong Industries
4th Floor, Hankow Centre
5-15 Hankow Rd.
Tsimshatsui
Kowloon, Hong Kong
Tel: (852)723-0818
Fax: (852)721-3494
Pages: Varies
Exhibits: None
Price: Contact for subscription prices

For the Hong Kong/China businessperson, this 60- to 70-page Chinese/English magazine provides general business articles on industry and technology topics and on business conditions in China. It also offers news about the member companies of the Federation of Hong Kong Industries.

Title: *Hong Kong Trader*
Date: Monthly
Format: Periodical
Editor: T.S. Tan
Publisher: Hong Kong Trade Development Council
36–39th Floors, Office Tower
Convention Plaza
1 Harbour Rd.
Wanchai, Hong Kong
Tel: (852)584-4333
Fax: (852)824-0249
Pages: Varies
Exhibits: None
Price: Contact for subscription prices

This 8-page color newspaper provides articles about successful Hong Kong export businesses, the Hong Kong and Chinese economy, upcoming conferences, and general Hong Kong business news.

The tone is upbeat (though perhaps a little too optimistic in political perspective, especially in regard to Mainland China), but the information is well researched and well written.

Title: *The Other Hong Kong Report*
Date: Annual
Format: Paperback
Editor: Sung Yun-wing and Lee Ming-kwan
Publisher: Chinese University Press
Chinese University of Hong Kong
Shatin
New Territories, Hong Kong
Tel: (852)695-2508
Fax: (852)604-6692
Pages: Varies
Exhibits: Photographs and tables

For businesspeople seeking a complete and readable overview of current trends and key events in Hong Kong under one cover, this annual compilation of perspective articles is highly recommended. The book is so named because its objective is to offer an alternative view to the government's annual report of events and developments in the territory. In other words, the well-written pieces in this volume pull no punches in regard to the China-Hong Kong relationship. The coverage includes the legal system, political parties, Americans in Hong Kong, Vietnamese boat people, law and order, economy, labor, transportation, and much more. This publication is recommended to the general business reader and the serious political analyst alike.

HISTORY AND SOCIETY

Title: *Macau: City of Commerce and Culture*
Date: 1987
Format: Hardcover
Editor: R.D. Cremer
Publisher: UEA Press, Ltd.
13th Floor, Office Tower
Shun Tak Centre
200 Connaught Rd.
Central, Hong Kong
Tel: (852)(5)859-9333
Pages: 202
Exhibits: Tables and photographs

Well written and well illustrated, this compilation of chapters from many authors explores Macao's history, culture, language, economy, trade, and institutional framework as the territory prepares to become part of China in 1999. This book is an engaging and colorful introduction for businesspeople preparing to visit and deal with Macao.

Title: *The Making of Hong Kong Society*
Date: 1991
Format: Hardcover
Author: Chan Wai Kwan
Publisher: Clarendon Press/Oxford University Press
Walton St.
Oxford 0X2 6DP, United Kingdom
Tel: (44)(865)56767
Fax: (44)(865)56646
Pages: 251
Exhibits: Tables

For those interested in Hong Kong's social history, this monograph, based on a Ph.D dissertation, offers a unique source. With all of the attention focused on the island's economic rise, little attention has been paid to the people who made the miracle possible. The readable chapters of this volume discuss the rise of the British merchant class, the emergence of leadership in the Chinese population, the rise of the Chinese merchant class, and Hong Kong's working class. This is an important contribution to the limited literature on this topic.

LAWS AND REGULATIONS

Title: *The Common System of Law in Chinese Context: Hong Kong in Transition*
Date: 1992
Format: Hardcover
Author: Berry Fong-Chung Hsu
Publisher: M.E. Sharpe, Inc.
80 Business Park Dr.
Armonk, N.Y. 10504
Tel: (914)273-1800
Fax: (914)273-2106
Pages: 284
Exhibits: Tables

The author of this study deals with the important question, To what extent has British Common Law been accepted by the citizens of Hong Kong?, in order to explore the changes in Hong Kong's legal environment that might come with the transition to Chinese sovereignty in 1997. The research is based on the results of a survey of attitudes and perceptions held by citizens. Selected chapters cover the introduction of Common Law in Hong Kong, the contrasts between Chinese culture and a "standard model Common Law judicial system," and the absorption of Common Law notions by the Chinese people in Hong Kong and in the Basic Law of Hong Kong.

Title: *Company Law in Hong Kong*
Date: 1986
Format: Hardcover
Author: Pauline Wallace
Publisher: Butterworth and Co. (Asia) Pte., Ltd.
30 Robinson Rd., #12-01
Tuan Sing Towers
Singapore, 0104
Tel: (65)220-3684
Fax: (65)225-2939
Pages: 366
Exhibits: None

Meant for lawyers, this volume treats the subject of law as it applies to companies in Hong Kong in great detail and with plentiful analysis of actual court cases. For the expert, the book is a recommended source of legal explanation on all aspects of a company's business activity, from incorporation to liquidation.

Title: *The Hong Kong Basic Law: Blueprint for "Stability and Prosperity" Under Chinese Sovereignty?*
Date: 1991
Format: Hardcover
Editor: Ming K. Chan and David J. Clark
Publisher: M.E. Sharpe, Inc.
80 Business Park Dr.
Armonk, N.Y. 10504
Tel: (914)273-1800
Fax: (914)273-2106

Pages: 310
Exhibits: None

Meant for analysts seeking to understand the process by which China and Britain came to agreement over the turning over of Hong Kong to Chinese sovereignty in 1997, this volume contains key "documents that chronicle the drafting process from the point of view of the various parties in the process." Researchers into Chinese affairs will find a complete draft of the Basic Law and the 1984 Sino-British Joint Declaration. A 55-page analysis examines the evolution of the Basic Law and the "one country, two systems" economic approach in Hong Kong in light of the Tiananmen uprising in Beijing and a growing democracy movement in Hong Kong.

MARKET DATA AND ANALYSIS

Title: *Hong Kong Annual Digest of Statistics*
Date: Annual
Format: Hardcover
Author: Census and Statistics Department, Hong Kong
Publisher: The Government Printer, Hong Kong
Publications Sale Counter of the Census and Statistics Department
19th Floor, Wanchai Tower 1
12 Harbour Rd.
Wanchai, Hong Kong
Tel: (852)823-4736
Pages: 293
Exhibits: Maps and tables
Price: $98

Compiled by the Census and Statistics Department, this is a first-choice source of raw statistical data about Hong Kong. The sections of clearly organized tables cover climate and geography, population, labor, industrial production, distributive trade, external trade, gross domestic product, public finance, and more.

Title: *Hong Kong Market Atlas*
Date: 1990
Format: Paperback
Author: Marcel Toussaint
Publisher: Business International Asia/Pacific, Ltd.
215 Park Ave. South
New York, NY 10003
Tel: (212)460-0600
Fax: (212)995-8837
Pages: 332
Exhibits: Maps and graphs

This attractive publication makes you ask, "Why aren't there more books like this one?" Covering Hong Kong's geography, economy, labor force, production, trade, budget, and so on, the book is a collection of graphs constructed from timely data collected by Hong Kong government organizations. From population by district to the household income of Wan Chai District, the business researcher will find in this large-format paperback a treasure trove of relevant data brought to visual life in user-friendly color graphs.

Title: *Supermap with the Data of the Hong Kong 1981 Census and 1986 By-Census*
Date: 1993

Format: CD-ROM
Author: Census and Statistical Department, Hong Kong
Publisher: Space-time Researcher Pty., Ltd.
Publications Sale Counter of the Census and Statistical Department
19th Floor, Wanchai Tower 1
12 Harbour Rd.
Wanchai, Hong Kong
Exhibits: Tables
Price: HK$7,800

This CD-ROM puts at your fingertips data collected for the 1981 and 1986 Hong Kong population census, including information about the age, sex, income, and housing of the population in each district. It is of great help to businesspeople planning their strategies for marketing to Hong Kong.

POLITICS AND GOVERNMENT

Title: *The Government and Politics of Hong Kong*
Date: 1991
Format: Hardcover
Author: Norman Miners
Publisher: Oxford University Press
18th Floor, Warwick House
Taikoo Trading Estate
28 Tong Chong St.
Quarry Bay, Hong Kong
Tel: (852)(5)516-3222
Fax: (852)(5)565-8491
Pages: 315
Exhibits: Maps and tables

Here is an erudite and readable explanation of how the Crown colony of Hong Kong is run, written by a political scientist at the University of Hong Kong. For those who work with the Hong Kong bureaucracy, this book provides ample background, including chapters on Hong Kong's government ideology, constitution, governing system, administrative and financial control, local government, pressure groups, political parties, and pressures from China. It includes an appendix of constitutional documents, such as the Joint Declaration and the Basic Law.

TAXATION

Title: *Hong Kong: International Tax and Business Guide*
Date: 1990
Format: Paperback
Publisher: Deloitte Ross Tohmatsu (DRT) International
1633 Broadway
New York, NY 10019-6754
Tel: (212)489-1600
Fax: (212)245-0839
Pages: 120
Exhibits: Maps and tables

This book about taxation in Hong Kong is perhaps the most complete, with a handy overview of the economy, employment practices, infrastructure (including a map of subway routes), business organization, intellectual property rights, and *then* five chapters about taxation. It is suggested as a handbook for expatriates and accountants.

Title: *Hong Kong Taxation*
Date: Annual

Format: Hardcover
Author: David Flux
Publisher: Chinese University Press
Chinese University of Hong Kong
Shatin
New Territories, Hong Kong
Tel: (852)695-2508
Fax: (852)604-6692
Pages: 579
Exhibits: Tables

Revised annually, this comprehensive and practical guide explains Hong Kong taxation in great detail. The author makes generous use of examples and cases to illustrate his points. The chapters include a handy overview of taxation in Hong Kong, property tax, salaries tax, interest tax, profits tax, depreciation allowances, personal tax, and more. This book is highly recommended for accountants and tax lawyers as well as serious businesspeople and expatriates.

Title: *Taxation in Hong Kong*
Date: 1990
Format: Hardcover
Publisher: KPMG Peat Marwick
345 Park Ave.
New York, NY 10154
Tel: (212)758-9700
Pages: 72
Exhibits: None

This slim volume clearly describes Hong Kong's tax policies and explains how to calculate them. It includes chapters on property tax, salary tax, profits tax, and depreciation allowances. It is recommended as a primer for expatriates and accountants. The book also includes many easy-to-understand examples of how to calculate taxes in special circumstances, for example: "A client had a number of sources of income liable to tax in Hong Kong. He owned a flat. . . ." You get the idea.

TAIWAN

OVERVIEW

Taiwan, once called Formosa, is an island empire about the size of Holland. It is the 12th largest trading nation in the world and the second most cash-rich country after Japan—and Japan has six times as many people. An economic powerhouse with a timid demeanor, the Taiwan stock market does as much business as both the New York and the Tokyo exchanges. One hundred and twenty countries don't recognize Taiwan diplomatically, yet Taiwan exports to virtually all of them.

Taiwan at a Glance

Population:	20.80 million
Religion:	Buddhist, Confucian, Taoist, Christian
Government:	Effective one-party rule
Language:	Mandarin (official language), Taiwanese, Hakka; many businesspeople speak English and Japanese as well
Currency:	New Taiwan (NT) dollar
Trade (1993):	\$81.5 billion total exports; \$72.0 billion total imports

The Taiwanese live under an authoritarian government that is still run by Chinese Nationalists who fled the Mainland before the bayonets of the Communists in 1949. Martial law was lifted in only 1987 after being in force since 1949. The Mainland's mandarinate, which ran the Kuomintang up until its defeat at the hands of the Communists in 1949, started arriving on the island of Formosa in the mid-1940s before the final fall of Chiang Kai-shek. Taiwan's Old Guard has been in control of Taiwan ever since. Although reforms in the 1980s broke the dictatorship in Taiwan, animosity between Mainlanders and Taiwanese has never faded completely, even as Taiwan's population grew from 8 million (including 2 million Mainlanders) in 1951 to 20 million in 1981. The U.S.-subsidized loans, expertise, military protection, and grants fueled Taiwan's rise. America's role in Taiwan's economy can be expressed numerically: Of Taiwan's $10.9-billion trade surplus in 1992, $10.4 billion was with the United States.

Economic Conditions

Fantastically productive, Taiwan's 316,712 factories are mostly small and family run; 85 percent of them employ fewer than 50 workers. Since the end of World War II, the island has experienced an average annual growth rate of almost 9 percent, swiftly moving from an agricultural to an industrial society during the 1950s and from an industrial society to one based firmly in capital-intensive high-tech manufacturing during the 1960s to 1980s. In the 1990s, the island is poised to become an important player in R&D and innovation as well as financial services. Taiwan has more money in reserves than any other country—more than $80 billion. In 1991, economic growth hummed along at 7.3 percent, and unemployment remained below 2 percent.

Taiwan's economy remains 40 percent dependent on exports, which help it to accrue its $13-billion trade surplus each year. Its trade continues to merge with that of Mainland China as Taiwan's offshore plants now located in China demand more imports from Taiwan. In fact, this dynamic has played an important role in maintaining the island's export balance while markets in the West have languished due to worldwide recession. Indicative of the island's tenacity in diversifying its trade, the United States is now its sixth largest trade partner, well behind first-place Japan, the only country that enjoys a sizable trade surplus with the island. America's share of Taiwan's export dropped from 44 to 29 percent between 1987 and 1991. Hong Kong's role as entrepôt between the island and the People's Republic (and its role as Taiwan's second largest export market) will likely fade after 1997.

Although the Taiwanese government promotes an "import substitution" industrial strategy for the country's large firms, most of Taiwan's companies are small, family-run businesses. Their entrepreneurial, resourceful, and export-driven managers tend to distrust officialdom and, for that matter, anyone who is not a member of the immediate family. In fact, Taiwanese companies are typically limited in size to the extended family, usually 5 to 15 employees. As elsewhere in Asia, rising wages and an appreciating currency are forcing Taiwan to shift from labor-intensive production to more capital-intensive production. This shift has fueled Taiwan's heavy investment in areas of Asia, such as South China, Vietnam, Indonesia, Thailand, and the Philippines, where semiskilled labor is still inexpensive. For example, more than 2,800 Taiwanese enterprises have set up in the People's Republic as of this writing.

Because Taiwan's companies are generally resistant to buying foreign products that are also made in Taiwan, to sell to them requires that Western suppliers have representation in Taiwan. Exhaustive searches for both buyers and distributors remain an absolute must for foreigners. Even with nontariff barriers to the market, Taiwan must increase its imports to avoid political problems with its trading partners and to slake heavy consumer demand for products that have remained unavailable because of import restrictions. The best prospects for U.S. sales include pollution-control equipment, computers and peripherals, laboratory instruments, semiconductors, medical equipment, telecommunications equipment, process controls, CAD-CAM manufacturing technologies, and power plants.

Because the United States does not recognize the Republic of Taiwan as a nation separate from Mainland China, U.S. government representation on the island is coordinated through the American Institute in Taiwan (AIT), a private, nonprofit corporation, with headquarters in Rosslyn, Virginia, and offices in Taipei and Kaohsiung. Commercial services similar to those provided by the U.S. Foreign Commercial Service can be obtained from AIT's commercial sections in Taipei and Kaohsiung.

ACCOUNTING, BANKING, AND FINANCE

Title: *The Republic of China: Monthly Statistics of Finance*
Date: Monthly
Format: Periodical
Publisher: Ministry of Finance
2 Aikuo
West Taipei 10046, Taiwan
Tel: (886)(2)351-1611
Pages: Varies
Exhibits: Graphs and tables
Price: Contact for subscription prices

Not of the highest publishing quality, this periodical carries Taiwan's government-issued body of economic indicators. It is of use to market trackers and researchers. Foreign trade figures are broken down by commodity.

COMPANY DIRECTORIES

Title: *Directory of Taiwan*
Date: Annual
Format: Paperback
Publisher: China News
11th Floor, 110 Yenping S. Rd.
Taipei, Taiwan
Tel: (886)(2)321-0882
Pages: 528
Exhibits: None
Price: $15.40

This is a useful phone book of key contacts in Taiwan, in part because all addresses and names are listed in both English and Chinese. The book is small in size but includes every conceivable listing that the foreign visitor might need, from English-speaking service centers to the Mayor of Taipei. This directory is recommended and reasonably priced.

Title: *Taiwan Importers Directory*
Date: Annual
Format: Hardcover
Publisher: Taiwan Yellow Pages Corp.
P.O. Box 81-02
Taipei 10047, Taiwan
Tel: (886)(2)781-8981
Fax: (886)(2)781-8982
Pages: Varies
Exhibits: None
Price: $80

A great resource for marketers, this 400-page directory is easy to use and attractively published. The first part lists all commodities and the Taiwanese firms that import them. The second part lists all of the companies in alphabetical order; each entry includes the address, the name of the general manager, and the main items the company imports.

COUNTRY PROFILES

Title: *Country Forecast: Taiwan*
Date: Quarterly
Format: Periodical; also available on-line
Publisher: The Economist Intelligence Unit
P.O. Box 154
Dartford
Kent DA1 1QB, United Kingdom
Tel: (44)(322)289-194
Fax: (44)(322)223-803
For on-line version, contact:
Maid Systems, Ltd.
Maid House
18 Dufferin St.
London EC1Y 8PD, United Kingdom
Tel: (44)(71)253-6900
Pages: Varies
Exhibits: Tables
Price: Contact for subscription prices

In this quarterly outlook report, businesspeople will find concise analyses and forecasts regarding Taiwan's politics, economy, and business environment. New developments in each area are noted, and tables provide current economic data. This resource will interest business prognosticators and potential investors in Taiwan.

Title: *The Republic of China Yearbook*
Date: Annual
Format: Hardcover
Author: Government Information Service, Republic of China
Publisher: Kwang Hwa Publishing Co.
2 Tien Tsin St.
Taipei 10041, Taiwan
Tel: (886)(2)341-9211
Pages: Varies
Exhibits: Maps, graphs, photographs, and tables
Price: $45

A handsome, fully illustrated yearbook of 800 to 900 pages, this volume provides a wide array of information about Taiwan in article form. Topics range from geography and history to national defense and foreign relations. This book is a comprehensive information sourcebook for businesspeople involved with Taiwan and a resource for building one's conversational skills on Taiwan-related topics.

ECONOMY

Title: *Quarterly National Economic Trends*
Date: Quarterly
Format: Periodical
Editor: Directorate-General of Budget, Accounting, and Statistics, Republic of China
Publisher: China Cultural Service
5 Lane 333
Section 3
Roosevelt Rd.
Taipei 10041, Taiwan
Tel: (886)(2)351-1611
Pages: Varies
Exhibits: Graphs and tables
Price: Contact for subscription prices

For anyone tracking Taiwan's economy, this is the government's quarterly report. It includes an introductory section that analyzes the data.

GENERAL BUSINESS

Title: *Doing Business in Taiwan*
Date: 1989
Format: Hardcover
Author: James Cheng
Publisher: Cheng and Cheng Law Offices
4th Floor, 624 Ming Chuan E. Rd.
Taipei, Taiwan
Tel: (886)(2)713-3233
Fax: (886)(2)713-3222
Pages: 218
Exhibits: Tables

This book provides a brief overview of the laws and regulations that affect foreign companies conducting business in Taiwan. It is a convenient reference guide for businesspeople setting up shop there. The legal aspects covered include the forms of commercial ventures allowed in Taiwan, the procedures for setting up a business, the general laws governing business activity, intellectual property rights, and trademark law.

Title: *Taiwan Trade Opportunities*
Date: Monthly
Format: Periodical
Publisher: China External Trade Development Council
8th Floor, 333 Keelung Rd.
Section 1
Taipei 10063, Taiwan
Tel: (886)(2)725-5200
Fax: (886)(2)757-6828
Pages: Varies
Exhibits: Tables
Price: $50/year

This 50- to 60-page magazine lists trading opportunities advertised by Taiwanese firms. The trade leads are divided into "Wish to Import" and "Wish to Export" categories and include products ranging from printed circuit boards to facial equipment. The funny thing is that the issue reviewed contained only a single "Wish to Import" entry out of hundreds of trade leads. The magazine also contains industry reports covering new products in selected industries.

MARKET DATA AND ANALYSIS

Title: *Imports and Exports of the Republic of China*
Date: 1993
Format: Hardcover
Publisher: China External Trade Development Council (CETRA)
8th Floor, 333 Keelung Rd.
Section 1
Taipei 10086, Taiwan
Tel: (886)(2)725-5200
Fax: (886)(2)757-6828
Pages: 1,768
Exhibits: None

This massive trade directory lists 15,580 Taiwanese companies in 6,065 products areas. You can look up a product classification and find a list of buying and selling companies, or you can look up the company to find out what they buy and sell. Company listings include contact information, the CEO's name, and the company's bank. An alphabetical list of product names by "key word" (for example, the key word for "shrimp, peeled, frozen" is simply *shrimp*) is a handy addition.

Title: *Statistical Yearbook of the Republic of China, 1992*
Date: Annual
Format: Paperback
Author: Directorate-General of Budget, Accounting, and Statistics
Publisher: Chen Chung Book Co.
3rd Floor, 20 Heng-yang Rd.
Taipei 10047, Taiwan
Tel: (886)(2)381-3980
Pages: 312
Price: NT$800

Published by the Taiwanese government, this is the best source of raw statistical data about Taiwan. Selected sections cover population and labor, wages, culture, education, industry, mining, construction, transportation, and telecommunications. Where appropriate, tables provide data from the early 1970s to the present.

Title: *Taiwan Products*
Date: Monthly
Format: Periodical
Editor: Y.L. Chang
Publisher: Far East Trade Service, Inc.
4–8th Floor, 333 Keelung Rd.
Section 1
Taipei 10548, Taiwan
Tel: (886)(2)725-5200
Fax: (886)(2)757-6828
Pages: Varies
Exhibits: Photographs
Price: $35/year

For buyers of goods made in Taiwan, this glossy 100-page magazine runs color advertisements for finished products offered by Taiwanese manufacturers. Text articles provide updates on new product lines, all of which are useful to the buyer of light manufactured goods.

POLITICS AND GOVERNMENT

Title: *Constitutional Reform and the Future of the Republic of China*
Date: 1991
Format: Hardcover
Editor: Harvey Feldman
Publisher: M.E. Sharpe, Inc.
80 Business Park Dr.
Armonk, N.Y. 10504
Tel: (914)273-1800
Fax: (914)273-2106
Pages: 173
Exhibits: None

Written under the auspices of the East Asian Institute at Columbia University, this is a compilation of academic essays and dialogues that were initially presented at a 1990 conference bearing the same title as the book. The focus is on institutional and constitutional change in Taiwan. Readers will find ample prognostications for the future of political development on the island. The text is presented in spoken rather than prose style.

Title: *Democratization of Taiwan and the Future of China's Unification*
Date: 1992
Format: Paperback
Author: John C. Kuan
Publisher: Democracy Foundation
10th Floor, 102 Kwang Fu S. Rd.
Taipei 10046, Taiwan
Tel: (886)(2)731-8920
Fax: (886)(2)771-1951
Pages: 161
Exhibits: None
Price: $20

Dealing with a very relevant topic for the China political watcher, this erudite set of essays by a well-known Taiwanese scholar and official provides insights into the volatile relationship between China and Taiwan and examines the chances for the future reunification of the countries. Of particular interest to political risk analysts, the book puts Taiwan's economic development experience in perspective, evaluates the island's slow evolution toward democracy, and hypothesizes that "without the cultivation of democratic values throughout mainland China, reunification is neither feasible nor desirable vis-à-vis the interests of the 20 million Chinese living on Taiwan." This book is recommended.

Title: *Issues and Studies*
Date: Monthly
Format: Periodical
Editor: James C. Shen
Publisher: Institute of International Relations, Republic of China
64 Wan Shou Rd.
Wenshan
Taipei 10041, Taiwan
Tel: (886)(2)939-4921
Fax: (886)(2)938-2133
Pages: Varies
Exhibits: Graphs and tables
Price: $30/year

This academic journal covers China and Taiwan, with some general coverage of East Asia. Businesspeople will find some articles of interest, especially those dealing with economic linkages between the "three Chinas": Hong Kong, the People's Republic of China, and Taiwan.

Title: *Political Change in Taiwan*
Date: 1992
Format: Hardcover
Editor: Tun-Jen Cheng and Stephan Haggard
Publisher: Lynne Rienner Publishers, Inc.
1800 30th St.
Boulder, CO 80301
Tel: (303)444-6684
Fax: (303)444-0824
Pages: 267
Exhibits: Tables

This compilation of well-integrated academic essays, written under the auspices of the Center for International Affairs at Harvard University, sets out to examine the future of democracy in Taiwan. The five parts of the book focus on social change; liberalization and democratization; the evolution of the KMT and the rise of a party system in Taiwan; the electoral system and the behavior of voters; and future prospects for democracy in Taiwan. This book is readable and extensively footnoted.

Title: *Taiwan Studies Newsletter*
Date: Quarterly
Format: Periodical
Editor: Jack Williams
Publisher: Taiwan Studies Group
China and Inner Asia Council
Association for Asian Studies
Asian Studies Center
Michigan State University
East Lansing, MI 48824
Tel: (517)353-1680
Fax: (517)336-2659
Pages: Varies
Exhibits: Tables
Price: $10/year

For the serious researcher of Taiwan, this newsletter provides abstracts of recently published books and articles on Taiwan, many of which businesspeople should be aware of. Although it needs a graphic face-lift, this publication is a useful monitor of the growing literature about Taiwan.

RESEARCH AND DEVELOPMENT

Title: *Directory of R&D Institutions in the Republic of China*
Date: 1992
Format: Paperback
Publisher: Science and Technology Information Center
National Science Council
16th Floor, 106 Hoping E. Rd.
Section 1
Taipei 10636, Taiwan
Pages: 691
Exhibits: None
Price: $20

Here is an indispensable directory for the technology hunter in Taiwan. The 1,600 institutions listed are divided into those under the Executive Yuan, provincial, county, and city research organizations; those under the Taipei and Kaohsiung city governments; and those under the auspices of universities, colleges, and military academies. Each entry includes the address, phone number, major research activities, annual budget, source of budget, and whether the organization cooperates with outside entities. This last bit of information will be of interest to foreign businesses seeking to acquire basic Taiwanese scientific research.

MONGOLIA

OVERVIEW

Mongolia is a vast country of high plains and mountain ranges the size of Alaska, landlocked between Russia and China. One-fourth of the country's population of 2.4 million, which is 90 percent Mongolian, lives in the capital of Ulan Bator. With the dissolution of the Soviet Union, the country is on its way toward creating a viable multiparty democracy. Foreign investment and joint ventures with foreign firms are encouraged, but the impediments to business are extreme: inefficient infrastructure, delays in approvals, power shortages, and a general lack of business law.

Mongolia at a Glance

Population:	2.18 million
Religion:	Tibetan Buddhist, shamanist
Government:	Multiparty democracy
Language:	Khalkha Mongolian; other Mongolian dialects
Currency:	Tugrik (Tug)
Trade (1993):	$368 million total exports; $399 million total imports

COUNTRY PROFILES

Title: *Mongolia: A Centrally Planned Economy in Transition*

Date: 1992

Format: Hardcover

Author: Asian Development Bank

Publisher: Oxford University Press
18th Floor, Warwick House
Tong Chong St.
Quarry Bay, Hong Kong
Tel: (852)(5)516-3222
Fax: (852)(5)565-8491

Pages: 250

Exhibits: Maps and tables

Attractive and well illustrated, this detailed introduction to Mongolia is a one-stop source for intrepid businesspeople entering the country. Selected chapters cover natural resources and the economic system, economic and social development, the financial sector, fiscal policy, and economic reform. Detailed "sectoral assessments" focus on agriculture, industry, social infrastructure, transportation and communication, energy, and natural resources. An appendix is loaded with statistics.

Part Two

Southeast Asia

SOUTHEAST ASIA

OVERVIEW

The member countries of the Association of Southeast Asian Nations (ASEAN)—Singapore, Philippines, Indonesia, Malaysia, Thailand, and Brunei—have emerged as important "mini-dragons" in the Asia-Pacific boom. The ASEAN member countries, which are home to more than 300 million people, make up one of the world's regional economic success stories. Scattered along the equator and extending 1,000 miles to the north and 500 miles to the south, the countries range from resource-rich Indonesia to the superindustrialized island-state of Singapore. All are tropical in climate, but mountain wilderness and hardwood forests are features of all of the countries except Singapore.

Every ASEAN country has pursued an export-led, market-oriented development strategy, and together they have sustained an average growth rate of 7 percent throughout the 1970s and close to that in the 1980s and early 1990s in the face of deteriorating oil prices and slackening world trade. As a trading bloc, ASEAN is one of the world's production, trade, and investment powerhouses, accounting for 88 percent of world rubber exports, 70 percent of copra, and more than 70 percent of palm oil. The region is a major supplier of tin, copper, coal, nickel, tungsten, and forest products, not to mention a key production base for electronics, textiles, food, and oil. Total trade between the United States and ASEAN members has soared from $23 billion in 1985 to $330 billion in 1992. American companies invested $9.3 billion in ASEAN countries in 1985; they invested $30.2 billion in the region in 1993.

ASEAN was founded in 1967 for the purpose of promoting regional cooperation and self-reliance among its original five members. Economic cooperation was a stated goal as well, but ASEAN has never been effective at accomplishing economic and social goals due to the diversity of interests and economic disparity between members. It has reduced internal trade barriers and established a number of industrial projects, however. Brunei became a member in 1984, just after winning its independence from the British.

Historical Background

Centuries-long migrations of Siamese, Annamese, and Burmese from Southwest China and Tibet through the dense valleys and rich alluvial plains to the sea populated the region that is now called Thailand. The Siamese arrived at the Chao Phya River and ejected the Khmer, Yuan, Jawa, and Mon peoples. Soon, the kingdom of Siam stretched all the way to Singapore. The Chinese followed the migrants by the 13th century via an overland trade route across the great gorges of the Lantsam, Lu Kiang, and Lung Kong in the northern region of Thailand.

The migrants from South China also became the predecessors of the Malayo-Indonesians, who populated the 10,000 islands of present-day Indonesia farther south. At the same time, however, starting 6,000 years ago, waves of Malayo-Polynesians (or Austronesians) began arriving on the Malay archipelago after sailing west from the region of the Philippines. They began mixing with those arriving down the neck of the archipelago from South China. This mixing occurred between Mongolian and Austronesian groups all across the islands of Indonesia.

Early Southeast Asians were agriculturalists, among the first to domesticate tubers and legumes. They used the ox and the water buffalo and worshiped ancestors and spirits associated with fields and streams. Inheritance was matrilineal. The *Orang Asli*, or "original people," who first came to the Malay peninsula migrated from Yunnan in South China. Proto-Malays followed in 2000 B.C., bringing with them their seafaring and navigational skills. Deutero-Malays followed them with their farming skills and self-contained village organization, which was to influence Malay ethnic patterns for centuries. They devised a system of social custom and tradition that was later given the name *adat* in Malaysia and Indonesia. *Adat* is equivalent to the western notion of common law. This *adat* culture became Muslim culture after the Islamization of the region in the 13th century. Through maritime trade, *adat*/Muslim culture spread east as far as present-day Mindanao, the southernmost island of the Philippines; to this day, the island is predominantly Muslim, whereas the rest of the Philippines are Christian.

The crescent of Islam was always mightier than the cross of Christianity in Southeast Asia. The spread of Islam started with the rise of Malacca as a locus of trading and commerce in Southeast Asia. Like a gentle breeze, the Islam religion blew across Southeast Asia and supplanted Hinduism and Buddhism. For the next century, Islam outstripped Catholicism in its spread over the archipelago. Where trade was conducted by Muslims, Islam was introduced. Indonesia is now home to the largest Muslim population in the world. Muslim Asians—whether in Malaysia, Indonesia, Singapore, or on Mindanao Island in the Philippines—live by the laws of the Koran, which forbids adherents from participating in certain activities and from eating certain food considered to be unclean. Muslim women observe strict rules as to their behavior, dress, and social roles.

In contrast, Thailand is the only country on the Asian Pacific Rim that is overwhelmingly Buddhist, and this makes the country a unique region of Asia in which to do business. Myanmar, formerly called Burma, shares many similarities with Thailand, including the fact that its population is almost entirely Buddhist.

Influence of the Chinese

The "sojourn" of overseas Chinese, called the *Nanyang*, began over a thousand years ago. Now, 47 million Chinese live outside of mainland China; they make up 10 percent of the population of Thailand, 2.5 percent of that of Indonesia, and 80 percent of that of Singapore. The great majority of overseas Chinese come from the Southeastern provinces of China, mostly Cantonese, Hakka, and Teochius peoples. Throughout Southeast Asia, the Chinese invested in farms, rubber estates, copra plantations, timber, shipping, and merchandizing. They quickly gained the dominant economic position wherever they settled. They maintained their own schools and separated themselves as much as possible from local populations. In Malaya, they entered into trade, supplied most of the labor in the mines, soon owning a third of them, and became well positioned in nearly every other industry in Malaya. In Thailand, they worked in tin and tungsten mines, on rubber plantations, and as shopkeepers and traders. In both Thailand and Indonesia, the Chinese came to control the retail district. They soon owned 80 to 90 percent of Thailand's rice mills, for example.

In some Asian countries, most notably Indonesia, Thailand, and Vietnam, discriminatory laws against the Chinese have been ratified not on racial bases, but to target them as capitalists who might monopolize strategic industries. Some of the world's richest people are overseas Chinese. Li Ka-shing, the richest man in Hong Kong, owns Canada's 12th largest oil company and Hong Kong International Terminals, controlling half of the shipping traffic through Hong Kong harbor. Y.K. Pao, from Hong Kong, is a shipowner and real estate financier who purchased the Omni Hotel chain in the United States for $135 million in 1988. Y.C. Wang, from Taiwan, owns Formosa Plastics Group, which had sales of $5.8 billion in 1988. Y.Z. Hsu, from Taiwan, is a textile kingpin. Overseas Chinese from Hong Kong and Taiwan own 10 percent of downtown San Francisco. Though public-sector companies usually have ethnically indigenous owners, like Thais or Malays, owners of Chinese descent who speak Mandarin or another Chinese dialect control most companies that do business in the private sectors in these countries. That said, it remains vital for Westerners to understand the indigenous cultures with which they will deal in Southeast Asia.

COUNTRY PROFILES

Title: *Southeast Asia Monitor*
Date: Monthly
Format: Periodical
Editor: Anthony Beachly
Publisher: Business Monitor International, Ltd.
56-60 Saint John St.
London EC1M 4DT, United Kingdom
Tel: (44)(71)608-3646
Fax: (44)(71)608-3620
Pages: Varies
Exhibits: Tables
Price: $380/year

Greatly overpriced yet recommended as a regional updater on commercial topics, this 10-page monthly newsletter provides news briefs on each Southeast Asian country as well as a feature article on a regional economic issue, such as the success or failure of the ASEAN Free Trade Area (AFTA). In each country briefing of 1 to 2 pages, a table of economic forecasts is given for the next two years. The commercial news about each country is a little sparse, but, for a brief updater, this publication succeeds.

Title: *Southeast Asian Affairs*
Date: Annual
Format: Hardcover
Editor: Sharon Siddque and Ng Chee Yuen
Publisher: Institute of Southeast Asian Studies
Heng Mui Keng Terrace
Pasir Panjang 0511, Singapore
Tel: (65)778-0955
Fax: (65)775-6259
Pages: 363
Exhibits: Maps and tables

Each edition of this book offers an anthology of expert articles on Asian politics and economic development. The approach is academic in style and coverage, but the solid, well-researched articles provide timely theoretical conclusions for the serious researcher of Asian political economics.

Title: *The Southeast Asian Investment Guide*
Date: 1992
Format: Paperback
Author: Neill T. Macpherson
Publisher: Longman Group (Far East), Ltd./Longman Professional
18th Floor, Cornwall House
Tong Chong St.
Quarry Bay, Hong Kong
Tel: (914)993-5000 (U.S.)
Fax: (914)997-8115 (U.S.)
Pages: 318
Exhibits: Maps and tables

Dealing with one country per chapter, this handsomely published guide provides a summary of the foreign investment climates and regulatory policies of Brunei, Indonesia, Malaysia, Philippines, Singapore, and Thailand as of early 1991. The author is a lawyer, but there is more here than a complete description of tax and legal environments, though this is the focus. There is a profile for each country, a commentary on the government's attitude about foreign investment, a look at economic trends, and coverage of financial matters. Each country receives

15 to 20 pages of discussion. This book is recommended for lawyers and accountants working in the region.

ECONOMY

Title: *ASEAN Economic Bulletin*
Date: Monthly
Format: Periodical
Editor: K.S. Sandhu
Publisher: Institute of Southeast Asian Studies
Heng Mui Keng Terrace
Pasir Panjang 0511, Singapore
Tel: (65)778-0955
Fax: (65)775-6259
Pages: Varies
Exhibits: Tables
Price: $35/year for individuals; $44/year for institutions

Here is a midsize journal that provides well-researched academic articles covering issues in trade, investment, and economic development in the member countries of ASEAN. The articles are readable and provide an analysis of issues for the serious business reader. The coverage of enterprise management in the region is particularly good and difficult to find elsewhere. The price of this monthly is a bargain for the specialist.

Title: *Booming Economies of South East Asia: Thailand, Malaysia, Singapore, and Indonesia*
Date: 1990
Format: Hardcover
Author: Alain Guillouet
Publisher: Longman Singapore Publishers (Pte.), Ltd.
25 First Lok Yang Rd.
Jurong Town, 2262 Singapore
Tel: (914)993-5000 (U.S.)
Fax: (914)997-8115 (U.S.)
Pages: 195
Exhibits: Maps, graphs, and tables

Made up of bulleted lists, graphs, and numbered paragraphs, this may not be an engrossing or enjoyable read, but it does provide much economic information about four key nations in Southeast Asia, all under one cover. Most chapters are country-specific, providing background and an overview of trade and investment trends or examining each country's adjustment to indebtedness and growth patterns. This is a handy one-stop source, but most of the information is available from the U.S. Department of Commerce.

Title: *Southeast Asia in the World Economy*
Date: 1991
Format: Hardcover
Author: Chris Dixon
Publisher: Cambridge University Press
Pitt Building
Trumpington St.
Cambridge CB2 1RP, United Kingdom
Tel: (44)(223)312-393
Fax: (44)(223)315-052
Pages: 281
Exhibits: Maps, graphs, and tables

Here is a well-written and well-illustrated volume that gives the businessperson headed for Southeast Asia a solid foundation in the region's geography, trade, development, politics, and relationship with the world at large. This is a highly recommended feat of scholarly research and synthesis. The writing style is clear, and the book is rich in factual detail.

HISTORY AND SOCIETY

Title: *Atlas of Southeast Asia*
Date: 1989
Format: Hardcover
Author: Richard Ulack and Guyla Pauer
Publisher: Macmillan Publishing Co.
866 Third Ave.
New York, NY 10022
Tel: (212)702-2000
Fax: (212)605-3099
Pages: 171
Exhibits: Maps, graphs, and photographs

An attractive atlas that includes country and metropolitan area maps, this volume features Burma, Vietnam, Cambodia, Laos, and Brunei as well as the more developed Southeast Asian countries. Each country section includes key facts, a historical overview, and a description of the physical environment, economy, transportation, and society. Some of the data are dated, but the rest are useful as a general cultural introduction to these countries.

Title: *A Short History of Malaysia, Singapore and Brunei*
Date: 1981
Format: Hardcover
Author: C. Mary Turnbull
Publisher: Grahmam Brash (Pte.), Ltd.
36-C Prinsep St.
Singapore, 0718
Tel: (65)861-1336
Fax: (65)861-4815
Pages: 320
Exhibits: Maps, photographs, and tables

Here is a recommended and very readable history of three countries that are not usually treated in the same volume. Coverage of Indonesia is also provided. The book offers a concise history of the region, covering Islam, the British colonial period, and the pursuit of nationalism and independence. Most important to businesspeople, it provides a clear explanation of Malaysia's government system, the ethnic makeup of the region, and the role of Chinese businesspeople there.

INDUSTRY

Title: *Computerworld—Southeast Asia*
Date: Weekly
Format: Periodical
Editor: Timothy J. Wilson
Publisher: Asia Computerworld Communications, Ltd.
80 Marine Parade Rd.
#13-09 Parkway Parade
Singapore, 1544
Pages: Varies
Exhibits: None
Price: $230/year

This large-format color news weekly provides quality information on hardware and software business developments as they affect the Asia-Pacific. The journalism and the graphic presentation are top-notch. The publication covers deals and new products and features editorials about the industry. It is highly recommended to marketers in the computer industry.

Title: *Southeast Asia Building*
Date: Monthly
Format: Periodical
Editor: Steven Ooi
Publisher: Trade Link Media Pte., Ltd.
470 No. Bridge Rd.
02-03 Singapore Finance House
Singapore, 0718
Tel: (65)334-0378
Fax: (65)334-0373
Pages: Varies
Exhibits: None
Price: $143/year

One hundred pages of gloss and blazing color, this monthly trade magazine, directed at those who are involved in the construction industry, carries articles on specifications, new products, building news, and chemical methods and offers complete coverage of industry events, such as trade shows and conferences. It is chock-full of product advertisements.

INFORMATION SOURCES

Title: *Index to Periodical Articles Relating to Singapore, Malaysia, Brunei, and ASEAN (Supplement 1990)*
Date: 1991
Format: Paperback
Author: Reference and Information Services Dept., Central Library/Hon Sui Sen Memorial Library
Publisher: Reference and Information Services Dept. Central Library
National University of Singapore
10 Kent Ridge Crescent
Singapore, 0511
Tel: (65)776-1148
Fax: (65)774-0652
Pages: 239
Exhibits: None

This is an extremely useful and well-organized bibliography of articles and books about the countries of Southeast Asia and the Philippines. The section that lists articles about business and industry is of special interest to anyone researching a company or business opportunity in these countries. An author and subject index is included.

MARKET DATA AND ANALYSIS

Title: *Preparing ASEAN for the Information Century*
Date: 1990
Format: Paperback
Author: Vivien M. Talisayon
Publisher: University of the Philippines
Gonzales Hall Dillman
Quezon City 3004, Philippines
Tel: (63)(2)992-558
Pages: 186
Exhibits: Tables

Of possible interest to market researchers, this slim volume compares the degree of computerization at the elementary, secondary, and teacher education levels in the six member countries of ASEAN. The author reviews computer policies and programs in each country and proposes areas in which regional cooperation should be pursued.

POLITICS AND GOVERNMENT

Title: *Annual Report of the ASEAN Standing Committee*

Date: Annual

Format: Paperback

Author: Standing Committee of the Association of Southeast Asian Nations

Publisher: ASEAN Secretariat
70-A Jalan Sisingamangaraja
P.O. Box 2072
Jakarta 12042, Indonesia

Pages: Varies

Exhibits: Photographs and tables

This ponderous and dry yearly report of the ASEAN Standing Committee is useful for businesspeople who need to follow ASEAN policy initiatives closely as they affect trade flows, development projects, and public works projects in member nations. ASEAN policy changes can also affect customs regulations, taxation, industrial policy, and numerous other regulatory areas that might have an effect on a foreign business operation in the region.

Title: *Behind the Myth: Business, Money and Power in Southeast Asia*

Date: 1989

Format: Hardcover

Author: James Clad

Publisher: Unwin Hyman, Ltd.
15-17 Broadwick St.
London W1V 1FP, United Kingdom

Pages: 275

Exhibits: None

It may come as a surprise to some, but the success of East Asia—Japan, South Korea, and Taiwan—is nearly equaled in terms of economic growth by the countries of Southeast Asia, including Indonesia, Singapore, Philippines, Malaysia, Brunei, and Thailand. In this book, an experienced journalist tells the story of economic success in the region and spotlights some of the warts as well, such as poor education, poverty, and corrupt government leaders. Therein lies the "myth" of free marketism in Southeast Asia; in fact, these economies are characterized by business-government linkages and favoritism and depend on outside capital, technology, management, and markets. For anyone doing business with the countries of ASEAN, this book offers a well-crafted and well-informed introduction to the commercial scene.

Title: *Contemporary Southeast Asia*

Date: Monthly

Format: Periodical

Author: Institute of Southeast Asian Studies

Editor: Derek da Cunha

Publisher: Singapore University Press
Heng Mui Keng
Pasir Panjang Terrace
Singapore, 0511
Tel: (65)776-1148
Fax: (65)774-0652

Pages: Varies

Exhibits: None

Price: $24/year for individuals; $30/year for institutions

This bargain-price 100-page monthly journal contains articles and book reviews. The articles tend to focus on political development, foreign policy, and analysis of Asian societies from a theoretical point of view. For those gauging political risk factors or formulating long-term corporate strategy in Asia, this journal can be useful.

Title: *Indochina Chronology*

Date: Quarterly

Format: Periodical

Author: Institute of East Asian Studies, University of California, Berkeley

Editor: Douglas Pike

Publisher: University of California Press
2120 Berkeley Way
Berkeley, CA 94720
Tel: (510)642-4247
Fax: (510)643-7127

Pages: Varies

Exhibits: None

Price: $25/year

This 35-page quarterly provides researchers and analysts with reliable information on current events in Cambodia, Laos, and Vietnam. The short articles are abstracts from credible wire services and published news accounts. This is a useful updater for businesspeople who lack the time to read more comprehensive sources of Indochina news.

Title: *Indochina Digest*

Date: Weekly

Format: Periodical

Publisher: Indochina Project
Suite 740
2001 S St., NW
Washington, DC 20009
Tel: (202)483-9222

Pages: Varies

Exhibits: None

Price: Contact for subscription prices

This two-page news briefing covers trade, investment, and policy developments in Cambodia, Laos, and Vietnam. As in the *Indochina Chronology*, the short articles are abstracts from credible wire services and published news accounts. This is a useful updater for businesspeople who lack the time to read more comprehensive sources of Indochina news.

Title: *Indochina Issues*

Date: Monthly

Format: Periodical

Publisher: Indochina Project
Suite 740
2001 S St., NW
Washington, DC 20009
Tel: (202)483-9222

Pages: Varies

Exhibits: None

Price: $20/year

This seven-page newsletter focuses on military, political, and international aid issues as they relate to Cambodia, Laos, and Vietnam. It is useful to political risk analysts and those in the international assistance field.

Title: *Indochina Journal*
Date: Irregular
Format: Periodical
Author: Indochina Human Rights Group
Publisher: Indochina Journal
P.O. Box 1163
Burlingame, CA 94011-1163
Tel: (415)952-4343
Pages: Varies
Exhibits: None
Price: $8/four issues

The purpose of this 20-page newsletter is to educate readers about human rights abuses in Cambodia, Laos, and Vietnam and about the status of refugees from these countries. Businesspeople engaged with counterparts in these countries might find that this publication enhances their perspective on Indochina and its people.

Title: *Indochina Report*
Date: Quarterly
Format: Periodical
Editor: M. Rajaretnam
Publisher: Information and Resource Center Pte., Ltd.
6 Nassim Rd.
Singapore, 1025
Tel: (65)734-9600
Fax: (65)733-6217
Pages: Varies
Exhibits: None
Price: Contact for subscription prices

This attractive 15-page newsletter "looks behind signal developments in one of the three countries [of Indochina] to discern key trends, explain events and assess their implications for the rest of Southeast Asia." Political analysts and macroeconomists will find selected issues of interest, but most businesspeople will find the newsletter esoteric in tone and approach.

Title: *The Overseas Chinese in ASEAN: Business Strategies and Management Practices*
Date: 1986
Format: Hardcover
Author: Victor Simpao Limlingan
Publisher: Vita Development Corp.
108 Celery Dr.
Valla Verde V
Pasig, Metro
Manila, Philippines
Tel: (63)(2)673-0336
Pages: 166
Exhibits: Tables

What this study lacks in publication quality it makes up for in originality and completeness. As the author states, the "objective of the book is to formulate a conceptual framework for explaining how the Overseas Chinese in the ASEAN countries have achieved remarkable economic performance." That performance, we learn, is not due purely to the so-called Trader hypothesis but is "attributed to the discovery of a superior strategy effectively implemented . . . and consistent with Chinese culture." The author describes Chinese business strategies in ASEAN with much detail and provides admirable analysis. This book is a must for managers who want to emulate the management style of the companies that have traditionally dominated the business communities of Southeast Asia.

TRAVEL ADVICE

Title: *The Business Travel Guide to ASEAN Nations: Indonesia, Malaysia, Philippines, Singapore, Thailand, Hong Kong*
Date: 1979
Format: Paperback
Publisher: Executive Squire, Ltd.
G.P.O. Box 2071
Bangkok, Thailand
Pages: 288
Exhibits: Maps and tables

This handbook may be hard to find, but it contains useful addresses, phone numbers, and logistical information for travelers to Southeast Asia. Your best bet in purchasing it is a business bookstore in Singapore or Hong Kong.

Title: *South-East Asia on a Shoestring*
Date: 1989
Format: Paperback
Author: Tony Wheeler
Publisher: Lonely Planet Publications
P.O. Box 2001A
Berkeley, CA 94702
Tel: (510)893-8555
Fax: (510)893-8563
Pages: 682
Exhibits: Maps
Price: $14.95

This fabulous travel guide includes travel advice for all of Southeast Asia, including Vietnam, Laos, and Kampuchea. The coverage of multiisland Indonesia is comprehensive. As with all Lonely Planet guides, the advice emphasizes bargain hunting and cultural sight-seeing; the typical businessperson might not be seeking a bargain hotel or have the time to sightsee. Still, this guide is useful and entertaining for those who want an inside view of the region. Remember, however, that when the author says a hotel offers "no frills," he means it.

Singapore

OVERVIEW

The island of Singapore, lying just off of the southern tip of the Malay peninsula, measures 250 square miles, is home to just under 3 million, and is endowed with virtually no natural resources. Its small size and dearth of resources haven't stopped Singapore from pursuing its export-led economic strategy, which is based on the two-way flow of trade, to become the richest country in Asia other than Japan. Singapore lies at the historical crossroads between East and West, and this is reflected in the island's population of 2.9 million, which is 77.7 percent ethnic Chinese, 14.1 percent Malay, 7.1 percent Indian, and 1.1 percent other ethnic groups. The Singaporeans are the most prosperous people in Asia after the Japanese.

Singapore at a Glance

Population:	2.92 million
Religion:	Buddhist, Muslim, Hindu, Christian
Government:	Parliamentary democracy
Language:	English, Mandarin, Malay, Tamil, various Chinese dialects
Currency:	Singapore dollar
Trade (1993):	\$63.4 total exports; \$72.1 billion total imports

Power in Singapore is vested among those of Chinese descent. As a foreign businessperson, you will most likely deal with highly educated, English-speaking, ethnic Chinese cosmopolites. The typical Singaporean is pragmatic, skillful, logical, and productive. The Singaporean government emphasizes personal sacrifice to nation-state goals, enforcing Confucian values of thrift, industry, and social cohesiveness. Mandarin is the chosen language for business and education. The typical Singaporean willingly trades some of what Westerners might define as inalienable rights in exchange for an extremely high standard of living and a clean, crimeless, urban environment.

Economic Conditions

Singapore's rampant economic growth of the 1980s slowed in the 1990s to a respectable 6.7 percent in 1991, a slowdown largely due to recession in the United States and its other Western markets. Unfortunately for the island, future resurgence of its manufacturing export growth depends on economic recovery in the United States, which, as of this writing, appears problematic. Singapore sells 25 percent of its exports to the United States.

The problem for the city-state is that labor is in short supply. As Hong Kong utilizes Chinese labor by setting up factories in Southern China, Singapore has had to use Indonesian labor to expand and become less dependent on multinationals, who fuel much of Singapore's growth. Singapore's continued growth, in conjunction with its low birth rate, signals increased pressure on labor and a concomitant rise in wages relative to productivity. In fact, wages rose 7.6 percent in 1991, whereas productivity declined 1.5 percent. Higher taxes and higher costs of doing business, in conjunction with rising wages, now threaten Singapore's potential as a regional center of Southeast Asian commerce in terms of its competitiveness as an export platform and as a site for locating corporate headquarters.

To address its labor problem, Singapore has launched, together with Malaysia and Indonesia, the Triangle of Growth, wherein Singapore and the adjacent areas of Malaysia's Johor state and Indonesia's Riau Islands will be integrated economically. This will provide Singapore with new sources of needed labor and natural resources. In the grand scheme of things, Singapore has the potential and the intention of developing from a production-intensive economy to one based on innovation and design. This shift must be made while gains are achieved in the rate of productivity and in foreign capital inputs. United States firms placed $572 million in investment in Singapore in 1991, which equaled 39 percent of total investment that year.

The Singapore market should not be ignored by American marketers. The island imports $72.1 billion in imports each year and imposes virtually no tariff or nontariff barriers on trade. Key imports include oil, telecommunications equipment, office and data-processing machines, general industrial machinery, and transport equipment. In this consumer market, the average Singaporean earns $13,000 annually. Business corruption and violent crime are virtually absent; commercial dealings take place in a "Western-style," no-nonsense, no-delays atmosphere. Another plus for American sellers and investment managers is that Singaporeans speak English. As a free port and a laissez-faire economy, Singapore has no capital gains tax, turnover tax, value-added tax, development tax, or surtax on imports. Attractive concessions are offered to investors as part of the development of the Triangle of Growth.

Historical Background

The island freed itself from British colonialism in 1963 and became part of Malaysia. Two years later, it split off from the Malaysia Federation and declared itself the Republic of Singapore. Singapore, which means "The Lion City," is an immigrant society. On its streets one hears the Malay, Tamil, Mandarin, Hokkien, Cantonese, and English languages as well as a combination of them all, which some jokingly call "Singlish."

Lee Kuan Yew ruled the country from independence until 1990. His leadership style was a unique blend of ancient Confucian patriarch and English gentleman. Not a single slum area exists in Singapore to spoil the fantastically cosmopolitan (some say artificial) atmosphere. Virtually everyone who wants a job has one. Officialdom is virtually corruption-free. The government doesn't run a deficit and possesses large cash reserves. Singaporeans save 42 percent of their money, more than any populace in the world.

Priding itself for its rock-stable parliamentary democratic political organization, the island is often the first choice among foreign investors setting up in Asia. Lee Kuan Yew's successor, Goh Chok Tong, has stayed the course toward maintaining Singapore's top-notch infrastructure, free-market economic system, skilled labor force, and hands-on approach to social policy.

COMPANY DIRECTORIES

Title: *Dun's Key Business Directory of Singapore*

Date: Annual

Format: Hardcover

Publisher: Dun & Bradstreet International
Publications Department
80 Anson Rd. #29-02
IBM Towers
Singapore, 0208
Tel: (65)334-2236
Fax: (65)334-2465 or 2469

Pages: 359 (2 vols.)

Exhibits: None

This directory contains a database of 1,500 Singaporean firms listed alphabetically and by business activity. A directory of directors and key executives is also provided. The companies included have an annual turnover of more than S$12 million and/or at least 50 employees. Each entry lists the number of employees, start-up date, turnover, auditor, banker, names of directors, and importing/exporting status.

Title: *KOMPASS Directory of American Business in Singapore*

Date: Annual

Format: Paperback

Author: U.S. Foreign Commercial Service

Editor: Florence Boon, Celaine Francis, Gloria Tan, and Linda Wong

Publisher: KOMPASS SouthEast Asia, Ltd.

326C King George's Ave.
Singapore, 0820
Tel: (65)296-9684

Pages: 334
Exhibits: Drawings
Price: $50

This directory lists not only American companies in Singapore, but also the principal agents and distributors representing U.S. firms there. Firms are cross-listed by product line and service. This book is attractively published and recommended as the best available source of this information.

Title: *Singapore Chinese Chamber of Commerce and Industry Directory*
Date: Annual
Format: Paperback
Editor: Fiona Hu
Publisher: Singapore Chinese Chamber of Commerce and Industry
47 Hill St.
Singapore, 0617
Tel: (65)337-8381
Fax: (65)339-0605
Pages: 415
Exhibits: Photographs

This directory lists the 5,300 member companies of the Singapore Chinese Chamber of Commerce and Industry, which dates back to 1906. The companies are listed by product classification and are cross-indexed by name. Company profiles include only addresses and business activities. The book includes advertising.

Title: *Singapore Industrial Directory*
Date: Annual
Format: Paperback
Author: Singapore Institute of Purchasing and Supply
Publisher: Promedia International
1302 Loring 1
Toa Payoh
#03-10 Siong Hoe Ind. Building
Singapore, 1231
Tel: (65)258-8255
Fax: (65)259-7651
Pages: Varies
Exhibits: None

Whether the reader is looking for a specific product, a specific company, or a specific trade name in Singapore, this directory will help. This 600-page volume is tabbed for easy use, and company profiles list contact information, key personnel, and scope of the business. The plethora of product advertisements might interest the buyers of Singaporean goods most of all.

Title: *Times Business Directory of Singapore (Buku Merah)*
Date: Annual
Format: Hardcover
Publisher: Times Trade Directories Pte., Ltd.
1 New Industrial Rd.
Times Centre
Singapore, 1953
Tel: (65)284-8844
Fax: (65)288-1186
Pages: 1,200
Exhibits: Photographs

A finer business directory does not exist. This three-inch-thick volume profiles local and foreign-owned companies, listing them alphabetically and indexing them by product. Personal names listed in profiles are also indexed—a handy feature. This resource provides a directory of government ministries and official bodies and an enormous classified section that is useful as a desktop phonebook. The text is divided by tabs for easy use.

COUNTRY PROFILES

Title: *Business, Society and Development in Singapore*
Date: 1990
Format: Hardcover
Editor: Chong Li Choy, Tan Chwee Huat, Wong Kwei Cheong, and Caroline Yeoh
Publisher: Times Academic Press
1 New Industrial Rd.
Times Centre
Singapore, 1953
Tel: (65)284-8844
Fax: (65)288-9254
Pages: 122
Exhibits: None

For readers seeking an analysis of Singapore's evolution into a highly modernized Asian nation featuring the best in business environments, this compilation will be of interest. Topics include Singaporean business ethics, corporate social responsibility, corporate government, trade unions, consumer interests, business-community relations, regulation of business, and human resource management. This is a provocative reader that provides important lessons about how and why Singaporean business works.

Title: *Country Report: Singapore*
Date: Quarterly
Format: Periodical; also available on microfilm
Publisher: The Economist Intelligence Unit
P.O. Box 154
Dartford
Kent DA1 1QB, United Kingdom
Tel: (44)(322)289-194
Fax: (44)(322)223-803
For microfilm version, contact:
World Microfilms Publications, Ltd.
2-6 Foscote Mews
London W92 HH, United Kingdom
Pages: Varies
Exhibits: Graphs and tables
Price: Contact for subscription prices

For anyone tracking political, economic, or business climate changes in Singapore, this is a recommended one-stop source. Starting with a very handy executive summary of the entire "outlook," the publication includes sections on the political scene, economic policy, trends in demand, employment and wages, industry, finance, and foreign trade as well as an appendix of current statistics.

Title: *Singapore*
Date: Annual
Format: Hardcover
Editor: Tan Han Hoe
Publisher: Information Division, Ministry of Communications and Information

460 Alexandra Rd., #39-00
PSA Building
Singapore, 0511
Tel: (65)270-7988
Fax: (65)279-9734

Pages: 328

Exhibits: Maps, photographs, and tables

Produced by the Singaporean government, this almanac-style volume contains well-written chapters on all aspects of Singaporean society, politics, and economy. Topics include trade, industry, finance, banking, law, international relations and other subjects of interest to businesspeople. This is a pithy introduction to Singapore, written from the positive perspective of the government.

Title: *Singapore Bulletin*

Date: Monthly

Format: Periodical

Editor: Ng Poey Siong

Publisher: Ministry of Information and the Arts
30th Floor, PSA Building
460 Alexandra Rd.
Singapore, 0511
Tel: (65)279-9832
Fax: (65)279-9860

Pages: Varies

Exhibits: Photographs

Price: Contact for subscription prices

This government-issued 20- to 25-page newsletter provides brief news updates on developments in Singaporean industry, trade, tourism, medicine, and education. It tracks trade deals, VIP meetings, economic performance, foreign investments, and general business news in a grab-bag format.

ECONOMY

Title: *Economic Survey of Singapore*

Date: Quarterly

Format: Periodical

Author: Ministry of Trade and Industry, Republic of Singapore

Publisher: SNP Publishers, Ltd.
303 Upper Serangoon Rd.
P.O. Box 485
Singapore, 1334
Tel: (65)380-8338
Fax: (65)285-4894

Pages: Varies

Exhibits: Graphs and tables

Pricc: S$150/year

For anyone who needs current economic statistical data on Singapore, this 100-page publication is the government's latest release of numbers. The data cover Singapore's industrial performance vis-à-vis the world, labor productivity, manufacturing, commerce, and services. This periodical features plenty of graphs, tables, and analysis and is recommended.

Title: *The Political Economy of Singapore's Industrialization*

Date: 1989

Format: Hardcover

Author: Garry Rodan

Publisher: Macmillan Press, Ltd.
Houndmills, Basingstoke
Hants RG21 2XS, United Kingdom
Tel: (44)(256)29242
Fax: (44)(256)479-476

Pages: 266

Exhibits: Tables

In this academic monograph, business researchers will find an extensively footnoted and erudite analysis of Singapore's political economy. The book's seven chapters focus on economic theory, preindustrial Singapore, political legacies, export-oriented manufacturing, advanced industrialization, the island's future, and conclusions. For those seeking in-depth economic analysis, this book is recommended.

ETIQUETTE AND PROTOCOL

Title: *Culture Shock: Singapore*
Date: 1993
Format: Paperback
Author: JoAnn Meriwether Craig
Publisher: Graphic Arts Center Publishing Co.
P.O. Box 10306
Portland, OR 97210
Tel: (503)226-2402
Fax: (503)226-2402
Pages: 296
Exhibits: Photographs

Meant for expatriates and travelers to Singapore, this readable volume is a recommended cultural tour of the island's multiethnic community. It covers customs, manners, and ceremonies for the Chinese, Malay, and Indian communities. The 25-page chapter covering business etiquette is thorough and accurate.

GENERAL BUSINESS

Title: *Doing Business in Singapore: Handbook for Businessmen*
Date: 1987
Format: Hardcover
Author: Goh Tianwah
Publisher: Rank Books
Block 1002
Toa Payoh Industrial Park #07-1423
Singapore, 1231
Pages: 141
Exhibits: None

For the businessperson setting up a business in Singapore, this now partially dated guidebook lists the relevant laws and regulatory procedures. It includes logistical advice for registering a company, hiring, paying wages and taxes, and entering into partnership agreements. This is one of only a few titles on this topic.

Title: *Guide to Doing Business in Singapore*
Date: 1991
Format: Paperback
Author: Deloitte & Touche
Publisher: SND Publishers Pte., Ltd.
6 Battery Rd. #27-01
Singapore, 0104
Tel: (65)224-8288
Fax: (65)224-7520
Pages: 175
Exhibits: Tables

This overview guide to Singapore's business environment has been compiled by a well-known accounting firm. The topics covered include the investment climate, business regulations, and taxation and investment incentives. It is useful to businesspeople entering Singapore as well as expatriates. A handy appendix of key economic data and addresses is included.

Title: *Investors' Guide to the Economic Climate of Singapore*
Date: 1992
Format: Paperback
Publisher: Singapore International Chamber of Commerce
50 Raffles Place #03-02
Shell Tower
Singapore, 0104
Tel: (65)224-1255
Fax: (65)224-2785
Pages: 197
Exhibits: Maps and tables

With this attractive booklet, the Singapore International Chamber of Commerce has produced a comprehensive guide for investors. The topics covered include an overview of Singapore's attractions, geography, economic policies, financial facilities, investment incentives, taxation, import regulations, labor rules, and other essential information for would-be investors. Not for general reading, the book presents facts and data in legalese.

HISTORY AND SOCIETY

Title: *A History of Singapore*
Date: 1991
Format: Hardcover
Editor: Ernest C.T. Chew and Edwin Lee
Publisher: Oxford University Press
200 Madison Ave.
New York, NY 10016
Tel: (212)679-7300
Pages: 442
Exhibits: Maps and tables

For those in need of a comprehensive and meticulous history of Singapore, this well-organized compilation of expert historical articles covers most of the salient themes: geography, British rule, Japanese occupation, the transition to independence, social issues, and foreign policy. Extensively footnoted.

Title: *Nation-building in Malaysia 1946–1974*
Date: 1985
Format: Hardcover
Author: James P. Ongkili
Publisher: Oxford University Press
800 Madison Ave.
New York, NY 10016
Tel: (212)679-7300
Fax: (212)725-2972
Pages: 275
Exhibits: None

The history of Singapore is inextricably bound to the history of Malaysia, from which it separated in 1965. Until then, the island's heritage was very much intertwined with the quest for independence and national unity that is the political and historic evolution of the Malay people. This important study tracks the process of nation-building in the Malay Federation from 1946 to 1974, against the obstacles of communalism and racial diversity. The chronicle leads nicely to the previous title, which specifically provides a detailed history of Singapore.

INFORMATION SOURCES

Title: *Singapore Periodicals Index*
Date: Annual
Format: Paperback

Publisher: National Library
Stamford Rd.
Singapore, 0617
Tel: (65)337-7355
Fax: (65)330-9611

Pages: 511

Exhibits: None

Price: $55

Each issue of this comprehensive periodical index lists more than 5,000 articles from about 150 Singapore publications printed in Malay, Chinese, and English. Articles of less than 750 words are not included. Each entry includes price, frequency, address, and language of contents, but no abstract. Listings are divided by language and are alphabetized by subject.

LAWS AND REGULATIONS

Title: *Construction Law in Singapore and Malaysia*

Date: 1988

Format: Hardcover

Author: Nigel M. Robinson and Anthony P. Lavers

Publisher: Butterworth and Co. (Asia) Pte., Ltd.
30 Robinson Rd. #12-01
Tuan Sing Towers
Singapore, 0104
Tel: (44)(732)884-567 (U.K.)
Fax: (44)(732)884-079 (U.K.)

Pages: 350

Exhibits: Tables

A readable volume and a useful reference source, this book will interest lawyers, dispute mediators, and executives involved in the construction industry in Singapore or Malaysia. The topics covered include all aspects of construction law, from content of construction materials and liability for design to risk management and arbitration. This well-organized, authoritative book includes a useful digest of relevant cases.

Title: *Securities Regulation in Singapore and Malaysia: A Primer on the Laws of the Stock Market with Cases and Materials*

Date: 1978

Format: Hardcover

Author: Tan Pheng Theng

Publisher: Stock Exchange of Singapore, Ltd.
Robinson Rd.
P.O. Box 2306
Singapore, 9043
Tel: (65)535-3788
Fax: (65)532-4476

Pages: 751

Exhibits: None

Consisting of text, selected cases, and other materials, this legal textbook about securities regulation in Singapore and Malaysia will interest the serious international lawyer and financier. Sections include regulation of the share market, public floatation, insider trading, and market manipulation. The prose is clearly written and extensively footnoted. Remember, however, that this is a legal textbook and not a guidebook.

Title: *The Singapore Legal System*

Date: 1989

Format: Hardcover

Editor: Walter Woon
Publisher: Longman Singapore Publishers Pte., Ltd.
25 First Lok Yang Rd.
Singapore, 2262
Tel: (914)993-5000 (U.S.)
Fax: (914)997-8115 (U.S.)
Pages: 356
Exhibits: None

This unique volume offers an in-depth overview of Singapore's legal system, which is often incorrectly held to be merely a colonial outgrowth of the British legal system. This source is meant to be a law school textbook rather than a practical how-to reader; it is jammed with cases and statutes to meet that objective. Chapters cover legal history, the making of law, state administation, the legacy of English law, the courts, precedent, and so on. Unfortunately, few other sources covering the island's legal system are written for nonlawyers.

MANAGEMENT

Title: *Singapore Management*
Date: Semiannual
Format: Periodical
Editor: You Poh Seng
Publisher: Singapore Institute of Management
Management House
41 Namly Ave.
Singapore, 1026
Pages: Varies
Exhibits: Tables
Price: S$24/year

With three to five articles in each issue written by Asian academics, this journal is for managers keeping tabs on managerial practice throughout Asia. Financial management and accounting practices receive as much coverage as leadership and strategic issues. The approach is theoretical.

POLITICS AND GOVERNMENT

Title: *Singapore Government Directory*
Date: 1993
Format: Paperback
Author: Ministry of Information and the Arts
Publisher: Singapore National Printers, Ltd./SNP Publishers Pte., Ltd.
97 Ubi Ave. 4
Singapore, 1440
Tel: (65)741-2500
Fax: (65)744-3770
Pages: 795
Exhibits: Tables
Price: S$42 (overseas orders)

Here is an indispensable directory of Singapore's entire government. If only a directory like this existed for every country! The volume lists ministries and departments alphabetically for easy use, and the text is divided by clearly labeled tabs. Each entry includes the address, a very useful description of the function of the department, names of key officers, and phone numbers. This first-class directory is essential for businesspeople working with Singapore.

TAXATION

Title: *Singapore Master Tax Guide, 1990*

Date: 1990

Format: Hardcover

Author: CCH Tax Editors

Publisher: CCH Asia, Ltd.
139 Cecil St.
Cecil House
#02-00 0106, Singapore
Tel: (65)225-2555

Pages: 800

Exhibits: Tables

Written "to assist taxpayers in understanding their liabilities and entitlements," this guide covers the rules of business and personal taxation in Singapore. Clear examples of how tax laws are reflected in a return make this a useful tool for expatriates and accountants. Indexing by numbered paragraph gives the book a rather foreboding legalese "feel," but it helps for easy use. This book is certainly comprehensive and authoritative.

INDONESIA

OVERVIEW

Indonesia's 13,677 "Spice Islands" comprise the largest archipelago in the world, known to geographers as the 3,000-mile-long Malay archipelago, the fabled East Indies. The country consists of seven major islands, all well-endowed with natural resources. Indonesia is home to an enormous and growing population of more than 170 million, the fifth largest in the world, with the largest middle class in all of Asia. There are more than 300 ethnic groups, such as the Batak, Balinese, Badui, Dayak, Javanese, and overseas Chinese, and they speak as many languages and dialects. The capital of Jakarta, on the island of Java, is the focal point of Indonesian business and decision making.

Indonesia at a Glance

Population:	186.3 million
Religions:	Muslim, Buddhist
Government:	Strong presidential government with 1,000-member People's Consultative Assembly
Language:	Bahasa Indonesian, English for business
Currency:	Rupiah (Rp)
Trade (1993):	\$34.0 billion total exports; \$27.3 billion total imports

The country's tight-knit bureaucrats have grown increasingly pragmatic in recent years, trying to deregulate the country's economy away from petroleum via foreign investment and reduce the cronyism and rampant corruption among government officials that have embarrassed Indonesia's leaders and tarnished the country's image for decades. (Mrs. Tien Suharto, the president's wife, was once dubbed "Madame Tien Per Cent" by the Indonesian public.) They have smashed state monopolies and begun to privatize large Indonesian *pribumi* (state corporations). Foreign investment is rising, mainly from Korean and Taiwanese investors who employ low-cost Indonesian labor. The conspicuous absence of Chinese investment is due to sentiment remaining from the slaughter of thousands of Chinese by the Javanese in the aftermath of the 1965 Communist coup attempt. Even so, Indonesians of Chinese descent wield great clout in Indonesian commerce. There are two strains of Chinese people living in Indonesia; the *Peranakan*, who were born there and have been totally assimilated into Indonesian culture, and the *Totoks*, who are newcomers to the archipelago, many of whom pay some personal allegiance to Mainland China.

Economic Conditions

Presently, Indonesia is experiencing the same kind of economic boom that other Asian nations experienced 20 years ago. Indonesia's large state-owned enterprises have been in the process of moving into private hands while the government has set about liberalizing the economy, bringing down trade barriers through a policy of deregulation and debureaucratization. Growth, expansion of trade, and an improved environment for Western investors have been the result. Total exports increased 68 percent between 1987 and 1991 to more than $28 billion; U.S. sales to Indonesia increased from $650 million in 1986 to $3.2 billion in 1991. Economic growth of 7 percent or more can be expected to continue in the years ahead, well above the 5 percent figure that the government needs to complete Replita V, its current, and sixth, five-year development plan.

Indonesia is the undisputed leader in Southwest Asian energy production, with oil production at 1.6 million barrels a day and natural gas reserves of 80 trillion cubic feet. However, energy plays a diminishing role in the economy as a result of rapid industrialization; it has fallen from 65 percent of export earnings in 1989 to 30 percent in 1992. This is not to say that the country's petroleum industry is in decline; in fact, it's expanding. Other parts of the economy have simply expanded faster.

Half of all Indonesians work on the highly labor-intensive farms, which are concentrated on Java, Madura, and Bali. Rubber is the country's primary agricultural export; other exports are palm oil, coffee, and forest resources. In fact, 75 percent of the country's landmass is covered by tropical forest, 10 percent of the world's total. Forest resources are Indonesia's second largest source of foreign exchange earnings, mostly from lumber sales to Japan, Singapore, Taiwan, and Italy. Indonesia has taken action to curtail the illegal destruction of its rain forests; clear-cutting has been outlawed completely, though the long-term success of these programs is uncertain.

Truly exciting developments are under way in Indonesia's manufacturing sector, which has grown by 44 percent since 1985 and experiences 7 to 9 percent growth each year. Consumer-goods manufacturing is the focus, including the production of foods, beverages, tobacco products, textiles, and home-use products. Larger enterprises produce cement, fertilizers, petrochemicals, pharmaceuticals, pulp and paper, and basic metal products. Tourism has grown into an important foreign exchange earner as well, with 2.2 million visitors bringing in $2.1 billion in 1990. More than 70 new large-chain hotels are planned for construction over the course of the 1990s.

Indonesia's Byzantine regulatory environment, however, continues to stymie foreigners. Corruption remains endemic, and requirements that, for example, force investors to form joint ventures and allow for at least 20 percent local ownership scare away potential investors. Recently, foreign investment in Indonesia has soared, even with the restrictions, with a total of 8,750 applications approved in 1991 alone. In that year, the U.S. companies invested $2.2 billion (excluding oil, gas, and banking).

Historical Background

Although Islamic traders had been trading with Indonesia since the fourth century, it was not until the fourteenth century that the religion of Islam took root in North Sumatra, spreading later to Java. The people of Java and its capital, Jakarta, are almost all nominal or devout Muslims, whereas Bali's 2.5 million people are mostly Hindus. Originating from its early village organization, cooperative village communalism, called *Mmsyawarah*, was imbedded in Indonesian character and culture. Tens of thousands of Indonesian villages are organized under the tradition of mutual assistance (*gotong royong*), a system based on an ancient model of joint responsibility and cooperation. When a person, a family, a village, or, for that matter, a state is in trouble or need, the people nearby drop their own work to come to its assistance without pay or coercion. This emphasis on harmony permeates social, commercial, and national affiliations. *Suku*, social adhesiveness among all ethnic groups, was made possible by the tolerant, all-inclusive doctrine of Islam and was further guaranteed by Indonesia's fervent nationalism. Indonesians are Indonesians first and members of their ethnic group second.

Like Malays in Malaysia, the Indonesian Malay believes that there are no "single monkeys," people who are islands unto themselves. Indonesian Malays are nonindividualistic and cooperative rather than competitive or self-interested. They adhere to proscribed group behavior and their individual duty (*fardu kifayah*). One duty is to never sever relationships due to altercation. Compromises are made to keep the group together, and materialism and worldly pleasures are denounced in favor of communal values. Indonesian Malays oppose the pursuit of wealth and power for their own sake but believe in hard work, industry, and self-reliance.

Indonesia instills in its population the values embodied in its *Pacascilla*, a five-point manifesto on which Indonesian politics and social life are based. The tenets include belief in one supreme god (any one is fine), a just humanity, the unity of Indonesia, democratic rule by representation, and social justice for all Indonesians, regardless of ethnicity. Through the so-called P-4 Program, educated Indonesians learn everything from the rules of flag etiquette to the fine points of the country's five-year development objectives. A person exits the program knowing the meaning of being an Indonesian citizen in tune with the country's national goals and collective spirit.

COMPANY DIRECTORIES

Title: *Key Business Directory of Indonesia/Thailand*

Date: 1990

Format: Hardcover

Publisher: Dun & Bradstreet (Singapore) Pte., Ltd.
80 Anson Rd.
#29-02 IBM Towers
Singapore, 0208
Tel: (65)334-2236
Fax: (65)334-2465 or 2469

Pages: 294

Exhibits: None

Listing Indonesian (and Thai) firms by name, product classification, and geographic region, this directory contains 1,500 companies selected on the basis of annual turnover of more than Rp 10 billion and/or at least 80 employees. Each listing includes the name of the CEO, turnover, number of employees, import/export status, auditor, and directors. This directory is perhaps the best available.

COUNTRY PROFILES

Title: *Country Forecast: Indonesia*

Date: Quarterly

Format: Periodical; also available on-line

Publisher: The Economist Intelligence Unit
P.O. Box 154
Dartford
Kent DA1 1QB, United Kingdom
Tel: (44)(322)289-194
Fax: (44)(322)223-803
For on-line version, contact:
Maid Systems, Ltd.
Maid House
18 Dufferin St.
London EC1Y 8PD, United Kingdom
Tel: (44)(71)253-6900

Pages: Varies

Exhibits: Tables

Price: Contact for subscription prices

For businesspeople involved in Indonesia, this 10- to 15-page publication assesses the political scene, the economy, and the business climate and provides forecasts for each for the next five years. Tables of economic data for the previous five years and projections for the next five years round out this useful updater.

Title: *Country Report: Indonesia*

Date: Quarterly

Format: Periodical; also available on microfilm

Publisher: The Economist Intelligence Unit
P.O. Box 154
Dartford
Kent DA1 1QB, United Kingdom
Tel: (44)(322)289-194
Fax: (44)(322)223-803
For microfilm version, contact:
World Microfilm Publications, Ltd.
2-6 Foscote Mews
London W9 2HH, United Kingdom

Pages: Varies

Exhibits: Graphs and tables

Price: Contact for subscription prices

For businesspeople tracking political, economic, or business climate changes in Indonesia, this 30- to 40-page quarterly is a recommended one-stop source. Starting with a very handy executive summary of the entire "outlook," the contents include sections on the political scene, economic policy, employment, industry, finance, and trade and an appendix of current statistics.

Title: *Indonesia: A Country Study*
Date: 1983
Format: Hardcover
Author: Foreign Area Studies, The American University
Publisher: The American University/ Department of the Army
4400 Massachusetts Ave., NW
McDowell 117
Washington, DC 20016
Tel: (202)885-3409
Fax: (202)855-3453
Pages: 343
Exhibits: Maps, photographs, and tables

Covering Indonesia's history, society, geography, economy, government, politics, and national security, this country overview (like the other books in the series) is the best single introduction to the country. Each chapter is compiled by a different author, the table of contents includes easy reference subheadings, and the book includes photographs, tables, a glossary, a bibliography, and an index. It is current as of 1982, although the bulk of its content remains up to date.

DICTIONARIES AND LANGUAGE STUDIES

Title: *An Indonesian-English Dictionary*
Date: 1989
Format: Hardcover
Author: John M. Echols and Hassan Shadily
Publisher: Cornell University Press
124 Roberts Place
Ithaca, NY 14850
Tel: (607)257-7000
Fax: (607)257-3552
Pages: 618
Exhibits: None

For the serious student interested in learning to read modern Indonesian, called Bahasa Indonesian, this is a desktop dictionary that includes a short analysis of the language and a pronunciation guide.

ECONOMICS

Title: *Bulletin of Indonesia Economic Studies*
Date: Triannual
Format: Periodical
Editor: Hal Hill
Publisher: Indonesian Project
Australian National University
Box 4 GPO
Canberra ACT 2601, Australia
Tel:(61)(62)49-5111
Pages: Varies
Exhibits: Graphs and tables
Price: $A 36/year

Each issue of this small-format 100-page journal contains 4 to 6 articles on varied subjects related to Indonesia's economy and development. Businesspeople will find an occasional article that provides practical insights into Indonesian management, political policy, and regulatory reform.

Title: *Indonesia Development News Quarterly*
Date: Quarterly
Format: Periodical
Editor: Sjamsoe Soegito
Publisher: Indonesia Development News/Hill & Knowlton
11th Floor, 420 Lexington Ave.
New York, NY 10017
Tel: (212)697-5600
Fax: (212)210-8885
Pages: Varies
Exhibits: Maps, photographs, and tables
Price: Contact for subscription prices

This is an attractive 6- to 10-page newsletter prepared for the Republic of Indonesia by Hill and Knowlton in Washington, D.C., to provide English-speaking readers with updates on Indonesian politics, economics, and business climate. The publication provides biographies of key government officials and descriptions of development plans, both of which are useful to businesspeople. A table of recent investment deals contains information not readily found elsewhere, and key economic indicators are also included. This periodical is recommended.

Title: *Unity and Diversity: Regional Economic Development in Indonesia Since 1970*
Date: 1989
Format: Hardcover
Editor: Hal Hill
Publisher: Oxford University Press
Unit 221, UBI Ave. 4
Intrepid Warehouse Complex
Singapore, 1440
Tel: (65)743-1066
Fax: (65)742-5915
Pages: 610
Exhibits: Graphs and tables

With chapters covering each of the numerous geographic regions of Indonesia, this hefty, well-researched book is for the business researcher looking for specific data on selected areas, such as Aceh, East Kalimantan, or Jakarta. Each regional profile examines the state of agricultural and industrial development, government policy in the area, the local economy, the standard of living, and key trends. This is a readable sourcebook.

ETIQUETTE AND PROTOCOL

Title: *Culture Shock! Indonesia*
Date: 1990
Format: Paperback
Author: Cathie Draine and Barbara Hall
Publisher: Time Books International
Graphic Arts Publishing Co.
P.O. Box 10306
Portland, OR 97210
Tel: (503)226-1410
Fax: (503)226-2402

Pages: 278

Exhibits: Cartoons and photographs

This book is perhaps the most concise and readable examination of Indonesian ethnic groups, cultural values, customs, and manners. It is recommended as a cultural orientation for expatriates. It includes a list of cultural do's and don'ts.

GENERAL BUSINESS

Title: *Doing Business in Indonesia*

Date: 1989

Format: Paperback

Publisher: Price Waterhouse
4th Floor, Ficorinvest Building
Jalan HR Rasuna Said Kav C-18
Kuningan
Jakarta Selatan 12950, Indonesia
Tel: (62)(21)513-516 or 518

Pages: 234

Exhibits: Graphs and tables

This concise guide to taxation policies and regulations in Indonesia was created by one of the leading accounting firms there. The book is recommended as an overview for executives, accountants, and prospective investors. Selected chapters cover the business environment, investment incentives, the regulatory environment, banking and finance, exporting, labor relations, and the tax system.

HISTORY AND SOCIETY

Title: *Indonesia: The Underdeveloped Freedom*

Date: 1974

Format: Hardcover

Author: S. Tas

Publisher: Pegasus
197 Rt. 18, Suite 3000
East Brunswick, NJ 08816
Tel: (908)214-2636
Fax: (908)246-2917

Pages: 388

Exhibits: Map

This fine history, translated from the Dutch, covers Indonesia's national development from the earliest settlers to the post-Sukarno period and the system of Guided Democracy. Selected chapters focus on the arrival of the Europeans, the nationalist movement against colonialism, the Japanese occupation, the struggle for democracy, and the coup attempt in 1965. For those looking for background, this is a readable volume.

Title: *Pribumi Indonesians, The Chinese Minority and China: A Study of Perceptions and Policies*

Date: 1978

Format: Hardcover

Author: Leo Suryadinata

Publisher: Heinemann Educational Books (Asia), Ltd.
41 Jalan Pemimpin #03-05
Singapore, 2057
Tel: (65)258-3255
Fax: (65)258-8279

Pages: 241

Exhibits: None

One important aspect of Indonesian commercial culture that the foreign businessperson must understand is the role of Chinese private entrepreneurs in the economy and how they interface with *pribumi* companies operated by ethnic Indonesians. This book provides a historical Overview of the uneasy relationship between Indonesians and the country's Chinese minority.

POLITICS AND GOVERNMENT

Title: *Indonesia Issues*
Date: Monthly
Format: Periodical; also available on e-mail and CompuServe
Editor: John A. MacDougall
Publisher: Indonesia Publications
7538 Newberry Lane
Lanham-Seabrook, MD 20706
Tel: (301)552-3251
Fax: (301)552-4465
Pages: Varies
Exhibits: None

This 20-page loose-leaf newsletter carries excerpted reports on the human rights situation in Indonesia. It might be of interest both to political analysts and to those traveling to East Timor, where the security situation is most tense. The overall publishing quality is poor.

Title: *Indonesia News Service*
Date: Weekly
Format: Periodical; also available on-line
Publisher: Indonesia Publications
7538 Newberry Lane
Lanham-Seabrook, MD 20706
Tel: (301)552-3251
Fax: (301)552-4465
Pages: Varies
Exhibits: None
Price: Contact for subscription prices

For those following Indonesian current events, this 5- to 10-page loose-leaf newsletter provides news abstracts from published sources. The material is presented in large block paragraphs, cited for source, and dated. The briefs are not organized in any way, and thus this is a rather frustrating reader for those who need weekly news reports from Indonesia.

Title: *Managing Indonesia: The Modern Political Economy*
Date: 1993
Format: Hardcover
Author: John Bresnan
Publisher: Columbia University Press
562 W. 113 St.
New York, NY 10025
Tel: (212)316-7100
Fax: (212)316-7169
Pages: 375
Exhibits: None

This clearly written history covers the period since the 1965 attempted coup against Sukarno. It is recommended for the businessperson who is looking for an overview of the political climate in Indonesia as it relates to commercial organization.

Title: *News and Views Indonesia*
Date: Monthly
Format: Periodical
Publisher: Department of Foreign Affairs

Directorate of Information
Republic of Indonesia
The Indonesia Embassy
2020 Massachusetts Ave., NW
Washington, DC 20036
Tel: (202)775-5200
Fax: (202)775-5365

Pages: Varies
Exhibits: Photographs
Price: Free

Published by Indonesia's Department of Foreign Affairs, this 7- to 10-page newsletter runs news briefs on political developments, aid and development, oil and energy, trade and investment, education, tourism, and the environment. This is a readable news source, and you can't beat the price.

TRAVEL ADVICE

Title: *Bali Handbook*
Date: 1990
Format: Hardcover
Author: Bill Dalton
Publisher: Moon Publications
722 Wall St.
Chico, CA 95928
Tel: (916)345-5473
Fax: (916)345-6751
Pages: 428
Exhibits: Diagrams, maps, and photographs

The author of this comprehensive insider's travel guide also wrote the first great guide to Indonesia, called *Indonesia Guide*. This book provides a complete cultural and historical overview of Bali as well as sightseeing and accommodation information about every terrace and bamboo grove in "this tiny Hindu island province" of neary 3 million people. The book features plentiful illustrations.

Title: *Indonesia: A Travel Survival Kit*
Date: 1986
Format: Hardcover
Author: Ginny Bruce
Publisher: Lonely Planet Publications
P.O. Box 2001A
Berkeley, CA 94702
Tel: (510)893-8555
Fax: (510)893-8563
Pages: 768
Exhibits: Maps and photographs

This guide for budget travelers offers a concise history of the country and excellent travel advice for those who want to get off the beaten path. It contains an informative chapter about Javanese history and cultural arts, as well. It is recommended.

Title: *Indonesia Handbook*
Date: 1988
Format: Hardcover
Author: Bill Dalton
Publisher: Moon Publications
722 Wall St.
Chico, CA 95928
Tel: (916)345-5473
Fax: (916)345-6751
Pages: 1,058
Exhibits: Drawings, maps, photographs, and tables

This budget traveler's guidebook contains a concise introductory overview of Indonesian history, politics, and religion, all of which are useful to the businessperson. It is also a rich source of information for the traveler in Indonesia who enjoys getting off the beaten path. It is recommended.

MALAYSIA

OVERVIEW

Malaysia is roughly the size of Japan but has only 18 million people. The country is divided geographically between Sabah, Sarawak, and the Malaysian peninsula, where the capital of Kuala Lumpur is located, with its Islamic minarets and onion-shaped cupolas rising above its traffic congestion. Sabah and Sarawak are located 400 miles offshore in the South China Sea.

Built of the fruits of the jungle, Malaysia is a major world producer of tin, rubber, lumber, palm oil, gold, and petroleum. It is also the third largest producer of semiconductors and has one of the highest standards of living in Asia. It doubles its exports every three years, more than 50 percent of which are electronic goods and components.

Malaysia at a Glance

Population	18.6 million
Religion:	Muslim, Buddhist, Confucian, Taoist, Hindu, Christian, folk/tribal
Government:	Constitutional monarchy
Language:	Bahasa Malaysian
Currency:	Ringgit or Malaysian dollar (M$ = 100 sen)
Trade (1993):	$40.6 billion total exports; $39.8 billion total imports

The population is 47 percent Malay, 33 percent Chinese, and 9 percent Indian. The Chinese are key players in the business community, and the Malays, who are predominantly Muslim, run the official government, which is centered in Kuala Lumpur. Malaysia's Indian population is employed mainly in the rubber industry and the medical and legal professions.

Economic Conditions

Malaysia's economic boom, so visible in the overnight construction of hotels and office buildings in its main cities, seems ready to cool off in the mid-1990s. Applications for building permits are down, auto sales have dropped, and retail sales have softened. The annual growth of Malaysia's economy peaked in 1990 at 9.8 percent and remains steady at 8 percent in 1993. The country's leaders are currently privatizing hundreds of companies in finance, agriculture, and utilities—30 percent of which are tagged for Malay, rather than Chinese, ownership.

As in Singapore, a shortage of labor in Malaysia hampers continued economic expansion. Full employment in Malaysia has driven wages up sharply, almost 10 percent in 1992, far ahead of productivity, which rose only 5.9 percent in 1992. Many doubt whether Malaysia can remain a competitive platform for export manufacturing in light of these trends; the government has pleaded with workers not to "take advantage" of the labor shortage to pursue wage increases.

Exports grew by 12 percent in 1992, fueled primarily by the expanding electronics industry. Malaysia has been attempting to diversify its export markets among ASEAN nations and in Africa and South America, but as of yet, Organization for Economic Cooperation and Development (OECD) countries continue to buy the lion's share of the country's exports. The European Community, the United States, and Japan combine to purchase two-thirds of Malaysia's exports. Malaysia is the world's leading exporter of room air-conditioners and is strong in televisions, semiconductors, crude oil, natural rubber, and palm oil. Malaysia has also moved rapidly to expand the makeup of its exports to include not only goods but also capital and services, such as its well-developed plantation management expertise.

The government actively uses concessionary laws and regulations in seeking foreign investment, especially in the areas of capital-intensive and high-tech industries. United States investors have placed $7 billion in Malaysia as of 1991, doubling U.S. in-country assets since 1987. United States investment is focused on petroleum exploration and production (65 percent of assets) and microelectronics (20 percent of assets) but has increased fourfold in other sectors to $750 million during the same period. The U.S. Department of Commerce estimates that U.S. investment will increase by 18 percent per year, with most currently planned inputs in the oil sector.

Most crucial to investors and marketers alike, the Malaysian economy is becoming increasingly streamlined as public agencies divest themselves of the operation of business. State-owned companies have been moving into private hands. Therefore, the procurement process on many large and small projects has been shortened. Of special interest to the West, Malaysians are being encouraged through fiscal incentives to invest abroad in selected industries, such as oil and gas exploration in Vietnam, Burma, and Syria.

Malaysian markets have opened, especially to companies that act aggressively to keep abreast of policy developments affecting them. Total two-way U.S.-Malaysia trade in 1991 equaled $11.5 billion. The United States is Malaysia's third-ranking trade partner after Singapore and Japan; much of this country's trade with Singapore is actually U.S.-Malaysia trade in which Singapore acts as an entrepôt. Opportunities for U.S. sales to Malaysia exist mainly in the following areas: oil and gas exploration, petrochemical and power projects, oil and gas equipment, telecommunications, computers and peripherals, software, hazardous waste disposal, medical equipment, aviation equipment, processed and high-value foods, and wheat products.

Historical Background

During colonial times, too few indigenous laborers were available to mine tin, tap rubber, or harvest the British plantations on the Malay peninsula. Thus, foreign labor, mainly Chinese and Indian, was brought in to help. The British left intact Malay customs and religion—except for a few non-Western features of the culture, such as arranged marriages and the subjugation of women—even allowing Malay rulers to hold their positions, at least symbolically.

Malaysians speak Bahasa Malaysian, but educated urban Malays speak English as well, usually impeccably. Islamic fundamentalism is strongest in the northern states, where whippings and canings are carried out against those found guilty of imbibing alcohol or participating in illicit sex. Women generally wear the *purdah*, an Arab-style robe, though few of them wear the veil. As might be expected, the Buddhist, Christian, and Hindu minorities in Malaysia live in some fear of Islamic religious revival, which could conceivably exclude them from the mainstream of Malaysian culture and politics. Malaysia is a democratic monarchy run by seven sultans, one of whom acts as king.

A Malay is a Muslim who speaks the Malay language and conforms to Malay social customs. Devout Muslims observe a strict praying protocol five times a day, which tends to unify the community. They observe Muslim laws about what is *haram* (forbidden), such as eating pork and drinking alcohol, and what is *mukruh* (allowed but not encouraged), such as smoking, eating crabs and shellfish, and touching dogs, which are considered unclean. Devout Muslims hope to make the *hajj*, a pilgrimage to Mecca, because this will bring them great personal satisfaction and respect in the community. As members of Malay society, they observe *adab*, the responsibility to show courtesy in word, deed, and action to all people at all times, and act to encourage social harmony, whether it be in the family, community, or society as a whole. It should be noted that Malay Muslims, even fundamentalists, are passive and nonviolent in comparison to Middle Eastern Muslims. The Malay phrase *tid'apa* is the equivalent of Thailand's *mai pen rai*, both expressing a nonchalant indifference to the mundane tasks of daily life.

As relative newcomers to the country, Chinese Malaysians are perceived by Malays as holding allegiances to Mainland China. Unlike the case in Thailand, Malays chose early on to segregate the Chinese and Malay populations in fear that the Malay minority would be threatened with extinction should the Chinese be permitted to become real equals in the society. After Communist Liberation in China, the Chinese threat to the Malays intensified, becoming the impetus for Malaysia to achieve independence from Britain in 1957 and separate itself from Singapore. A degree of resentment exists to this day between the Malay and the Chinese populations of the country.

ACCOUNTING, BANKING, AND FINANCE

Title: *Malaysia's Capital Market: Growth and Opportunities*
Date: 1991
Format: Hardcover
Author: Kuala Lumpur Stock Exchange
Publisher: Pelanduk Publications Sdn. Bhd.
24 Jalan 20/16A
46300 Petaling Jaya
Selangor Darul Ehsan, Malaysia
Tel: (60)(3)776-613
Fax: (60)(3)776-855
Pages: 165
Exhibits: Graphs and tables

This compilation of papers, presented at the 1990 Convention and Exposition on Malaysia's Capital Growth Opportunities, is the most recently published book to cover Malaysia's capital market in a comprehensive manner. It discusses public-listed companies, stock brokerages, financial institutions, and state-run corporations. Selected chapters focus on the Malaysian economy, the capital market, privatization, the petrochemical industry, the textile industry, the timber industry, the tourism industry, and the telecommunications industry. The articles are presented in a clear and readable style.

Title: *Securities Regulation in Singapore and Malaysia: A Primer on the Laws of the Stock Market with Cases and Materials*
Date: 1978
Format: Hardcover
Author: Tan Pheng Theng
Publisher: Stock Exchange of Singapore, Ltd.
Robinson Rd.
P.O. Box 2306
Singapore, 9043
Tel: (65)535-3788
Fax: (65)532-4476
Pages: 751
Exhibits: None

Consisting of text, selected cases, and other materials, this legal textbook about securities regulation in Singapore and Malaysia will interest the serious international lawyer and financier. It discusses the regulation of the share market, public floatation, insider trading, market manipulation, and so on. The prose is clear and extensively footnoted. Remember, however, that this is a legal textbook and not a guidebook.

COMPANY DIRECTORIES

Title: *Importers, Exporters and Manufacturers in Malaysia*

Date: Annual

Format: Hardcover

Publisher: MDC Sdn. Bhd.
2717 and 2718 Jalan Permata Empat
Wisma MDC, Taman Permata
Kuala Lumpur 53300, Malaysia
Tel: (60)(3)408-6600, 6601, or 6602

Pages: 856

Exhibits: None

Price: M$50

This full-length directory lists Malaysian importers, exporters, and manufacturers in three alphabetized sections. Each entry provides contact information and a list of products imported, exported, and produced. It is handy for marketers and buyers dealing with Malaysia.

Title: *Key Business Directory of Malaysia*, Vol. 2

Date: 1990

Format: Hardcover

Publisher: Dun & Bradstreet Singapore Pte., Ltd.
80 Anson Rd.
#29-02 IBM Towers
Singapore 0208
Tel: (65)334-3336
Fax: (65)334-2465

Pages: 320

Exhibits: None

This directory includes 1,500 Malaysian companies with an annual turnover of more than M$18,000 and/or at least 50 employees. Firms are listed by name, product classification, and geographic region. Each listing includes the name of the CEO, turnover, number of employees, import/export status, auditor, and directors. This directory is recommended.

COUNTRY PROFILES

Title: *Global Forecasting Service: Malaysia*

Date: Quarterly

Format: Periodical

Publisher: The Economist Intelligence Unit
P.O. Box 154
Dartford
Kent DA1 1QB, United Kingdom
Tel: (44)(322)289-194
Fax: (44)(322)223-803
For on-line version, contact:
Maid Systems, Ltd.
Maid House
18 Dufferin St.
London ECIY 8PD, United Kingdom
Tel: (44)(71)253-6900

Pages: Varies

Exhibits: Tables

Price: Contact for subscription prices

This 25- to 30-page periodical provides an overview of Malaysia's political, economic, social/demographic, and business climate outlook for the next five years. The large-format publications in this series are expensive, but for the executive decision maker with little chance to read widely on Malaysia, this is a recommended updater and forecaster. It includes fact sheets and a summary of predictions.

Title: *Malaysia: A Country Study*
Date: 1985
Format: Hardcover
Author: Foreign Area Studies Center, The American University
Editor: Frederica M. Bunge
Publisher: The American University/ Department of the Army
4400 Massachusetts Ave., NW
McDowell 117
Washington, DC 20016
Tel: (202)885-3409
Fax: (202)885-3453
Pages: 366
Exhibits: Charts, graphs, and photographs

Covering Malaysia's history, society, geography, economy, government, politics, and national security, this country Overview (like the other books in the series) is the best one-stop introduction to the country. Each chapter is compiled by a different author, the table of contents includes subheadings for easy reference, and the book includes photographs, government organization charts, a glossary, a bibliography, and an index. It is current only as of 1984, though the bulk of it is still timely.

ECONOMY

Title: *The Forest Resources of Malaysia: Their Economics and Development*
Date: 1986
Format: Hardcover
Author: Raj Kumar
Publisher: Oxford University Press
Walton St.
Oxford OX2 6DP, United Kingdom
Tel: (44)(865)56767
Fax: (44)(865)56646
Pages: 268
Exhibits: Tables

Erudite and theoretical, this research monograph is of use to businesspeople involved in the lumber business in Malaysia. The author examines in detail the role of the forestry industry in Malaysia's economy, the history of forestry in the various regions of the country, employment in the industry, financial issues, and the future of forest policy. This is an impressive study for the industry analyst.

Title: *Growth and Structural Change in the Malaysian Economy*
Date: 1990
Format: Hardcover
Author: Jomo Kwame Sundaram
Publisher: Macmillan Press, Ltd.
4 Little Essex St.
London WC2R 3LF, United Kingdom
Tel: (71)836-6633
Fax: (71)379-4204
Pages: 262
Exhibits: Tables

Written by a Malaysian professor, this clearly articulated analysis of Malaysia's economy is yet another readable choice for the businessperson seeking background knowledge of this subject. The topics covered include the colonial legacy, economic growth through international trade, employment and income distribution, past development plans, industrialization, and a complete analysis of current political and economic policy.

Title: *The Malaysian Challenges in the 1990's—Strategies for Growth and Development*
Date: 1990
Format: Paperback
Author: Fong Chen Onn and others
Publisher: Pelanduk Publications (m) Sdn. Bhd.
24 Jalan 20/16A
46300 Petaling Jaya
Selangor Darul Ehsan, Malaysia
Tel: (60)(3)776-1613
Fax: (60)(3)776-8551
Pages: 251
Exhibits: Graphs and tables

This book, published in Malaysia, is a compilation of lectures given by Malaysian analysts on the country's economic and cultural policies. It might prove useful as a source of background information on political and social policies in the country, as viewed by local observers. Also, political risk analysts might want to consider it for its overview of future scenarios in the Malaysian political realm.

Title: *Malaysian Economic Outlook*
Date: Semiannual
Format: Periodical
Publisher: Malaysian Institute of Economic Research
P.O. Box 12160
Kuala Lumpur 50768, Malaysia
Pages: Varies
Exhibits: Graphs and tables
Price: Contact for subscription prices

This economic updater and forecaster, published in Malaysia, provides semiannual illustrated analysis of the world economy and Malaysia's economic outlook for the near term. It includes good coverage of exchange rates, investment flows, industrial production, prices, and balance of payments. In short, this is a recommended source for analysts and researchers who seek current, credible data.

Title: *The Malaysian Economy: Pacific Connections*
Date: 1991
Format: Hardcover
Author: Mohamed Ariff
Publisher: Oxford University Press
Unit 221, Ubi Ave. 4
Singapore, 1440
Tel: (65)743-1066
Fax: (65)742-5915
Pages: 216
Exhibits: Maps, graphs, and tables

An erudite monograph written by a professor at the University of Malaya, this volume provides a well-researched overview of Malaysia's economic integration with Pacific Rim countries. It discusses the structure and profile of the economy, management of the economy, trade flows, foreign investment and its impact, and more and provides an analysis of Malaysia's economic relations to the Asia-Pacific region. Clear charts and tables visually depict Malaysian bureaucratic decision making, expansion of trade, and so on. For the serious businessperson, this is a great introduction to Malaysia's political economy and development imperatives.

Title: *The Malaysian Economy: Spatial Perspectives*
Date: 1990
Format: Hardcover
Author: George Cho
Publisher: Routledge, Chapman and Hall, Inc.
29 W. 35th St.
New York, NY 10001
Tel: (212)244-3336
Fax: (212)563-2269
Pages: 314
Exhibits: Maps, graphs, and tables

For the businessperson seeking readable background information on Malaysia's economy and industrial development, this volume, written by a Malaysian professor, is recommended. Without being too theoretical, the author covers the characteristics of the economy and its colonial legacy, reviews past development plans, rural and urban development, and industrial structure and growth and analyzes some of the potential political and social obstacles that Malaysia faces, namely, handling its diverse population and the geographic division of its territory. The book is written in clear, extensively footnoted prose.

ETIQUETTE AND PROTOCOL

Title: *Culture Shock! Malaysia*
Date: 1991
Format: Hardcover
Author: Heidi Munan
Publisher: Graphic Arts Center Publishing Co.
P.O. Box 10306
Portland, OR 97210
Tel: (503)226-2402
Fax: (503)226-1410
Pages: 240
Exhibits: Cartoons and photographs

An enjoyable reader on etiquette and customs, this book provides an armchair tour of Malaysian society, ways of communicating, and ceremonies. It includes sections on making a good first impression, dining etiquette, language, and work; a fun cultural quiz; and a set of tips. It is recommended to anyone who plans to visit Malaysia, though business protocol is not the focus here.

Title: *Malaysian Protocol*
Date: 1986
Format: Hardcover
Author: Abdullah Ali
Publisher: Times Books International
Times Centre
1 New Industrial Rd.
Singapore, 1953
Tel: (65)284-8844
Fax: (65)285-4871
Pages: 213
Exhibits: Maps, charts, photographs, and tables

Elegantly written and published, this is the definitive source for those dealing with high officials and royalty in Malaysia. The detail is astounding. It covers invitations, greetings and salutations, government titles, and so on. It is highly recommended for the protocol officer in charge of coordinating high-level diplomatic or business missions; it is not for the general business visitor.

GENERAL BUSINESS

Title: *Malaysian Business*
Date: Biweekly
Format: Periodical
Editor: Ahmad Rejal Arbee
Publisher: Berita Publishing Sdn. Bhd.
22 Jalan Liku
Kuala Lampur 59100, Malaysia
Tel: (60)(3)282-4322
Fax: (60)(3)282-1605
Pages: Varies
Exhibits: Graphs and tables
Price: Contact for subscription prices

Colorful and packed with articles, this 70- to 80-page general business magazine covers the Asian business scene from the point of view of the Malaysian businessperson. It includes interviews, opinion, travel tips, stock information, and marketing tips. It is recommended as a reader for marketers and investors who are significantly involved with Malaysia.

HISTORY AND SOCIETY

Title: *Malaysia*
Date: 1965
Format: Hardcover
Author: Victor Purcell
Publisher: Walker Company
720 Fifth Ave.
New York, NY 10019
Tel: (212)265-3632
Pages: 224
Exhibits: Maps and photographs

A great many volumes are to be found that chronicle the colorful story of Malaysia and her rich cultural heritage. Perhaps the best known author in the field is Victor Purcell, whose 1948 landmark study, *The Chinese in Malaya*, remains an important work on the subject. I include his history of Malaysia in this unforgivably short list for its ease of reading, completeness, and its marvelous illustrations, which serve to bring the country alive and make it real for the business reader lacking time to pursue the stacks at a university library. If you can't locate this book, the next one listed will do the trick almost as well.

Title: *Malaysia: Economic Expansion and National Unity*
Date: 1981
Format: Hardcover
Author: John Michael Gullick
Publisher: Ernest Benn Limited
25 New Street Square
Fleet Street
London EC4A 3JA
Pages: 290
Exhibits: Maps, photographs, and tables

Again, many good historical accounts of Malaysia are available, but this one is easily readable and covers all the territory essential for the business person. Chapters cover early history (1400–1786), British rule, ethnic makeup of the country, the transition to independence, politics, economy, foreign policy, and cultural aspects. A still-current primer.

Title: *Malaysian World-View*
Date: 1985

Format: Hardcover
Editor: Taib Osman
Publisher: Southeast Asian Studies Program
Institute of Southeast Asian Studies
Heng Mui Keng Terrace
Pasir Panjang
Singapore, 0511
Tel: (65)778-0955
Fax: (65)775-6259
Pages: 284
Exhibits: None

This academic monograph provides a rough outline of Malay values and personality and includes a bibliography of related materials. It can still be found in some college libraries.

INFORMATION SOURCES

Title: *Malaysian Periodicals Index*
Date: Annual
Format: Paperback
Publisher: University of Malaya
P.O. Box 1127
Jalan Pantai Baru
Kuala Lumpur 59700, Malaysia
Tel: (60)(3)757-887
Fax: (60)(3)757-3661
Pages: Varies
Exhibits: None
Price: M$53/year

This periodical index lists articles published in Bahasa Malaysian English, Chinese, and Tamil in selected Malaysian periodicals. Articles of less than 750 words are not included, with the exception of poems and short stories. Each entry lists subject, title, periodical name, date, and number of pages, but there are no abstracts. The index is weak in the areas of business and industry.

LAWS AND REGULATIONS

Title: *Construction Law in Singapore and Malaysia*
Date: 1988
Format: Hardcover
Author: Nigel M. Robinson and Anthony P. Lavers
Publisher: Butterworth and Co. (Asia) Pte., Ltd.
30 Robinson Rd. #12-01
Tuan Sing Towers
Singapore, 0104
Tel: (65)220-3684
Fax: (65)225-2939
Pages: 350
Exhibits: Tables

A readable volume and a useful reference source, this book will interest lawyers, dispute mediators, and executives who are involved in the construction industry in Malaysia or Singapore. The topics covered include all aspects of construction law, from the content of construction materials and the liability for design to risk management and arbitration. It is well organized and authoritative and includes a useful digest of relevant cases.

Title: *General Principles of Malaysian Law*
Date: 1990
Format: Hardcover
Author: Lee Mei Pheng
Publisher: Penerbit Fajar Bakti Sdn. Bhd.

3 Jalan 13/3
46200 Petaling Jaya
Selangor Darul Ehsan, Malaysia
Tel: (60)(3)757-0000
Fax: (60)(3)757-6688

Pages: 474

Exhibits: None

Meant for lawyers and law students, this book discusses the basic principles of Malaysian Law as they relate to bankers. The author has collected hundreds of important cases and has set them down in summarized, readable form in layperson's language. The book covers the law of the contract, company law, agency law, the sale of goods law, and other topics that might intrigue the general business reader. Two introductory chapters provide a fine overview of the roots of Malaysian law and the country's judicial system.

Title: *Malaysian Laws on Banking and Finance*

Date: Annual

Format: Hardcover

Publisher: International Law Book Services
14, 1st Floor, Larong Bunus Enam
Off Jalan Masjid India
Kuala Lumpur 50100, Malaysia
Tel: (60)(3)293-9862 or 9864
Fax: (60)(3)292-8035

Pages: 676

Exhibits: None

For international lawyers working with Malaysia, this hefty text is a compilation of the legal acts, amendments, and agreements that make up the country's banking and financial law. This is strictly a desktop reference for legal professionals or students of international law.

MANAGEMENT

Title: *Malaysian Management: The Story of the Malaysian Institute of Management*

Date: 1991

Format: Hardcover

Author: D.J.M. Tate

Publisher: Malaysian Institute of Management
7th Floor, Wisma HLA
SF Jalan Raja Chulan
Kuala Lumpur 50200, Malaysia
Tel: (60)(3)242-5255 or 268-6500

Pages: 116

Exhibits: Graphs, photographs, and tables

Since 1966, the Malaysian Institute of Management has promoted higher standards of enterprise management in Malaysia. This history of the organization is wise preparatory reading for Westerners who will become involved with the institute or with groups of Malaysian managers who are associated with it.

TAXATION

Title: *Malaysian Master Tax Guide*

Date: Annual

Format: Hardcover

Publisher: CCH Asia, Ltd.

139 Cecil St.
Cecil House #02-00
Singapore, 0106
Tel: (65)225-2555

Pages: 830

Exhibits: Tables

This comprehensive tax guide is written "to assist taxpayers in understanding their tax liabilities and entitlements" in Malaysia. It includes complete coverage of business tax laws and tax rates and is highly recommended to accountants and tax lawyers.

THAILAND

OVERVIEW

Bangkok, Thailand's capital city on the Chao Phraya River, is called *Krung Thep*, the "City of Angels." Its balmy heat soothes, and the legendary Thai hospitality calms the nerves. One hears the phrase *Men pai ren* at every turn: "No problem. It doesn't really matter." Besides these benefits of being in Thailand, there are extremely attractive investor incentives for businesses to set up shop there. Thailand has become a site for low-cost export manufacturing; labor can be hired for as little as 35 cents an hour. The government actively supports business and does everything in its power to attract foreign investment.

Thailand at a Glance

Population:	59.4 million
Religion:	Buddhist, Muslim, Christian, other
Government:	Constitutional monarchy
Language:	Thai
Currency:	Bhat
Trade (1993):	$32.2 billion total exports; $36.3 billion total imports

Until recently, stability has come easy to Thailand, in part because the country escaped the destructive impact of foreign colonialism. The country's leaders have been politically fortunate in that 90 percent of the population shares the same ethnic background, religion, and language; this reduces the potential for ethnic conflict. The Chinese, who virtually control Thailand's private sector, have suffered neither discriminating social policy, as in Indonesia and Malaysia, nor violent persecution, as in Indonesia during the 1960s.

Thailand's traditionally stable constitutional monarchy has been in place for more than 60 years. Under it, civilian and military officials have worked in symbiosis to manage and regulate the transition of the country's economy from one based on agriculture to one based increasingly on manufacturing, tourism, and trade. The military bureaucracy, the main bastion of Thai (rather than

Chinese) power, has not moved rapidly enough, however, in pushing through pro-democracy political reforms to match the economic reforms and their resulting prosperity among Thai urbanites. It is hoped that the king has taken this lesson in hand and will push now for political reforms alongside the liberalization and deregulation of the economy.

Economic Conditions

Thai business conditions sustained a terrible jolt in May 1992, when civilian pro-democracy protesters clashed with the military. The protesters demanded the resignation of Prime Minister Suchinda Kraprayoon, a former general, and the amendment of the constitution to guarantee that future prime ministers be elected members of Parliament. At least 500 protesters were killed or reported missing after being mowed down in a barrage of machine-gun fire. Suchinda resigned less than a week later. King Bhumibol then appointed a new prime minister to lead an interim government. Observers point to the pervasive role of the king in quelling what could have escalated into civil war.

Thailand's average annual growth rate of 10 percent, which it sustained from 1987 to 1991, fell off to a still respectable 7 to 8 percent in 1992. Investment applications dropped off in 1991 by 50 percent due to diminishing investment from Japan, Hong Kong, and Taiwan. Much of the investment once targeted for Thailand is now destined for South China, Dalien China, and Mexico (in anticipation of the passage of the North American Free Trade Agreement). This is not to say that Thailand's attractions—a large consumer market, homogeneous populations, and a low-cost, skilled labor force—will not continue to lure investors. However, the heady days of 1987 and 1988, when the country was awash with Japanese investment, are gone—at least until a pro-business government can ensure long-term political stability through real democratic reforms.

Recently, wages in Thailand have risen 15 percent a year, from $3.12 a day in 1989 to $4.60 a day in 1992. Manufacturers of low-cost exports might find Thai labor too expensive now in comparison to the Philippines, South China, and Indonesia. Moreover, the infrastructure is strained to the limit, air pollution only gets worse, and the AIDS epidemic is predicted to affect 7 percent of the population by the year 2000, which will put heavy pressure on health care and reduce the size and cost-competitiveness of the skilled labor force.

Historical Background

Through the fortunes of history and the will of its people to remain independent, *Muang Thai*, the "Land of the Free," has remained free from domination by colonial powers throughout its history, unlike any of its neighbors. Thais are, almost to a person, devoted Buddhists, which makes them almost inhumanly tolerant. In fact, Thailand and Burma are the only countries in the Asia-Pacific that are overwhelmingly Buddhist.

Buddhism can be summed up in one simple belief: All life is suffering. In Thailand, it means that everyone should be tolerant and easy-going because material possessions and personal achievement don't matter much in the grand scheme of things. Personal well-being is more important than career position. Economic position is the result of karma accumulated over the course of past existences. Buddhism's five major commandments are these: (1) Do not take life. (2) Do not steal. (3) Do not commit adultery. (4) Do not tell untruths. (5) Refrain from intoxicants. Most Thais follow all but the last one closely. They also live by the Buddhist principle of following a middle path and avoiding extremes in business, in social life, and in their opinions. For the Thai, time itself is cyclical rather than linear, like Buddhism's Wheel of Life. Thais accept the authority of those in positions of power because these people must have acquired the merit to deserve such power through successive past lives in which they transgressed to a state of karma closer to Nirvana. However, they expect those in power to look out for the common folk as a parent looks after a child. Buddhist values also teach them to be frugal. All of this is not to suggest that the Thais don't work hard; they do, and this is one of the reasons that foreign investment has come into Thailand at such a rapid pace.

Until the dissolution of the Thai monarchy in 1910, Thai society was built on a class system based on hereditary lineage. The king was political leader and head of the Buddhist order, supplying both spiritual and material protection and aid. The king became a symbol invested with religious meaning and respect. Ethnic Chinese occupy all Thai social classes except government and military positions. Although one out of every ten Thais is of Chinese descent, the Chinese control the business community and own the banks and prominent factories.

ACCOUNTING, BANKING, AND FINANCE

Title: *Bangkok Bank Monthly Review*

Date: Monthly

Format: Periodical

Publisher: Bangkok Bank, Ltd.
33 Silom Rd.
Bangkok 10500, Thailand
Tel: (66)(2)234-3333
Fax: (66)(2)221-9800

Pages: Varies

Exhibits: Graphs and tables

Price: Contact for subscription prices

Containing quarterly economic data and stock market statistics, this 30- to 40-page publication is a credible source for investors and researchers. It also includes analytical articles on subjects that bear on the Thai financial sector, such as the effects of establishing an ASEAN Free Trade Area on Thailand. Although a bit awkward in writing style, this is a useful source for data collectors.

Title: *Bank of Thailand Quarterly Bulletin*
Date: Quarterly
Format: Periodical
Publisher: Bank of Thailand
273 Samsen Rd.
Bangkok 10200, Thailand
Tel: (66)(2)282-7599, ext. 2617 or 2618
Fax: (66)(2)280-0626
Pages: Varies
Exhibits: Tables
Price: $13/year

Inexpensive and packed with 100-pages of statistical data, this publication is a highly recommended source of current Thai economic information. It includes an analysis of production, population, wages, prices, trade, fiscal conditions, and monetary developments. The statistical data cover every aspect of trade, production, and investment.

Title: *Thai Capital Market*
Date: 1988
Format: Hardcover
Author: Somjai Phagaphasvivat
Publisher: S.S. Consultant and Research
37/140 Soi Yenchit
Chan Road
Yanawa
Bangkok 10120, Thailand
Pages: 247
Exhibits: Tables

For those seeking an understanding of the Securities Exchange and the securities business in Thailand, this is one of the few sources available in English. The first part of the volume describes the evolution of the Securities Exchange, and the second contains articles on issues related to the development of Thailand's capital market. As a grab-bag reader, this is a useful source, but it is quickly becoming dated.

COMPANY DIRECTORIES

Title: *American Chamber of Commerce in Thailand Handbook Directory*
Date: Annual
Format: Paperback
Publisher: American Chamber of Commerce in Thailand
140 Wireless Rd.
Bangkok 10330, Thailand
Tel: (66)(2)251-9266
Fax: (66)(2)255-2454
Pages: 378
Exhibits: Photographs

For those who plan to move to Thailand, this booklet can provide personal contacts in that country. The profiles of members include a portrait, address, phone number, job title, and function.

Title: *Key Business Directory of Indonesia/Thailand*
Date: 1990
Format: Hardcover
Publisher: Dun & Bradstreet (Singapore) Pte., Ltd.
80 Anson Rd.
#29-02 IBM Towers
Singapore, 0208
Tel: (65)334-336
Fax: (65)334-2465 or 2469
Pages: 294
Exhibits: None

This directory includes 1,500 companies that have an annual turnover of more than 150 million bahts and/or at least 50 employees. Thai and Indonesian firms are listed by name, product classification, and geographic region. Each listing includes the name of the CEO, turnover, number of employees, import/export status, auditor, and directors. This directory is recommended.

Title: *Leading Companies in Thailand*
Date: Annual
Format: Hardcover
Publisher: International Business Research (Thailand) Co., Ltd.
Address: Not available.
Pages: 440
Exhibits: Photographs

This attractive directory ranks approximately 350 Thai firms that have more than one billion baht in annual revenue. The company profiles include address, nature of business, the year's highlights, bankers, shareholders, history, directors, and managers. A facing page provides a biography of the company's CEO, including a portrait. The directory carries advertising. It is hoped that future editions will provide contact information and subscription prices.

Title: *Thailand Company Information*
Date: Annual
Format: Paperback
Publisher: Advanced Research Group Co., Ltd.
109 Surawong Rd.
8th Floor, CCT Building
Bangkok 10500, Thailand
Tel: (66)(2)236-2902-4
Fax: (66)(2)236-2900 or 237-6900
Pages: Varies
Exhibits: None

This attractive directory of the top 2,000 Thai firms is divided by industry and has an index of companies by name. The book is tabbed for easy use. Each entry lists the type of business, the major shareholders, the nationality of the firm (e.g., Thai 85%, Chinese 15%), and financial data.

Title: *Thailand Export Monitor*
Date: Annual
Format: Hardcover
Publisher: Alpha Research Co., Ltd.
16/69 Soi Thong Lor
Wipawadee Rangsit Rd.
Jatujak
Bangkok 10900, Thailand
Tel: (66)(2)513-0661 or 512-5111
Fax: (66)(2)513-0661
Pages: 868
Exhibits: Maps and tables

Meant for buyers of goods and services offered in Thailand, this volume provides a directory of exporters listed by product classification. It also contains much information about export services, including a complete presentation of data about Thailand export performance for the past year. It is useful to buyers and anyone researching Thai export capability in general. The directory carries advertising and includes a complete list of government and trade organizations involved in trade.

Title: *Thailand Import Monitor*
Date: Annual
Format: Hardcover
Publisher: Alpha Research Co., Ltd.
16/69 Soi Thong Lor
Wipawadee Rangsit Rd.
Jatujak
Bangkok 10900, Thailand
Tel: (66)(2)513-0661 or 512-5111
Fax: (66)(2)513-0661
Pages: 850
Exhibits: Graphs and tables

Meant for exporters of goods and services to Thailand, this volume provides a directory of importers, listed by product classification, and much information about import services, including a comprehensive body of data on Thailand's import performance for the past year. It is useful to sellers and anyone researching the Thai import market in general. It includes a list of government and trade organizations involved in importing.

Title: *Thailand Industrial Buyer's Guide*
Date: Annual
Format: Paperback
Publisher: Business Publications Co., Ltd.
9/42 Petchaburi 10
Soi Kingpetch
Bangkok 10400, Thailand
Tel: (66)(2)215-0926-9
Fax: (66)(2)215-6865
Pages: 751
Exhibits: None

Following an introductory section that provides a rich overview of Thailand's trade services and government offices, this directory lists 7,500 Thai exporters by product category. Exporters also appear by name in an index. Meant for importers of Thai goods, this volume offers additional information about organizations that play a role in trade, including associations, chambers, embassies, shipping companies, and airlines. It is recommended to importers.

Title: *Thailand's Exporters Selected List*
Date: Annual
Format: Hardcover
Publisher: Ministry of Commerce
Royal Thai Government
22/77 Rachadapisek Rd.
Bangkok 10900, Thailand
Tel: (66)(2)511-5066 or 5077
Fax: (66)(2)512-1079
Pages: Varies
Exhibits: None

"Designed to showcase the Kingdom's major export sectors," this directory lists Thai exporting companies by product and service. There are full-color advertisements from many of the firms.

COUNTRY PROFILES

Title: *Country Report: Thailand, Myanmar (Burma)*
Date: Quarterly
Format: Periodical; also available on microfilm
Publisher: The Economist Intelligence Unit

P.O. Box 154
Dartford
Kent DA1 1QB, United Kingdom
Tel: (44)(322)289-194
Fax: (44)(322)223-803
For microfilm version, contact:
World Microfilm Publications, Ltd.
2-6 Foscote Mews
London W92HH, United Kingdom

Pages: Varies
Exhibits: Tables
Price: Contact for subscription prices

For businesspeople tracking political, economic, or business climate changes in Thailand or Burma, this is a recommended source. Following a very handy executive summary of the entire "outlook," the contents include sections on the political scene, economic policy, employment, industry, finance, and trade. An appendix of current statistics is also included.

Title: *Global Forecasting Service: Thailand*
Date: Quarterly
Format: Periodical
Publisher: The Economist Intelligence Unit
P.O. Box 154
Dartford
Kent DA1 1QB, United Kingdom
Tel: (44)(322)289-194
Fax: (44)(322)223-803
For on-line version, contact:
Maid Systems, Ltd.
Maid House
18 Dufferin St.
London ECIY 8PD, United Kingdom
Tel: (44)(71)253-6900

Pages: Varies
Exhibits: Tables
Price: Contact for subscription prices

This 25- to 30-page periodical provides an overview of Thailand's political, economic, social/demographic, and business climate outlook for the next five years. The large-format publications in this series are expensive, but for the executive decision maker with limited time to read widely on Thailand, this is a recommended updater and forecaster. It includes fact sheets and a summary of predictions.

Title: *Thailand: A Country Study*
Date: 1989
Format: Hardcover
Author: Federal Research Division, Library of Congress
Editor: Barbara Leitch LePoer
Publisher: Library of Congress/Department of the Army
101 Independence Ave., SE
Washington, DC 20540
Tel: (202)707-5079
Fax: (202)707-3585

Pages: 365
Exhibits: Charts, maps, photographs, and tables

Covering Thailand's history, society, geography, economy, government, politics, and national security, this country overview (like the other books in the series) is the best single introduction to the country. Each chapter is compiled by a different author, the table of contents includes subheadings for easy reference, and the book includes photographs, government organization charts, a glossary, a bibliography, and an index. It is current only as of 1987, but the bulk of the contact is still timely.

Title: *Thailand's Turn: Profile of a New Dragon*
Date: 1992
Format: Hardcover
Author: Elliott Kulick and Dick Wilson
Publisher: St. Martin's Press
175 Fifth Ave.
New York, NY 10010
Tel: (212)674-5151
Fax: (212)420-9314
Pages: 212
Exhibits: Table

Businesspeople will find this compact reader about Thailand's fast rise as an economic powerhouse in Asia to be an entertaining and well-researched primer on Thai society, politics, and economy. The authors include a who's who of key Thai officials and a glossary of Thai terms, and they lace the discussion with engaging anecdotes. This is a recommended introduction.

ETIQUETTE AND PROTOCOL

Title: *Culture Shock! Thailand*
Date: 1990
Format: Paperback
Author: Robert Cooper and Nanthapa Cooper
Publisher: Graphic Arts Center Publishing Co.
P.O. Box 10306
Portland, OR 97210
Tel:(503)226-2402
Fax: (503)226-1410
Pages: 255
Exhibits: Cartoons and photographs

For the businessperson and others preparing to live and/or work in Thailand, this book contains a readable and fully illustrated description of Thai character, customs, and ceremonies. It contains a helpful index and useful "critical incident" exercises to help readers steer clear of etiquette mine fields. This resource is recommended.

GENERAL BUSINESS

Title: *Business Review*
Date: Monthly
Format: Periodical
Editor: Laurie Rosenthal
Publisher: Nation Publishing Group Co., Ltd.
44 Moo 10 Bangna-Trat Rd.
K.m. 4.5 Bangna
Prakanong
Bangkok 10260, Thailand
Tel: (66)(2)317-0420
Fax: (66)(2)317-1384
Pages: Varies
Exhibits: None
Price: $115/year

Covering Thai business in general, this 100-page magazine is useful to expatriates and managers working in Thailand. Its shotgun coverage includes industry, agriculture, profiles of businesspeople, relevant commercial news, and even a horoscope. This is one of the few sources of general Thai business news.

Title: *Doing Business in Thailand*
Date: 1987
Format: Hardcover
Publisher: BIC Publishing Co., Ltd.
7 Phaholyothin Soi 4
Phaholyothin Rd.
Bangkok 10400, Thailand
Tel: (66)(2)270-1691 or 1117
Pages: 233
Exhibits: Photographs and tables

Now a bit dated, this is one of the few general business guidebooks that covers profiting as an investor in Thailand. It contains a useful list of Thai cultural values that affect business dealings, a profile of the country, an overview of laws affecting foreign investment, and useful addresses.

Title: *Importing from Thailand*
Date: 1989
Format: Hardcover
Publisher: Trade Media, Ltd.
The Asian Sources Media Group
22nd Floor, Vita Towers
29 Wong Chuk Hang Rd.
Wong Chuk Hang, Hong Kong
Mailing Address:
GPO Box 11411
Hong Kong
Tel: (852)555-4777
Fax: (852)873-0488
Pages: 191
Exhibits: None

Offered as a "buyer's manual for selecting suppliers, negotiating orders and arranging methods of payment for more profitable purchasing," this compact and densely packed book provides a look at Thai exports, customs and trade regulations, shipping protocol, trade support services, and banking operations and offers tips for business travelers. It is a recommended guidebook for buyers.

HISTORY AND SOCIETY

Title: *Interact: Guidelines for Thais and North Americans*
Date: 1980
Format: Paperback
Author: John Paul Fieg
Publisher: Intercultural Press
Box 768
Yarmouth, ME 04096
Tel: (207)846-5168
Fax: (207)846-5181
Pages: 118
Exhibits: None

This detailed and erudite exploration into Thai values and character is of great use to expatriates and managers in Thailand. The author proves that Thais and Americans have more in common than you might have expected.

Title: *Thailand—Its People, Its Society, Its Culture*
Date: 1974
Format: Paperback
Author: Frank J. Moore
Publisher: HRAF Press
New Haven, CT
Pages: 170
Exhibits: None

A bit dated now, this book provides a concise overview of Thai culture, customs, and etiquette. The book is out of print, but can be found in some large libraries.

INDUSTRY

Title: *TDRI Quarterly Review*
Date: Quarterly
Format: Periodical
Author: Thailand Development Research Institute
Editor: Anne Johnson
Publisher: Thailand Development Research Institute
16th Floor, Rajapark Building
163 Asoke Rd.
Sukhumvit
Bangkok 10110,Thailand
Tel: (66)(2)258-9012-7
Fax: (66)(2)258-9046
Pages: Varies
Exhibits: Graphs and tables
Price: $14/year

This 30- to 40-page large-format quarterly contains 5 to 7 articles and a news brief. The articles offer well-illustrated profiles and analyses of selected Thai industries, such as the auto industry or railways. Two or more articles focus on the Thai economy. This is a useful reader for a low price.

POLITICS AND GOVERNMENT

Title: *Power and Politics in Thailand*
Date: 1989
Format: Paperback
Author: Kevin Hewison
Publisher: Journal of Contemporary Asia Publishers
c/o University of The Philippines
37 Gonzales Hall, Dilliman
Quezon City, Philippines 3004
Tel: (63)(2)992-558
Pages: 177
Exhibits: Tables and graphs

Authored by a consultant-sociologist based in Northeast Thailand, this short analysis of Thai political power is extensively footnoted and academic in style. Now becoming dated and difficult to find, it provides an interesting cultural analysis of politics in Thailand, the relationship between capitalist development and the state, and Thai industry. It is useful as an in-depth introduction to Thai political economy, with the caveat that the essays included were written between 1980 and 1988.

TRAVEL ADVICE

Title: *Thailand and Burma*
Date: 1988
Format: Hardcover
Author: Frank Kusy and Frances Capel
Publisher: Globe Pequot Press
6 Business Park Rd.
Old Saybrook, CT 06475
Tel: (203)395-0440
Fax: (203)395-0312
Pages: 392
Exhibits: Maps

For the traveler who wants to spend more than a few days in Thailand or Burma and wants to get off the beaten track, this thoughtful and complete guide by a travel writer and a novelist is a recommended source. It offers plenty of background information and covers all of the regions in both countries. Country and city maps, a dining guide, and hotel information are included.

PHILIPPINES

OVERVIEW

The Philippines archipelago consists of 7,100 islands and inlets divided into the areas of Luzon, Visayan, and Mindanao. More than 64.27 million people live on the Philippine islands, and they speak more than 70 distinct languages and dialects. The Philippines is the only Christian, English-speaking democracy in Asia. Unfortunately, the country is also one of the riskiest places in the region for a foreigner to live, work, or invest money. Regional allegiances based on lineage, language, and ethnic makeup remain in force today, at times a force of national cooperation and, just as often, of international conflict and competition. However, foreign investment in the islands tripled during 1988, with exports rising 27 percent, mainly due to Japanese firms moving their processing and assembly work to the islands.

Philippines at a Glance

Population:	64.27 million
Religion:	Roman Catholic
Government:	Constitutional democracy
Language:	Tagalog; English is widely spoken
Currency:	Peso
Trade (1993):	$9.8 billion total exports; $14.5 billion total imports

The election of former Defense Secretary Fidel V. Ramos, who was Corazon Aquino's choice, to the Philippine presidency in May 1992 was probably the fairest and certainly the most peaceful election in the country's history. With a pro-business moderate in power and threats from the right and the left at a minimum, the potential for growth and prosperity in the country is high. The challenge is to build up the country's insufficient electric power capacity to fuel economic growth. Power outages arise from too little investment in power generation, plant breakdowns, and insufficient rainfall to sustain hydro-generated power. Lack of power prevents production from meeting the growing domestic demand and resulted in increased imports—good news for foreign suppliers but bad news for the Philippine economy. An underdeveloped telecommunications network impedes economic growth as well. The government is tapping the public and private sector, not to mention international financial institutions, in an attempt to alleviate the country's lacking infrastructure. Another drag on the economy is its debt burden of $29 billion, which requires 20 percent of the country's export receipts just to service.

Economic Conditions

The Philippine economy appears to be turning a corner in the mid-1990s. Inflation has been pulled down to single-digit levels. Interest rates and the trade deficit are now under control. The gross national product rose slightly in 1992 after remaining flat in 1991, though industrial output dropped off slightly due to power shortages. Economic problems over the past five years have resulted in long-awaited reforms of the regulatory environment, which has kept the economy relatively closed to foreigners. Tariff rates and import barriers have been lowered, offering up a wide range of sales opportunities to U.S. firms.

Philippine imports are concentrated in supplying the country's key industries: electronics, garments, power generation, telecommunications equipment, and oil for the production of energy. The United States increased its trade with the Philippines in 1992 by 16 percent and is the country's largest export market, purchasing 40 percent of its exports. In that year, the Philippines expanded its electronics and apparel sectors in the face of power shortages, though its 1992 trade imbalance reached upward of $5 billion. The best trade prospects for U.S. suppliers include electrical power systems, telecommunications equipment, industrial chemicals, and computers and peripherals. Without a doubt, and ignoring political risk factors, the Philippines offer one of the largest, most skilled, and cheapest labor forces in Asia. Due to a lack of opportunity in the technical and scientific areas, available employees await offers from foreign companies in these sectors.

Historical Overview

After two decades of dictatorship under Ferdinand Marcos, a democratic electoral system was restored under President Corazon Aquino's administration. The Aquino years were fraught with seven coup attempts, security concerns due to Communist insurgency, and a Senate unwilling to ratify progressive legislation. Moreover, widespread and persistent government corruption continued to compromise officials after Aquino established the Presidential Commission on

Good Government when she took office. One systemic political problem for the country has been its armed forces, elements of which have been behind coup attempts and have been unwilling to give up the privileges that they were accustomed to after 20 years of martial law.

The country's 50-year status as a colony of the United States (1898–1947), the widespread knowledge of English, and the predominance of the Catholic Church bring the islands closer culturally with the United States than any other ASEAN country. Filipinos tend to associate American products with quality and technological excellence.

There are three different cultures in the Philippines: Filipino, Hispanic, and Chinese. Filipino culture is the result of four separate cultural legacies: centuries of village agriculture based on tribal kinship; 300 years of exposure to Spanish Catholicism; 50 years of exposure to American free enterprise; and an enduring Chinese ethnic presence in the business community. The English language was brought to the islands by American occupiers in the early 1900s, along with a U.S.-style public school system that eventually helped replace Tagalog (Filipino) with English as the language of business.

Early Filipino tribal society was organized along kinship lines. With colonization by the Spanish, Catholicism was superimposed on this kinship-based social system. The blood-brother covenant was mixed with the "compadre" system of Spanish Catholicism, which produced enormous families based on both blood line and godparent relationships, a tradition that is very popular in the Philippines. Connections and alliances were created between those who were related by blood as well as those "ritual kinfolk" linked together by ceremony. Family and group membership became all-important, especially in business. These and other ancient values are part of the modern Filipino: respect for elders, deference to superiors, kindness and tolerance toward those of inferior status. The typical Filipino understands that family and group connections can produce tax breaks, kickbacks, and even elusive business contracts, and this applies to politics as well as business. Without family connections or political influence, an aspiring leader has little chance of ascending the hierarchy. Cory Aquino, who won her 1986 presidency on a platform of popularism, is the offspring of one of the largest sugar plantation families in the country. As Filipinos say, "An American politician kisses babies. In the Philippines, we finance their education."

COMPANY DIRECTORIES

Title: *American Chamber of Commerce of the Philippines Directory*

Date: Annual

Format: Paperback

Publisher: American Chamber of Commerce of the Philippines, Inc.
2nd Floor, Corinthian Plaza
Paseo de Roxas
C.P.O. Box 1578
Makati
Metro Manila 1299, Philippines
Tel: (63)(2)818-7911
Fax: (63)(2)816-6359

Pages: Varies

Exhibits: Photographs

For experts headed for the Philippines, this book can provide personal contacts in the country. The profiles of members include a portrait, address, phone number, and job function and title.

Title: *Kompass: Philippines*

Date: Annual

Format: Hardcover

Publisher: Croner Publications, Inc.
211-03 Jamaica Ave.
Queens Village, NY 11428
Tel: (718)464-0866
Fax: (718)465-6171

Pages: Varies

Exhibits: Tables

Perhaps the most comprehensive directory of Philippine companies, this list is divided by products and services offered. Company profiles include office hours, trademarks, subsidiaries, board of directors, number of employees, and a coded list of products and services offered.

Title: *Philippine Agribusiness Factbook and Directory*

Date: Annual

Format: Paperback

Publisher: Center for Research and Communication
Southeast Asian Science Foundation, Inc.
Pearl Drive
Ortigas Complex
Pasig
Metro Manila, Philippines
Tel: (63)(2)631-0935

Pages: 439

Exhibits: Graphs and tables

Besides providing a directory of agricultural firms in the Philippines, this volume also offers a comprehensive set of statistics on the performance of the country's rural sector. The book lists fishery production, forest production, the price of commodities, lending, agricultural trade status, and commodity profiles. This is a great resource for those who need this information.

Title: *Philippine Export Directory*

Date: Annual

Format: Paperback

Editor: William L. Ogan

Publisher: Pacific Asia Publications
Dona Felisa Syjuco Building, Suite 407
Remedois St. and Taft Ave.
Malate, Manila 1004, Philippines
Tel: (63)(2)521-9784

Pages: Varies
Exhibits: None

Meant for buyers of Philippine products, this directory lists suppliers by product and service and by company name. A list of government and trade associations is also provided, and the book is tabbed for easy use. It includes lists of airlines, personnel agencies, banks, and communications services and is recommended to any company buying from the Philippines. The directory carries advertisements.

Title: *Philippine Manufacturers Directory*
Date: Annual
Format: Paperback
Editor: William L. Ogan
Publisher: Pacific Publishing House, Inc.
Dona Felisa Syjuco Building, Room 407
Remedios St. and Taft Ave.
Malate
Manila 1550, Philippines
Pages: 296
Exhibits: Photographs

Meant for buyers of goods manufactured in the Philippines, this directory lists the top manufacturing firms by product and by name. It includes lists of employment agencies, financial institutions, and shipping companies and carries advertisements.

COUNTRY PROFILES

Title: *Country Forecast: Philippines*
Date: Quarterly
Format: Periodical; also available on-line
Publisher: The Economist Intelligence Unit
P.O. Box 154
Dartford
Kent DA1 1QB, United Kingdom
Tel: (44)(322)289-194
Fax: (44)(322)223-803
For on-line version, contact:
Maid Systems, Ltd.
Maid House
18 Dufferin St.
London EC1Y 8PD, United Kingdom
Tel: (44)(71)253-6900
Pages: Varies
Exhibits: Tables
Price: Contact for subscription prices

For businesspeople involved in the Philippines, this 10- to 15-page booklet assesses the political scene, the economy, and the business climate and provides forecasts for each. Tables of economic data for the previous five years and projections for the next five years round out this useful updater.

Title: *Country Report: Philippines*
Date: Quarterly
Format: Periodical; also available on microfilm
Publisher: The Economist Intelligence Unit
P.O. Box 154
Dartford
Kent DA1 1QB, United Kingdom
Tel: (44)(322)289-194
Fax: (44)(322)223-803

For microfilm version, contact:
World Microfilm Publications, Ltd.
2-6 Foscote Mews
London W92 HH, United Kingdom
Tel: (44)(71)266-2202
Fax: (44)(71)266-2314

Pages: Varies

Exhibits: Tables

Price: Contact for subscription prices

For businesspeople tracking political, economic, or business climate changes in the Philippines, this is a recommended one-stop source. Following a very handy executive summary of the entire "outlook," the contents include sections on the political scene, economic policy, employment, industry, finance, and trade as well as an appendix of current statistics.

Title: *Philippine Almanac*

Date: Annual

Format: Hardcover

Editor: Juan Luis Z. Luna, Jr.

Publisher: Aurora Publications
927 Quezon Ave.
Quezon City
Philippines 1104
Tel: (63)(2)9213788
Fax: (63)(2)951091

Pages: 1,061

Exhibits: Maps, graphs, photographs, and tables

Meant for researchers or businesspeople who need general factual information about the Philippines at their fingertips, this almanac covers all things Philippine, from economic statistics to famous composers, from fisheries to the first Philippine newspapers. It is recommended.

DICTIONARIES AND LANGUAGE STUDIES

Title: *Concise English-Tagalog Dictionary*

Date: 1969

Format: Hardcover

Author: Jose Villa Panganiban

Publisher: Charles E. Tuttle Co.
2-6, Suido 1-chome
Bunkyo-ku
Tokyo 112, Japan
Tel: (81)(3)811-7106-9

Pages: 170

Exhibits: None

This hand-size English-to-Tagolog dictionary includes sections on terms of measurement, geographic names, and a guide to pronunciation.

Title: *Filipino-English/English-Filipino Dictionary*

Date: 1988

Format: Hardcover

Author: Sam Bickford and Angelina Bickford

Publisher: Hippocrene Books
171 Madison Ave.
New York, NY 10016
Tel: (212)685-4371
Fax: (212)779-9338

Pages: 389

Exhibits: None

Pocket-size and of very low quality, this two-way English-Tagolog dictionary contains definitions that are typically only one or two words long, making it a simple and convenient traveler's companion.

ECONOMY

Title: *Journal of Philippine Development*
Date: Semiannual
Format: Periodical
Editor: Jennifer P.T. Liguton
Publisher: Philippine Institute for Development Studies
NEDA sa Makati Building
106 Amorsolo St.
Legaspi Village
Makati 1229, Philippines
Pages: Varies
Exhibits: Graphs and tables
Price: $32.50/year

The highly theoretical articles in this small-format journal focus on serious analysis of microeconomic issues affecting Philippine modernization and development. Meant for economists or financiers, the articles are extensively footnoted and clearly written.

Title: *Philippine Development*
Date: Bimonthly
Format: Periodical
Editor: Edwin P. Daiwey
Publisher: Office of the Director-General of the National Economic and Development Authority
NEDA Bookstore
Development Information Staff
NEDA sa Pasig Building
Amber Ave.
Pasig
Metro Manila, Philippines 1000
Tel: (63)(2)631-3281
Pages: Varies
Exhibits: Photographs

This inexpensively published 30-page magazine contains updates on development projects in the Philippines, agriculture and infrastructure, science and technology, the environment, and issues in trade and industry. For businesspeople involved in large public projects, this is a useful reader. It includes readable articles on the Philippine economy, technology assimilation, and sources of project financing.

ETIQUETTE AND PROTOCOL

Title: *Culture Shock! The Philippines*
Date: 1992
Format: Paperback
Author: Alfredo Roces and Grace Roces
Publisher: Graphic Arts Publishing Co.
Box 10306
3019 N.W. Yeon Ave.
Portland, OR 97210
Tel: (503)226-2402
Fax: (503)226-1410
Pages: 248
Exhibits: Cartoons, photographs, and maps

Another readable and recommended book in its series, this one provides detailed advice on Philippine special occasions, daily life, and personality. For anyone who plans to visit the Philippines, this book provides an essential cultural orientation. It contains 10 pages on business behavior and protocol.

GENERAL BUSINESS

Title: *Advertising in the Philippines: Its Historical, Cultural and Social Dimensions*
Date: 1989
Format: Hardcover
Author: Visitacion R. de la Torre
Publisher: Tower Book House
P.O. Box 14485
Austin, TX 78761
Tel: (512)459-4521
Pages: 474
Exhibits: Photographs

This one-of-a-kind tabletop picture book will interest advertising and marketing people who are heading for the Philippines. Its many photographs and its readable text provide a complete history and commentary on advertising in the Philippines from the time of the town crier to that of the jingle writer. The author profiles the island's most notable advertising professionals with plentiful reproductions of their work.

Title: *Doing Business in the Philippines*
Date: 1989
Format: Hardcover
Publisher: Price Waterhouse
1251 Avenue of the Americas
New York, NY 10020
Tel: (212)489-8900
Pages: 213
Exhibits: Tables

This concise guide on taxation policies in the Philippines was created by one of the leading accounting firms there. It is recommended as an overview for executives and prospective investors. Selected chapters cover the business environment, investment incentives, the regulatory environment, banking and finance, exporting, labor relations, and the tax system.

Title: *Marketing Mix: Strategy in the Philippines Setting*
Date: 1993
Format: Paperback
Author: Josiah Go
Publisher: Josiah Go Foundation, Inc.
P.O. Box 428
Greenhills
Metro Manila, Philippines
Pages: 292
Exhibits: Graphs, photographs, and tables

This self-published volume follows on the heels of the author's first title, *Contemporary Marketing Strategy in the Philippines Setting*, first published in 1992. For serious marketers headed for the Philippines, this book is a gold mine. (If only you could find books loaded with so much hands-on detail about selling and advertising in other Asian countries.) Chapters cover every aspect of marketing goods and services in the Philippines, starting with an erudite introduction to marketing, market segmentation, marketing mix, product strategy, distribution, customer service, selling cycles, pricing, and promotion. The author is academically trained and has experience as a marketing professional in the Philippines. What the book lacks in publishing quality and ease of reading style it makes up for in the richness of examples and anecdotes from inside the Philippine market.

Title: *Philippine Business Report*
Date: Monthly
Format: Periodical
Publisher: Trade and Industry Information Center
Department of Trade and Industry
4th Floor, Industry and Investments Building
385 Sen. Gil J. Puyat Ave.
Makati
Metro Manila, Philippines 1005
Tel: (63)(2)8-36-11
Fax: (63)(2)85-64-87
Pages: Varies
Exhibits: None
Price: Contact for subscription prices

Providing a potpourri of commercial news and announcements of upcoming business events, this 7- to 8-page newsletter, issued by the Philippine Department of Trade and Industry, is a handy source of scuttlebutt concerning recent Philippine-foreign deals, such as "Nissan Invests in Car Engine Assembly." It also notes developments in loan policy, export zones, and investment incentives.

Title: *U.S.-Philippine Business News*
Date: Bimonthly
Format: Periodical
Publisher: Philippine-U.S. Business Committee
U.S. Chamber of Commerce
1615 H St., NW
Washington, DC 20062
Tel: (202)463-5668
Pages: Varies
Exhibits: Photographs
Price: Contact for subscription prices

This seven-page briefing in the form of a newsletter provides businesspeople with updates on the Philippine investment climate, economy, newly appointed U.S. officials working in the country, new projects, recent deals, policy legislation, and upcoming trade shows and conferences. The publication also lists a series of available marketing reports sold by the U.S.-Philippine Business Committee. (Write to the address above to receive the list.)

HISTORY AND SOCIETY

Title: *Imelda: Steel Butterfly of the Philippines*
Date: 1988
Format: Hardcover
Author: Katherine Ellison
Publisher: McGraw-Hill
1221 Avenue of the Americas
New York, NY 10020
Tel: (708)615-3360
Fax: (708)614-3363

Pages: 290
Exhibits: Photographs

Through this readable biography of the former first lady, readers get a firsthand glimpse of Philippine high society yesterday and, for the most part, today.

Title: *In Our Image: America's Empire in the Philippines*
Date: 1989
Format: Paperback
Author: Stanley Karnow
Publisher: Foreign Policy Association/ Random House
201 E. 50th St.
New York, NY 10022
Tel: (212)751-2600
Fax: (212)872-8026
Pages: 71
Exhibits: Charts, maps, and photographs

This readable book is the best available exploration of Philippine history and the U.S.-Philippine relationship. It provides a useful background for those who plan to move to the islands.

Title: *The Philippines: Fire on the Rim*
Date: 1989
Format: Hardcover
Author: Joseph Collins
Publisher: The Institute for Food and Development Policy
145 Ninth St.
San Francisco, CA 94103
Tel: (415)864-8555
Fax: (415)864-3909
Pages: 316
Exhibits: Photographs

This book contains 50 profiles of Filipinos, who, to quote the author, "describe the social turmoil that makes their country one of the most explosive in the world." The profiles are set up in question-and-answer form; the life stories are poignant and of interest to political analysts and businesspeople who wish to understand the common Filipino.

LAWS AND REGULATIONS

Title: *Philippine Law Journal*
Date: Quarterly
Format: Periodical
Editor: Angelica Pai F. Pena
Publisher: College of Law
University of the Philippines
Gonzales Hall
Dilman Library
Quezon City, Philippines 3004
Tel: (63)(2)992-558
Fax: (63)(2)992-863
Pages: Varies
Exhibits: None
Price: $25/year

Each issue of this attractive, small-format legal journal includes 3 to 5 long articles on topics related to the Philippine legal environment. It is useful to international lawyers and to those who are interested in the philosophical and historical roots of Philippine law; it is not, however, useful to the businessperson who needs practical legal information.

Title: *Philippine Laws*
Date: 1989
Format: Paperback
Author: M.H. Casenas
Publisher: J.M. Robles
P.O. Box 838 MCPO Pasay Rd.
Makati
Metro Manila, Philippines 1550
Pages: 222
Exhibits: None

This one-of-a-kind book "attempts to elicit and simplify for its readers the rather complex interplay of the various existing laws, rules and regulations" that affect foreign nationals in the Philippines. The types of laws explained in this essential expatriate companion include those applicable to immigration, deportation, naturalization, arrest, bail, search warrants, rights and guarantees, marriage and property, leases, and investment.

Title: *Philippine Legal Encyclopedia*
Date: 1986
Format: Hardcover
Author: Jose Agaton R. Sibal
Publisher: Central Lawbook Publishing Co.
927 Quezon Ave.
Quezon City, Philippines 3410
Tel: (63)(2)993-897
Pages: 1,187
Exhibits: None

This legal encyclopedia provides a comprehensive list of definitions of terms, topics, words, and phrases to assist both lawyers and laypeople in making sense of pleadings, contracts, and other legal documents in the Philippines. From *abaca* (Manila hemp) to zoning laws, this tome is a helpful reference book for those who make legally binding commitments in the country.

MARKET DATA AND ANALYSIS

Title: *Philippine Statistical Yearbook*
Date: Annual
Format: Paperback
Publisher: National Statistical Coordination Board
The Secretary General
7th Floor, Marvin Plaza Building
2153 Chino Roces Ave.
Makati
Metro Manila, Philippines 1550
Tel: (63)(2)851-778
Fax:(63)(2)816-6941
Pages: 600
Exhibits: Maps, graphs, and tables

Issued by the Philippine government each year, this is the most complete and current source of raw economic data on the country's population, housing, economy, resources, industry, and social services. The well-organized tables of data are clearly rendered and often accompanied by graphs.

POLITICS AND GOVERNMENT

Title: *The Philippine Revolution: The Leader's View*
Date: 1989

Format: Hardcover

Author: Jose Maria Sison

Publisher: Taylor and Francis New York, Inc.
79 Madison Ave.
New York, NY 10016
Tel: (212)785-5800
Fax: (212)785-5515

Pages: 241

Exhibits: Maps and photographs

This book comprises questions posed to and answered by Jose Maria Sison, a key revolutionary figure in the fight to oust Ferdinand Marcos. It provides an inside account of the resistance movement from the point of view of a partisan participant and is useful to the political analyst looking at the future of the Philippines. The book includes a glossary.

VIETNAM

Vietnam at a Glance

Population:	69.1 million
Religion:	Buddhism, Taoism, Confucian
Government:	One-party socialist rule
Language:	Vietnamese
Currency:	New dong
Trade (1993):	\$2.46 (million \$US) total exports; \$2.38 (million \$US) total imports

Vietnam, with its hard-working population of nearly 70 million, has emerged as the hottest new business frontier on the Asian Pacific Rim. Hundreds of foreign business executives and entrepreneurs have taken notice of the country's current economic boom and imminent entry into the club of economic dragons thriving in the Asia-Pacific. At the government-sponsored Asia-Pacific Outlook Conference at the University of Southern California in March 1993, the Vietnam seminar was rated number one in importance by the 400 U.S. business executives who participated. Even before the U.S. embargo on Vietnam was lifted, numerous Fortune-500 companies were conducting discussions in Vietnam for the future or were signing deals through their foreign subsidiaries.

All of the excitement is understandable when one considers the facts surrounding the "new" Vietnam. The country's reform program has prompted an explosion of private business activity and record rates of economic growth. As the latest "dragon" of Asia, Vietnam is an opportunity that marketers and investors should quickly act on. With annual growth exceeding 30 percent, almost zero inflation, and a stabilized currency, Vietnam offers a huge market to producers through government spending and an expanding consumer class. At the same time, Vietnam's labor rates, the lowest in Asia, present attractive opportunities for investors. Now that the Clinton administration has lifted the U.S. ban on business with Vietnam, a host of American companies—including PepsiCo, Coca-Cola, and American Express—are leading the way toward U.S. reengagement with its former enemy.

Vietnam's growth has encouraged a stampede of foreign investment. In December 1992, there were 556 foreign projects in operation in Vietnam, representing a total value of $4.63 billion in contracts. Since the relaxation of the U.S. trade restrictions at that time, many U.S. firms have applied to open offices in Vietnam, and hundreds more have begun negotiations with their Vietnamese counterparts. Ho Chi Minh City (formerly Saigon) has exploded with new hotels, offices, and investment zones. More than 500,000 businesspeople now travel to Vietnam every year. The future for Vietnam looks bright, indeed.

COMPANY DIRECTORIES

Title: *Vietnam Business Directory*
Date: 1990
Format: Paperback
Publisher: Chamber of Commerce and Industry in Vietnam
33 Ba Trieu St.
Hanoi 8, Vietnam
Tel: (84)(4)52961 or 53023
Fax: (84)(4)56446
Pages: 368
Exhibits: None

One of the few directories of Vietnamese enterprises and government organizations, this small-format bilingual volume lists several hundred entities and their business activities. The publishing quality is poor.

Title: *Vietnam Opportunities*
Date: 1992
Format: Hardcover
Author: Youth Advertising House, Vietnam
Editor: Dinh Ba Thanh
Publisher: Longman Group (Far East), Ltd.
18th Floor, Cornwall House
Tong Chong St.
Hong Kong
Tel: (914)993-5000 (U.S.)
Fax: (914)997-8115) (U.S.)
Pages: 403
Exhibits: Maps and photographs

This attractive directory provides prospective investors with 4,000 government-approved contacts in each of Vietnam's 43 provinces. Each entry lists the company name, address, telephone and telex numbers, CEO, and the nature and scope of the business, for example, mechanical manufacturing. The book also includes business information on travel, investment law, taxation, import controls, work permits, and the Vietnamese market. It is recommended.

COUNTRY PROFILES

Title: *Vietnam: A Country Study*
Date: 1989
Format: Hardcover
Author: Federal Research Division, Library of Congress
Publisher: Library of Congress/ Department of the Army

101 Independence Ave., SE
Washington, DC 20540
Tel: (202)707-5079
Fax: (202)707-3585

Pages: 386

Exhibits: Charts, maps, graphs, photographs, and tables

Covering Vietnam's history, society, geography, economy, government, politics, and national security, this country overview (like the other books in the series) is the best single introduction to the country. Each chapter is compiled by a different author, the table of contents includes subheadings for easy reference, and the book includes photographs, government organization charts, a glossary, a bibliography, and an index. It is current as of 1989.

Title: *Vietnam: Politics, Economics and Society*

Date: 1988

Format: Hardcover

Author: Melanie Beresford

Publisher: Printer Publishers, Ltd.
25 Floral St.
London WC2E 9DS, United Kingdom

Pages: 242

Exhibits: None

This book is part of the anachronistically titled Marxist Regimes Series, published and sponsored by the University College in Cardiff, England. Though quickly becoming dated, this volume covers Vietnam's history, social system, political system, economy, and international relations. Businesspeople will find this book to be a useful source of background. The writing is crisp, fact-packed, and formal.

DICTIONARIES AND LANGUAGE STUDIES

Title: *Vietnamese-English Dictionary*

Date: 1986

Format: Hardcover

Author: Le-Ba-Khanh and Le-Ba-Kong

Publisher: P. Shalom Publishers, Inc.
5409 18th Ave.
Brooklyn, NY 11204
Tel: (718)256-1954

Pages: 388

Exhibits: None

Compact and recently published, this Vietnamese-to-English dictionary is meant for Vietnamese speakers who want to find English words and their pronunciation. New dictionaries for Westerners who want to learn Vietnamese will be published in the near future.

ECONOMY

Title: *National Unification and Economic Development in Vietnam*

Date: 1989

Format: Hardcover

Author: Melanie Beresford

Publisher: Macmillan Press, Ltd.
4 Little Essex St.
London WC2R 3LF, United Kingdom
Tel: (44)(256)29242
Fax: (44)(256)479-476

Pages: 296

Exhibits: Graphs and tables

This research monograph, written by an academic, focuses on the subject of economic unification in Vietnam since 1975, linking the process of reunification to Vietnam's overall course of economic development. Selected chapters deal with the colonial period, the period of 1955 to 1975, agriculture, industrialization, and socialist-oriented production. This is an erudite study for economists and business researchers seeking to understand the historical background behind the economic transformation in Vietnam today.

Title: *Reinventing Vietnamese Socialism:* Doi Moi *in Comparative Perspective*
Date: 1993
Format: Paperback
Editor: William S. Turkey and Mark Seldon
Publisher: Westview Press, Inc.
550 Central Ave.
Boulder, CO 80301-2877
Tel: (303)444-3541
Fax: (303)449-3356
Pages: 368
Exhibits: Tables

For businesspeople who want an in-depth background in Vietnam's economic evolution and the current transition to market socialism, this is a good source. The five parts of this thick anthology of long articles cover the origins of economic reform in Vietnam, the economy, agriculture, politics, and society. The articles are academic in style and analysis.

Title: *Vietnam's Economic Policy Since 1975*
Date: 1990
Format: Hardcover
Author: Vo Nhan Tri
Publisher: Institute of Southeast Asian Studies
Heng Mui Keng Terrace
Pasir Panjang
Singapore, 0511
Tel: (65)778-0955
Fax: (65)775-6259
Pages: 253
Exhibits: None

This readable monograph, written by an academic, explains Vietnam's economic evolution since the end of the Vietnam War in five chronologically oriented chapters. This is a useful historical analysis for economists and business researchers who want to understand the backdrop of the country's current development agenda.

GENERAL BUSINESS

Title: *Guide to Doing Business in Vietnam*
Date: 1991
Format: Hardcover
Author: Chu Van Hop
Publisher: CCH International
Talavera and Khartoum Rds.
North Ryde NSW 2113, Australia
Tel: (61)(2)888-2555
Fax: (61)(2)888-7324
Pages: 176
Exhibits: None

This volume is a compilation of regulations rather than a readable guidebook. It covers foreign investment policy, land law, exchange control, accounting issues, import controls, taxation, and other topics that are important to businesspeople. It contains transcriptions of foreign investment laws and decrees.

Title: *Vietnam Foreign Trade*
Date: Irregular
Format: Periodical
Editor: Nguyen Tam
Publisher: Chamber of Commerce and Industry of Vietnam
33 Ba Trieu St.
Hanoi 8, Vietnam
Tel: (84)(4)52961, 53023
Fax: (84)(4)56446
Pages: Varies
Exhibits: Tables
Price: Contact for subscription prices

Published by the Chamber of Commerce and Industry of Vietnam, this 30-page inexpensively published magazine presents articles highlighting Vietnamese industrial and agricultural successes, including the profits of commercial companies, deals with foreigners, and chamber news. Published in Hanoi, this is a fairly readable source of government-approved statistics and commercial information.

POLITICS AND GOVERNMENT

Title: *Vietnam Commentary*
Date: Bimonthly
Format: Periodical
Publisher: Information and Resource Center Pte., Ltd.
6 Nassim Rd.
Singapore, 1025
Tel: (65)734-9600
Fax: (65)733-6217
Pages: Varies
Exhibits: None
Price: Contact for subscription prices

This 15- to 20-page nicely published newsletter offers an analysis of important political, military, economic, and other developments in Vietnam. Meant for business decision makers, area specialists, and political risk analysts, the articles, written by experts, offer in-depth appraisals of Vietnam's infrastructure, industry, and political climate. For serious researchers, especially those looking for predictions about where Vietnam is heading, this is a useful source.

Title: *Vietnam Insight*
Date: Monthly
Format: Periodical
Editor: Tran Dieu Chan
Publisher: National United Front for the Liberation of Vietnam General Directorate of Overseas Affairs
P.O. Box 7826
San Jose, CA 95150
Tel: (408)226-2261
Pages: Varies
Exhibits: None
Price: Contact for subscription prices

This 10-page newsletter is sponsored by the National United Front for the Liberation of Vietnam. As such, it provides editorial articles on political and human rights developments, with an emphasis on the prisoner of war issue. It is highly critical of Vietnamese military leaders and opposed to U.S.-Vietnam commercial ties. Political risk analysts might find this publication useful.

Title: *Vietnam News*
Date: Weekly
Format: Periodical
Publisher: Vietnam News Agency
79 Ly Thuong Kiet
Hanoi 5, Vietnam
Tel: (84)(4)254-693
Fax: (84)(4)259-617
Pages: Varies
Exhibits: Drawings and photographs
Price: Contact for subscription prices

Published by the Vietnam News Agency, this 10- to 15-page newspaper is a recommended source of general news, business headlines, production statistics, and economic indicators. Note, however, that its editorial focus is government-influenced. The business news concentrates on the oil industry and technology. This recommended reader is well illustrated with photography and graphics.

Title: *Vietnam Studies Bulletin*
Date: Irregular
Format: Periodical
Editor: David Hunt
Publisher: History Department and William Joiner Center
University of Massachusetts
100 Morrissey Blvd.
Boston, MA 02125
Tel: (413)545-2217
Fax: (413)545-1226
Pages: Varies
Exhibits: None
Price: Contact for subscription prices

This low-budget 10-page newsletter provides information about Vietnam-related course offerings at universities, upcoming conferences, recent publications, and academic work in progress. This is a fine source for businesspeople who seek specialists and talented researchers to assist with commercial projects in Vietnam.

TRAVEL ADVICE

Title: *Guide to Vietnam*
Date: 1989
Format: Paperback
Author: John R. Jones
Publisher: Hunter Publishing, Inc.
300 Raritan Center Pkwy., CN 94
Edison, NJ 08810
Tel: (908)225-1900
Fax: (908)417-0482
Pages: 196
Exhibits: Diagrams, maps, and photographs

Those who are going to Vietnam will find this traveler's guide useful for its description of the country and of cultural sites in all regions. The publication quality is low, however, and other business travel guides should appear soon.

MYANMAR (BURMA)

OVERVIEW

The country of Myanmar (formerly Burma), located on the Bay of Bengal and sharing borders with China, Thailand, Laos, Bangladesh, and India, has a population of more than 42 million. In elections in 1990, the people voted to end military rule by giving 82 percent of the National Assembly seats to the National League of Democracy (NLD), the country's main opposition party. The military remains unwilling to hand over power, however. It has also ignored election results calling for the release of NLD leaders, including Aung San Sun Kyi, the daughter of the country's independence leader, Aung San.

Myanmar at a Glance

Population:	42.4 million
Religion:	Buddhist, Animist, Christian
Government:	Military dictatorship
Language:	Burmese, ethnic dialects
Currency:	Kyat (Kt = 100 pyas)
Trade (1992):	$607 million total exports; $1 billion total imports

The international community has acted to curtail aid to Myanmar and trade. Naturally the government went broke as exports plunged 42 percent in 1989. It resorted to selling off the country's assets, including a part of its Tokyo embassy building to real estate developers, timber concessions, fishing rights, oil and exploration rights, and mineral rights. Foreign companies have been permitted for the first time to set up distribution for outlets and joint ventures with state enterprises.

Myanmar's primary exports are teak, rice, minerals, and gems. Its imports include capital, intermediate goods, and consumer items, mainly from Japan, China, and Singapore.

COUNTRY PROFILES

Title: *Totalitarianism in Burma: Prospects for Economic Development*

Date: 1992

Format: Hardcover

Author: Mya Maung

Publisher: Paragon House
90 Fifth Ave.
New York, NY 10011
Tel: (212)620-2820
Fax: (212)633-0518

Pages: 277

Exhibits: Graphs and tables

This book focuses "on the damaging impact of military dictatorship on the social propensity of Burma to develop into a modern industrial state." Its core prediction for Burmese economic development is bleak in light of the "enormous damage the military dictatorship has inflicted upon the country's human capital for nearly three decades." Chapters cover the Burmese totalitarian state, student revolts of 1988, the plight of dissidents, human rights violations, and the military command economy. This book pulls no punches and will interest anyone who is thinking about becoming involved with Myanmar.

POLITICS AND GOVERNMENT

Title: *The Future of Burma: Crisis and Choice in Myanmar*

Date: 1990

Format: Hardcover

Author: David I. Steinberg

Publisher: University Press of America, Inc.
4720 Boston Way
Lanham, MD 20706
Tel: (301)459-3366
Fax: (301)459-2118

Pages: 100

Exhibits: Maps

This slim volume offers the intrepid Myanmar-bound businessperson a fine introduction to the country's political atmosphere, which remains turbulent. The five sections of the monograph focus on the 1988 coup and its aftermath, with a thorough explaination of the economic factors underlying the country's instability. The writing style is formal but not stiff or theoretical.

TRAVEL ADVICE

Title: *Burma*

Date: 1989

Format: Hardcover

Author: Wilhelm Klein

Editor: John Gottberg Anderson

Publisher: ADA Publications (HK), Ltd.
Graphic Arts Center Publishing
3019 N.W. Yeon
P.O. Box 10306
Portland, OR 97210
Tel: (503)226-2402
Fax: (503)226-1410

Pages: 332

Exhibits: Maps and photographs

This traveler's guide is part of the exquisitely illustrated Insight Guides Series. The book is too heavy to take along to Myanmar, but as a source of background information, it's a great reader. One section covers tourist information and customs and provides important addresses.

CAMBODIA (KAMPUCHEA)

OVERVIEW

Cambodia, also known as Kampuchea, is an extremely poor country with virtually no industrial base at all other than some timber and mining activity. The country's economy remains almost entirely agricultural. Rubber, rice, and pepper are the most important exports.

Cambodia at a Glance

Population:	8.3 million
Religion:	Theravada Buddhist, Muslim, Animist, Atheist
Government:	Constitutional monarchy
Language:	Khmer and French
Currency:	Riel (R = 100 Sen)
Trade (1991):	$25 million total exports; $178 million total imports

Beset by government corruption and food shortages that, without international aid, would likely result in famine, Cambodia has yet to fully recover from decades of war and genocide under the Khmer Rouge. In 1990, the United Nations took control of the functioning of the government; in 1993, elections were held and a assembly was formed to draft a new constitution and a human rights charter. It is hoped that a return to free democracy will increase the country's chances of joining its neighbors in economic development.

COUNTRY PROFILES

Title: *Cambodia: A Country Study*
Date: 1990
Format: Hardcover
Author: Federal Research Division, Library of Congress
Publisher: Library of Congress/ Department of the Army
101 Independence Ave., SE
Washington, DC 20540
Tel: (202)707-5097
Fax: (202)707-3585
Pages: 362
Exhibits: Charts, maps, graphs, photographs, and tables

Covering Cambodia's history, society, geography, government, politics, and national security, this country overview (like the other books in the series) is the best single introduction to the country. Each chapter is compiled by a different author, the table of contents includes subheadings for easy reference, and the book includes photographs, government organization charts, a glossary, a bibliography, and an index. It is current only as of the late 1980s, but the bulk of its content remains timely.

Title: *Cambodia: Post-Settlement Reconstruction and Development*
Date: 1989
Format: Hardcover
Author: Robert J. Muscat
Publisher: East Asian Institute
Columbia University
562 W. 113 St.
New York, NY 10025
Tel: (212)316-7100
Fax: (212)316-7169
Pages: 143
Exhibits: Tables

Researchers and businesspeople seeking an analysis of Cambodia's industrial and agricultural performance and its reconstruction and development since the destruction of the 1970s will find this monograph to be a clearly written overview.

LAOS

OVERVIEW

The official name of Laos is the Lao People's Democratic Republic. It occupies a strip of mountainous jungle between Vietnam and Cambodia. The Communist government has been trying to ratify the constitution since 1976. Eighty-five percent of the country's population of 3.9 million works in agriculture, though private enterprise is being encouraged under a market-oriented economic reform program called *jin tana khan mai* or "new thinking." Laos is heavily dependent on foreign aid, and it exports only electricity, wood products, coffee, and tin in large quantities.

Laos at a Glance

Population:	4.24 million
Religion:	Buddhist
Government:	Communist
Language:	Lao, Vietnamese, French
Currency:	Kip (K = 100 at)
Trade (1991):	$97 million total exports; $228 million total imports

Beset by low educational levels and a lack of skills, the country's nonagricultural work force is concentrated in the small-scale manufacturing of beer, cigarettes, detergents, bricks, plywood, matches, salt, animal feed, and so on. Laos has been successful in attracting foreign investment, though rising inflation, bureaucratic delays, uncertain tax policies, and the legal climate are pitfalls. More than 75 projects were initiated by 1989, with 300 proposals received in that year. Most foreign-invested projects are in timber and other resource exploitation. More than half of these small-scale projects involve Thai partners.

COUNTRY PROFILES

Title: *Laos: A Country Study*
Date: 1986
Format: Hardcover
Author: Foreign Area Studies Center, The American University
Publisher: The American University/ Department of the Army
4400 Massachusetts Ave., NW
McDowell 117
Washington, DC 20016
Tel: (202)885-3409
Fax: (202)885-3453
Pages: 337
Exhibits: Maps, graphs, and tables

Covering Laos's history, society, geography, government, politics, and national security, this country overview (like the other books in the series) is a one-stop introduction to the country. Each chapter is compiled by a different author, the table of contents includes subheadings for easy reference, and the book includes government organization charts, a glossary, a bibliography, and an index. It is current only as of 1971, but as a historical and cultural overview, it remains timely.

Title: *Laos: Beyond the Revolution*
Date: 1991
Format: Hardcover
Editor: Joseph J. Zasloff and Leonard Unger
Publisher: St. Martin's Press
Scholarly and Reference Division
175 Fifth Ave.
New York, NY 10010
Tel: (212)674-5151
Fax: (212)420-9314
Pages: 348
Exhibits: Maps and tables

Here is a compilation of articles on a country that receives little attention. The book's five sections cover politics, economics, society, external relations, and U.S. policy toward Laos. The contributors include academics, consultants, and journalists. Businesspeople seeking background information about this emerging player in Asia will find this volume useful. The prose is not overly theoretical and is extensively footnoted.

DICTIONARIES AND LANGUAGE STUDIES

Title: *English-Lao/Lao-English Dictionary*
Date: 1983
Format: Paperback
Author: Russell Marcus
Publisher: Charles E. Tuttle Co.
2-6, Suido 1-chome
Bunkyo-ku
Tokyo 112, Japan
Tel: (81)(2)811-7106-9
Pages: 416
Exhibits: None

This two-way dictionary of Lao was first published in 1966. Since then the dictionary has been the basic communication tool between Lao- and English-speaking people. Included in the hand-size book is a tone code table and rules on Lao alphabetical order and spelling.

Papua New Guinea

OVERVIEW

Papua New Guinea is the largest and certainly the most resource-endowed of all of the Pacific island countries. The country is made up of more than 600 islands which together form a land mass the size of Oregon and Idaho combined. Papua New Guinea's population of 3.70 million is made up of Melanesians, Australians, Chinese, and other ethnic groups, some of whom are only recently emerging into the industrial age. More than 700 languages are spoken on this densely forested island of several thousand villages. Traditional Papua New Guinea social organization was based on a subsistence economy, recognition of kinship bonds and obligations that extend beyond the family group, egalitarian relationships, and a attachment to the land.

Papua New Guinea at a Glance

Population:	3.70 million
Religion:	Christian, Animist
Government:	Parliamentary Democracy
Language:	Melanesian Pidgin, English, Motu
Currency:	Kina (K = 100 toea)
Trade (1992):	$1.8 billion total exports; $1.3 billion total imports

The island's democracy is genuine and rooted in widely diffused Christian values and Melanesian traditions of village-level leadership based on merit and charisma. Unfortunately, economic growth has not produced the jobs needed to employ the 50,000 people who enter the job market every year. Rebellion has broken out on the country's copper-rich island of Bougainville, sapping export income and tossing the country into recession and negative economic growth in 1991.

Foreign investment in the country is limited mainly to resource exploitation, and the country purchases only $100 million worth of U.S. goods per year, including manufactured goods, machinery, equipment, oil, and food.

GENERAL BUSINESS

Title: *Doing Business in Papua New Guinea*
Date: 1988
Format: Hardcover
Publisher: Ernst and Whinney International
787 Seventh Ave.
New York, NY 10019
Tel: (212)830-6000
Pages: 61
Exhibits: Graphs and tables

Concise and relatively up-to-date, this taxation guide contains chapters covering the country's history and government, foreign investment incentives, taxation, auditing practices, and useful business contacts. Subsections are numbered for easy use.

Title: *Doing Business in Papua New Guinea*
Date: 1984
Format: Hardcover
Publisher: Price Waterhouse
1251 Avenue of the Americas
New York, NY 10020
Tel: (212)489-8900
Pages: 125
Exhibits: Tables

This is a brief guide covering taxation policies and regulations in Papua New Guinea. The booklet provides an overview for executives, accountants, and prospective investors. Selected chapters cover the business environment, investment incentives, the regulatory environment, banking and finance, and the tax system.

Appendix 1

Asia-Pacific Information Networks

Network (World Trade Center of San Francisco)
110 Sutter St., Suite 408
San Francisco, CA 94104
Tel: (415)392-2705

OLIADS

Intellibanc Corp.
2214 Torrance Blvd.
Torrance, CA 90501
Tel: (213)618-6900

Pacific Connections

Pacific Rim Commercial Exchange Program (PRCEP)
Management Development Institute
School of Business Administration
California State University
6000 J St.
Sacramento, CA 95819
Tel: (916)278-7141
(916)278-6346

Pacific Information Exchange

Asia Pacific Foundation of Canada
666-999 Canada Place
Vancouver, B.C.
V6C 3E1, Canada
Tel: (604)684-5986

Pacific Rim Data Bank International Program

Pacific Rim Relations
University of Utah
252 Orson Spencer Hall
Salt Lake City, UT 84112
Tel: (801)581-6267

Resources and Information Program

Research Institute for Asia and the Pacific
University of Sydney
Sydney 2006 NSW, Australia
Tel: (61)(2)692-2805

Appendix 2

Libraries Specializing in the Asia-Pacific

Hamilton Library
East Asia Collection
2550 The Mall
Honolulu, HI 96822
Tel: (808)948-8042

Harvard University
Harvard-Yenching Library
2 Divinity Ave.
Cambridge, MA 02138
Tel: (617)495-3395

Indiana University
East Asian Collection
Indiana University Library
410 E. 17th St., Room E860
Bloomington, IN 47405
Tel: (812)335-9695

Japanese Technical Information Service (JTIS)
University Microfilms International
300 N. Zeeb Rd.
Ann Arbor, MI 48106
Tel: (800)325-0295

Library of Congress
Science and Technology Division
101 Independence Ave., SE
Washington, DC 20540
Tel: (202)707-5639

Massachusetts Institute of Technology
77 Massachusetts Ave., Room 14S-216
Cambridge, MA 02139
Tel: (617)253-5651

The National Trade Data Bank (NTDB)
U.S. Department of Commerce
Main Commerce Building
14th and Constitution Ave., NW
Washington, DC 20230
Tel: (202)482-1405

National Translation Center
John Crear Library of the University of Chicago
5730 S. Ellis Ave.
Chicago, IL 60637-1403
Tel: (312)702-7060

Princeton University
Gest Oriental Library and East Asian Collections
317 Palmer Hall
41 Williams St.
Princeton, NJ 08544
Tel: (609)452-4729

U.S. Agency for International Development (AID) Library
Department of State
2201 C St., NW, Room SA-18
Washington, DC 20523
Tel: (703)235-1000

U.S. Army Corps of Engineers Library
Department of Defense
72 Lyme Rd.
Hanover, NH 03755-1290
Tel: (603)646-4221

U.S. Geological Survey (USGS)
Department of Interior
904 National Center
Reston, VA 22092
Tel: (703)648-6078

U.S. National Technical Information Service (NTIS)
5285 Port Royal Rd.
Springfield, VA 22161
Tel: (703)487-4929

U.S. Patent and Trademark Office
Scientific Library, Room 2C01
Crystal Plaza 3-4
Washington, DC 20231
Tel: (703)557-2957

University of Arizona
Oriental Studies Collection
University Library
1140 N. Colombo Ave.
Sierra Vista, AZ 85635
Tel: (602)621-6380

University of California, Berkeley
East Asiatic Library
208 Durant Hall
2223 Fulton St.
Berkeley, CA 97420
Tel: (510)642-2556

University of Chicago
Far Eastern Library
1100 E. 57th St.
Chicago, IL 60637
Tel: (312)702-8434

University of Chicago
John Crear Library
5730 S. Ellis Ave.
Chicago, IL 60637
Tel: (312)702-7715

University of Hawaii
Thomas Hale Hamilton Library
2550 The Mall
Honolulu, HI 96822
Tel: (808)948-8263

University of Maryland
East Asia Collection
McKeldin Library
College Park Campus
College Park, MD 20742
Tel: (301)454-5459

University of Michigan
Asia Library
Ann Arbor, MI 48109-1205
Tel: (313)764-0406

University of Pittsburgh
East Asian Library
201 Hillman Library
501 Bigelow Blvd.
Pittsburgh, PA 15260
Tel: (412)648-7573

University of Washington
Asian Library
322 Gowen Hall, DO-27
Seattle, WA 98195
Tel: (206)543-4490

Yale University
East Asian Collection
Sterling Memorial Library
120 High St.
New Haven, CT 06520
Tel: (203)432-1790

APPENDIX 3

JAPAN-U.S. BUSINESS ORGANIZATIONS

Alaska Kai
Shinkokusai Building, Room 405
4-1, Marunouchi 3-chome
Chiyoda-ku
Tokyo 100, Japan
Tel: (81)(3)211-0974

Japan-Hawaii Economic Council
Marunouchi Building, Room 834
4-1, Marunouchi 2-chome
Chiyoda-ku
Tokyo 100, Japan
Tel: (81)(3)214-6978

Japan-Midwest (U.S.) Association
c/o Keizai Doyukai
4-6, Marunouchi 1-chome
Chiyoda-ku
Tokyo 100, Japan
Tel: (81)(3)211-1271

Japan-Southern U.S. Association
c/o Japan-U.S. Economic Council
Otemachi Building, Room 772
6-1, Otemachi 1-chome
Chiyoda-ku
Tokyo 100, Japan
Tel: (81)(3)216-5823

Japan-U.S. Economic Council
Otemachi Building, Room 772
6-1, Otemachi 1-chome
Chiyoda-ku
Tokyo 100, Japan
Tel: (81)(3)216-5823

Japan-U.S. Southeast Association
c/o Keizai Doyukai
4-6, Marunouchi 1-chome
Chiyoda-ku
Tokyo 100, Japan
Tel: (81)(3)211-1271

JCA Japan-Western U.S. Association
c/o Japan-U.S. Economic Council
Otemachi Building, Room 772
6-1, Otemachi 1-chome
Chiyoda-ku
Tokyo 100, Japan
Tel: (81)(3)216-5823

Washington Kai
c/o State of Washington Tokyo Office
Kowa No. 2 Building, West, Room 205
11-39, Akasaka 1-chome
Minato-ku
Tokyo 107, Japan

APPENDIX 4

ASIA-PACIFIC RESEARCH ORGANIZATIONS AND UNIVERSITY PROGRAMS

The following is adapted from a list appearing in *The Pacific Rim Almanac* by Alexander Besher (New York: Harper Collins, 1991), pp. 747–753.

American Graduate School of International Management
Thunderbird Campus
Glendale, AZ 85306
Tel: (602)987-7244

Asian Management Center
685 Commonwealth Ave., Room 129
Boston, MA 02215
Tel: (617)353-2670

Asian Studies Center
214 Massachusetts Ave., NE
Washington, DC 20002
Tel: (202)546-4400

Aspen Institute for Humanistic Studies
Wye Plantation
P.O. Box 222
Queenstown, MD 21658
Tel: (301)827-7168

Berkeley Roundtable on the International Economy (BRIE)
2234 Piedmont Ave.
University of California
Berkeley, CA 94720
Tel: (415)642-3067

Boston University
Economics Department
212 Bay State Rd.
Boston, MA 02215
Tel: (617)353-4454

Brandeis University
Sachar Building
415 South St.
Waltham, MA 02254
Tel: (617)736-2000

Center for Korean Studies
University of California at Berkeley
2223 Fulton St., Room 512
Berkeley, CA 94720
Tel: (510)642-5674

Center for Pacific Rim Studies
University of California at Los Angeles
1250 Bunche Hall
405 Hilguard Ave.
Los Angeles, CA 90024
Tel: (213)206-0223

Center for the Pacific Rim and the Institute for Chinese-Western Cultural History
University of San Francisco
Lone Mountain, Room 282
513 Parnassus Ave.
San Francisco, CA 94117-1080
Tel: (415)666-6357
Fax: (415)666-2291

Columbia University
Department of East Asian Languages and Cultures
407 Kent Hall
Haven Ave.
New York, NY 10027
Tel: (212)280-2574

Cornell University
Department of Asian Studies
Rockefeller Hall
Ithaca, NY 14853
Tel: (607)255-4144

Council on East Asian Studies
Yale University
New Haven, CT 06520
Tel: (203)624-3426
Director: Conrad Totman

David M. Kennedy Center for International Studies
Brigham Young University
237 HRCB
University Hill
Provo, UT 84602
Tel: (801)378-3378
Publications Office
Tel: (801)378-6528

Dominican College
Pacific Basic Studies Program
1520 Grand Ave.
San Rafael, CA 94901
Tel: (415)457-4440, ext. 330
Director: Fran LePage

East Asian Institute
Columbia University
420 W. 118th St.
New York, NY 10027
Tel: (212)280-2591

East Asian Studies Program
Massachusetts Institute of Technology
77 Massachusetts Ave., Room 4209
Cambridge, MA 02139
Tel: (617)253-1354

East Asia Resource Center
University of Washington
Seattle, WA 98195
Tel: (206)543-1921

East-West Center (EWC)
1777 East-West Rd.
Honolulu, HI 96848
Tel: (808)944-7111

Georgetown University
School for Foreign Service
3701 O St., NW
Asian Studies Program
Intercultural Center, Room 506A
Washington, DC 20057
Tel: (202)625-4216

George Washington University
2025 F St., NW
Washington, DC 20052
Tel: (202)994-1000

George Washington University
Political Science Department
2221 I St., NW
Washington, DC 20052
Tel: (202)994-6290

Graduate School of International Relations and Pacific Studies
University of California at San Diego
100 Gilman Dr.
La Jolla, CA 92093
Tel: (619)534-6074

Harvard Business School
1301 Massachusetts Ave.
Cambridge, MA 02138
Tel: (617)495-6000

Harvard Institute for International Development
1737 Cambridge St.
Cambridge, MA 02138
Tel: (617)495-2161

Harvard University
1301 Massachusetts Ave.
Cambridge, MA 02138
Tel: (617)495-1000

Henry M. Jackson School of International Studies
University of Washington
411 Thompson Hall
Seattle, WA 98195
Tel: (206)543-4370

Illinois Institute of Technology
3300 S. Federal St.
Chicago, IL 60616
Tel: (312)567-5122

Indiana University
410 E. 17th St.
Bloomington, IN 47405
Tel: (812)332-0211

Indiana University
Department of East Asian Languages
Goodbody Hall
Bloomington, IN 47405
Tel: (812)335-1992

Indiana University
Department of Economics
901 Ballantine Hall
410 E. 17th St.
Bloomington, IN 47405
Tel: (812)335-1021

Institute for International Economics (IIE)
11 Dupont Circle, NW
Washington, DC 20036
Tel: (202)328-0583

Institute of East Asian Studies (IEAS)
University of California at Berkeley
Sixth Floor, 2223 Fulton St.
Berkeley, CA 94720
Tel: (510)642-2809

Institute of International Studies
Bradley University
200 W. Madison Ave.
Bradley Hall 303
Peoria, IL 61625
Tel: (309)676-7611

International Business and Economics Program
1800 K St., NW
Washington, DC 20006
Tel: (202)775-3227

International Business Education and Research Program (IBEAR)
Graduate School of Business Administration
3502 S. Hoover
University of Southern California
Los Angeles, CA 90089-1421
Tel: (213)743-2272

International Education and Programs
Western Michigan University
2090 Friedman Hall
Kalamazoo, MI 49008
Tel: (616)383-0483

Investor Responsibility Research Center (IRRC)
1755 Massachusetts Ave., NW, Suite 600
Washington, DC 20004
Tel: (202)939-6500

John K. Fairbank Council on East Asian Studies
1737 Cambridge St.
Cambridge, MA 02138
Tel: (617)495-4657

Korea Institute
1737 Cambridge St.
Cambridge, MA 02138
Tel: (617)495-9602

Massachusetts Institute of Technology
Political Science Department
30 Wadsworth St.
Cambridge, MA 02139
Professor: Lucian Pye
Tel: (617)253-5262

National Center for Export-Import Studies (NCEIS)
1242 35th St., NW, Suite 501
Washington, DC 20057
Tel: (202)625-4797

Olin Research Library
Wason Collection
Cornell University
Ithaca, NY 14853
Tel: (607)255-4144

Population Reference Bureau (PRB)
P.O. Box 96152
Washington, DC 20090
Tel: (202)639-8040

Princeton University
Asian Studies Department
211 Jones Hall
41 Williams St.
Princeton, NJ 08544
Tel: (609)452-4729

Starr East Asian Library
Columbia University
300 Kent Hall
100 Haven Ave.
New York, NY 10027
Tel: (212)280-4318
Director: Marsha Wagner

Trinity University
History Department
715 Stadium Dr.
San Antonio, TX 78284
Tel: (512)736-7621

University of Chicago
Department of History
1126 E. 59th St.
Chicago, IL 60637
Tel: (312)702-8398

University of Cincinnati
Political Science Department
Crosley Tower, Room 1013
220 Victory Pkwy.
Cincinnati, OH 45221
Tel: (513)475-3211

University of Detroit
Finance Department
4001 W. McNichols Rd.
Detroit, MI 48221
Tel: (313)927-1160

University of Hawaii at Manoa
1881 East-West Rd.
Honolulu, Hi 96822
Tel: (808)948-7041

University of Illinois at Chicago
Political Science Department
1102 Behavioral Science Building
412 S. Peoria St.
Box 4348
Chicago, IL 60680
Tel: (312)996-3108

University of Maryland
Department of East Asian Languages and Literature
University of Maryland
College Park Campus
College Park, MD 20742
Tel: (301)454-5152

University of Pennsylvania
Department of International Relations
246 Stiteler Hall
3401 Walnut
Philadelphia, PA 19104
Tel: (215)898-7657

University of Southern California
East Asian Library
3502 S. Hoover
Los Angeles, CA 90089
Tel: (213)743-2311

University of Southern California
History Department
Los Angeles, CA 90089-0034
Tel: (213)743-7522

University of Texas at Dallas
Department of International Management Studies
P.O. Box 830688
Richardson, TX 75083-0688
Tel: (214)543-2033

University of Washington
Seattle, WA 98195
Tel: (206)543-2100

University of Washington School of Law
JB-20
Seattle, WA 98195
Tel: (206)543-4550

Western Michigan University
1450 Dunbar
Kalamazoo, MI 49008
Tel: (616)383-1600

Western Michigan University
Political Science Department
3028 Friedman Hall, NN
Kalamazoo, MI 49008
Tel: (616)383-0483

William S. Richardson School of Law
2515 Dole St.
Honolulu, HI 96822
Tel: (808)948-6363

Woodrow Wilson School of Public and International Affairs
Princeton University
41 Williams St.
Princeton, NJ 08544
Tel: (609)452-4804

World Environment Center (WEC)
419 Park Ave., Suite 1403
New York, NY 10016
Tel: (212)683-7000

APPENDIX 5

COUNTRY DESK OFFICES, U.S. DEPARTMENT OF COMMERCE, WASHINGTON, DC

ASEAN	(202)377-3875
Australia	(202)377-3647
Bangladesh	(202)377-2954
Bhutan	(202)377-2954
Brunei	(202)377-3647
Burma (Myanmar)	(202)377-5334
Cambodia (Kampuchea)	(202)377-2462
Hong Kong	(202)377-2462
India	(202)377-2954
Indonesia	(202)377-3875
Japan	(202)377-4527
Korea, North	(202)377-3583
Korea, South	(202)377-4958
Laos	(202)377-2462
Macao	(202)377-2462
Malaysia	(202)377-3875
Mongolia	(202)377-3583
Nepal	(202)377-2954
Pacific Islands	(202)377-3647
Belau	
Cook Islands	
Federated States of Micronesia	
Fiji	
French Polynesia	
Kiribati	
Marshall Islands	
Nauru	

New Caledonia	
Niue	
Papua New Guinea	
Tokelau	
Tonga	
Tuvalu	
Vanuatu	
Wallis and Futana	
Western Samoa	
Pakistan	(202)377-2954
People's Republic of China	(202)377-3583
Philippines	(202)377-3875
Singapore	(202)377-3875
Sri Lanka	(202)377-2954
Taiwan	(202)377-4957
Thailand	(202)377-3875
Vietnam	(202)377-2462

Appendix 6

Headquarters of World Trade Centers Association (WTCA)

One World Trade Center, Suite 7701
New York, NY 10048
Tel: (212)313-4610
Fax: (212)488-0064
Telex: 285 472 WTNY UR
Network mail code: PENNY

APPENDIX 7

PACIFIC RIM CHAMBERS OF COMMERCE IN THE UNITED STATES

China

Chinese Chamber of Commerce
Confucius Plaza
33 Bowery, Room C203
New York, NY 10002
Tel: (212)226-2795

Chinese Chamber of Commerce
730 Sacramento St.
San Francisco, CA 94108
Tel: (415)982-3000

India

India Chamber of Commerce of America
18th Floor, 445 Park Ave.
New York, NY 10022
Tel: (212)755-7181

Indonesia

American-Indonesian Chamber of Commerce, Inc.
17th Floor, 711 3rd Ave.
New York, NY 10017
Tel: (212)687-4505

Japan

Honolulu-Japanese Chamber of Commerce
74-4 S. Beretania St.
Honolulu, HI 96826
Tel: (808)949-5531

Japanese Business Association of Southern California
45 S. Figueroa St., Room 206
Los Angeles, CA 90071
Tel: (213)485-0160

Japanese Chamber of Commerce and Industry of Chicago
401 N. Michigan Ave., Room 602
Chicago, IL 60611
Tel: (312)332-6199

Japanese Chamber of Commerce of New York, Inc.
1451 W. 57th St.
New York, NY 10019
Tel: (212)246-9774

Japanese Chamber of Commerce of Northern California
World Affairs Center
312 Sutter St., Room 408
San Francisco, CA 94108
Tel: (415)986-6140

Japanese Chamber of Commerce of Southern California
244 S. San Pedro St., Room 504
Los Angeles, CA 90012
Tel: (213)626-3067

Korea

Korean Chamber of Commerce
981 S. Western Ave., Suite 201
Los Angeles, CA 90006
Tel: (213)733-4410

U.S.-Korea Society
7th Floor, 725 Park Ave.
New York, NY 10021
Tel: (212)517-7730

Pakistan

U.S.-Pakistan Economic Council
c/o Morton Zuckerman
17 Battery Place, Room 1128
New York, NY 10004
Tel: (212)943-5828

Philippines

Philippine-American Chamber of Commerce, Inc.
17th Floor, 711 Third Ave.
New York, NY 10017
Tel: (212)972-9326

Philippine-American Chamber of Commerce
c/o Philippine Consulate
447 Sutter St.
San Francisco, CA 94102
Tel: (415)433-6666

APPENDIX 8

ASIAN REGIONAL ORGANIZATIONS

ASEAN-U.S. Trade Council
40 E. 49th St., Suite 501
New York, NY 10017
Tel: (212)688-2755

Asian Society
725 Park Ave.
New York, NY 10021
Tel: (212)288-6400

Asia Society
1785 Massachusetts Ave., NW
Washington, DC 20036
Tel: (202)387-6500

APPENDIX 9

AMERICAN CHAMBERS OF COMMERCE AND U.S. EMBASSIES IN ASIA

American Chamber of Commerce Directory for the Asia-Pacific

Australia

American Chamber of Commerce in Australia
3rd Floor, 50 Pitt St.
Sydney NSW 2000, Australia
Tel: (61)(2)241-1907
Fax: (61)(2)251-5220
Telex: 72729 ATTIAU
Cable: AMCHAM SYDNEY

Guam

Guam Chamber of Commerce
102 Ada Plaza Center
Agana 96910, Guam
Tel: (671)472-6311 or 8001
Fax: (671)472-6202
Telex: 6160 BOOTH GM
Cable: CHAMAGANA

Hong Kong

American Chamber of Commerce in Hong Kong
10th Floor, Swire House, Room 1030
Central, Hong Kong
Tel: (852)260-165
Telex: 83664 AMCC HX
Cable: AMCHAM HONG KONG
Fax: (852)810-1289

Indonesia

American Chamber of Commerce in Indonesia
22nd Floor, The Landmark Center
Suite 2204
Jln Jendral
Sudirman Kav 70A
Jakarta 10002, Indonesia
Tel: (62)(21)578-0656
Fax: (62)(21)819-8362
Telex: 48116 CIBSEM IA

Japan

American Chamber of Commerce in Japan
Fukide Building, No. 2
4-1-21, Toranomon
Minato-ku
Tokyo 105, Japan
Tel: (81)(3)433-5381
Fax: (81)(3)436-1446
Telex: J 2425104
Cable: AMCHAM TOKYO

American Chamber of Commerce in Okinawa
Sheraton Okinawa Hotel, Room 125
1520 Kishaba
23 Kitanakagusuku-son
Okinawa City 904, Japan
Tel: (81)(98)935-2684
Telex: J79828 SHEROKA
Cable: AMCHAM OKINAWA
Fax: (81)(98)935-3546

Korea, South

American Chamber of Commerce in Korea
Chosun Hotel Room 307
87 Sokong-Dong, chung-Gu
Seoul 100, Korea
Tel: (82)(2)753-6471, 753-6516, or 752-3061
Fax: (82)(2)755-6577
Telex: K28432 CHOSUN
Cable: AMCHAMBER SEOUL ATTN AMCHAM-K

Malaysia

American Business Council Malaysia
1501, 15th Floor
AMODA
22 Jalan Imbi
Kuala Lumpur 55100, Malaysia
Tel: (60)(3)248-2407 or 2540
Telex: MA 32956 FCSKL
Fax: (60)(3)243-7682

New Zealand

American Chamber of Commerce in New Zealand
5th Floor, Agriculture House
Featherstone and Johnston Sts.
P.O. Box 3408
Wellington 1, New Zealand
Tel: (64)(4)727-549
Fax: (64)(4)712-153
Telex: 3514 INBUSMAC NZ
Cable: AMCHAM NEW ZEALAND

Philippines

American Chamber of Commerce of the Philippines
2nd Floor, Corinthian Plaza
Paseo de Roxas
P.O. Box 1578
MCC, Makati
Metro Manila 3117 Philippines
Tel: (63)(2)818-7911
Fax: (63)(2)817-6582
Telex: (ITT) 45181, 22748 AMCHAM PH
Cable: AMCHAMCOM MANILA

Saipan

Saipan Chamber of Commerce
P.O. Box 806
Saipan, CM 96950
Tel: (670)234-6132
Fax: (670)234-7151
Telex: 657-JMC SPN

Singapore

American Business Council Singapore
1 Scotts Rd., No. 16-07
Shaw Centre
Singapore, 0922
Tel: (65)235-0077

Taiwan

American Chamber of Commerce in the Republic of China
N-1012 Chia Shin Building
1196 Chung Shan No Rd.
Section 2
P.O. Box 17-277
Taipei 10764, Taiwan
Tel: (886)(2)551-2515
Fax: (886)(2)542-3376
Telex: 27841 AMCHAM TPF
Cable: AMCHAM TAIPEI

Thailand

American Chamber of Commerce in Thailand
7th Floor, Shell House
140 Wireless Rd.
P.O. Box 11-1605
Bangkok 10500, Thailand
Tel: (66)(2)251-9266
Fax: (66)(2)253-7388
Telex: 82778 KGCOM TH
Cable: AMERCHAM BANGKOK

Asia/Pacific Affairs
International Division
1615 H St., NW
Washington, DC 20062, USA
Tel: (202)463-5486
Fax: (202)463-3114
Telex: 248302 CCUS UR

Embassies of the United States of America Located in Asia

China

Beijing American Embassy
Tel: (86)(1)523-831
Telex: 22701 AMEMB CN
Street address:
Xiu Shui Bei Jie 3
Mailing address:
FPO San Francisco, CA 96655

Guangzhou American Consulate
Tel: (86)(20)699-00, ext. 1000
Telex: 44439 G2DSHCN
Street address:
China Hotel
Liu Hua Lu
Mailing address:
Box 100
FPO San Francisco, CA 96659

Shanghai American Consulate General
Tel: (86)(21)379-880
Street address:
1469 Huai Hai Middle
Mailing address:
Box 200
FPO San Francisco, CA 96659

Shenyang American Consulate General
Tel: (86)(24)290-038
Telex: 80011 AMCS CN
Street address:
40 Lane 4
Section 5
Sanjing St.
Heping District
Mailing address:
Box 45
FPO San Francisco, CA 96559-0002

Hong Kong

Hong Kong American Consulate General Officer
Tel: (852)523-9011
Telex: 63141 USDOC HX
Street address: 26 Garden Rd.
Mailing address:
Box 30
FPO San Francisco, CA 96659

India

Bombay American Consulate General
Tel: (91)(22)822-3611 or 828-0571
Telex: 011-6525 ACON IN
Street address:
Lincoln House
78 Bhulabhai Desai Rd.
Mailing address:
U.S. Department of State (Bombay)
Washington, DC 20520-6240

Calcutta American Consulate General
Tel: (91)(33)443-611 or 443-616
Street address:
5/1 Ho Chi Minh Sarani
Calcutta 700071
Mailing address:
U.S. Department of State (Calcutta)
Washington, DC 20520-6250

Madras American Consulate General
Tel: (91)(44)473-040
Street address:
Mount Rd. 600006
Mailing address:
U.S. Department of State (Madras)
Washington, DC 20520

New Delhi American Embassy
Tel: (91)(11)600-651
Telex: 031-65269 USEM IN
Street address:
Shanti Path
Chanakyapuri 110021
Mailing address:
U.S. Department of State (New Delhi)
Washington, DC 20520-9000

Indonesia

Jakarta American Embassy
Tel: (62)(21)360-360
Telex: 44218 AMEMB JKT
Street address:
Medan Merdeka Selatan 5
Mailing address:
APO San Francisco, CA 96356

Japan

Fukuoka American Consulate
Tel: (81)(92)751-9331
Telex: 725679
Street address:
5-26, Ohori 2-chome
Chuo-ku Fukuoka 810
Mailing address:
Box 10
FPO Seattle, WA 98766

Osaka-Kobe American Consulate General
Tel: (81)(6)361-9600
Telex: 5623023 AMCONJ
Street address:
9th Floor, Sankei Bldg.
4-9, Umeda 2-chome
Kita-ku Osaka 530
Mailing address:
APO San Francisco, CA 96503

Sapporo American Consulate
Tel: (81)(11)641-1115
Telex: 935338 AMCONSJ
Street address:
Kita 1-Jyo Nishi 28-chome
Chuo-ku Sapporo 064
Mailing address:
APO San Francisco, CA 96503

Tokyo American Embassy
Tel: (81)(3)583-7141
Telex: 2422118
Street address:
10-1, Akasaka 1-chome
Minato-ku 107
Mailing address:
APO San Francisco, CA 96503

Korea

Seoul American Embassy
Tel: (82)(2)732-2601
Telex: 23108 AMEMB
Street address:
82 Sejong-Ro Chongro-Ku
Mailing address:
APO San Francisco, CA 96301

Malaysia

Kuala Lumpur American Embassy
Tel: (60)(3)248-9011
Telex: 32956 FCSKL MA
Street address:
376 Jalan Tun Razak
Mailing address:
U.S. Department of State (Kuala Lumpur)
Washington, DC 20520-4210

Philippines

Manila American Embassy
Tel: (63)(2)818-6674
Telex: 22708 COSEC PH via RCA
Street address:
395 Buendia Ave.
Extension Makati
Mailing address:
APO San Francisco, CA 96528

Singapore

Bangkok American Embassy
Tel: (66)(2)251-9260
Telex: 20966 FCSBKK
Street address:
R Floor, Shell Building
140 Wireless Rd.
Mailing address:
APO San Francisco, CA 96346

Taiwan

The American Institute in Taiwan
Tel: (886)(2)709-2000
Telex: 23890 USTRADE
7 Lane 134 Hsinyi Rd., Section 3
Taipei

Appendix 10

U.S. Department of Commerce, International Trade Administration

Director General
U.S. and Foreign Commercial Service
HCH Building, Room 3802
14th and Constitution Aves., NW
Washington, DC 20230
Tel: (202)377-5777
Fax: (202)377-5777

Alabama

Berry Building, Room 302
2015 2nd Ave. North
Birmingham, AL 35203
Tel: (205)731-1331
Fax: (205)229-1331

Alaska

701 C St.
P.O. Box 32
Anchorage, AK 99513
Tel: (907)271-5041
Fax: (907)271-5041

Arizona

Federal Building, Room 3412
230 N. First Ave.
Phoenix, AZ 85025
Tel: (602)261-3285
Fax: (602)261-3285

Arkansas

Suite 811, Savers Federal Building
320 W. Capital Ave.
Little Rock, AR 72201
Tel: (501)378-5794
Fax: (501)740-5794

California

11777 San Vicente Blvd., Room 800
Los Angeles, CA 90049
Tel: (213)209-6707
Fax: (213)793-6707

116 W. 4th St., Suite 1
Santa Ana, CA 92701
Tel: (714)836-2461
Fax: (714)799-2461

6363 Greenwich Dr., Suite 250
San Diego, CA 92101
Tel: (619)557-5395
Fax: (619)895-5395

450 Golden Gate
Box 36013
San Francisco, CA 94102
Tel: (415)556-5860
Fax: (415)556-5860

Colorado

1625 Broadway, Suite 600
Denver, CO 80202
Tel: (303)844-3246

Connecticut

Federal Office Building, Room 610B
450 Main St.
Hartford, CT 06109
Tel: (203)240-3530
Fax: (203)244-3530

Delaware

Contact Philadelphia, PA, office.

District of Columbia

Department of Commerce
HCH Building, Room 1066
14th and Constitution Aves., NW
Washington, DC 20230
Tel: (202)377-3181
Fax: (202)377-3181

Florida

128 N. Osceola Ave.
Clearwater, FL 34615
Tel: (813)461-0011
Fax: (813)826-3738

3100 University Blvd. South, Suite 200A
Jacksonville, FL 32216
Tel: (904)791-2796
Fax: (904)946-2796

Federal Building, Suite 224
51 S.W. First Ave.
Miami, FL 33130
Tel: (305)536-5267
Fax: (305)350-5267

111 North Orange Ave., Suite 1439
Orlando, FL 32802
Tel: (407)648-1608
Fax: (407)820-6235

Collins Building, Room 401
107 W. Gaines St.
Tallahassee, FL 32304
Tel: (904)488-6469
Fax: (904)965-7194

Georgia

1365 Peachtree St., NE, Suite 504
Atlanta, GA 30309
Tel: (404)347-7000
Fax: (404)257-4872

120 Barnard St., A107
Savannah, GA 31401
Tel: (912)944-4204
Fax: (912)248-4204

Hawaii

P.O. Box 50026
300 Ala Moana Blvd.
Honolulu, HI 96850
Tel: (808)541-1782
Fax: (808)551-1782

Idaho (Portland, OR, District)

2nd Floor, Hall of Mirrors
700 W. State St.
Boise, ID 83720
Tel: (208)334-3857
Fax: (208)554-9254

Illinois

Mid Continental Plaza Building, Room 1406
55 E. Monroe St.
Chicago, IL 60603
Tel: (312)353-4450
Fax: (312)353-4450

W.R. Harper College
Roselle and Algonquin Rds.
Palatine, IL 60067
Tel: (312)398-3000, ext. 2532

515 N. Court St.
P.O. Box 1747
Rockford, IL 61110-0247
Tel: (815)987-8123
Fax: (815)363-4347

Indiana

One North Capitol, Suite 520
Indianapolis, IN 46205
Tel: (317)226-6214
Fax: (317)331-6214

Iowa

817 Federal Building
210 Walnut St.
Des Moines, IA 50309
Tel: (515)284-4222
Fax: (515)862-4222

Kansas (Kansas City, MO, District)

River Park Place, Suite 580
720 N. Waco
Wichita, KS 67203
Tel: (316)269-6160
Fax: (316)752-6160

Kentucky

Gene Snyder Courthouse and
Customhouse Building, Room 636B
601 W. Broadway
Louisville, KY 40202
Tel: (502)582-5066
Fax: (502)352-5066

Louisiana

432 World Trade Center
2 Canal St.
New Orleans, LA 70130
Tel: (504)589-6546
Fax: (504)682-6546

Maine (Boston, MA, District)

77 Sewall St.
Augusta, ME 04330
Tel: (207)622-8249
Fax: (207)833-6249

Maryland

413 U.S. Customhouse
40 S. Gay St.
Baltimore, MD 21202
Tel: (301)962-3560
Fax: (301)922-3560

Massachusetts

World Trade Center, Suite 307
Commonwealth Pier Area
Boston, MA 02210
Tel: (617)565-8563
Fax: (617)835-8563

Michigan

1140 McNamara Building
477 Michigan Ave.
Detroit, MI 48226
Tel: (313)226-3650
Fax: (313)226-3650

300 Monroe, NW, Room 409
Grand Rapids, MI 49503
Tel: (616)456-2411
Fax: (616)372-2411

Minnesota

108 Federal Building
110 S. Fourth St.
Minneapolis, MN 55401
Tel: (612)348-1638
Fax: (612)777-1638

Mississippi

328 Jackson Mall Office Center
300 Woodrow Wilson Blvd.
Jackson, MS 39213
Tel: (601)965-4388
Fax: (601)490-4388

Missouri

7911 Forsyth Blvd., Suite 610
St. Louis, MO 63105
Tel: (314)425-3302
Fax: (314)279-3302

601 E. 12th St., Room 635
Kansas City, MO 64106
Tel: (816)426-3141
Fax: (816)867-3141

Montana

Contact Denver, CO, office.

Nebraska

11133 O St.
Omaha, NE 68137
Tel: (402)221-3664
Fax: (402)864-3664

Nevada

1755 E. Plumb Lane, No. 152
Reno, NV 89502
Tel: (702)784-5203
Fax: (702)470-5203

New Hampshire

Contact Boston, MA, office.

New Jersey

Building 6
3131 Princeton Pike, Suite 100
Trenton, NJ 08648
Tel: (609)989-2100
Fax: (609)483-2100

New Mexico

517 Gold, SW, Suite 4303
Albuquerque, NM 87102
Tel: (505)766-2386
Fax: (505)474-2386

c/o Economic Development and
Tourism Department
1100 St. Francis Drive
Santa Fe, NM 87503
Tel: (505)827-0264

New York

1312 Federal Building
111 W. Huron St.
Buffalo, NY 14202
Tel: (716)846-4191
Fax: (716)437-4191

26 Federal Plaza, Room 3718
New York, NY 10278
Tel: (212)264-0634
Fax: (212)264-0634

121 E Ave.
Rochester, NY 14604
Tel: (716)263-6480
Fax: (716)963-6840

North Carolina

324 W. Market St.
P.O. Box 1950
Greensboro, NC 27202
Tel: (919)333-6345
Fax: (919)699-5345

North Dakota

Contact Omaha, NE, office.

Ohio

9504 Federal Building
550 Main St.
Cincinnati, OH 45202
Tel: (513)684-2944
Fax: (513)684-2944

668 Euclid Ave., Room 600
Cleveland, OH 44114
Tel: (216)522-4750
Fax: (216)942-4750

Oklahoma

5 Broadway Executive Park, Suite 200
6601 Broadway Extension
Oklahoma City, OK 73116
Tel: (405)231-5302
Fax: (405)736-5302

440 S. Houston St.
Tulsa, OK 74127
Tel: (918)581-7650
Fax: (918)745-7650

Oregon

1220 S.W. Third Ave., Room 618
Portland, OR 97204
Tel: (503)221-3001
Fax: (503)423-3001

Pennsylvania

475 Allendale Rd., Suite 202
Philadelphia, PA 19406
Tel: (215)962-4980
Fax: (215)486-7954

2002 Federal Building
1000 Liberty Ave.
Pittsburgh, PA 15222
Tel: (412)644-2850
Fax: (412)722-2850

Puerto Rico

Federal Building, Room G-55
San Juan (Hato Ray), PR 00918
Tel: (809)766-5555
Fax: (809)498-5555

Rhode Island (Boston, MA, District)

7 Jackson Walkway
Providence, RI 02903
Tel: (401)528-5104
Fax: (401)838-5104

South Carolina

JC Long Building, Room 128
9 Liberty St.
Charleston, SC 29424
Tel: (803)724-4361
Fax: (803)677-4361

Strom Thurmond Federal Building, Suite 172
1835 Assembly St.
Columbia, SC 29201
Tel: (803)765-5345
Fax: (803)677-5345

South Dakota

Contact Omaha, NE, office.

Tennessee

Falls Building, Suite 200
22 N. Front St.
Memphis, TN 38103
Tel: (901)521-4137
Fax: (901)222-4137

Parkway Towers, Suite 1114
404 James Robertson Pkwy.
Nashville, TN 37219-1505
Tel: (615)736-5161
Fax: (615)852-5161

Texas

816 Congress Ave., Suite 1200
P.O. Box 12728
Austin, TX 78711
Tel: (512)482-5939
Fax: (512)770-5939

1100 Commerce St., Room 7A5
Dallas, TX 75242-0787
Tel: (214)767-0542
Fax: (214)729-0542

515 Rusk St., Room 2625
Houston, TX 77002
Tel: (713)229-2578
Fax: (713)526-4578

Utah

U.S. Courthouse, Room 340
350 S. Main St.
Salt Lake City, UT 84101
Tel: (801)524-5116
Fax: (801)588-5116

Vermont

Contact Boston, MA, office.

Virginia

8010 Federal Building
400 N. Eighth St.
Richmond, VA 23240
Tel: (804)771-2246
Fax: (804)925-2246

Washington

3131 Elliott Ave., Suite 290
Seattle, WA 98121
Tel: (206)442-5616
Fax: (206)399-5615

West 808, Room 623
Spokane Falls Building
Spokane, WA 99201
Tel: (509)456-4557
Fax: (509)439-4557

West Virginia

3402 Federal Building
500 Quarrier St.
Charleston, WV 25301
Tel: (304)347-5123
Fax: (304)930-5123

Wisconsin

517 E. Wisconsin Ave., Room 606
Milwaukee, WI 53202
Tel: (414)291-3473
Fax: (414)362-3473

Wyoming

Contact Denver, CO, office.

Appendix 11

Asia-Pacific Trade Associations

The following is adapted from the business contact lists contained in *Directory of International Sources of Business Information* by Sarah Ball (London: Pitman Publishing, 1989).

Hong Kong

Chinese Manufacturers' Association of Hong Kong
CMA Building
64-66 Connaught Rd.
Central, Hong Kong
Tel: (852)545-6166
Telex: 63526 MAFTS HX

Federation of Hong Kong Industries
Hankow Centre, Room 408
5-15 Hankow Rd.
Tsimshatsui
Kowloon, Hong Kong
Tel: (852)724-2855
Telex: 30101 FHKI HX

Hong Kong Tourist Association
35th Floor, Connaught Centre
Hong Kong
Tel: (852)722-5555

Indonesia

Association of Fertiliser and Petrochemical Producers
8th Floor, PUSRI Building
Jalan Kemanggisan Raya
Jakarta Barat
Tel: (62)(21)548-1208, ext. 498

Association of Indonesian Coffee Exporters (AEKI)
Jalan Gondangdia Lama 2
Jakarta Pusat, Indonesia
Tel: (62)(21)342-385
Telex: 44135 ABKIJA

Association of Indonesian Exporters (GPEI)
Jalan Krama Raya 4-6
Jakarta Pusat, Indonesia
Tel: (62)(21)350-099

Association of Indonesian Food and Beverages Enterprises
Jalan Kopi 33
Jakarta Barat, Indonesia
Tel: (62)(21)363-797 or 883-038

Association of Indonesian Palm Oil Producers (GAPKI)
Jalan Guru Patimpus 3P
Jalan Sumatra Utara, Indonesia
Tel: (62)(21)516-508

Association of Indonesian Textile Traders (APPTI)
CV Setia
Jalan Senopati 7
Denpasar
Bali, Indonesia
Tel: (62)361-26766

Association of National Oil Enterprises
4th Floor, Glodok Baru, Room 7-D
Jalan Hayam Wuruk
Jakarta Pusat 10230, Indonesia
Tel: (62)(21)655-139

Association of Rattan Producers
c/o PT Panca Niaga, 5th Floor
Kramat Raya 94-96
Jakarta 10710, Indonesia
Tel: (62)(21)377-853 or 346-071, ext. 412
Telex: 44208 Centrad la

Association of State Owned Trading Companies
c/o PT Pantja Niaga
Jalan Kramat Raya 94-96
Jakarta Pusat 10230, Indonesia
Tel: (62)(21)346-071

Federation of Industries for Electro-Technical and Home Electrical Appliances
3rd Floor, Galva Building
Jalan Hayam Wuruk 27
Jakarta Pusat 10350, Indonesia
Tel: (62)(21)351-131 or 356-695
Telex: 45105 CABELIA

Federation of Rubber Producers (GAPKINDO)
Jalan Cideng Barat 62A
Jakarta Barat 11470, Indonesia
Tel: (62)(21)346-811 or 813
Telex: 44963 GAPKINDO

Federation of Steel and Iron Manufacturers (GAPBESI)
Wisma Baja Krakatau Steel
Jalan Gatot Subroto Kav 54
P.O. Box 174
Jakarta 10420, Indonesia
Tel: (62)(21)511-796 or 510-881
Telex: 54958 / 45959 PTAS IA

Indonesian Essential Oil Trade Association (INDESSOTA)
c/o PT Djasuls Wangi
Jalan Garuda 99
Jakarta Pusat 10350, Indonesia
Tel: (62)(21)412-808

Indonesian Textile Association (API)
Wisma Fairbanks Block A-1
Jalan Pintu I Gelora Senayan
Jakarta 10270, Indonesia
Tel: (62)(21)581-560, 586-197, or 586-198
Telex: 46380 APTEKIA

Indonesian Tobacco Association (ITA)
c/o NV Ismail
Jalan H Agus Salim 85
Jakarta Pusat 10350, Indonesia
Tel: (62)(21)350-626 or 336-627

Indonesian Tyre Manufacturers' Association
c/o PT Goodyear Indonesia
Jalan Abdul Muis 16
Jakarta Pusat 10350, Indonesia
Tel: (62)(21)360-409

Indonesian Wire Manufacturers Association
(APKABEL)
Jalan Gajah Mada 13A
Jakarta 10320, Indonesia
Tel: (62)(21)377-777

Japan

All Japan Lead Pipe and Sheet Industrial Association
Murakami Tatemono Building
11-1, Shinbashi 2-chome
Minato-ku
Tokyo 107, Japan
Tel: (81)(3)501-0502

All Japan Machinist Hand Tool Manufacturers' Association
Kikai Shinko Kaikan
5-8, Shibakoen 3-chome
Minato-ku
Tokyo 107, Japan
Tel: (81)(3)432-2007

Communications Industries Association of Japan
Annex Sankei Building
7-2, Otemachi 1-chome
Chiyoda-ku
Tokyo 102, Japan
Tel: (81)(3)231-3156

Electronic Industries Association of Japan
Tosho Building
2-2, Marunouchi 3-chome
Chiyoda-ku
Tokyo 102, Japan
Tel: (81)(3)211-2765

Federation of Pharmaceutical Manufacturers' Association of Japan
9, Nihonbashi Hon-cho 2-chome
Chuo-ku
Tokyo 104, Japan
Tel: (81)(3)270-0581

Japan Aluminum Federation
Nihombashi Asahi Seimei Building
1-3, Nihombashi 2-chome
Chuo-ku
Tokyo 104, Japan
Tel: (81)(3)274-4551

Japan Automobile Manufacturers Association, Inc.
Otemachi Building
6-1, Otemachi 1-chome
Chiyoda-ku
Tokyo 102, Japan
Tel: (81)(3)216-5771

Japan Chemical Industry Association
2-6, Kasumigaseki 3-chome
Chiyoda-ku
Tokyo 102, Japan
Tel: (81)(3)580-0751

Japan Iron and Steel Federation
Keidanren Kaikan Building
9-4, Otemachi 1-chome
Chiyoda-ku
Tokyo 102, Japan
Tel: (81)(3)279-3611

Japan Machinery Federation
Kikai Shinko Building
5-8, Shibakoen 3-chome
Minato-ku
Tokyo 107, Japan
Tel: (81)(3)434-5381

Japan Paper Association
Kami Pulp Kaikan Building
9-11, Ginza 3-chome
Chuo-ku
Tokyo 104, Japan
Tel: (81)(3)543-2411

Japan Petrochemical Industry Association
Lino Building
1-1, Uchisaiwai-cho 2-chome
Chiyoda-ku
Tokyo 102, Japan
Tel: (81)(3)501-2151

Japan Plastics Industry Federation
Tokyo Club Building
2-6, Kasumigaseki 3-chome
Chiyoda-ku
Tokyo 102, Japan
Tel: (81)(3)580-0771

Japan Printers' Association
Nihon Insatsu Kaikan
16-8, Shintomi 1-chome
Chuo-ku
Tokyo 104, Japan
Tel: (81)(3)551-2223

Japan Textile Council
9, Nihonbashi Honcho 3-chome
Chuo-ku
Tokyo 104, Japan
Tel: (81)(3)241-7801

Japan Textile Machinery Association
Kikai Shinkoen 3-chome
Minato-ku
Tokyo 107, Japan
Tel: (81)(3)434-3821

Korea

Agriculture and Fishery Development Corp.
65-228 Hangangno 3ka
Yongsan-ku
Seoul 110-290, Korea
Tel: (82)(2)792-8201
Telex: AAFDC K23297

Electronic Industries Association of Korea
648 Yoksam-dong
Kangnam-ku
Seoul 110-102, Korea
Tel: (82)(2)553-0941

Federation of Korean Industries
28-1 Youido-dong
Yongdeungpo-ku
Seoul 110-510, Korea
Tel: (82)(2)783-0821
Telex: FEKOIS K25544

Korea Advanced Institute of Science and Technology
39-1 Hawolgok-dong
Songbuk-ku
Seoul 100-120, Korea
Tel: (82)(2)967-8801
Fax: (82)(2)963-4013
Telex: KISTROK J27380

Korea Auto Industries Association
35-4 Youido-dong
Yongdeungpo-ku
Seoul 121-130, Korea
Tel: (82)(2)784-8261
Telex: KAIASK K22373

Korea Computers Cooperative
427-5 Kongdok-dong
Mapo-ku
Seoul 110-062, Korea
Tel: (82)(2)712-6990

Korea Consumer Goods Exporters Association
159 Samsung-dong
Kangnam-ku
Seoul 110-102, Korea
Tel: (82)(2)757-3161
Fax: (82)(2)755-0782

Korea Electronic Industries Cooperative
813-5 Pangbae-dong
Kangnam-ku
Seoul 110-102, Korea
Tel: (82)(2)533-2309

Korea Metal Industry Cooperative
13-31 Youido-dong
Yongdeungpo-ku
Seoul 110-510, Korea
Tel: (82)(2)783-7811

Korean Federation of Textile Industries
159 Samsung-dong
Kangnam-ku
Seoul 110-102, Korea
Tel: (82)(2)778-0821
Telex: KOFOTI K22677

Korean Foods Industry Association, Inc.
1174-4 Socho-dong
Kangnam-ku
Seoul 110-102, Korea
Tel: (82)(2)585-5052

Korea Paper Manufacturers' Association
76-28 Hannam-dong
Yongsan-ku
Seoul 110-290, Korea
Tel: (82)(2)798-5861
Telex: KPASSO K25921

Korea Pharmaceutical Industry Association
19-20 Kwanchol-dong
Chongno-ku
Seoul 135-010, Korea
Tel: (82)(2)734-2401

Korea Telecommunication Industry Cooperative
Hanam Building, Room 910
44027 Youido-dong
Yongdeungpo-ku
Seoul 121-130, Korea
Tel: (82)(2)784-3621

Malaysia

Association of Natural Rubber Producing Countries
2nd Floor, Wisma Getah Asli
148 Jalan Ampang
Kuala Lumpur 50100, Malaysia
Tel: (60)(3)248-1735 or 8716

Automotive Federation of Malaysia/ Malaysian Motor Vehicles Assemblers Association
c/o Amim Holding Sdn. Bhd.
Batu Tiga Industrial Estate
Jalan Sesiku
4000 Shah Alam
Selangor 46300, Malaysia
Tel: (60)(3)243-5576

Federal Agricultural Marketing Authority
5th–8th Floors, Bangunan KUWASA
Jalan Raja Laut
Kuala Lumpur 50350, Malaysia
Tel: (60)(3)293-2622 or 2626

Federation of Malaya Timber Exporters Association
c/o Hew & Co.
3rd Floor, Straits Trading Building
Leboh Pasar Besar
Kuala Lumpur 59200, Malaysia
Tel: (60)(3)298-6266

Federation of Malaysian Manufacturers
17th Floor, West Wing, Wisma Sime Darby
Jalan Raja Laut
P.O. Box 12194
Kuala Lumpur 50350, Malaysia
Tel: (60)(3)293-1244
Telex: MA 32437 FMM

Federation of Rubber Trade Associations of Malaysia
138 Jalan Bandar
Kuala Lumpur 50000, Malaysia
Tel: (60)(3)238-4006

Fisheries Development Authority
Tingkat 7, Wisma PKNS
Jalan Raja Laut
Kuala Lumpur 50628, Malaysia
Tel: (60)(3)292-4044

Furniture Manufacturers and Traders Federation of Malaysia
75-1 Jalan Mega Mandung
Kompleks Bandar, Batu 5
Jalan Kelang
Kuala Lumpur 50782, Malaysia
Tel: (60)(3)782-5708

Malayan Edible Oil Manufacturers Association
134-1 Jalan Brickfield
Kuala Lumpur 50250, Malaysia
Tel: (60)(3)274-7420

Malaysian Association of Malay Exporters
c/o Rosdin Corp. Snd. Bhd.
35 Mezzanine Floor, KL Hilton
Jalan Sultan Ismail
Kuala Lumpur 50250, Malaysia
Tel: (60)(3)248-0255
Telex: MA 30763

Malaysian Automotive Component Parts Manufacturers Association
c/o Malaysian Sheet Glass Bhd.
Batu 13 Sungei Buloh
4700 Sungei Buloh
Selangor 46300, Malaysia
Tel: (60)(3)656-1001

Malaysian Garment Manufacturers Association
9B Jalan Lengkongan Brunei
Pudu
Kuala Lumpur 50350, Malaysia
Tel: (60)(3)242-2491

Malaysian International Shipping Corp.
P.O. Box 10371
Kuala Lumpur 50712, Malaysia
Tel: (60)(3)242-8088

Malaysian Oil Palm Growers Council of Malaysia
3rd Floor, Wisma Getah Asli 1
148 Jalan Ampang
Kuala Lumpur 50470, Malaysia
Tel: (60)(3)242-5088

Malaysian Plastics Manufacturers Association
37 Jalan 20/14
Paramount Garden
Petaling Jaya 47301
Selangor 46100, Malaysia
Tel: (60)(3)776-3027

Malaysian Plywood Manufacturers Association
36 and 36A Jalan Telawi
Bangsar Baru
Kuala Lumpur 56100, Malaysia
Tel: (60)(3)254-8062

Malaysian Rubber Research and
Development Board
Bangunan Getah Asli
148 Jalan Ampang
P.O. Box 10508
Kuala Lumpur 50716, Malaysia
Tel: (60)(3)248-4422 or 4690

Malaysian Timber Industry Board
5th Floor, Bangunan Sateras
Jalan Ampang
P.O. Box 10887
Kuala Lumpur 50728, Malaysia
Tel: (60)(3)248-6233 or 4791

North Borneo Timber Producers
Association
Block XLI
Jalan Tiga
Sandakan, Malaysia
Tel: (60)(89)213-7787

Palm Oil Refiners Association of
Malaysia
10th Floor, Room 1006
Wisma MPI
Jalan Raja Chulan
Kuala Lumpur 6000, Malaysia
Tel: (60)(3)248-8916 or 8893

Palm Oil Registration and Licensing
Authority (PORLA)
4th Floor, Block B
Damansara Office Complex
Jalan Dungan
P.O. Box 12184
Kuala Lumpur 50770, Malaysia
Tel: (60)(3)254-7122

Persatuan Bank Dalam Malaysia
23rd Floor, West Wing
Bangunan Datuk Zainal
Jalan Melaka
Kuala Lumpur 50350, Malaysia
Tel: (60)(3)292-2143 or 2243

Sarawak Manufacturers Association
23 Jalan Ang Cheng Ho
Kuching 50350, Malaysia
Tel: (60)(82)24682

Selangor Chinese Textile General
Goods Merchant Association
59B Jalan Sultan
Kuala Lumpur 50250, Malaysia
Tel: (60)(3)238-4170

Timber Association of Sabah
Bandar Ramai Ramai
Sandakan, Malaysia
Tel: (60)(89)43847

Timber Exporters Association of
Sarawak
81 Kampung Nyabor Rd.
Sibu 43200, Malaysia
Tel: (60)(84)333-317

Timber Trade Federation of Malaysia
c/o Rothmans International
Snooker Centre
5th Floor, Wisma HLA
Jalan Raja Chulan
Kuala Lumpur 50200, Malaysia
Tel: (60)(3)248-6605 or 6606

Tin Industry Research and
Development Board
9th Floor, Ming Building
Jalan Bukit Nanas
P.O. Box 12560
Kuala Lumpur 50782, Malaysia
Tel: (60)(3)232-8461

Singapore

Rubber Association of Singapore
14 Collyer Quay #13-00
Singapore Rubber House
Singapore, 0104
Tel: (65)535-3333
Telex: RS 20554 AB RASING

Singapore Association of Ship Suppliers
10 Anson Rd. #11-02
International Plaza
Singapore, 0207
Tel: (65)220-1205

Singapore Building Materials Suppliers Association
490C Jln Besar
Singapore, 0820
Tel: (65)298-4660

Singapore Contractors Association, Ltd.
Construction House
1 Bt Merah Lane 2
Singapore, 0315
Tel: (65)278-9577
Telex: RS 22406 SCAL

Singapore Freight Forwarders Association
6001 Beach Rd. #11-07/08
Golden Mile Tower
Singapore, 0719
Tel: (65)296-4645

Singapore Manufacturers' Association
The SMA House
20 Orchard Rd.
Singapore, 0923
Tel: (65)338-8787
Telex: RS 24992 SMA

Taiwan

Chinese National Association of General Contractors
10th Floor, Hsin-Foo Building
21 Chang-An E. Rd.
Section 1
Taipei 10764, Taiwan
Tel: (886)(2)581-8014

Chinese National Federation of Industry
17th Floor, 30 Chungking S. Rd.
Section 1
Taipei 10764, Taiwan
Tel: (886)(2)314-9405 or 9409

Importers and Exporters Association of Taipei
3rd Floor, 65 Nanking E. Rd.
Section 3
Taipei 10764, Taiwan
Tel: (886)(2)581-3521

Taipei Computers Association
3rd Floor, 201 Fu Hsing N. Rd.
Taipei 10764, Taiwan
Tel: (86)(2)713-2661

Taipei Industrial Association
2nd–3rd Floor, 117-1 Chengsun Rd.
Section 1
Pan Chiao City
Taipei Hsien 10764, Taiwan
Tel: (886)(2)962-5504

Taipei Office Appliances Association
9th Floor, 386 Yun Hua S. Rd.
Taipei 10656, Taiwan
Tel: (886)(2)771-9287

Taiwan Association of Machinery Industry
3rd Floor, 110 Hwai Ning St.
Taipei 10656, Taiwan
Tel: (886)(2)381-3722

Taiwan Electrical Appliance Manufacturers Association
7th Floor, 315-317 Sung Chiang Rd.
Taipei 10764, Taiwan
Tel: (886)(2)541-0122

Taiwan Electrical Engineering Association
11th Floor, 76 Sung Chiang Rd.
Taipei 10656, Taiwan
Tel: (886)(2)571-9238

Taiwan Food Industrial Association
6th Floor, 10 Chungking S. Rd.
Section 1
Taipei 10756, Taiwan
Tel: (886)(2)371-9848

Taiwan Importers and Exporters Association
14th Floor, 2 Fu Shing N. Rd.
Taipei 10764, Taiwan
Tel: (886)(2)773-1155

Taiwan Paper Industry Association
5th Floor, Taize Building
20 Pa Teh Rd.
Section 3
Taipei 10766, Taiwan
Tel: (886)(2)752-6352

Taiwan Plastics Industry Association
7th Floor, 162 Chang An E. Rd.
Section 2
Taipei 10764, Taiwan
Tel: (886)(2)771-9111

Thailand

Association of Chemical Traders
2nd Floor, Siam Science Service Building
4862/4-5 Rama IV Rd.
Prakhanong
Bangkok 10110, Thailand
Tel: (66)(2)391-9695 or 9048

Association of Finance Companies
3rd Floor, Sinthorn Building
Wireless Rd.
Bangkok 10500, Thailand
Tel: (66)(2)250-0129

Association of International Trading Companies
394/14 Samsen Rd.
Bangkok 10300, Thailand
Tel: (66)(2)280-0951

Association of Members of the Securities Exchange
3rd Floor, Sinthorn Building
Bangkok 10500, Thailand
Tel: (66)(2)252-2380, ext 337

Association of Thai Steel Industry
36/5-7 Soi 39
Sukhumvit Rd.
Bangkok 10110, Thailand
Tel: (66)(2)392-3898

Automotive Industries Association
394/14 Samsen Rd.
Bangkok 10300, Thailand
Tel: (66)(2)280-0951

Bangkok Chinese Importers and Exporters Association
869-875 Songwad Rd.
Bangkok 10100, Thailand
Tel: (66)(2)221-1594

Bangkok Shipowners and Agents Association
227 Tarua Rd.
Klong Toey
Bangkok 10110, Thailand
Tel: (66)(2)286-3101

Book Importers and Distributors Association
292/15-16 Luklaung Rd.
Near Paris Theater
Bangkok 10300, Thailand
Tel: (66)(2)282-0583

Coffee Manufacturers Association
185 Soi 39
Sukhumvit Rd.
Bangkok 10110, Thailand
Tel: (66)(2)392-3185

Cosmetic Manufacturers Association
1091/22-23 Soi Charurat
Makkasan
Petchburi Rd.
Bangkok 10400, Thailand
Tel: (66)(2)222-2559 or 223-9572-3

Cosmetics Association
1765 Ramkhamheang Rd.
Huamak
Bangkok 10240, Thailand
Tel: (66)(2)314-1415

Department Stores Association
Central Department Store Building
306 Silom Rd.
Bangkok 10500, Thailand
Tel: (66)(2)233-6930-9 or 235-4430-9

Oil Traders Association
603/4-6 Nakhon Chaisri Rd.
Dusit
Bangkok 10300, Thailand
Tel: (66)(2)241-0771

Pharmaceutical Products Association
75 Sukhumvit 42 Rd.
Prakhanong
Bangkok 10110, Thailand
Tel: (66)(2)391-8204

Rice Exporters Association
37 Soi Ngamduplee
Rama IV Rd.
Yannawa
Bangkok 10120, Thailand
Tel: (66)(2)286-3258, 5279, or 5105

Siam International Mining Association
204/3 Visudhikasat Rd.
Bangkok 10200, Thailand
Tel: (66)(2)282-3373, 0534, or 5214

Thai Agricultural Merchants Association
582-584 Anuwongse Rd.
Bangkok 10100, Thailand
Tel: (66)(2)222-0301

Thai Aquaculture Development and Exporting Association
1575 Chareon Nakorn Rd.
Klongsarn
Bangkok 10500, Thailand
Tel: (66)(2)437-1262 or 7866

Thai Bankers Association
14th Floor, Sathorn Thani Building
90 Sathorn Nua Rd.
Bangkok 10500, Thailand
Tel: (66)(2)234-1818

Thai-Chinese Promotion of Investment and Trade Association
15th Floor, Asoke Tower Building
219/48-51 Sukhumvit 21 Rd.
Bangkok 10110, Thailand
Tel: (66)(2)251-2059

Thai Convention Promotion Association
15th Floor, Bangkok Bank Building, Room 1509/2
333 Silom Rd.
Bangkok 10500, Thailand
Tel: (66)(2)235-0731-2

Thai Finance and Security Association
312/203 Silom Rd.
Bangkok 10500, Thailand
Tel: (66)(2)233-5586

Thai Garment Manufacturers' Association
17th Floor, Sathorn Thani 2 Building
92/48 N. Sathorn Rd.
Bangkok 10500, Thailand
Tel: (66)(2)235-4222 or 234-2948
Fax: (66)(2)234-2943

Thai Gem Exporters Association
277/1-2 Rama I Rd.
Bangkok 10500, Thailand
Tel: (66)(2)214-2641-4

Thai Handicraft Promotion Association
4th Floor, Ministry of Industry Building, Room 423
Rama VI Rd.
Bangkok 10400, Thailand
Tel: (66)(2)282-4149, ext. 221

Thai Industrial Promotion Association
90/17 Rajprarop Rd.
Bangkok 10400, Thailand
Tel: (66)(2)245-7773

Thai Mining Association
79 Prachatipatai Rd.
Banpanthom
Pranakorn
Bangkok 10200, Thailand
Tel: (66)(2)282-8947
Fax: (66)(2)280-3786 or 282-7372

Thai Orchid Exporters Association
245/53 Soi Yudhasilip, Arun Amarin
Bangyeekhan, Bangkok Noi
Bangkok 10700, Thailand
Tel: (66)(2)433-2870

Thai Pharmaceutical Manufacturers Association
2884 Rattapaitoon Building
New Petchburi Rd.
Bangkok 10310, Thailand
Tel: (66)(2)314-7461

Thai Plastic Industries Association
3rd Floor, Mahatun Building
215-217 Rajawongse Rd.
Bangkok 10100, Thailand
Tel: (66)(2)223-6183-6, ext. 45

Thai Rubber Traders Association
57 Rongmuang Soi 5
Pathumwan
Bangkok 10500, Thailand
Tel: (66)(2)214-3420

Thai Ship Builders and Repairers Association
158/2 Sukhothai Rd.
Dusit
Bangkok 10300, Thailand
Tel; (66)(2)241-0686 or 0540

Thai Silk Association
Soi Klauynamthai
Rama IV Rd.
Bangkok 10110, Thailand
Tel: (66)(2)391-2896

Thai Textile Manufacturing Association
454-460 Sukhumvit Rd.
Near Washington Theatre
Bangkok 10110, Thailand
Tel: (66)(2)258-2044 or 2023

Appendix 12

Asia-Pacific Currencies

Country	*Currency Unit*	*Units per U.S. Dollar*[a]
Cambodia	Riel	3,513
China	Renminbi yuan	8.8
Fiji	Dollar	1.5
Hong Kong	Dollar	7.75
India	Rupee	33.8
Indonesia	Rupiah	2,184
Japan	Yen	105
Korea, North	Won	.97
Korea, South	Won	807
Laos	Kip	723
Macao	Pataca	8
Malaysia	Ringgit	2.53
Myanmar	Kyat	6.36
Papua New Guinea	Kina	1.03
Philippines	Peso	30
Singapore	Dollar	1.57
Taiwan	Dollar	26.1
Thailand	Baht	25.6
Vietnam	Dong (new dong)	10,860

[a]Current as of January 1994.

Appendix 13

International Dialing Codes for Asia-Pacific Countries and Cities

Australia	61
Melbourne	3
Sydney	2
Brunei	673
China	86
Beijing	1
Guangzhou	20
Shanghai	21
Hong Kong	852
Hong Kong	5
Kowloon	3
India	91
Bombay	22
New Delhi	11
Indonesia	62
Jakarta	21
Japan	81
Nagoya	52
Osaka	6
Tokyo	3
South Korea	82
Seoul	2
Malaysia	60
Kuala Lumpur	3
New Zealand	64
Auckland	9
Wellington	4
Philippines	63
Manila	2
Singapore	65
Taiwan	886
Taipei	2
Thailand	66
Bangkok	2
Vietnam	84
Ho Chi Minh	8
Hanoi	4

Codes for other cities can be obtained from an international operator by dialing 00.

Appendix 14

Time Differences

	Difference in Hours[a]		
City	*Los Angeles*	*New York*	*London*
Bangkok	–15	–12	–7
Tokyo	–17	–14	–9
Beijing	–16	–13	–8
Hanoi/Ho Chi Minh	–16	–13	–8
Hong Kong	–16	–13	–8
Taipei	–16	–13	–8
Seoul	–17	–14	–9
Singapore	–15.5	–12.5	–7.5
Kuala Lumpur	–15.5	–12.5	–7.5
Jakarta	–15	–12	–7
Manila	–16	–13	–8

[a]For example, Los Angeles time is 15 hours behind Bangkok time. If it is noon on Friday in Los Angeles, it is 3 A.M. Saturday in Bangkok (count ahead 15 hours).

Appendix 15

Weather Planner

City	Jan.	Feb.	Mar.	Apr.	May	Jun.	Jul.	Aug.	Sept.	Oct.	Nov.	Dec.
	Month											
Bangkok												
Ave. temp. (°F)	80	82	84	87	86	85	84	84	83	83	80	78
Days of rain	1	3	4	6	17	18	19	19	21	17	7	3
Beijing												
Ave. temp. (°F)	31	32	42	57	68	76	80	80	69	58	41	31
Days of rain	3	3	3	4	6	9	13	11	7	4	2	2
Hong Kong												
Ave. temp.(°F)	60	59	64	71	77	82	83	83	81	77	70	63
Days of rain	6	8	11	12	16	21	19	17	14	8	6	5
Jakarta												
Ave. temp. (°F)	79	80	81	81	81	80	80	81	80	80	79	79
Days of rain	17	19	14	11	8	7	5	4	5	7	12	13
Kuala Lumpur												
Ave. temp. (°F)	81	81	82	82	82	81	81	81	81	81	81	81
Days of rain	13	16	16	20	15	12	11	13	17	19	20	17
Manila												
Ave. temp. (°F)	76	77	80	81	82	82	80	80	80	80	78	77
Days of rain	5	3	3	4	10	16	21	22	21	17	12	9
Seoul												
Ave. temp. (°F)	21	32	40	51	60	70	77	64	56	49	40	32
Days of rain	8	7	7	8	9	10	16	12	10	6	9	8
Singapore												
Ave. temp. (°F)	80	81	81	82	82	82	82	82	82	81	81	80
Days of rain	16	11	14	15	14	14	13	14	13	16	18	19
Taipei												
Ave. temp. (°F)	60	63	67	70	75	80	85	79	74	70	65	61
Days of rain	8	15	11	14	11	13	9	11	10	8	7	7
Tokyo												
Ave. temp. (°F)	39	39	45	55	62	70	76	79	73	62	52	42
Days of rain	7	8	13	14	14	16	15	13	17	14	10	7

APPENDIX 16

AIR DISTANCES

	London	*New York*	*San Francisco/ Los Angeles*	*Honolulu*	*Beijing*	*Bangkok*	*Taipei*
London	—	3,463	5,442	7,225	5,059	5,917	6,075
New York	3,463	—	2,248	4,958	5,942	7,521	7,782
San Francisco/ Los Angeles	5,442	2,248	—	2,558	5,139	6,888	6,280
Honolulu	7,225	4,958	2,558	—	4,398	5,730	5,046
Beijing	5,059	5,942	5,139	4,398	—	1,779	1,065
Bangkok	5,917	7,526	6,888	5,730	1,779	—	1,568
Taipei	6,075	7,782	6,776	5,046	1,065	1,568	—
Jakarta	7,261	10,030	8,965	6,705	3,223	1,432	2,358
Hong Kong	5,981	7,013	6,009	4,824	1,071	924	502
Manila	6,666	8,489	7,291	5,294	1,764	1,372	719
Seoul	5,507	6,868	5,955	4,539	594	775	919
Singapore	6,733	8,288	7,343	5,836	2,417	775	2,011
Tokyo	5,192	5,887	4,486	3,350	1,131	2,476	1,308
Kuala Lumpur	6,540	9,379	8,771	6,801	2,687	730	1,996

	Jakarta	*Hong Kong*	*Manila*	*Seoul*	*Singapore*	*Tokyo*	*Kuala Lumpur*
London	7,261	5,981	6,666	5,507	6,733	5,192	6,540
New York	10,030	7,013	8,489	6,868	9,516	6,739	9,379
San Francisco/ Los Angeles	8,965	6,009	7,291	5,955	8,764	5,473	8,771
Honolulu	6,705	4,824	5,294	4,539	5,836	3,350	6,801
Beijing	3,223	1,071	1,764	594	2,417	1,131	2,687
Bangkok	1,432	924	1,372	775	885	2,476	730
Taipei	2,358	502	718	919	2,611	1,308	1,996
Jakarta	—	2,011	1,723	3,271	550	3,581	730
Hong Kong	2,011	—	691	1,300	1,389	1,555	1,553
Manila	1,723	691	—	1,621	1,483	1,858	1,530
Seoul	3,271	1,300	1,621	—	2,893	719	2,853
Singapore	550	1,389	1,483	2,893	—	2,860	197
Tokyo	3581	1,555	1,858	719	2,860	—	3,298
Kuala Lumpur	730	1,553	1,530	2,853	197	3,298	—

APPENDIX 17

ELECTRICAL CURRENTS

Country	*Voltage (Volts)*	*Frequency (Hertz)*
China	220-240	50
Hong Kong	200	50
Indonesia	110-127	50[a]
Japan	100	50
Korea, South	100	66
Malaysia	220	50
Philippines	220[b]	60
Singapore	220	50
Taiwan	220	50
Thailand	220	50
Vietnam	110 and 220	50

[a]In most places.

[b]In hotels in Manila, 110-volt electricity might also be available.

Appendix 18

Feature-Length Motion Pictures about Asia and Japan

The following Western feature films might be useful in broadening your perspective on Asian culture, history, and social values. I have ranked them from 1 to 4 (with 4 being the highest ranking), according to the degree to which they acquaint the viewer with Asian customs, values, history, and personality.

To obtain a list of nonfiction films that deal with Asia-related subjects, contact the International Documentary Association in Los Angeles, California, tel: (310)284-8422.

Film	Rank
Apocalypse Now	1
Black Rain	3
The Bridge on the River Kwai	3
China Cry	4
China Rose	1
Empire of the Sun	4
The Good Earth	3
Good Morning Vietnam	2
Heaven and Earth	3
Indochine	3
The Joy Luck Club	4
The Killing Fields	3
The Last Emperor	4
Love Is a Many Splendored Thing	3
M Butterfly	3
Midway	2
Mr. Baseball	3
The Mikado	3
Oil for the Lamps of China	2
The Quiet American	2
The Sand Pebbles	3
The Scent of Green Papaya	4
The Seven Samurai	4
Rising Sun	2
Shogun	4
Tai-pan	3
Teahouse of the August Moon	3
The World of Suzy Wong	3
The Yakuza	2
The Year of Living Dangerously	3
The Year of the Dragon	2

APPENDIX 19

ASIAN BUSINESS HOLIDAYS

Holidays in Asia are many and varied. If taken to one of them by an Asian host, the Westerner will normally be a spectator rather than a participant. It is important, however, to know when the major festivals occur so as not to schedule business meetings during these times. (If you doubt the correctness of this advice, just ask the American flower grower who arrived in Taipei during the Ching Ming Festival—called the Tomb Sweeping Festival in Taiwan—which is celebrated in the first week of April. Entire families make their way to the resting places of their forebears and celebrate the family lineage. The American was picked up at the airport by a disgruntled host and spent the next 10 hours in a traffic jam of Taipei city dwellers heading south for the holiday.) The following holiday calendar is included as a guide.

Notes:

The italicized dates should be avoided as hosting dates, if at all possible.

Adapted from information on Asian holidays in *The Traveler's Guide to Asian Customs and Manners*, by Elizabeth Devine and Nancy L. Braganti (New York: St. Martin's Press, 1986) and *The Business Travel Guide to ASEAN Nations* (Executive Squire, Ltd., 1979).

Country	*January–March*	*April–June*
Taiwan	Foundation Day (Jan. 1) *Lunar New Year* (Jan./Feb.) Youth Day (Mar. 29)	*Tomb-Sweeping Day and the Death of Chiang Kai-shek* (Apr. 15) Dragon Boat Festival (late May or early June)
China	New Year's Day (Jan. 1) *Lunar New Year and Spring Festival* (late Jan. and early Feb.)	Labor Day (May 1)
Thailand	New Year's Day (Jan. 1) *Lunar New Year* (Jan./Feb.) Magha Puja Day (Feb.)	Chakri Day (Apr. 6) *Songkran Water Festival* (Apr. 13–15) Coronation Day (May 5) Visakha Puja (celebrating Buddha's birth, enlightenment, and entry into nirvana—May/June)
Hong Kong	New Year's Day (Jan. 1) *Lunar New Year* (2- to 4-day celebration in early Feb.)	*Ching Ming* (early Apr.) Easter Weekend Queen's Birthday (Apr. 21) Dragon Boat Festival (late May)
South Korea	New Year Holidays (Jan. 1–3) *Lunar New Year* (Jan./Feb.) Independence Movement Day (Mar. 1)	Arbor Day (Apr. 5) Children's Day (May 5) *Buddha's Birthday* (May) Memorial Day (June 6) Farmer's Day (June 15) Constitution Day (June 17)
Japan	*New Year's Day* (Jan. 1) Bank Holidays (Jan. 1–3) Adult's Day (Jan. 15) National Foundation Day (Feb. 11) *Vernal Equinox* (around Mar. 21)	May Day (May 1) Constitution Memorial Day (May 3) Children's Day (May 5) (*Many firms close from Apr. 29 to May 5*)

July–September	*October–December*
Confucius's Birthday and Teacher's Day (Sept. 28) *Mid-Autumn Moon Festival* (Sept./Oct.)	Double-Ten National Day (Oct. 10) Taiwan Restoration Day (Oct. 25) Chiang Kai-shek's Birthday (Oct. 31) Sun Yat-sen's Birthday (Nov. 12) Constitution Day (Dec. 25) *Christmas* (Dec. 25)
Founding of the Communist Party (July 1) People's Liberation Day (Aug. 1)	National Day (Oct. 1)
Queen's Birthday (Aug. 12)	Chulalongkorn Day (Oct. 23) Loy Krathong Festival of Lights (Oct./Nov.) The King's Birthday (Dec. 5) Constitution Day (Dec. 10) *Christmas* (Dec. 25)
Mid-Autumn Moon Festival (late Sept. or early Oct.)	*Christmas* (Dec. 25) Boxing Day (Dec. 26)
Liberation Day (Aug. 15) Thanksgiving (Sept./Oct.)	Armed Forces Day (Oct. 1) National Foundation Day (Oct. 3) Hangul Day (Oct. 9) *Christmas* (Dec. 25)
Respect for the Aged Day (Sept. 15) Autumnal Equinox Day (around Sept. 23)	Health and Sports Day (Oct. 10) Cultural Day (Nov. 3) Labor Thanksgiving Day (Nov. 23) *Happy New Year's Holidays* (Dec. 28 for 5–10 days)

Country	*January–March*	*April–June*
Philippines	*New Year's Day* (Jan. 1)	*Maundy Thursday* (3 days before Easter) *Good Friday* Labor Day (May 1) Independence Day (June 12)
Singapore	New Year's Day (Jan. 1) *Lunar New Year* (Jan./Feb.)	Good Friday Labor Day (May 5) Wesak Day (celebrates Buddha's birth, enlightenment, and entry into nirvana)
Indonesia	New Year's Day (Jan. 1) Good Friday (Mar. or Apr.) Iaul Adha: Moslem Day of Sacrifice (Jan.) *Maulid Nabi: Mohammed's Birthday* (Jan./Feb.)	Feast of the Ascension (40 days after Easter) *Waicak Day* (delebrates Buddha's birth, enlightenment, and entry into nirvana—in May)
Malaysia	New Year's Day (Jan. 1) Taipusam (Jan. or Feb.) *Lunar New Year* (Jan./Feb.) Federal Day (Feb. 1)	*Prophet Mohammed's Birthday* (Mar.) Labor Day (May 1) *Wesak Day* (May/June) King Vang di-Pert van Agong's Birthday (June 4)

July–September	*October–December*
Philippine-American Friendship Day (July 4) Thanksgiving (Sept. 21)	All Saints Day (Nov. 1) National Heroes Day (Nov. 30) *Christmas* (Dec. 25) Rizal Day (Dec. 30)
National Day (Aug. 9) Hari Raya Haji (Sept./Oct.)	Deepavali (Nov.) *Christmas* (Dec. 25)
Independence Day (Aug. 17) Mi'raj Nabi Mohammed (Aug.) *Idul Fitr* (2 days of celebration of the end of Ramadan) (Aug./Sept.)	*Christmas* (Dec. 25)
National Day (Aug. 31)	Deepavali (Oct./Nov.) *Christmas* (Dec. 25) Hari Raya Haji (Dec.)

Author Index

Title Index